Of One Blood

Of One Blood

Abolitionism and the Origins of Racial Equality

Paul Goodman

UNIVERSITY OF CALIFORNIA PRESS
Berkeley · Los Angeles · London

University of California Press
Berkeley and Los Angeles, California

University of California Press, Ltd.
London, England

© 1998 by
The Regents of the University of California

Library of Congress Cataloging-in-Publication Data

Goodman, Paul, 1934–1995.
    Of One Blood: abolitionism and the origins of
    racial equality. / Paul Goodman.
        p.   cm.
    Includes bibliographic references and index
    ISBN 0–520–20794–7 (cloth : alk. paper)
    1. Antislavery movements—United States—
    History—19th century.   2. United States—
    Race relations.   3. Afro-Americans—Civil
    rights—History—19th century.   I. Title.
E449.G67   1998
973.7'114—dc21   97–45560

Printed in the United States of America
9 8 7 6 5 4 3 2 1

The paper used in this publication meets the mini-
mum requirements of American National Standard
for Information Sciences—Permanence of Paper for
Printed Library Materials, ANSI Z39.48–1984.

For
David and Susan Brody
and
Jonathan, Pamela, and Sara

"God hath made of one blood all nations of men for to dwell on all the face of the earth."

Acts, xviii, 26

Contents

Foreword

Paul Goodman's groundbreaking scholarship combined a passionate radical humanism with conservative empiricism and methodological rigor. His zeal for the facts in all their complexity made his first book, *The Democratic-Republicans of Massachusetts: Politics in a Young Republic* (Cambridge, Mass., 1964), a major innovation in American political historiography. Skeptical of the traditional scholarship that took partisan rhetoric at face value, he incisively delineated the cross-cutting business and career interests that permeated both major parties from the beginning of our two-party system. Thus he prefigured a political history, now no longer so "new," that brought a new realism to the subject.

This gifted empiricist also pioneered a new social/cultural history when his wealth of facts on Jeffersonian New England showed him that political facts were not enough to explain even politics. This prompted him to undertake a research program tracing political linkages to family, gender, and religion, landmark articles reported significant additions to the empirical record—the states' little-known "homestead exemption" laws, for example, that protected homes, farms, and tools from creditors, or the fugitive New England poll books that recorded individual votes, revealing unexpected correlations of political preference with occupation, class, and religious orientation.

Soon Goodman's widening and deepening inquiries were revealing a pattern of profound upheaval in every department of Yankee life.

Tracking this "great transition" to its culmination during the 1820s and 1830s in a ferment of social reform, he focused on Antimasonry as the critical nexus between social/cultural change and political change. In *Towards a Christian Republic: Antimasonry and the Great Transition in New England* (New York, 1988) he showed this transition to be rooted in capitalist transformations, anticipating the idea of a market revolution as the driver of change in the Jeffersonian/Jacksonian republic.

Eventually the paramount American evil of slavery engaged this humane historian, as inevitably as it had the great transition's benevolent activists. By now facing terminal cancer, Goodman devoted himself with luminous serenity to explaining the sources of abolitionist zeal. Writing as always for engaged readers, he derived a sophisticated argument from a dense evidential base, gave full credit to exceptions and ambiguities, and scrupulously eschewed oversimplification and special pleading. *Of One Blood* is Goodman's crowning achievement, transfiguring our understanding of American abolitionism and placing it in the newest light since Gilbert Barnes's *Antislavery Impulse* three generations ago.

New insights abound. While building on Barnes's crucial discovery of the centrality of Protestant evangelicalism, Goodman corrects and expands this interpretation at critical points. His mastery of religious history extends the evangelical propensity for abolitionism beyond the New York revivalism of Charles Grandison Finney to include especially New England's Hopkinsianism, as well as William Lloyd Garrison's evangelical Baptist tradition. Consequently, he shows, similarities far outweighed differences between the Garrisonian wing of the movement and Barnes's Finney/Tappan/Weld wing.

Goodman is the first historian, moreover, to offer a persuasive answer to the crucial questions raised by the evangelical sources of abolitionism: Why didn't more evangelicals become abolitionists? What distinguishes the minority who did? Essential here is his understanding of how the market revolution (as he relabeled his great transition) transformed family, religion, gender, and class. The commitment of so many male abolitionists arose, his close analysis reveals, from alarm over the corrosion of traditional notions of equality, labor, and manhood. Scrutinizing women's unusual prominence in abolitionism, he similarly concludes that their ranks were drawn heavily from those evangelical women most sensitive to changes in women's roles.

Likewise, Goodman shows that workers' varied reactions reflected the varied experiences of the working classes. Abolitionism got strong support from artisans defending their threatened independence and moral economy. Although sharpening competition for society's crumbs made them susceptible to the racist incitement of anti-abolitionist elites, unskilled and immigrant whites were persuaded by a latent ideology of free labor to repudiate the slave power. All these coinciding propensities, Goodman concludes, along with antimaterialist strains in the abolitionist persuasion itself, indicate that abolitionism was most compelling to those evangelicals most upset about the market revolution's effects.

These insights alone deepen our understanding of American abolitionism more than the whole outpouring of abolitionist historiography inspired by the civil rights movement of the 1960s and 1970s. Yet through those decades, the sources for an even more profound insight likewise lay manifest, but unnoticed in the record. As African-American perspectives began at long last to penetrate the historical consciousness, Goodman first perceived that white abolitionism was galvanized by free black militancy.

The African-American community found its united voice in denouncing the inherent racism of the movement to colonize American blacks in Africa. Colonization had been embraced by slaveholders and racists to get rid of free blacks and by much of the conservative establishment as a moral fig leaf to claim antislavery virtue without disturbing the economic/political status quo. But it was also embraced at first by many benevolent evangelicals in the forlorn hope of eroding slavery by encouraging voluntary emancipation and emigration. Abolitionism was launched, Goodman demonstrates, by evangelical reformers who were shocked into renouncing colonization because they could hear what the African American community was saying.

The abolitionists' radicalism lay not just in their commitment to abolition rather than colonization, or even, as Barnes thought, in their commitment to immediatism rather than gradualism. They challenged white American society fundamentally, Goodman shows us, by championing full human equality. Abolitionist historiography has been strangely insensitive to the uncompromisingly egalitarian credo that abolitionists regularly laid down, publicly and privately, as their fundamental premise.

Goodman's final contribution is to explain how this critical moral breakthrough was possible. What enabled the pioneer white abolitionists to hear the black critique of racism, he demonstrates, was the experience, almost unknown to whites, of meeting and dealing with blacks as equals. Doubting history's ability to convey the obduracy of racist segregation to people who weren't there, I venture in support of this insight a personal note about the segregationist South of my youth. Introduced

by a high-school friend to two Quaker settlement-house women, likely
the only whites in my large Southern city who knew blacks as equals, I
was taken to a packed meeting of the NAACP, of which I (like most
whites) had never heard. There I was overwhelmed by the eloquent orator, a bishop of the AME Zion Church, of which I also had never heard.
It was one of those rare transformative moments when the scales fall
from one's eyes. As real fellow humans presented themselves in this fortuitous haven from the segregationist charade, stereotypes evaporated,
and I heard what they were saying. I could never accept my social environment so uncritically again, and few experiences, for good or ill, have
affected my life and values more.

Delineating the variety of similar experiences that galvanized most
of the pioneer abolitionists, Paul Goodman reminds us of the transformative power of lived equality, a power attested to by his own
fearless activism. During four decades at the mushrooming University
of California, Goodman led the battle against bureaucratic/political
subversion of equity and academic integrity. Under his devoted leadership, the university-wide American Federation of Teachers targeted the
"old-boy" system of confidential personnel decisions that too often
blocked tenure and promotion for women, minorities, and noncon-
formists. Goodman's tenacious campaign was not vindicated until the
university, after overturning an AFT-sponsored state law in the courts,
finally bowed to recent court decisions sustaining open files and giving
faculty members access to their evaluations. Goodman endowed a fellowship and a professorship for his department at Davis, memorializ-
ing, respectively, the American radical Eugene Debs and Emanuel
Ringelblum, the martyred historian of Jewish resistance to Nazi terror
in the Warsaw ghetto.

Modest and generous to a fault, Paul Goodman delighted in sharing
with colleagues and students his pleasure in his garden, in fine cookery,
and in music. His hospitality was especially memorable for conversation
energized by his wide-ranging curiosity, dogged intellectual honesty, and
passion for justice and equality. His magnificent final legacy, strengthening us in historical understanding, scholarly aspiration, and moral
commitment, is a fitting memorial to a widely cherished brother and
friend who gave the last full measure of devotion to his ideals and
his craft.

Charles Sellers
September 1997

Preface

This is a book about origins. It focuses on beginnings, before the anti-slavery movement became more complex and divided, in the hope that, by narrowing the temporal focus and emphasizing originating ideas and social impulses, we can answer key questions that, despite a vast body of writing, have eluded convincing treatment.

Abolitionism stumped Charles A. Beard, the pioneering exponent of economic interest and class forces in American history, and probably the most important American historian of the twentieth century. "The sources of this remarkable movement are difficult to discover," Beard admitted, unwittingly revealing limits to the explanatory power of his version of the economic interpretation of history.[1]

A major breakthrough in understanding came with the discovery by Gilbert H. Barnes of the correspondence of Theodore Dwight Weld with Sarah and Angelina Grimké and the James G. Birney correspondence, which revealed the importance of religion and which emphasized the role played by abolitionists in the Midwest who had been swept up in the Second Great Awakening under the charismatic revivalist preaching of Charles Grandison Finney and his followers.[2] The identification of a specific religious influence—the Finneyite revival—led Barnes to downgrade the importance of William Lloyd Garrison and other New Englanders in abolitionism's formative development. In fact, the two regional movements were interdependent. Many of the early leading Midwesterners were of Eastern origins; moreover, Garrison's early work, especially *Thoughts on African Colonization* (1832), played a major role in converting the Weldites, Finneyites, and others. Still another, more serious weakness marred Barnes's emphasis on the religious sources of abolition: while most early immediatists had evangelical roots, most evangelical Christians rejected abolition as a radical, ultraist movement. We need to identify the missing variables that explain why Christians, and even Finneyites, differed so sharply over the slavery question.

The same problem troubles the inconclusive, extended debate over the relationship between capitalism and abolitionism, which suggests that historians have not yet adequately specified that relationship.[3] Even if one accepts the argument that the dominance of a market mentality expanded "the sphere of causal perception within which everyday affairs proceeded, pushing people over a threshold of perception such that the most sensitive moralists among them no longer found passive sympathy an adequate response to the misery of slaves," one must still explain why the new humanitarian sensibility nourished by capitalism led only a small minority—and not many capitalists—in the United States to go beyond "passive sympathy" and embrace immediatism. On the contrary, elites, especially businessmen, were intensely and even violently hostile to the spread of abolitionism. Here, as with the Barnes thesis, the key is to identify missing variables that differentiate, contextualize, and historicize the culture of capitalism.

The most striking omission from standard historical treatments of abolitionism's origins is the near absence of African Americans and their role in converting whites to racial equality and immediatism. At the center of this story is the battle over African colonization, which, as nothing else did, galvanized the organization and opposition of free blacks in the North.

After the American Revolution, the abolition of slavery in the North left unanswered the question of the future of race relations in the young republic. African Americans were busy constructing communities, and not for some decades was their potential for claiming equal citizenship apparent. By the early nineteenth century a white backlash against black improvement erupted, together with the fear that such progress, if not checked, could lead to demands for equality. At the same time, the enormous growth and spread of slavery in the South disappointed expectations that somehow slavery would go into spontaneous decline. The rise of King Cotton, of course, made that absurd. Finally, an abortive slave revolt in Virginia in 1801 made many more realize that bondage was a time bomb.

To the rescue came the American Colonization Society, formed in 1816 by leading public figures, with strong backing from Virginia notables, including the Jeffersonian president, James Madison, and the Federalist chief justice, John Marshall, backed by leading public figures, including many of the country's foremost clergymen. The ACS crystallized what for many was latent in their thinking, that the United States was a white's man republic. Its program advocated the removal of free blacks to Africa. Colonizationists assumed that blacks were unassimilable because of white prejudice. Some blamed prejudice on the inherent inferiority of colored people, whereas the more sophisticated held that inferiority was a condition produced by prejudice. In either case, it seemed as if nothing could alter belief in black inferiority. Either that belief was held to be "natural," in the nature of things, or it was believed to be an unavoidable social fact.

In the 1820s, the ACS made considerable progress. It obtained funds from the United States government, which helped to establish a colony in West Africa—Liberia. Henry Clay, as a leader of the National Republican party, incorporated colonization in his platform of economic nationalism and sought further federal funding. The ACS became more activist, publishing a monthly and establishing auxiliary societies in the states to gain wider support.

Black alarm mounted as African colonization seemed poised to make the transition from a theoretical idea to one that many thought a practical plan, a plan deserving significant support from public resources. From the beginning, blacks met to oppose colonization. But their voices commanded no attention because most whites regarded them, even where they voted, as outside the civic community. Throughout the 1820s, as the colonizationist threat mounted, blacks persisted in their fierce opposition while continuing to build a black community. Indeed, the two went together. The more impressive the free American black community became, the less plausible or morally justifiable was colonization.

Many of the leading early immediatists, such as Garrison, Arthur and Lewis Tappan, Elizur Wright Jr., and Gerrit Smith, had been sympathetic to colonization. It seemed the only way out. Black opposition eventually caught their attention and changed their minds. They came to realize that the bedrock issue was racial equality. They also began to have first-hand contacts, however limited, with the black community and became convinced of the absurdity, let alone the immorality, of racial prejudice, resting as it did on the denial of the very humanity of black people. Black writings, especially in the *Colored American* (1827–29) and in Benjamin Lundy's pioneering *Genius of Universal Emancipation* (1821–37), also exercised a powerful effect and furnished white abolitionists with much of the argument that would advance the cause in the movement's formative years. Finally, Andrew Jackson's election as president in 1828, which relied heavily on Southern and Western votes, deepened the dilemma of Northerners troubled by the continued vitality and power of the peculiar institution.

As important as was the rise of a free black community and its struggles against colonization, it remains necessary to explain why only a few whites listened, let alone responded with sympathy. This question is explored by means of an examination of the social origins of abolitionism. Here, critical and ambivalent reactions by Americans to the market revolution hold a promising clue. Collective study of early abolitionist leaders shows how they identified slavery, and the bedrock on which it rested, racial prejudice, with the vices attributed to that great transformation in American life. They saw evils steadily and powerfully creeping into every aspect of American life, in the North as much as the South, which they identified with the excesses of the acquisitive spirit, the advances of secularism, and the reassertion of aristocratic influences and values. Close studies of the little-known but important antislavery leader, William Goodell, combined with a collective biography of male and female leaders, reveal a close connection between the spread of capitalism and the rise of demands for racial equality and immediate abolition, but not through the social processes suggested by Thomas Haskell in his highly abstract account of the rise of capitalism and the humanitarian sensibility. On the contrary, a critical view of the market revolution was central to the rise of the antislavery movement.

For its day, abolition was a mass movement that attracted tens of thousands of Americans into an organization that charged dues, published newspapers and pamphlets, held monthly meetings, conventions, and debates, sent out paid organizers through the country, engaged women in the cause, conducted the most extensive mass petition campaigns in American history, and worked closely with the free black community. Unlike temperance or missionary organizations, this mass movement rose in the face of fierce opposition that made membership unrespectable and, for those who had to face anti-abolitionist mobs, even risky. Yet over one hundred and twenty-five thousand people braved such dangers at the movement's height in the mid- and late 1830s.

No study of origins could fail to try to learn more about the anti-slavery rank and file.[4] Demographic studies are fraught with problems because of the difficulty of learning anything about obscure people, and one should be warned not to read my statistical findings as definitive, as much as quantitative findings encourage that. The results suggest that the prevailing notion that abolition was a movement of the "middle class" suffers from a failure to define the "middle class" or to recognize its complex and heterogeneous character. Most of the middle class, however defined, opposed abolition. Moreover, it becomes evident from the data on Lowell and Lynn, Massachusetts, the largest textile-factory town and largest shoe-manufacturing town, respectively, that immediatism could command support among hundreds, if not thousands, of wage earners. This view is buttressed by a careful reading of the country's leading labor newspaper in the 1830s, George Henry Evans's *Working Man's Advocate,* and by an examination of the career of William Leggett. If one considers that radical Jacksonian antibank, hard-money doctrine had special appeal to workingmen, Leggett's conversion to abolition is illuminating because he was one of the earliest and staunchest champions of Jacksonian bank policy. In terms of social class, abolitionism exercised a heterogeneous appeal to both middle-class and wage-earning citizens. Methodist leadership in Lowell, Quaker leadership in Lynn, and fierce labor struggles in both towns played important roles in disposing wage earners in these communities to support the antislavery struggle. As E. P. Thompson taught, but many of his worshippers have forgotten, working-class consciousness is a product of historical context and varies from group to group of workers with different experiences.

One of the most important contexts for understanding the social sources of abolitionism was the churches. In the churches of the North, fierce struggles raged over racial equality and abolition. The Protestant evangelical churches, where abolition made its greatest inroads, were no more homogeneous than was the social class of those attracted to abolitionism. Churches split bitterly on these questions, both ministers and rank and file. But because many churches were at first open to abolitionist argument, the movement had access to a large public, many of whom had embraced colonization because as Christians they were troubled by slavery. Because abolitionists themselves had undergone disillusionment, believing that colonization had hoodwinked them, they thought they could convince other Christians that it was contrary to God's teaching. As long as northern Christians subscribed to racial prejudice, abolitionists argued, they participated in the sins of slavery.

Abolitionists also believed that once undeceived about the immorality of
the ACS, people would realize how impractical it was to colonize two
million people, especially in the face of the opposition from the Deep
South slaveholders and free blacks everywhere. Yet only a minority, even
among the evangelicals, responded. Who that minority was and what it
had in common is not a simple question.

Important as the Weldite heirs of the Finney revival were, they failed
to carry the bulk of the evangelical churches in the 1830s. Finney himself never preached abolition, though he personally supported the cause.
As president of Oberlin, he tried to divert Weldite students from antislavery agitation to religious revivalism, arguing that once converted,
Christians were bound to embrace immediatism.

Abolition appealed particularly to that fraction of the pious who were
critical of the market revolution because they viewed it from a religious
perspective variously informed by antinomianism, pietism, and the
Social Gospel. Although formalism and doctrinalism, tendencies opposed to these, have been equally powerful forces in the mainstream
Protestant churches, the more individualistic and anti-authoritarian doctrines repeatedly have demonstrated popular appeal because they have
been demanding on personal beliefs and behavior and consequently have
seemed to many spiritually more satisfying. Many Protestants who held
such beliefs were deeply troubled by what they saw as the dark consequences of the market revolution: secularism, excesses of consumption,
the love of luxury and material display, the growth of poverty, inequality, and aristocracy, the increase in intemperance, criminality, and prostitution, and the commercialization of sex that all were concomitant with
the growth of cities with slums and large underclass populations. Those
who worried most about such developments were reacting to the perceived decline of the nation from the remembered days of simpler, wholesome, agrarian communities. For many, however, it was not the capitalist transformation of the cities, but slavery that seemed to sum up and
exemplify this long list of ills, and for them, abolition came to be the way
to attack and eradicate them all.

The first clergymen to respond in large numbers to the abolitionist
appeal in 1834 were not antinomians, pietists, or advocates of the Social
Gospel, however, but old-fashioned, mostly well-established New
Englanders with strong orthodox leanings. As defenders of the status
quo, they, too, deplored the consequences of the market revolution. Their
religious beliefs led them to sharp criticisms of the decline of commu-

nity, now being fractured by class differences, tumultuous demographic shifts, and religious heterogeneity. They attacked the indifference and laxity of the churches toward the evils of the day, including slavery, the ultimate commercialization of human values and human beings.

The evangelical churches were highly feminized by the early nineteenth century, and women joined the abolition movement in fair numbers, especially when husbands and ministers were sympathetic to the cause. Their labors in raising funds and circulating petitions were far out of proportion to their numbers because of their zeal and leisure time. They, too, were socially heterogeneous, including middle-class women who did not work outside the home and wage earners who did. Like their male counterparts, abolitionist women were a small minority. Most women remained aloof from organizational ties. The militants can best be explained by the long-term changes in gender relations in the half-century that had passed since the American Revolution. Subtly, slowly, and unevenly, women's sense of themselves and their place in society changed. Some women by the 1820s developed a protofeminism as they faced contradictions between their new aspirations for their sex and the barriers that stood in their way. That protofeminism made them critical of gender stereotypes that limited female potential. It also made them critical of racial stereotypes, which just as arbitrarily limited black potential, contrary to biblical teaching and empirical observation. From their struggles as abolitionists, their insistence over heated opposition on playing a role in public life on the most controverted question of the day, some female abolitionists underwent radicalization and asserted a full-blown feminism that led Elizabeth Cady Stanton and Lucretia Mott to call the meeting at Seneca Falls, New York, in 1848 that launched the long battle for women's suffrage.

Abolitionists expected those who joined their movement to accept and advance the principle of racial equality, regardless of the walk of life, social stratum, and religious background from which they came. The constitutions of antislavery societies in the early years specified that racial equality was second only to immediate abolition as an organizational objective. Abolitionists insisted that one cannot oppose slavery without opposing racial prejudice, its foundation and justification. And they found that racial prejudice transcended social status, that, high and low, Americans shared prejudice toward black people. Finally, they made innumerable efforts to work with African Americans to end their social isolation, to raise their self-esteem, and to build their communities, especially their schools, which they helped to finance and staff. For some white antislavery folk, it was not easy to overcome prejudice, even if they thought it wrong. The social gulf between white and black and the deep-seated nature of prejudice were formidable. But never before had so many white Americans labored with black Americans to lessen the distance between the races and to reconstruct a republic based on the Scriptural command "That God hath made of one blood all the nations of men for to dwell on the face of the earth."

I am grateful to the many who have helped to support this study. The Committee on Research, University of California, Davis, provided funds for travel, microfilm, and research assistants. Interlibrary loan at the University of California, Davis, library, though understaffed, efficiently responded to many requests cheerfully, never giving up on difficult titles.

The collective resources of the University California libraries, now more accessible through an on-line catalog, were vital, as were the microform collections of antislavery imprints made available by the Oberlin Library collection and Lost Cause Press collection. The many librarians at depositories in the Northeast also deserve acknowledgment, especially those at the American Antiquarian Society, New Hampshire Historical Society, Boston Public Library, Massachusetts Public Library, Oberlin College Library, Rhode Island Historical Society, and Connecticut Historical Society.

Because the author has had to confront a terminal disease during the entire composition of this book, others, too, require my thanks. The staff administering clinical trials for lung cancer patients at the University of California, Davis, provided the initial experimental treatments that allowed me to write Part 1 and about half of the remainder of the book. These include Dr. David Gandara and Corinne Turrell, Coordinator of Clinical trials; and more recently my care has been in charge of Dr. Norman Cohen, Comprehensive Cancer Center, Alta Bates Hospital, Berkeley, California.

In a different category have been the special concerns extended by friends and colleagues: Susan and David Brody, Sam Bottone and Toni Propotnik, Pat St. Lawrence, Norma Landau, Bill Bowsky, Barbara Metcalf, Naomi Janowitz, and Andrew Lazarus. I am also grateful to Clarence Walker for his patience and encouragement, serving as a wonderful sounding board for sometimes heretical ideas, but then Clarence has a bias for heresy. Charles Sellers read part 1 in draft, and his encouragement has been immeasurable.

• • •

Paul Goodman died on October 6, 1995. The manuscript he left was at
once complete and unfinished. It contained everything Paul intended to
say, but set down in great gusts of energy (and delight) as he battled his
illness, and with no second chance to revise what he had written. It fell
to me, and the superb editor assigned by the Press, Bud Bynack, to stand
in for Paul and prepare his book for publication. The reader will sympathize with our predicament. Paul had high hopes for this book; he
wanted it to be read—very much so. But in this, of all circumstances, the
author's voice is precious. As we have negotiated between the need for
revision and the desire to honor that voice, we have done our utmost to
respect Paul's intentions. Nothing concerning his views or conclusions
has been amended, and, except for the opening paragraphs of chapter
13, no material has been added. But we subtracted two chapters: a previously published article on the manual labor movement (its treatment
of Theodore Dwight Weld has been added to chapter 8) and a con-
cluding piece on the political obstacles facing abolition, written when
Paul's powers finally began to flag. We have revised the book's structure
somewhat to give the sections greater symmetry and thematic unity. And
the writing has been edited with an eye to an economy of language and
the avoidance of repetition. The original printout of the manuscript, with
Paul's own corrections, is deposited in Special Collections, Shields
Library, at the University of California, Davis.

Nicholas Marshall, a doctoral candidate at Davis and Paul's former
student, generously came to his assistance by compiling the notes for all
but the first section, and afterward he came to mine by putting the notes
into finished form and checking Bud Bynack's many factual queries. I
want also to thank Nicholas's father, Lynn Marshall, an old friend and
disputant of Paul's on the fine points of abolitionist history, for wise counsel, and likewise the outside readers, James B. Stewart and William E.
Gienapp, although they will note that I have not always followed their
advice. Bud Bynack's editing was of course invaluable, beyond the call of
duty. Finally, I have to express heartfelt thanks to Scott Norton, the
production editor, and, especially, to Lynne Withey, the associate direc-
tor of the Press. When she learned of Paul's manuscript, Lynne agreed at
once to read it herself. As a result, I was able to tell Paul days before he
died that the Press would publish his book and go all out for it. In the circumstances, I can't imagine what better gift I could have conveyed to him.

David Brody

PART I

Beginnings

"Finally, let us urge upon you a total abandonment of prejudice against color," abolitionist leaders instructed the thousands of rank and filers who had enlisted in the cause by 1837. Were slaves white skinned, they told them, no one would tolerate their bondage for an instant. White abolitionists who harbored color prejudice never could be efficient advocates of the cause because American slavery was racial in character and justification. "The abandonment of prejudice is required of us as a proof of our sincerity and consistency," abolitionists affirmed. Seven years earlier, at the outset of his conversion to immediate abolition, William Lloyd Garrison had reached the same conclusion: "O that [my countrymen] might feel as keenly for a black skin as for a white skin." The black leader Samuel Cornish understood the significance for his people of the emergence of these white immediatists, despite their shortcomings: "They have shown that God created all men EQUAL."[1]

In the 1830s, for the first time in American history an articulate and significant minority of white Americans embraced racial equality as both a concept and a commitment, although it was an ideal far more difficult to live up to than to profess. Earlier proponents of racial equality were isolated voices that left few traces. This new development marked a change in the history of race relations in America—and in the struggle for racial justice—at a time when the dominant view among elites and common folk held that there was no future for free blacks in the United States. For nearly a century, from Thomas Jefferson in the 1770s

to Henry Clay in the 1820s and Abraham Lincoln in the 1860s, the idea
of colonization, relocating African Americans elsewhere, preferably to
their ancestral lands, seemed the only practical solution to the American
race problem. Freeing the slaves, were that feasible, would settle nothing, according to received opinion, since few believed that the two races
could live productively or harmoniously in the same country. The first
wave of emancipations at the end of the eighteenth century reinforced
this conviction.

In the half-century following the American Revolution, a large free
black population emerged for the first time in American history, the
fruit of state-sponsored abolition north of the Mason-Dixon line and
individual manumissions in the slave states. By 1830 their numbers
had grown to three hundred thousand. These free blacks proved to be a
troubling presence. To Henry Clay, echoing common opinion in the
1820s, they were "the most corrupt, depraved and abandoned" people
in the country. Whether one attributed their condition to inherent
defects of character and intelligence or to white prejudice that prevented
them from developing their capacities, Clay believed that blacks would
forever remain a degraded people as long as they lived in the United
States. "No talents however great, no piety, however pure and devoted,
no patriotism, however ardent," Clay was certain, ever could earn
African Americans equal rights or respect in the land of their birth.
White prejudice was permanent, unalterable, "invincible." In African
repatriation lay the only hope.[2]

By 1817, African colonization had become more than a speculative
idea. In the next decade, hundreds of prominent Americans—political
leaders including Presidents Madison and Monroe and religious leaders
in most of the large denominations, from Presbyterian Lyman Beecher of
Massachusetts to Episcopalian bishop William Mead of Virginia—threw
their prestige and influence behind the America Colonization
Society(ACS), which established the colony of Liberia in West Africa.
One of the most impressive voluntary societies of its day, the ACS
boasted over two hundred state and local auxiliaries by 1830. It was
quietly assisted by President Monroe and endorsed by state legislatures
and the major religious denominations, as well as by an illustrious
panoply of notables.[3]

The ACS unintentionally mobilized black opposition, however, and
though this opposition was ignored at first, it eventually made profound
inroads on white opinion. From the outset, African Americans in the free
communities from Boston to Baltimore defiantly rejected colonization,

warning that they never would freely abandon the land of their birth, which they had drenched with their blood and sweat. They would struggle for full equality, encouraged by the impressive advances they already had made in the decades since winning their freedom. By the 1820s, the free black communities of the large Northern cities had developed resources, leadership, self-confidence, and militancy that proved formidable, even against so weighty an opponent as the ACS. By 1830, African American leaders had begun to convince whites who supported colonization that racism underpinned slavery and colonization, that colonization stood in the way of emancipation, and that as long as Northern whites embraced both, there was no prospect for ending slavery in the United States. By insisting on their inherent equality, by acknowledging but explaining black deficiencies as the result of slavery and persisting white prejudice afterward, and by pointing with pride to their patriotism and piety and to their achievements through education and industry, blacks affirmed bourgeois values that they shared with whites. Black confidence that whites could overcome prejudice if they only opened their eyes to black aspiration and accomplishment thus challenged a core assumption of colonization.

By the early 1830s, free blacks had convinced a small but prophetic vanguard of white men and women to repudiate colonization and embrace immediate emancipation and racial equality. By virtue of their personal example and through the power of their argument, they created the modern biracial abolitionist movement. Their faith in the ability of white people to change, to abandon colonization for integration and racial prejudice for equality, was the triggering force behind the emergence of racial egalitarianism. Yet the fact that only a small sector of white opinion proved susceptible to African American persuasion necessarily complicates any explanation of the origins of racial equality in Jacksonian America. Along with the story of the fight against racial prejudice, the story of that prejudice also must be told.

Racial Equality in the Era of the American Revolution

The American Revolution launched the debate over the future of blacks in the United States. As long as most blacks had been slaves, law and custom had fixed their place, fastening the institution on colonial America without confronting conscience, save for isolated exceptions. The American Revolution, however, inspired the first wave of emancipations. Republican natural-rights ideology reinforced latent Christian benevolence to abolish slavery everywhere north of Maryland, thereby endowing the new revolutionary order with a glow of moral legitimacy and ideological consistency. The vanguard republic became the vanguard emancipator, at least in half of the new nation.[1]

Yet the first wave of abolitionism suffered from severe limits. It failed to penetrate those states where slavery was the foundation of the labor and property systems and where the size of the black population made emancipation seem an unthinkable danger. Even in the new "free states," few gave much thought to the status and future of the newly emancipated. In Pennsylvania (1780) and New York (1799), gradual emancipation laws stretched out and blurred the transition from bondage to freedom. In 1800, over half of Philadelphia blacks still resided in white households, and many remained indentured for a term of service. So while legal status had changed, the life experience of many freed people of color remained closely linked with the past.[2]

Massachusetts abolished slavery in 1784 by judicial interpretation of its new republican constitution, but in 1788, the state sought to discourage any further settlement of blacks under a warning-out law adopted that year. When hundreds of Bay State blacks expressed interest in African colonization in the 1780s, Samuel Adams, patriarch of the Revolution, favored state assistance. A generation later, Massachusetts whites remained troubled by the influx of free blacks, regarded by many as degraded and dangerous. In 1822, a legislative investigation explored the desirability of halting further growth of the black population, but factional divisions stalled action.[3] Elsewhere, too, states made clear that blacks should avoid their territory. Three years after Ohio entered the Union as a free state, it prohibited blacks from settling, but because the law went unenforced, blacks continued to flow north across the Ohio River into Cincinnati. A white backlash erupted in the late 1820s, forcing hundreds of frightened African Americans to find refuge in lower Canada.[4]

In the slave states, too, the growth of a large free black population triggered a reaction, especially after the bloody events in Haiti in the 1790s and Gabriel's Revolt in Virginia in 1800. In 1806, Virginia repealed the post-Revolutionary manumission law under which conscience-stricken masters had freed nearly thirty thousand slaves. Thereafter, no newly emancipated slave could remain in Virginia for more than one year, at risk of reenslavement. Neighboring Kentucky also excluded free blacks, as did all the new states of the lower South.[5]

Everywhere, the presence of blacks posed anomalies for white emancipators, who had not thought through the implications, civic or spiritual, of emancipation. The first abolitionist societies formed after the American Revolution affirmed that God had "made no essential distinction in the human race, and that all the individuals of the great family of mankind have a common claim upon the general feeling of natural bounties." Accordingly, the abolitionist societies exhorted whites to aid the freed blacks to raise themselves up, but except for the work of the state societies, especially in providing for schooling, this appeal fell on unreceptive ears. What is the good of "removing the sorrows of slavery," the abolitionists wondered, "if the new made man is relieved from the power of one, only to be sensible of his hopeless inferiority to all?" The abolitionists themselves were a feeble band, made up of a handful of benevolently minded men, some notable, others obscure. Though a few of the state societies displayed some vigor, notably in Philadelphia and New York City, the national meetings never attracted more than twenty-five delegates and sank to as few as nine in attendance during the first eight conventions held between 1794 and 1803. It is doubtful that such numbers exerted much influence on white opinion, let alone on social policy, despite the earnestness of their appeals.[6]

Outside these ranks, even among Northerners opposed to slavery, free blacks fared poorly. Support for abolition did not imply belief in racial equality. When Quakers liberated their slaves to conform with the new antislavery ethic that became part of the denomination's discipline after 1750, they did not welcome blacks as members of the faith. Not until 1790 did the bar formally come down, but by then, blacks who had been freed by Quaker masters had found spiritual nourishment elsewhere. In other denominations, blacks were expected to worship with whites, but to occupy segregated spaces in the galleries and far corners, the more out of sight the better. When blacks, denied opportunities to buy pews, no longer could tolerate the humiliation, they withdrew and formed all-black congregations and in time new black denominations.[7]

When it came to schooling, they were also largely on their own, though a few whites offered help. Eager for educational opportunities, the first generation of free blacks found most public schools closed and their requests for tax revenues for black schools refused. Opportunities in the job market proved equally meager. Freed blacks were anxious to learn a trade, hire on as an apprentice, demonstrate their talents, and work their way up, but few masters could overcome their own prejudices or those of the journeymen to give industrious blacks a chance.[8]

So unprepared were whites for black citizenship that the suffrage laws enacted during the Revolutionary era failed to specify whites only until a wave of black voting triggered a wave of exclusions, in Maryland in 1783 and again in 1810, in Connecticut in 1814 and in the 1818 constitution, in New York in 1821, in Rhode Island in 1832, and in Pennsylvania in 1838. When a black ran for office in Maryland in the 1790s, the anomalous silence of the law was quickly remedied. Likewise, the militia laws failed to bar blacks, but when patriotic blacks rallied to the flag, they were turned away, in Maryland in 1810 and, a decade later, in Rhode Island, though in times of dire need whites relented to allow blacks to defend the country, for example when the British threatened New York City and assaulted New Orleans during the War of 1812.[9]

Even those few whites sympathetic to black uplift and integration qualified their commitment to racial equality in crucial ways. Anthony Benezet, the pioneer Quaker antislavery agitator who opened a school for free blacks in the 1780s in his last years, worried whether any pious person could be found to continue the work at the school endowed in his will. Pride and ignorance fostered racial prejudice, even among

Quakers. Perhaps, Benezet thought, some blacks would be better off migrating abroad.[10]

Samuel Hopkins, the Edwardean theologian and pioneer abolitionist in Newport, Rhode Island, reached a similar conclusion. Though Hopkins had appealed to the Continental Congress in 1775 and later to the federal Constitutional Convention to take action against slavery on Christian and republican grounds, and though several blacks gained full membership in his Newport church and he mingled with African Americans in public, Hopkins doubted that integration was practical, even though he thought the races equal. Because of the physical differences between the races, white prejudice seemed inveterate, and Hopkins concluded that some blacks would prosper better in Africa, although he opposed forced colonization and linked colonization with emancipation.[11]

Even the two most important defenders of the unity of mankind and the equality of races in the young republic could not conquer color phobia. Benjamin Rush was an early supporter of black self-help and uplift. He aided blacks in establishing their own places of worship, fought for schooling, and participated in the 1790s in an integrated funeral for a black worthy in Philadelphia and in a roof-raising party for a black church at which whites and blacks took turns serving dinner to one another. Here were surely heroic, symbolic efforts at bringing the races together in everyday life. Yet Rush, one of the early republic's foremost scientists, believed blackness to be a disease, an affliction related to leprosy. Someday a cure would lift the curse of color. Princeton's Rev. Samuel H. Smith was no better able to conceive that black skins are beautiful. While arguing on biblical grounds the unity of humanity, as the product of a single act of creation, Smith believed white skins to be the norm and blackness an accident, a deformity of nature caused primarily by climate. In North America's temperate climate, Africans were whitening, Smith soothingly assured his countrymen. Time dealt unkindly with Smith's theory.[12]

Few publicly challenged Hopkins, Rush, Smith, and others who adhered to the prevailing eighteenth-century Enlightenment belief in environmental explanations of racial difference. Yet few accepted racial equality as a matter of social policy or practice. Thomas Jefferson was notable for admitting his "suspicion" that blacks were created inherently inferior to whites in intellect, though many shared his conclusion that colonization offered the solution to the race question. Jefferson appealed to the evidence offered by history and recent experience. Neither in

Africa nor America, he believed, had Africans achieved a level of civilization remotely comparable to the levels that the once-backward European peoples had reached—the Germanic tribes, for example, "civilized" by the Romans—levels that Jefferson predicted Native Americans some day would achieve.[13]

By the 1820s, forty years of freedom had reshaped the African American communities in the large cities north of Baltimore. Black preachers, school graduates, craftsmen, businessmen, and property holders, upwardly mobile folk who through hard labor and sacrifice had achieved respectability by any white, bourgeois standard, backed articulate and militant black leaders who forcefully challenged Jefferson's "suspicion" and rejected Jefferson's favorite panacea, colonization, in favor of integration and equality. These African Americans offered impressive new evidence for judging the inherent nature and potential of dark-skinned Americans. And while most free blacks remained mired in poverty and ignorance, the progress of the minority suggested that Jefferson's doubts rested on shaky evidence. In 1801, St. George Tucker, acknowledging the unity of mankind, prophetically warned that once freed, blacks "would never rest satisfied with anything short of perfect equality." By 1830, Tucker's statement was no longer prophecy.[14]

The environmentalist argument for racial equality in the eighteenth century had not rested on strong contemporary empirical evidence. In the half-century after the American Revolution, black progress gave environmentalism strong empirical grounding for the first time. Blacks themselves persisted in the quest for equality, however daunting the obstacles. In New York, where a gradual-emancipation law delayed the end of slavery, black self-manumissions and industriousness persuaded whites of blacks' devotion to freedom and led the legislature to advance the end of slavery in 1827, touching off joyous celebrations of this new day of Jubilee. In Baltimore, blacks, aided by white businessmen who also preferred a freer market in labor services, successfully fought the white cartmen who had sought in the late 1820s to secure legislative sanction for their monopoly of the trade.[15] The dozens of black churches, schools, Masonic lodges, and benefit and improvement societies established by 1830 all testified to black devotion to self-improvement through hard work, sacrifice, and institution building.

These developments within the free black community in the early nineteenth century precipitated the first great crisis in American race relations. Some whites now began forcibly to resist black advances and aspirations. Until 1805, the Fourth of July in Philadelphia had brought blacks and whites together to celebrate the national birthday, but race relations had soured as blacks advanced, Irish immigrants swelled the growing working class, and insecure whites no longer welcomed black participation. Elsewhere, white resistance took a violent turn. Rioters in Boston in 1826, Providence in 1823 and 1831, Cincinnati in 1829, and Philadelphia in 1829, 1834, and 1835 sought to reassert white supremacy in the face of black advances and to remind the former slaves of their status as an inferior caste, forever excluded from the promise of American life. The target of the rioters' rage was typically some symbol of black achievement, such as a church or home.[16]

The idea of America as a "*Herrenvolk* republic" did not spring Medusa-like out of the minds of white folk. It emerged only after the progress and demands of free blacks compelled whites to clarify and make explicit their understanding of American republicanism as the white race's exclusive gift.

The most important effort to construct a *Herrenvolk* republic was the formation in 1816 of the American Colonization Society, which aimed to remove free blacks to Africa. Black resistance to colonization culminated in a struggle between 1826 and 1833 that left the ACS badly wounded and Garrisonian immediatism in the ascendancy in the North. The ideas of black removal, inherent inferiority, and the invincibility of white prejudice remained powerful, even dominant in antebellum America, but now these ideas faced an unprecedented challenge from below. In the course of this struggle, African Americans forged the first biracial alliance with a mass movement among white people committed to the idea and practice of racial equality.

Toward a *Herrenvolk* Republic

The Meaning of African Colonization

In 1789, James Madison warmly endorsed William Thornton's pioneering scheme for African colonization. Thornton, a British West Indies planter who settled in the United States in the 1780s and became a versatile public servant and friend of President George Washington, had sought an outlet for the slaves on his Tortola plantation, whom he emancipated and wished to settle in West Africa. Madison, like Thornton, envisioned colonization as Jefferson had, as a necessary part of any scheme for freeing and relocating American slaves.[1] Madison's planter father was one of the largest slaveholders in his county, and the son accumulated a substantial slave labor force of his own. Madison never freed any of his slaves during his lifetime. Nor did he sell any until near the end of his life, and then to a relative who had migrated to the Alabama frontier. Madison's failure to free himself of slavery and his decision to sell surplus slaves from Virginia to a cousin residing in the Black Belt were paradigmatic; his generation, which could not reconcile slavery with republican principles, nonetheless desired to profit from a slave trade that was almost universally condemned, save in the newer South. Yet while some Southern slaveholders wrestled with the dilemmas of conscience—and, like George Washington, freed their slaves or moved to the free states—most Southerners supported bold action to protect and expand the peculiar institution on which their own and their region's wealth and power rested. The Louisiana Purchase (1803), the single most important achievement of Thomas Jefferson's presidency, hung like the forbidden

11

fruit over the early American republic, for it opened enormous possibilities, both for the expansion of slavery and for sectional conflict. In 1819, with the Missouri crisis, the dangers became evident. Nonetheless, this was a fruit few outside New England could resist plucking.[2]

Increasingly after 1800, the expansion of slavery in the territories and its intensification in those older states suitable for cotton culture undermined the view held by many Southerners, from Jefferson to Clay, that although slavery was a misfortune and was likely to threaten the Union, in time it would die out and the danger would subside. This always was wishful thinking, but when people confront an intractable problem that deeply plagues the conscience and see no readily available solution, the vague hope that in the long run the problem will take care of itself can prove irresistible. Colonization, an old idea that had surfaced in the South as well as in the North during the first wave of abolitionist sentiment inspired by the American Revolution, refurbished hopes and gained fresh plausibility from the formation of the ACS, which was dedicated to turning dreams into practical realities.

Before the creation of the Federal Union in 1789, the future of slavery lay with state government. Everywhere north of Maryland, slavery was headed for extinction. The Federal Union would of necessity be a divided Union, half slave and half free. The first emancipations added a new, potent difference between the Northern and Southern states, heightening consciousness of sectional diversity and crystallizing the regional differences that originally had forced revolutionaries to create a loose confederation that shared sovereignty with the states. The Articles of Confederation, however, had proved defective in part because state government could not effectively protect or advance sectional and particularistic interests, nor was centralized power available to revive the sagging postwar economy. This required, among other measures, the opening of the Trans-Appalachian West to settlement by deploying national military power to remove Indian obstacles and by engaging in diplomacy or war to remove British, French, and Spanish constraints on the development of the Ohio and Mississippi Valleys and the plains of the Gulf. It also required access to foreign markets for American export surpluses, excluded by mercantilist controls, access that only a stronger, more centralized government could possibly wrest in a world trading system populated by protectionist rivals.

Southerners were willing to risk the transfer of power from the states to the national government because economic development was central to the security and prosperity of white citizens and lay beyond the capacity of local government. Yet they proceeded uneasily in the face of a national ideological consensus that slavery violated natural rights, the justifying principle of the young republic. They gained confidence, however, from the equally compelling reasons that drew the free states toward the new Federal Union and that created the grounds for a grand compromise to satisfy regional interests.

The outcome of the Constitutional Convention left Southerners confident. The slave states won partial recognition of their slave populations, 60 percent of which were to be counted for purposes of Southern representation in the House of Representatives and the Electoral College; Congress could not impose duties on the export of Southern staples or interfere with the importation of slaves from abroad for twenty years, during which time planters might replenish losses incurred during the Revolutionary War and acquire the additional field hands needed to open up new lands in the West; finally, the federal government received the power to recapture runaway slaves who crossed state lines.

The need for a Fugitive Slave Law, adopted in 1793, was no small matter. The abolition of slavery in the North in the 1780s, especially in Pennsylvania, bordering on Maryland and close to even larger slave populations in northern Virginia, posed new security problems for masters. Slaves could now seek refuge in states that had outlawed bondage and whose growing free black communities could provide runaways with help and refuge. For all these reasons, the Federal Union had much to offer slaveholders. John Adams speculated that the Southern states did not expel the free states from the Union only because of fear for the security of their human chattels.[3]

Madison and other Southern leaders entered the new Union confident that the slave states would occupy a dominant position. The diffusion of slavery held the key to the future security and well-being of the old colonial South—from Maryland and Delaware to North Carolina. The Federal Constitution, Madison believed, did not authorize the nation to exclude slavery from the territories, save in the states carved out of the territory covered by the Northwest Ordinance adopted by the Confederation Congress in its waning hours in 1787. Any effort to contain the expansion of slavery, as in Jefferson's Ordinance of 1785, Madison thought, would have caused a storm at the federal convention and probably would have doomed it to failure.

The economic and demographic trends in the South in the late eighteenth century also pointed toward a Southern-dominated Union. Southern populations had surged in the late colonial period and after the war, pouring into the southern parts of the Trans-Appalachian West. Virginia long had been the largest colony and now became the original "Empire State." For a time, North Carolina became more populous than New York, South Carolina more populous than New Jersey. Kentucky and Tennessee were the first new territories to attract sufficient numbers to qualify for admission to the Federal Union in the 1790s. The opportunity to migrate west, especially from the old colonial South, enabled yeomen and planters to trade worn-out holdings for virgin lands. The diffusion of slavery from the stagnant or laggard economies of the upper South to these new, expanding economies, where the production of cotton rapidly spread in the late 1790s, not only relieved the old, settled regions of a dangerously high proportion of blacks, but also allowed slaveholders to employ their slaves more profitably or to sell surplus slaves to others trekking into the Southwest. The Louisiana Purchase seemed to seal Southern dominance of the Union, for it removed the major foreign constraints on expansion in the Cotton and Sugar Belts, securing New Orleans as the great entrepôt of the Ohio and Mississippi Valleys. Southern calculations, however, proved mistaken.[4]

By 1820, the white population of the Northern states and territories was double that of the Southern states and territories. Madison and others had failed to estimate accurately the potential for economic development and population growth within the Northeast and the spread of farming into unsettled regions in western New York, northern New England, and the Old Northwest. They failed also to foresee the flow of Southern yeomen across the Ohio River into the free Northwest, draining the South of a substantial pool of white citizens who preferred to live where slavery fell under federal ban. These trends, which confounded Southern expectations and calculations, elevated the struggle over the expansion of slavery into Missouri to epic proportions. The sudden eruption in Congress in 1818 of latent Northern sentiment to curb the spread of slavery, coming without warning or popular antislavery organization and agitation, justified the apprehensions that had impelled Southerners a generation earlier to seek protection of their "peculiar institution" in the constitutional settlement of 1789.[5]

Southerners played the principal role in conceiving and organizing the American Colonization Society in 1816, and though none could foresee with precision the imminence of the dangerous sectional debate that the admission of Missouri unleashed, there already were ample grounds for taking steps to avoid slavery's destabilizing threats to the Union. The problem began within the heart of the Old South itself—the Jeffersonian

South—where the majority defended slavery in fact while opposing it ostensibly. As we have seen, Gabriel's Revolt in Virginia, coming on top of the bloody revolution in Haiti, also had aroused new interest in colonizing free blacks, who now appeared a growing threat to white security.

The number of free blacks in the South swelled to over one hundred thousand by 1810. Whites regarded them as dangerous fomenters of discontent among those in bondage. After meeting in secret session so that neither whites nor blacks would be aware of how troubled the abortive uprising had left Virginia's leaders, the Virginia legislature instructed Governor Monroe to seek President Jefferson's advice on the practicality of colonizing free blacks abroad. Jefferson was encouraging, but nothing happened until new events gave new urgency to colonization.[6]

In 1808, the United States dealt a blow to the international slave trade by banning further importations, a year after Great Britain had taken parallel action. To antislavery men and women throughout the Atlantic world, this seemed like a victory in the struggle against slavery, but it proved Pyrrhic because illicit trading continued, and would continue indefinitely, until demand dried up or the sources of slaves in West Africa were blocked. British antislavery forces hoped that establishment of the British colony of Sierra Leone, aided by patrols off the African coast by the Royal Navy, would cut off the slave trade at the source. American colonizationists proposed to support that strategy by establishing a parallel colony, Liberia. Colonization thus offered a plan for ending the international slave trade by bringing West Africa under Anglo-American influence.

In going along with a ban on the foreign slave trade, Southerners demonstrated their ostensible desire to contain the growth of an evil not readily susceptible to abolition, though the end of legal importation also reduced supply and propped up the price of slaves. Here was a painless, even profitable way of reaffirming their abstract antislavery sentiment. Eight years later, in founding the American Colonization Society, Southern elites, who dominated the board of managers, provided fresh evidence of the ostensible desire of slaveholders to limit expansion of the peculiar institution. Leading Southern colonizationists could thus bask in the glow of humanitarian benevolence, celebrated by pious Northern allies as "advocates of bleeding Africa."

The expansion of slavery in the United States did not depend, however, on fresh imports of human chattel from abroad. Even though imports surged in the half-dozen years before the federal ban went into effect, the growth of the domestic slave population and the internal slave trade satisfied most of the demand for slave labor emanating from the developing regions of the South, though the prices tended to rise. During the first four decades of the Federal Union, the slave population grew from seven hundred thousand to two million. In that same period, Virginia exported over two hundred thousand and Maryland over one hundred thousand slaves, part of one of the largest population transfers in American history up to that time. By 1820, slavery's expansion had reached Missouri and the Floridas, which the United States acquired from Spain in 1819, and soon made inroads into Mexico's northeastern province, Texas.[7]

The American Colonization Society provided political and ideological cover for an expansionist slave South. From its inception, the ACS renounced any intention of interfering with slavery in the United States. The timing of the society's founding in 1816, some fifteen years after Virginians first had displayed serious interest in colonization, offers further clues to its purposes. The end of the War of 1812 unleashed powerful forces of economic development, setting off in the next two decades a wave of economic nationalism that gave birth to a second Bank of the United States, rising demands for tariff protection, and proposals for a system of federally financed internal improvements. Henry Clay, who staked his political future on an integrated program of federally guided economic development—"The American System"—was also a prime mover in founding and managing the ACS. Clay incorporated colonization as an integral part of The American System, assuming, as did other colonization leaders, that federal funds were necessary to carry out any large-scale colonization enterprise.[8]

The first three decades of the nineteenth century were the heyday of American voluntarism. National and local groups, such as Bible, temperance, missionary, Sunday school, and educational societies, flourished. Unlike other voluntary associations, however, the American Colonization Society did not expect to rely primarily on private contributions and efforts. The task of removing tens of thousands of free blacks to an undeveloped region in Africa thousands of miles away required vast resources. Only the federal government had those resources; the initial role of the ACS was to demonstrate the feasibility of the project. By the mid-1820s, sufficient progress in Liberia warranted more ambitious efforts.

During its first decade, the ACS made only modest efforts to garner public support. Its founders did not conceive of it as a popular organization or make much effort to establish state and local societies, publicize the cause, recruit a mass membership, or raise substantial funds through traveling agents and publications. Endorsed by luminaries in the nation's capital, drawing its leadership and supporters from former presidents, Supreme Court justices, congressmen, senators, and distinguished divines, the ACS was an elite institution and fittingly held its annual meetings in the hall of the House of Representatives.[9]

With connections to some of the most influential politicians in Washington, the ACS relied on pulling strings to advance its cause. In 1819, Congress passed the Slave Trade Act, which authorized the president to assist Britain in suppressing the slave trade off the west coast of Africa. Few who voted for the measure imagined that they were appropriating funds to establish a colony for former slaves in West Africa, but that was precisely the intent of Congressman Charles Fenton Mercer, a key figure in the formation and management of the ACS and a close ally of House Speaker Henry Clay. Mercer had been instrumental in pushing through reendorsement of colonization by a closed session of the Virginia legislature in 1816 and enlisting key supporters for the new organization, including Robert Finley, an influential Presbyterian minister from Basking Ridge, New Jersey. The alliance of Mercer and Finley symbolized the alliance of elite politicians and influential clergymen that was the ACS's principal strength.[10]

Once the new law against the slave trade reached the executive branch, Treasury Secretary William Henry Crawford, an ACS stalwart who served on its board of managers, convinced the rest of the cabinet, except Secretary of State John Quincy Adams, that the law allowed the president to expend a portion of the $100,000 Congress had appropriated to assist the ACS in establishing a colony to receive Africans captured in the course of suppressing the slave trade. For the ACS, this was an invaluable windfall. Thus, through the assistance of the United States government, the ACS launched its project, though not without suffering painful setbacks.

At home, the ACS picked up steam. In 1825, a vigorous new executive secretary, Rev. Ralph R. Gurley, took charge of day-to-day operations. He traveled extensively, began to raise more money, initiated a monthly, *The African Repository,* published pamphlets, encouraged the formation of state societies and other local auxiliaries, enlisted the support of the leading religious denominations, and secured endorsements from over a dozen states.[11]

During its first forty years, the ACS relocated a mere thirty-six hundred blacks. A sympathetic historian, Early Lee, blamed the paucity of colonizationist-inspired manumissions on the domestic slave trade: he argued that the ACS would have freed many more but for the opening of the Cotton Kingdom in the Southwest, which made it too profitable to sell or transfer slaves there. Yet most of the society's founding leaders—including Clay, Monroe, Madison, and Jefferson—supported the expansion of slavery into the Southwest and proved staunch defenders of slavery in Missouri. The ACS's first president, Bushrod Washington, sold slaves in the interregional slave trade that he no longer needed on his Virginia plantations. Thus, during the ACS's first decade, while tens of thousands of slaves trudged in chains from the Old South to the rising Cotton Kingdom, only eleven slaves in 1825 and ten in 1826 won their freedom and moved to Liberia. And though the numbers increased in the following decade, they remained pathetically small.[12] To critics such as the African Americans in Lyme, Connecticut, in 1831, the ACS was simply "one of the wildest projects ever patronized by a body of enlightened men"; to Garrison, after he saw the light in 1832, the society was a "labyrinth of sophistry"; and to James G. Birney, formerly a traveling agent for the society and another convert to immediatism, the ACS was just "an opiate to the conscience."[13] Yet hardly any whites shared these views during the organization's first fifteen years, when its actual functions were hidden behind professions of concern for the plight of black slaves and conscientious white slaveholders. Only in retrospect did the extraordinary, chameleonlike character of colonization ideology become evident, though it has long continued to mislead and confuse historians. In fact, colonizationist ideology formed a remarkable web of argument that justified the perpetuation of slavery.

The most important function of the ACS was to ensure sectional harmony by offering a platform sufficiently broad and vague on which both slaveholders and nonslaveholders, professed abolitionists and anti-abolitionists, North and South, could stand: the removal of free blacks to Africa. This was its professed purpose, but in fact, colonization served another purpose as well: removing the onus of slavery from the shoulders of Southerners. For Southerners, no objective was more important than to forestall and repress latent agitation against slavery in the free states. Colonization's architects hoped to achieve this by persuading people that gradual emancipation was feasible only if masters were encouraged to free their slaves. In colonizationist propaganda, gradual emancipation thus was made hostage to colonization. It insisted that any agitation that placed masters under moral scrutiny or political pressure or questioned their Christian benevolence would chill the inclination to manumit. Northern sensitivity to the slaveholders' feelings, therefore, was essential if the process of gradual emancipation was to go forward. Nor must one ever speak too harshly of slavery itself, the suffering of the victims and the cruelty of the master, lest slavery became a moral issue for public discussion.[14]

Colonizationists also were able to preach patience. Since free blacks were dangerous and degraded, and few whites wanted them as neighbors, no conscientious master should be expected to free slaves until there was adequate provision for resettlement abroad. Once again, any prospects for gradual emancipation therefore hinged on the success of colonization. Until there were flourishing settlements in Africa capable of receiving thousands of freed men and women, Southerners could claim to be justified in doing nothing.

Colonizationists tirelessly argued that because slavery was a national, not a regional problem, it required national action and resources. A central theme of colonizationist propaganda held that Britain had committed the original sin of enslavement and had imposed slavery on the innocent, unwitting colonies. Subsequent generations of Americans had inherited, not originated, the peculiar institution, and therefore Southerners bore no responsibility for its survival until some suitable means of dismantling it came into view. Once slavery had been fastened on the colonies, colonizationists argued, Northern slave traders and merchants shared responsibility with Southern planters for sustaining the institution. They shared, too, a vital interest in removing their own free black populations.

Yet the extraordinary expansion of slavery after the American Revolution and its spread across the Southwest strained the plausibility of British culpability, for however much the original onus fell on the English, responsibility for slavery's enormous growth fell exclusively on the American conscience after independence. Yet by endlessly reiterating the doctrine of a British original sin and by arguing that turning slaves loose without colonization was cruel and irresponsible, colonizationists hoped to divert attention from slavery's expansionist dynamic and from slaveholders' responsibility for it.

By proposing to remove free blacks, wherever they lived, colonizationists formally conceptualized the American republic in racial terms and offered a program for purifying the nation, North and South. In fact, a majority of blacks who migrated to Liberia came from the free states.

An Ohio politician, Thomas Corwin, explained his region's enthusiasm for a practical means for securing a *Herrenvolk* republic: colonization removed the one class that stood in the way of "the perfection of our social and political system" by eliminating "the only evil" confronting the republic: the growing presence of free blacks.[15]

Such racialist utopianism formed one of colonizationism's strongest bisectional appeals. Colonizationists never tired of describing free blacks as an outcast and isolated race, shunned and despised by whites, filling up the prisons, serving at best as menials, a people with whom one never mingled, even in church. No wonder kindly masters protected their charges from such a fate, the colonizationists claimed. The cause of free black wretchedness was their color, neither their fault nor that of the white race, but an unchangeable circumstance, imposed by "nature," that blacks could not "surmount" or whites "demolish." In this view, white color prejudice was as rooted in nature as dark skins.[16]

Defamation of black character thus emerged as a central theme in colonization discourse. Yet many leading spokesmen denied blacks to be inherently inferior in intellect or character. "It is not inferiority of acuity, but the force of condition, that has produced this degradation," Rev. Eliphalet Nott, president of Union College and the New York State Colonization Society, explained. "We have endeavored, but endeavored in vain to restore them either to self respect, or to the respect of others." The fault was neither theirs nor ours, he said, but "resulted from a cause over which neither they, nor we, can ever have control." The salvation of blacks lay elsewhere. They were "qualified" only "for colonizing Africa," which "is their country," where "they may be blessed, and be a blessing." Once restored to their ancestral land, Nott argued, blacks would be "capable of as intuitive a perception, as sublime an energy, and as dauntless a fortitude, as the residue of the species."[17]

Whether all or most colonizationists subscribed to this environmentalist view of black degradation is impossible to say. It was a view repeatedly expressed by many of the society's leading figures, notably Clay, its chief functionary, Rev. Ralph Gurley, and many others. For that reason, some have exonerated the ACS of racism, though the shrewdest student of the organization, George Fredrickson, qualified his exoneration by acknowledging that at the grass roots, colonization societies were little more than black removal societies whose emotions and rhetoric verged on "proto-racism."[18]

African Americans were unambivalent. To them, there was nothing "proto" about colonizationist racism. By dwelling unceasingly on the degradation of the African race in America, the ACS functioned as a defamation society that fed, reinforced, and gave elite respectability to popular prejudice, which easily overlooked or brushed aside the environmentalist explanations of black degradation. And by insisting, as did all colonizationist spokesmen, that white prejudice was irremediable, the society elevated irrational bias against color into a "natural," reasonable sentiment.

The systematic defamation of black character and behavior was a necessary element in any defense of slavery once the achievements of a free black community threatened racist stereotypes and made more problematic any racial justification of the peculiar institution. The result was a furious white backlash in the early nineteenth century. Southerners' hysteria at efforts to prevent the expansion of slavery in Missouri revealed an intense insecurity and profound anxiety. Colonizationism responded to this backlash with its doctrines of shared sectional responsibility, no emancipation without colonization, Britain's original sin, and the "natural" and irremediable degradation of black people in a white republic.

In March 1820, in the aftermath of the Missouri debates, Secretary of State John Quincy Adams, who unlike his colleagues in the Monroe cabinet did not support the American Colonization Society, acknowledged the extent to which slavery had perverted the republic's founding principles. Walking home one day with Secretary of War John C. Calhoun, he listened as the South Carolinian explained that domestic labor back home was strictly the province of slaves. Adams responded that "this confounding of the ideas of servitude and labor was one of the evil effects of slavery." Calhoun answered that on the contrary, by confining manual labor to slaves, slavery guaranteed equality among whites. Adams thought this a perversion of the truth, "mistaking labor for slavery, and dominion for freedom." Adams believed that the Missouri crisis had "betrayed the secret" of the slaveholders' "souls." In the abstract, they admitted slavery to be an evil and blamed Britain for fastening it on the country, but in reality, Adams believed, Southern pride and self-esteem rested on slavery. "They think they are more noble hearted and generous than the plain freemen who labor," and consequently "they look down on Yankee simplicity." Slavery thus tainted "the very source of moral principles" by enshrining "false estimates of virtue and vice." Nothing could "be more false and heartless than this doctrine which makes the first and holiest rights of humanity to depend upon the color of the skin." Tainted at birth by "the bargain between freedom and slavery," the Union was "morally and politically vicious, inconsistent with the principles upon which alone our Revolution can be justified." These sentiments appeared in Adams's diary; in public, he supported the Missouri Compromise and the perpetuation of a system under which "this slave representation has governed the union." Unlike other leading members of President Monroe's cabinet, however, Adams did not believe in the principle or practicality of colonizationism or support the initial efforts to enlist the help of the federal government in founding a colony in West Africa, though he did not advocate racial equality.[19]

Adams was an ambitious politician, and after the chaotic election of 1824 that put him in the White House with the aid of Henry Clay, he shifted ground to align himself with the colonizationist Clay. Adams and Clay launched a campaign for congressional funding for the ACS's efforts, conceiving of African colonization as one part of a program for national development under the guidance of the federal government. The campaign, however, aroused bitter opposition, especially in South Carolina and Georgia. If left unchecked, Southerners believed, expanded federal power in effect threatened interference with slavery, thanks to the free states' growing demographic preponderance in the nation.[20]

Andrew Jackson's election in 1828 was a triumph for the South and West, his principal electoral base, and a defeat for the advocates of colonization. Whereas Jackson's predecessors had taken a sympathetic interest in the establishment of the colony of Liberia, the Old Hero accepted the opinion he received from "Kitchen Cabinet" advisor Amos Kendall that federal aid to the ACS was illegal. When an ACS lobbyist, the Quaker Elliott Cresson from Philadelphia, visited the White House to rebut Kendall, Old Hickory barely could contain the contempt in which he held the idea of colonization.[21] Though Congress passed Clay's distribution bill in 1832, which granted a portion of the federal land-sales revenues to the states to use for colonization, among other projects, Jackson's pocket veto killed further prospects of federal support for the ACS, just as the Maysville Road bill and U.S. Bank recharter vetoes sealed the fate of Clay's American System.

The Black Struggle for Racial Equality, 1817–1832

In 1823, the New York City black minister John Gloucester predicted: "We are on the edge of a period when we shall be elevated to equality."[1] There was much tangible evidence to justify such optimism. In Philadelphia, for example, the number of black churches grew from five to sixteen between 1813 and 1837, monuments, however modest architecturally, to black devotion to Christian faith. Likewise, the number of beneficial societies throughout the country mushroomed from 11 in 1811 to 43 by 1831 and 110 by 1838, as blacks pooled resources to aid one another. Blacks long had looked to education as a key to uplifting the race, and despite white resistance, by 1837 two-thirds of the black children of Philadelphia attended public schools. Despite the formidable obstacles blacks faced in the job market, by 1812 12 percent of black families owned property in Philadelphia, while vagrancy rates and poorhouse data reveal blacks were less likely to become dependent than Irish immigrants.[2]

Black leaders did not ignore the many who remained impoverished and ignorant, but they took pride from the minority of achievers and were confident that their numbers would expand vastly if only white prejudice relented. By insisting that blacks were hopelessly degraded, however, the colonization movement loomed as a major obstacle to further black progress because it reinforced, intensified, and justified white prejudice. Combating that prejudice, therefore, became a top priority.

By the late 1820s a new self-confidence, rooted in the achievements of a half-century, galvanized the African-American counterattack against

the ACS, a counterattack also spurred on by fear that colonization had
made deep inroads into white public opinion and stood poised to secure
support from the federal government. Even a devoted friend of gradual
emancipation such as Benjamin Lundy gave persistent if qualified support to African colonization as useful, but not sufficient unless colonization was linked to emancipation, a linkage about which the ACS remained steadfastly ambivalent without losing Lundy's endorsement.
Lundy remained friendly to African colonization, though he mustered
much more enthusiasm for Haitian colonization, organizing a boatload
of blacks, part of some six thousand who removed to the Caribbean island in the 1820s. Even after the emergence of immediatism in 1831,
Lundy pursued colonization, this time in Texas. During the last years of
his life, he made two arduous journeys to Texas to explore the possibilities of establishing a colony with Mexican blessing.[3]

Colonization also long had demonstrated an appeal for some blacks
discouraged by the obstacles they faced in the United States. Paul Cuffee,
a black merchant and ship captain from Westport, Connecticut, had
sought for some time to establish a colony in West Africa for commercial and benevolent reasons. He also endorsed the ACS. At the founding
of the ACS, the organization received support from a few other prominent black leaders, including the wealthy Philadelphia businessman
James Forten, who reversed himself only after a mass meeting of
Philadelphia blacks uncompromisingly denounced colonization two
weeks after the formation of the ACS. Haiti especially commanded special attraction for blacks because it was a black-governed state, a source
of pride among American blacks. In the 1820s, Haiti's rulers sought to
lure African-American immigrants with the promise of prosperity and
freedom, but once they had arrived in Haiti, disappointed expectations
of access to land and economic opportunity, combined with the contempt
of the native black elites and the strangeness of the Catholic culture,
soured settlers and sent many fleeing back to the United States.[4] Though
hostility to colonization remained the dominant sentiment among
African Americans, there were always some lured by the prospects of
instant escape from white prejudice, such as the Baltimore black
Methodist preacher Daniel Coker, who migrated to Liberia in the 1820s,
and, most shockingly, John Russwurm, coeditor of the militantly anti-
colonizationist *Freedom's Journal.*

The founding of *Freedom's Journal* in March 1827, the first black
newspaper in the United States, was a momentous event. It represented
a new stage in the development of black consciousness and organization.

Edited in New York by Rev. Samuel Cornish, who withdrew from his church to take on this more important task, and by Russwurm, a recent graduate of Bowdoin College, the paper sought to give blacks their own voice. For too long, others had spoken for them, misrepresenting their history, condition, experiences, and aspirations. In 1826, for example, a group of Baltimore blacks published a "Memorial of Free People of Color" that the ACS claimed to be an endorsement of African colonization, and that seemed a dangerous breach in the normally united black front against the ACS. The endorsement, however, had been written by two leading Baltimore white colonizationists, C. C. Harper and Benjamin Latrobe. As part of its militant campaign to discredit the ACS, *Freedom's Journal* exposed the fraud.[5] *Freedom's Journal* allowed blacks to break "the deceptive silence in public print regarding black opposition" to colonization.[6]

Even professed friends, such as the philanthropic whites who joined the ACS, "represent us disadvantageously, without becoming personally acquainted with the true state of things, nor discerning between virtue and vice among us," the editors declared. Nothing threatened or disturbed blacks more than systematic defamation of black character, the undergirding argument for slavery and removal. "The virtuous part of our people feel themselves sorely aggrieved," they asserted. "Our vices and our degradation are ever arranged against us, but our virtues are passed over." Worst of all, even sympathetic whites had "fallen into the current of popular feeling" and were being swept along "actually living in the practice of prejudice, while they abjure it in theory, and feel it not in their hearts." How to make benevolently minded whites who had been seduced by colonization's religious and philanthropic appeals conscious of their prejudice became a crucial objective.[7]

Black writers assaulted prejudice frontally. Free blacks had advanced impressively in just a few decades, their argument went. That progress was uneven, but it nourished strong hopes for continued improvement. In no other land, blacks affirmed, could they find such opportunity. Were colonizationists sincerely devoted to the welfare of black people, they would not display such stubborn ignorance of black advancement, engage in such relentless defamation of black character, or demonstrate so little interest in encouraging continued improvement in the United States.[8]

In a country with three hundred thousand free blacks, there had been pressing need for a publication devoted to black struggle. *Freedom's Journal* had complex ambitions. While it systematically refuted colonizationist defamation, mustering historical evidence of black achievement, environmentalist explanations for black shortfalls, and the religious argument that dark-skinned people were part of God's creation, it relentlessly campaigned on behalf of self-improvement: the key to the race's advance was rigorous education and hard work, embracing the virtues of industry, temperance, and order, thereby convincing "the world by uniform propriety of conduct . . . that we are worthy of esteem and patronage."[9]

It also sought to link together black communities, especially in the large cities, and to give expression to nationwide black sentiment. In Boston, David Walker and others gathered in Walker's home to commit their support to *Freedom's Journal*, with Walker becoming the paper's Boston agent, joined by agents in other cities. Editor John Russwurm visited black communities in New Haven, Hartford, and Boston and sent back detailed, thoughtful reports on local conditions. Likewise, Rev. Samuel Cornish, who visited Boston, reported that the city offered blacks more opportunity than other places, though prejudice abounded there, too.[10] The paper provided a powerful forum for black voices in New York, Philadelphia, and especially Baltimore, where William Watkins wrote an extraordinary series attacking the ACS.

The newspaper not only reflected, but also helped to shape black consciousness. As blacks read stirring polemics, historical essays, and moralistic appeals for self-improvement, their pride and determination swelled. The paper also exemplified the self-confidence of its black leaders, who opened the pages of *Freedom's Journal* to blacks who favored African colonization.[11]

Freedom's Journal also aimed at a white audience. In fact, it was nearly as important to force whites to confront black opinion they preferred to ignore as to mobilize black opinion. The two objectives were inextricably intertwined. The increasing threat from the ACS was the driving force behind this latest expression of black resistance, which sought to shore up black opposition and put white support for colonization on the defensive. Blacks were genuinely puzzled that decent men and women embraced such an indecent cause, and they persisted in regarding many colonizationists as friends to be enlightened.

Freedom's Journal was only the most important manifestation of this new consciousness. Blacks had recognized that the time had come for new militancy and better organization. In 1826, a year before the paper's founding, black churches in Massachusetts formed the Massachusetts General Colored Association. They came out squarely for immediate emancipation and racial equality, frontally challenging colonization doctrine. In 1826, Jacob Greener harassed a colonization speaker in Baltimore, and speakers at new protest meetings in New York and Philadelphia in 1827 contended there was no evidence that colonization promoted emancipation. In 1829, Rev. Samuel Cornish challenged Rev. Theodore Gallaudet at a colonization meeting in New York City. *Freedom's Journal* simply amplified such sentiment manyfold. James Forten published an attack on Henry Clay, the country's leading colonizationist politician. Mordecai Noah, an editor promoting New York City's Democratic Party, also came under attack, as did David Hale, editor of the *New York Commercial Journal*. Black voters received advice to vote independently, advice aimed at questioning past support for Adams, Clay, and company now that colonization, integrated into the administration's program for economic development, threatened to become national policy backed by the resources of the United States.[12]

Such unprecedented defiance of white opinion triggered a white counterattack. At Princeton Theological Seminary, Samuel Miller and other Presbyterians became incensed at the black challenge to one of the denomination's favored philanthropies. Rev. Theodore Wright, who succeeded Cornish at the First Colored Presbyterian Church in New York City, attended Princeton, where *Freedom's Journal* appeared as a "thunderclap" to the white students and faculty. Miller sent a defense of colonization for publication that Cornish and Russwurm printed, but he also dropped his subscription to *Freedom's Journal*, announcing in the *New York Observer* that the black paper vilified the wise and the good. Cornish and Russwurm then pointed to Miller as an example of colonizationist "friends" who held blacks in as much contempt as their enemies. In New York, in October 1827, Gerrit Smith, a wealthy landowner and philanthropist who had contributed generously to the ACS, also expressed indignation at the attacks on colonization in *Freedom's Journal*: "The turn that negro learning takes in this country is not always favorable. It is certainly not with the editors of *Freedom's Journal*, a paper I was at first disposed to patronize." Smith eventually embraced immediatism in 1835, but he long had adhered to the colonizationist view that "the country ... must hasten to clear out the entire black population whose necessarily abused condition was at war with American institutions."[13] And in New York, the Episcopal bishop Onderdonck silenced Peter Williams, the black minister of St. Phillip's, for his anticolonizationist sentiments.[14]

White disapproval did not intimidate blacks. *Freedom's Journal* was only the opening gun in the renewed African American campaign against colonization. Now, at last, whites were forced to pay attention to black opinion. The next great blast, David Walker's *Appeal to the Colored Citizens of the World,* riveted attention as never before.

David Walker (1785–1830), the son of a white mother and a slave father, was born in Wilmington, North Carolina. A free black, Walker traveled extensively in the South, observing the cruelty of slavery first-hand. Walker eventually settled in Boston, where he sold new and used clothing. He quickly became a leader in Boston's black community, a member of the Methodist Church, active in the Massachusetts General Colored Association, and an agent of *Freedom's Journal.* In his mind, organization was essential to militant resistance: "The very derision, violence and oppression, with which we as a part of the community are treated by a benevolent and Christian people, ought to stimulate us to the greatest exertion for the acquirement of both literature and property."[15]

Walker typified a new generation forged by the experience of creating the first developed free black communities in the United States in the urban centers during the half-century after the American Revolution. These communities, boasting churches, schools, mutual aid and fraternal societies, and a cadre of leaders—ministers, educators, and businessmen—emboldened people to challenge white supremacy. In an address delivered before the General Colored Association of Massachusetts, Walker laid out a strategy for doing so. Walker understood the need to overcome resistance to organization among African Americans, whether out of timidity, fear, or lack of self-confidence. Formal association was essential to advance the race by uniting "the colored population, so far, through the United States of America, as may be practicable and expedient; forming societies, opening, extending, and keeping up correspondence." Lack of unity had been fatal to black prospects in the past. Thus presaging the *Appeal,* Walker sought to arouse blacks to mutual aid and self-help and to put an end to passive acquiescence in injustice. He also sought to persuade them that they would possess power once they mobilized.[16]

Mobilizing individuals and organizations was Walker's major purpose in the *Appeal.* It was more than a cry of conscience. For all its impassioned rhetoric, prophetic denunciations of white cant and injustice, and apocalyptic predictions, the *Appeal* advanced a complex, cogent argument with an immediate political purpose: to persuade blacks to struggle with whites to abandon colonization for racial equality.

Walker developed two themes simultaneously, the reasons for black pride and the need for blacks actively to resist the conditions that oppressed them. The first theme focused on those blacks in history whose achievements rebutted the view of them as degraded that was popularized by colonizationist defamation propaganda and by Thomas Jefferson. While combating this defamation, Walker singled out Jefferson for special attention. Jefferson's suspicion of black mental inferiority had done incalculable harm to the reputation of black people and required refutation by blacks themselves. Urging blacks to place copies of *Notes on the State of Virginia* in the hands of their children to stimulate rebuttal, Walker showed the way by refuting Jefferson's misuse of history. The examples Jefferson cited of achievement by the Roman former slaves Terence and Epictetus proved nothing, Walker argued. Neither Roman law nor custom oppressed the emancipated as color prejudice held back free blacks in the United States. Lessons in comparative history competed with Walker's instruction in Christian faith: Jefferson had described God's creation of black people as a "misfortune," a view that Walker characterized as steeped in human arrogance and bordering on blasphemy. God "has been pleased to make us black," Walker affirmed, and "we will not take his [Jefferson's] say so, for the fact" that our color is our misfortune. God makes no mistakes.[17]

At the same time that he sought to arouse black pride and self-esteem, Walker also stressed the need for resistance. Walker admitted that African Americans themselves bore complicity in their enslavement and degradation. He was determined to speak the truth, however painful. Africans enslaved Africans and others, he reminded people; dark-skinned Egyptians had enslaved Jews. In America, African drivers whipped other slaves and aided masters in securing their control, and free blacks helped to capture runaways. The failure of blacks to resist allowed a relatively small number of whites to keep thousands in chains and lent support to Jefferson's view that blacks, unlike Native Americans, were biologically inclined to servitude. Resistance, therefore, became a test for Walker of human equality. Once whites stood in mortal fear of slave revolt, slavery would crumble. Yet black disunity, complicity, and passivity frustrated Walker's hopes. He justified physical resistance as self-defense and denounced a coffle of slaves that had broken free in Kentucky but allowed their master, aided by a black woman, to escape with his life. "How sixty could let one escape unkilled, I cannot imagine," he exclaimed.[18] Though readers singled out Walker's defense of resistance for attention, Walker was too realistic to place his hopes on insurrection.

What gives unity to Walker's polemic is the argument for racial equality and for the active part to be taken by black people in achieving it.
The American Colonization Society, the principal enemy, systematically
"abused and held up the [African] Americans as the greatest nuisance to
white society, and throat-cutters in the world." Doubts about black
capacity for advancement lay at the heart of colonization doctrine, and
colonization, Walker concluded, was a cause of "our wretchedness."[19]
Such defamation emanated not from the gutters of New York or
Philadelphia, but from the pulpit, the halls of Congress, and from the
thoughts and writings of the republic's most prominent statesmen and
divines. Walker singled out Henry Clay as the prime mover in the
enterprise, quoting him extensively to refute Clay's reputation as a friend
of "bleeding Africa." Clay, like Jefferson, Walker argued, advocated
colonization for the purpose of better securing slavery. He cited John
Randolph, who candidly acknowledged that colonization had little to
do with gradual emancipation. He also condemned Elias B. Caldwell, a
Northern collaborator of Clay's who was close to Northern evangelicals
and who argued that the more one cultivated the minds of blacks, the
more miserable they would become. Three times in the essay, Walker
singled out the policies of Northern churches, making clear that white
prejudice and Christian hypocrisy, not just slavery, were his targets.

In fact, Christian hypocrisy provoked Walker's sharpest barbs.
While pious evangelicals formed numerous associations to combat
Freemasonry, intemperance, infidelity, and Sunday mail, they maintained
silence on the cruelties of slavery. The Gospel is supposed to be color-
blind, yet white color phobia caused Christians to oppress blacks in the
churches themselves, confining them to "nigger pews" and thereby "daring God" himself. In contrast, Walker lavished extravagant praise on
Bishop Richard Allen for his courageous struggle against expatriation.
The United States, Allen preached, had become African Americans'
"mother country," watered by their sweat and tears.

Turning the tables on black defamers, Walker countered that whites
were "the seed of Cain," judged by their behavior in history. Whereas
the Greeks, Romans, French, and British repeatedly had cut one another's throats, the people of Africa and Asia "never were half so avaricious, deceitful, and unmerciful."[20] Walker then advanced his "suspicion"—mocking Jefferson—that whites were created inherently inferior
morally to blacks. Until they abandoned slavery, whites hardly could
claim to be Christian or expect to convert the globe. Emancipation thus
became the means of securing the white race's redemption.

In promoting that redemption, black people played a central role. At the heart of Walker's *Appeal* lay the radical notion that the conversion of whites rested with blacks, an astonishing reversal that must have thrilled blacks as much as it infuriated whites. Free blacks occupied the strategic ground, enjoying opportunities denied slaves. Too many were smugly content to enjoy their own freedom, ignoring their larger responsibilities, accepting the too-limiting role carved out by white prejudice. They should aim at becoming skilled and educated. Nothing so frightened whites as "the bare name of educating the colored people," for a truly educated people decisively would give the lie to Jefferson's "suspicions."

Living in an evangelical age filled with millenarian apprehensions, Walker warned that unless whites repented and abandoned slavery and colonization, they faced providential punishment. Appealing with "tenderness" toward white friends who mistakenly had embraced colonization, Walker offered friendship, confident that either white prejudice would succumb in the face of black struggle or "the Lord our God will bring other destructions upon them."[21] On the Declaration of Independence, he hoped, both races could occupy common ground.

Walker circulated copies of the *Appeal* through the mails and via black and white seamen, who carried them to Southern cities in Virginia, North Carolina, Georgia, and Louisiana. Southern white leaders became alarmed and enacted new laws against teaching free blacks to read or write and demanded that Boston's mayor, Harrison G. Otis, take action against Walker. Otis assured Southerners that whites had no sympathy with Walker, but said he had violated no laws, so nothing could be done. Georgians, however, placed a large sum on Walker's head. In 1830, Walker died from causes unknown amid suspicion, never confirmed, of foul play.[22]

Few documents in American history elicited such contradictory contemporary and historical evaluations as the *Appeal*. The ACS quarterly took notice of its publication without comment; Benjamin Lundy condemned Walker for inciting to violence, but William Lloyd Garrison was more sympathetic. He admired Walker's "impassioned and determined spirit" and his "bravery and intelligence," but thought the *Appeal* "a most injudicious publication, yet warranted by the creed of an independent people."[23] The black leader H. H. Garnet in 1848 proclaimed it "among the first, and . . . the boldest and most direct appeals in behalf of freedom, which was made in the early part of the Anti-Slavery Reformation."[24] For one twentieth-century white historian, however, the

Appeal was "a most bloodthirsty document," while Saunders Redding, a modern black scholar, thought it "scurrilous, ranting, mad—but these were the temper of the times."[25] In their biography of their father, the Garrison children came closer to the truth about Walker: "His noble intensity, pride, disgust, fierceness, his eloquence and his general intellectual ability, have not been commemorated as they deserve."[26] In the short run, however, the significance of Walker's *Appeal* lay in giving voice to the new black militancy of the 1820s, to the struggle against African colonization and the growing awareness of the necessity of black unity and organization. And a key element of that militancy was his contention that blacks could and should take the initiative in advocating their cause.

Walker's attack on colonization did not sweep the field. A continuing division among blacks over whether to support colonization in some form triggered the calling of the first national black convention in 1830. Frederick Grice, a Baltimore iceman and hog butcher, originated the idea in response to the Ohio expulsions of blacks. Grice had seen a copy of David Walker's *Appeal* in the office of Lundy's *Genius of Universal Emancipation* sometime during 1829–30, which was where Garrison remarked that the pamphlet was premature. In Baltimore, the debate over colonization had raged throughout the 1820s and the dominant sentiment had come down on the side of Walker. But the expulsion of blacks from Ohio posed a cruel dilemma: should a principled stand against colonization anywhere outside the United States extend to Canada, where black refugees from this Ohio persecution had found shelter?

Settlement in Canada became a central question facing the first national conventions of African Americans which met in the 1830s. Grice's call met only a feeble response at first, but Bishop Richard Allen of Philadelphia recognized the need to unite black opinion and gave it his endorsement. Assembling in Philadelphia, a small band of blacks from several eastern-seaboard cities formed "The American Society of Free Persons of Color, for improving their condition in the United States; for purchasing lands; and for the establishment of a settlement in Upper Canada." The lengthy title revealed mixed purposes and deep divisions.[27]

At the convention, speeches affirmed the quest for equality while acknowledging the deplorable conditions blacks faced in striving to elevate themselves, including their own disunity. The American Colonization Society, put forward by its proponents as the most valuable means to raise up blacks, attracted many sincere friends of the black race, one speaker acknowledged, but it was one of the causes "of many of our unconstitutional, unchristian, and unheard sufferings."[28]

The alternative to African colonization was black uplift, but emphasis on black self-development, which became the dominant theme at the conventions by the mid-1830s, could not settle the question of Canadian colonization, and blacks remained torn. The conventions in effect pursued both resistance to colonization in Africa and support for colonization in Canada. At every convention during the first decade, delegates tirelessly emphasized the centrality of education and occupational training for advancement, along with the need for a black temperance movement, further underlining black commitment to bourgeois values. But even though most leaders remained committed to the pursuit of equality within the United States, in opposition to colonizationist efforts, they could not abandon those forced to flee for safety north of the border. The second convention, in 1832, reported the establishment of two thousand settlers in Canada and the purchase of eight hundred acres and called for additional funds to aid the Canadian brethren.

By 1832, however, Canada had receded in importance. The conventions still supported the refugees, but the center of the struggle lay elsewhere. Whites in Canada in 1831 sought to block further black influx, and this threw cold water on black colonization there. Canada remained preferable for those who felt they must migrate, but uncertainty that blacks could acquire property under Canadian law discouraged any further financial efforts, except to help those already living there. There was only one real answer to persecution.[29]

That was the continuing struggle for equality in the United States, and this required the destruction of the ACS. It was up to blacks themselves, the delegates had affirmed in 1831, whether they would "assume a rank and standing among the nations of the earth, as men and freemen."[30] The key was to educate a rising generation of black leaders, and the appearance at the 1831 convention of three white men, William Lloyd Garrison, Simeon Jocelyn, a preacher to blacks in New Haven, Connecticut, for over a decade, and the wealthy, evangelical, philanthropic businessman, Arthur Tappan, New York City's largest silk importer, proved to be a momentous development. The emergence of these white opponents of colonization was another reason for turning away from Canada so as not to discourage white commitment to the struggle for equality in the United States.[31] Garrison, Jocelyn, and Tappan proposed to join hands with blacks to establish a manual labor college in New Haven to train a new generation of black leaders. Manual labor schools were egalitarian efforts to wed physical labor on farms and in workshops to an academic regimen to produce physically, mentally, and morally fit citizens, both white and black. The college, by opening opportunity to black youth, would "remove prejudice and jealousy in the community, and lead to mutual respect and confidence between our white and colored population." Surely, the education of African Americans would provide "one of the signs of glory which shall fill the earth in Messiah's glorious day."[32]

For a long time, the ACS had usurped the field of white philanthropy, attracting men like Garrison, Tappan, and others who later became pillars of immediatism. Jocelyn, Garrison, and Tappan came to the 1831 convention thinking that colonization was mistaken, and they were intent on embarking on a new course. The proposed manual labor college in New Haven was intended as a joint venture, with half the funds raised by blacks, the rest from whites, and with blacks making up a majority of the trustees. True philanthropy, blacks affirmed, rejects prejudice against "any people which have no better foundation than accidental diversities of color, and refuses to determine without substantial evidence and incontestable fact as the basis of her judgment." New Haven, Jocelyn's base and the home of Yale University, seemed an ideal location for testing black potential. The manual labor system was especially well adapted to poor black students since it offered them a means of working while learning. Here, "the children of the poor may receive a regular classical education, as well as those of their more opulent brethren, and the charge will be so regulated as to put it within the reach of all."[33] Tappan was a member of the board of managers of the national Society for the Promotion of Manual Labor, which in 1831 had engaged Theodore Dwight Weld, Charles Grandison Finney's most important convert in the great revivals that had fired New York's Burned-Over District in the 1820s, to canvass the country as agent on behalf of the manual labor idea.

The challenge to colonization from African Americans alarmed ACS leaders, who requested an opportunity to address the third convention in 1833. Rev. Ralph Gurley tried eloquently to remove erroneous impressions that blacks held against the ACS, but Garrison's reply only confirmed black hostility, as did speeches by black leaders, though nine argued on each side of the colonization question, evidence of continued black divisions, which were further underlined by the refusal of the convention to publish, at the urging of Pittsburgh's militant anticolonizationist John Vashon, the tribute paid by General Andrew Jackson to the free blacks who had fought against the British at New Orleans.[34]

By the 1834 African-American convention, all mention of Ohio colonization disappeared, for now the issue was joined: racial prejudice was the principal enemy, and the ACS, its most potent disseminator, had to be crushed. By this time, African Americans sensed that thanks to their labors and those of friends like Garrison, the ACS lay wounded. Echoing David Walker, the convention reaffirmed the necessity of black self-discipline, education, and occupational advancement as key to the struggle. That year, reflecting a new unity, the convention published Andrew Jackson's Proclamation to the Free Colored Inhabitants of Louisiana of 1814, which had offered promises of bounties to blacks who fought for their country "as sons of Freedom," thereby affirming the convention's integrationist faith.[35] Integration also led the convention to endorse the newly formed New England Antislavery Society, the latest fruit of white-black collaboration. Earlier white antislavery societies, formed in the post-Revolutionary era, had not included blacks, whereas the new immediatist movement was the result of black efforts to convert whites. New hope now infused the rhetoric of black leaders: "Let no man remove from this, our native land, for our principles come from the Bible and the Declaration of Independence."[36]

The Conversion of William Lloyd Garrison

In May 1837, at the peak of white abolitionism's strength, Rev. Samuel Cornish reminded readers of the *Colored American* that credit for turning back the colonizationist tide belonged to African Americans. Garrison and others had performed yeoman service, but blacks always unwaveringly had opposed expatriation, convinced that they would "some day possess in our native land, *a perfect equality, in all respects* with our white brethren." Cornish was not ungrateful for the heroic labors of white abolitionists, but he recalled that "this doctrine is neither Tappan nor Garrison but is BIBLEISM, and we claim some instrumentality in teaching it to both these good men."[1] Cornish then reprinted essays that he and James Forten had written attacking colonization. These had first appeared in *Freedom's Journal*, 18 May 1827, and anticipated every argument of their white allies, although Cornish recognized that winning white support had been an essential development.

By the early 1830s, the decade-long struggle by African Americans against colonization had converted a crucial cadre of whites. These converts owed their transformation to personal relations and firsthand contacts with blacks that opened their eyes to the evils of colonization, its shameless defamation of African American worth and achievement, and its incompatibility with Christian republican norms. Among those first converted to abolitionism by their contact with black opponents of colonization was the editor of the *Liberator* himself. There can be no better example of the role played by blacks and black opposition to colonization in setting in motion the abolitionist movement than the conversion of William Lloyd Garrison.

There were a number of influences that prepared Garrison for his conversion to abolitionism and immediatism, but it was his encounter with black opposition to colonization that proved decisive. Garrison already had doubts about colonization. When he had been hired to edit a pro-Adams newspaper in Bennington, Vermont, during Adams's unsuccessful 1828 campaign against Andrew Jackson, Garrison had supported colonization along with other moral causes typically endorsed by high-minded Northern evangelical Protestants. But up to this time, Garrison had displayed only modest interest in the slavery question. Benjamin Lundy, the veteran gradualist antislavery newspaperman, had visited Garrison in Boston in 1827 and Bennington in 1828, hoping to impress on him his vision of slavery as the preeminent moral issue. Although Garrison's commitments to the cause of President Adams kept him preoccupied from October 1828 until March 1829, Andrew Jackson's victory confirmed for Garrison Lundy's long-held view that the slave states held a virtual lock on the presidency.[2] By 1830, Garrison, who like his friend John Greenleaf Whittier, another National Republican editor and admirer of Clay, was souring on Clay, the National Republican Party, and on the American Colonization Society as well.

The slaveholders' victory in the 1828 election, restoring a planter to the White House, not only alienated Garrison from politics, but it converged with his experience among African Americans in Baltimore, where he went to work after the election for eight months as coeditor with Benjamin Lundy of the *Genius of Universal Emancipation*. That experience opened his eyes to the sinfulness of African colonization and racial prejudice and to the unflinching opposition of free blacks to removal to Africa. Until blocked by Andrew Jackson's victory, African colonization had begun to acquire a dynamic momentum that alarmed and mobilized free blacks. Their counterattack produced far-reaching unanticipated consequences.

Garrison's doubts about colonization first surfaced in public in a Fourth of July address he delivered at Boston's Park Street Church in 1829. The Park Street Address was a prophetic landmark in his evolution toward immediatism and his lifelong commitment to racial equality. Who selected Garrison and why for the Park Street Church oration, a showcase celebration of Christian philanthropy, is not clear, but as a frequent worshipper at Lyman Beecher's Hanover Street Church and as a great admirer of Beecher's success as a Boston revivalist, Garrison must have come to the attention of orthodox Congregational leaders because of his role as a journalist devoted to the fusion of morals and politics, his devotion to temperance, antislavery, and Sabbatarianism, all causes embraced by the evangelicals.[3]

Garrison approached the pulpit with fear and trembling. It was an important audience and occasion. His friends John Greenleaf Whittier and the maverick Unitarian, Rev. John Pierpont, were in attendance. Whittier formed part of an important, new circle of editors and printers to whom Garrison had gravitated in Boston in the 1820s. They included Oliver Johnson, who became editor of an anti-Universalist paper, the *Christian Soldier,* and later served as a faithful collaborator at the *Liberator;* William C. Collier, a Baptist who sponsored the *National Philanthropist,* for which Garrison served as printer and editor from 1827 to 1828; William Goodell, who left Providence, where he edited the *Investigator,* for Boston to edit the *Philanthropist;* David Lee Child, who edited the *Massachusetts Journal,* a National Republican organ with moralistic leanings; and Stephen Foster, a printer on the Child paper and later foreman at the *Christian Examiner,* the Unitarian weekly, who lent Garrison the type to print the first three issues of the *Liberator.*

This circle is important for understanding Garrison's evolution, for it nurtured and shaped his ambition. From the time Garrison completed his apprenticeship as a printer, he sought to edit a newspaper. Those ambitions received impetus from his early writings for the press, which revealed his talents to his superiors. They sponsored him as editor of a series of newspapers through which he advanced the interests of the Timothy Pickering–William Henry Crawford forces in Massachusetts in 1824, then collaborated with Caleb Cushing, an ambitious young Essex County, Massachusetts, politician, until he fell out with him. He then worked in Bennington, Vermont, as editor of the *Journal of the Times,* established to promote the reelection of John Quincy Adams in 1828.

As a hired gun in the service of elites who supplied the capital, Garrison had to echo others' opinions. He could be dropped whenever it suited his sponsors' convenience. President Adams's defeat, for example, left him dangling; a dispute with Cushing sent him packing. For a man of ambition and strong moral opinions, Garrison found his position anomalous. Yet he found in the Boston circle of printers and journalists stability and fellowship. The intense moralism that they shared transcended denominational differences, offset their dependency on the favor of employers, and reinforced their sense of importance as moral sentinels. An editor must never be a "political adventurer or a loose

moralist," Garrison insisted, and though the profession had been corrupted by many such men, Garrison thought that now "a new race of
editors, with better qualifications and nobler views, are entering the
ranks," namely, his friends.[4]

Garrison first had published Whittier in 1826 as editor of the
Newburyport *Free Press;* in turn, Whittier's optimism and sympathies
for the underprivileged influenced Garrison. In 1827, Garrison took up
residence with his fellow Baptist William Collier, editing his paper until
he went to work for the Adams campaign. At the *National
Philanthropist,* Garrison took an ultra line on temperance and the
Sabbath, demanding teetotalism toward alcohol and strict observance of
the Lord's Day, well in advance of mainstream evangelical opinion.
Similarly ultra views on temperance got Goodell into trouble with the
religious backers of the temperance newspapers he edited, first in
Massachusetts and then in New York. Garrison himself best exemplified
the moralism of the circle in a letter to the *Boston Courier* in 1827 that
attacked lotteries and "whatever has a tendency to create an unusual
thirst for gain."[5]

This ultraist brand of moralism lay the groundwork for Garrison's
conversion to belief in immediate abolition. "I speak not as a partisan
or an opponent of any man or measures," Garrison proclaimed near the
beginning of the Park Street Church Address, "when I say that our politics are rotten to the core." Politics were corrupt because public morals
were corrupt. Citizens went "shackled to the polls, year after year, by
tens and hundreds and thousands" like "the merest automata" to vote
for "unprincipled jugglers!" Political corruption only reflected a deeper
corruption that allowed desecration of the "holy Sabbath," widespread
infidelity, ravaging intemperance, "a profligate press," and indifference
to the nation's gravest national sin, slavery. "The republic does not bear
a charmed life," Garrison warned, if such evils, especially slavery, remained unattended.[6]

Although the evil of slavery was acknowledged by "Christians and
Philanthropists," their response was equivocal. "What has Christianity
done, by direct effort, for our slave population?" Garrison asked.
"Comparatively nothing," he answered. The country was awash in
"charitable societies" that formed "golden links of benevolence," but
"they bring no sustenance to the perishing slaves."[7]

If Americans faltered as Christians, they stumbled as republicans, paying smug, sanctimonious tribute each Fourth of July to the sacred doctrine of the Declaration of Independence that all men are created equal

while ignoring "such a glaring contradiction as exists between our creed and practice the annals of six thousand years cannot parallel." If the audience had anticipated the customary patriotic praise the occasion typically elicited from the day's orator, Garrison surprised them: "I am ashamed of my country. I am sick of our unmeaning declamation in praise of liberty and equality, of our hypocritical cant about the unalienable rights of man."[8]

Garrison then broke ranks with the conventional wisdom in the North that slavery was a Southern problem and responsibility. "Sir, this is a business in which, as members of one great family, we have a common interest; but we take no responsibility, either individually or collectively," because "our hearts are cold, our blood stagnates in our veins." Reminding his listeners of their obligation to the slaves under the Golden Rule, he insisted that the free states "demand a gradual abolition of slavery, because, by its continuation, they participate in the guilt thereof, and are threatened with ultimate destruction." Alluding to the recent election, Garrison noted that the free states had nearly double the population of the slave states, yet the constitutional provision for slave representation, combined with party manipulation, had deprived the free states "of their just influence in the councils of the nation." Such a situation was "absurd and anti-republican." Garrison recognized the limits of federal power over domestic institutions such as slavery, but there were no limits on prayer, charity, and persuading slaveholders to abandon slavery.[9]

The crux of the matter was race. "Would you shut your eyes upon their sufferings, and calmly talk of Constitutional limitations" were the slaves to "suddenly become white?" And on the grounds of race, "the prejudices of the North are stronger than those of the South." Until Northerners conquered those prejudices, they would continue to help forge the chains that bound the slaves.

Paying tribute to his friend Lundy, Garrison proclaimed himself a gradualist, claiming that emancipation would take more than a generation to accomplish But he also echoed Lundy's demand that the work of emancipation begin now. Delay was dangerous, he told his audience. The nation stood atop an erupting volcano. "A cry of horror, a cry of revenge, will go up to heaven," and "blood will flow like water,—the blood of guilty men and of innocent women and children," unless "republican America" moved toward "the glorious day of universal emancipation." Now was "perhaps the last opportunity that will be granted us by a long-suffering God."[10]

In seconding Lundy's gradualism, Garrison still endorsed colonization, if only in passing. Garrison called on the press, the churches, and
the clergy, on "our New England women," and on "auxiliary colonization societies in every State, county, and town" to take up the challenge.
He thus broke no new ground on these crucial issues, but by insisting
that slavery was "strictly a national sin," that Northern racial prejudice
was at the crux of the matter, and that a bloody apocalypse lay over the
horizon, he endorsed essential elements of the immediatist perspective
toward which he was moving. And in setting forth a vision of a society
based on racial equality, he was implicitly challenging the cardinal assumption of colonization, even as he refused to break with it. Most "of
our colored population were born on our soil," he reminded people,
"and are therefore entitled to all the privileges of American Citizens."
The United States was "their country by birth, not by adoption," "their
children possess the same inherent and unalienable rights as ours, and it
is a crime of the blackest die to load them with fetters."[11] It was not until he had firsthand experience of blacks as equals and as obdurate opponents of colonization that he became fully committed to the immediatist doctrines that made him one of abolitionism's most ardent
advocates.

Within two months after the Park Street Church Address, Garrison
had reached Baltimore and appeared for the first time as coeditor with
Lundy of the *Genius of Universal Emancipation*.[12] In Baltimore,
Garrison socialized among Lundy's Quaker and African-American
friends. The two men soon agreed to sign their editorials separately because their views were diverging on adherence to colonization and gradualism, with Garrison becoming more skeptical of the former and more
impatient with the latter. Baltimore possessed the largest and one of the
most impressive African-American communities in the United States.
Men such as William Watkins and Jacob Greener were powerful spokesmen for the race. Watkins, the son of a trustee of the Sharp Street
Methodist Church, took over the Baltimore school for blacks after Rev.
Daniel Coker, a Methodist, left for Liberia. Self-taught, with a fine command of English, Watkins's intelligence and dignity confounded prejudice and impressed Garrison immensely.[13] Watkins's essays attacking colonization provided much of the argument that later appeared in
Garrison's *Thoughts on African Colonization*. Yet even before reaching
Baltimore, Garrison probably had become more conscious of the depths
of black opposition to colonization, for the first issue of the *Genius* co-
edited by Garrison published an account by "A Traveler in the North"

of a July 4 annual Jubilee of Boston blacks that Garrison may have
attended. In any event, the writer, perhaps Garrison himself, praised
the blacks for their temperance, in comparison with the riotous
intemperance whites exhibited on July 4, and then described a meeting
at Rev. Nathaniel Paul's church, where efforts to promote colonization
by an agent of the ACS aroused murmurs of dissent, which the writer
thought amply provoked by the insult imparted by the argument that
ignorance and moral degradation justified enslavement until removal
was practical.[14]

Still, Garrison's encounter with the free black population of Baltimore
was what ultimately converted him from colonizationist to abolitionist.
There, the influence of black anticolonization opinion and the argument
for racial equality pushed him further in the direction he already had
taken in Boston. It did not prove easy to break with colonization, and
even in Baltimore, Garrison still echoed the Lundy line that colonization
was a useful auxiliary if it promoted gradual emancipation. But in
October 1829, he visited a black school and challenged readers: "We
should like to have those, who persist in debasing the intellect and capacity of our colored population, to stop into this school, and try if they
can argue against the fact."[15] In January, he praised the formation of the
African Temperance Society, which was organized on teetotal principles,
a cause ever dear to his heart, and one that most white evangelicals still
hesitated to embrace, seeing it as ultraist.[16]

The debate over colonization, however, had assumed center stage. In
November 1829, Watkins launched a powerful series rebutting a procolonization series that had begun in the *Genius*. David Walker's *Appeal*
already had appeared, and Garrison read it, but he must have been familiar with the line of argument, since he vouched for the authenticity
of Walker's authorship, which came under challenge, by affirming that
Walker had been studying the subject diligently for years and had expressed himself orally in substance similar to the views found in the
Appeal. In Baltimore, as we have seen, Frederick Grice noticed a copy
in Garrison's office.

By December 1829, Garrison's thoughts turned back to politics as a
new session of Congress approached. As he saw it, moral conflict undergirded all the major issues facing the new session: the South Carolina
proslavery attacks against tariff protection, the proslavery implications
of Texas independence from Mexico and Cherokee removal, which
would clear the way for further unchecked expansion of the Cotton
Kingdom into the Southwest, and the petitions calling for abolition of

slavery in the District of Columbia and for a halt to Sabbath mails. The new strength of the Jacksonians, now in command of the White House, seemed to bode ill for any containment of slavery or of moral corruption in public life. President Jackson and the Deep South were also hostile to colonization, which marred prospects for receiving federal funding, the only strategy that gave plausibility to the idea of transporting tens of thousands annually to Africa. Bankrupt morally, bankrupt politically, and now bankrupt financially, colonization together with its political mastermind, Henry Clay, no longer commanded Garrison's support.[17]

Garrison left Baltimore a changed man. When he announced his departure from the *Genius*, Garrison admitted that his views on slavery were only imperfectly developed because he had been too preoccupied with running the newspaper to think the issue through fully, and he promised to do better in the near future. In fact, he had gained new respect for the progress of free blacks; he had encountered impressive examples of black intelligence; and he had fallen increasingly under the sway of black anticolonization arguments and the touching faith of blacks in the capacity of whites to change. Rejecting the view that white prejudice against blacks was invincible—Clay's argument and that of every advocate of colonization—Garrison now regarded it as a libel upon the American people, for it assumed that white citizens possessed "a moral incapacity to do justice, love mercy, and walk uprightly."[18] In Baltimore, too, he had seen victims of whippings and witnessed firsthand the slave trade in all its brutality. Finally, he had suffered imprisonment for exposing Northern complicity in the expansion of slavery, making him a martyr to truth and more determined than ever to take the cause to the North. His jailing received wide notice in some one hundred Northern newspapers.

As Garrison cast about for a new strategy after leaving Lundy, he first thought of establishing a paper in the nation's capital. He now realized more clearly that racial prejudice was the principal stumbling block— the intolerance motivating colonization efforts and justifying the continued enslavement of millions. As he traveled from Baltimore to Boston, he encountered white indifference to the condition of the slaves, except among a few Quakers. He also encountered other impressive black leaders, such as James Forten and Robert Purvis in Philadelphia, who confirmed his views of black ability, already deepened in Baltimore. But when he tried to arouse whites in New Haven, Hartford, Providence, and Boston, he "found contempt more bitter, opposition more active, detraction more relentless."[19]

Garrison realized that others must undergo the same conversion that he had undergone and learn to view African Americans for their true worth. That battle lay in the North. By August 1830, when he announced the prospectus of a new antislavery newspaper, spurred on by the dangers of Jacksonianism, and then in January 1831, when the *Liberator* finally appeared, Garrison had launched the next phase of his career, as colonization's mortal enemy, racial equality's best friend.

"The Hidden Springs of Prejudice"

Rev. Simeon Jocelyn preceded William Lloyd Garrison in the conversion to abolitionism by contact with black anticolonizationists and the free black community. Yet Jocelyn's experiences also brought him face to face with the sources of colonizationist strength and the underlying motives for white resistance to the cause of freedom and equality for African Americans in the United States. It brought him face to face with the pervasiveness of white racial prejudice.

Like virtually every important white convert—Garrison in 1830, James G. Birney in 1834, Gerrit Smith in 1835—Jocelyn had embraced colonization. Jocelyn was an engraver who with his brother, Nathaniel, operated a firm in New Haven, Connecticut, and New Haven was a colonizationist stronghold at the time.[1] A man of deep piety, he studied with Rev. Nathaniel W. Taylor, pastor of the Center Church in New Haven, who subsequently became professor of theology at the founding of Yale Divinity School. Taylor was the foremost theologian engaged in the work of reconstructing Calvinism in the early nineteenth century to accommodate a new, more optimistic view of human ability in the search for salvation.[2] Given the meliorist tendencies in Taylor's famous dictum that people possess a "power to the contrary" to combat sin, the Taylor circle in New Haven became a center of colonizationist sentiment, regarding the transporting of freed blacks as the only practicable way to combat the sin of slavery. And with the arrival of Leonard Bacon as Taylor's successor at the Center Church, colonizationist sentiment among New

Haven elites found a new advocate. Bacon was a prize student from
Andover Theological Seminary and one of Congregationalism's most
promising young talents.

Bacon had developed a strong feeling against slavery and an interest
in colonization while still at Andover, seeing the ACS as the most promising means for gradually abolishing slavery. He attended an annual meeting of the ACS in Washington to urge new organizational efforts and to
reassure himself that colonizationists shared his gradualist beliefs about
abolition. The most important Northern clerical leader attracted by the
ACS throughout the 1820s and 1830s, Bacon became a powerful advocate in sermons such as *A Plea for Africa* and in writings in the
Christian Spectator.

Taylorite meliorism led to an emphasis on self-help. In New Haven,
as a member of the Taylorite circle close to Yale, Bacon organized a group
of young white men into an African Improvement Society in 1826. They
threw their support behind New Haven's black church, which had been
originated a few years earlier by Jocelyn, who had hoped to encourage
black self-improvement. The board of the society was biracial, a notable
breach of caste, but Bacon's interest in black education always remained
closely linked to colonization, to prepare African Americans for the arduous job of spreading Christianity and civilization upon their repatriation. In 1828, Bacon helped to establish the Connecticut Colonization
Society and served as its first secretary.[3]

Freedom's Journal reported the formation of New Haven's African
Improvement Society and sent its junior editor, John Russwurm, to de-
scribe the condition of the city's blacks. There were about eight hundred
free blacks in the city, but only five or six owned any property, and many
of the rest were vagabonds and a disgrace to the community, Russwurm
observed. The African Improvement Society received verbal support
from many of the town's leading citizens, but it had not yet accomplished
much and already had run into opposition. The black church was a
rough, unfinished wooden building, and its two schools operated only
three months a year, much too short a time. The condition of New
Haven's blacks, Russwurm concluded, hardly made them suitable material for the colonizationists' mission of rescuing Darkest Africa.[4]

Russwurm found that the American Colonization Society enjoyed
broad support among the town's leading citizens. Everywhere he went,
colonization was on people's lips. Russwurm may have tried to counter
white opinion: the ACS, he wrote, had been successful in imposing its
foolish, impractical views on many whites, and whites must face the truth

that blacks were unwilling to emigrate. He had highest praise for Jocelyn, whom he described as a warm friend of black people.

Jocelyn's close association with New Haven's African Americans, his dedication to their advancement in the United States, and his knowledge of how hard some strove to improve themselves made him especially susceptible to black opposition to colonization. By 1827, these influences had their effect. Jocelyn rejected colonization in favor of equality.[5] By 1831, as we have seen, Jocelyn was in the forefront of the anti-colonizationist efforts to establish the manual labor college in New Haven.[6] For this early convert, it was an early lesson in the obstacles abolitionism faced.

New Haven roundly repudiated the effort to provide blacks with a means for self-help and eventual equality. In September 1831, the town fathers, including the foremost National Republican and Jacksonian leaders, together with the voters of New Haven, assembled in a town meeting, and with only four or five dissenting, Jocelyn among them, voted to "resist the establishment of the proposed College in this place, by every lawful means."[7]

The nearly unanimous decision at New Haven stunned the blacks and their white allies. As the home of Yale University, with an elite devoted to a meliorist theology and professing a strong interest in combating the sin of slavery, no other city had seemed to offer such fair prospects. The grounds of the rejection pulled the rug from under any hope of black improvement. The town meeting perceived the manual labor school as part of a program for immediate emancipation, as merely "an auxiliary thereto," constituting "an unwarrantable and dangerous interference with the internal concerns of other States" that "ought to be discouraged." Not only did black self-improvement threaten the Union, the citizens of New Haven claimed, but it also threatened the "the prosperity if not the existence of the present institutions of learning, and will be destructive of the best interests of the city," an acknowledgment that Southern patronage of Yale deserved careful tending and that the city's female schools would be less attractive if New Haven were overrun by hot-blooded black teenagers.[8]

Jocelyn had not anticipated the opposition. For years he had worked for black uplift in New Haven with the endorsement of leading men. Just two years before the idea of a manual labor college surfaced, the idea of a high school received approval from "our literary men," those surely "who were from their peculiar situation, supposed to be better able to judge of its effect upon Yale College and the female schools, than other persons in the city."⁹ Jocelyn denied the alleged links between the manual labor college and immediatism. One of its most generous benefactors was a slaveholder, he pointed out, and "some of the friends . . . are in favor of immediate emancipation, and some of them are opposed to it. Some of them are opposed to the Colonization Society, and some of them are its advocates." The objective was "simply education in literature, the sciences and the arts, without respect to peculiar denomination." Jocelyn had expected "that men of influence and literature would favor the undertaking." Instead, it encountered "the influence of prejudice and a slavery-accommodating spirit."

But Jocelyn could not foresee Nat Turner's insurrection, between 13 and 23 August 1831, which left fifty-seven whites dead and resulted in the execution of twenty blacks. This slave revolt suddenly affected sectional comity and Southern self-confidence, resulting in demands for Northern reassurances. Even more important, Jocelyn failed to appreciate that any scheme designed to promote the long-term advancement of African Americans in the United States directly repudiated colonization and therefore appeared to be a step toward immediatism and racial equality. Furthermore, Jocelyn gave away the tendency of the scheme when he admitted that the college hoped also to educate young blacks from the British West Indies, soon to be freed by Parliament, by bringing them to New Haven. Finally, Jocelyn glossed over the radical implications of the manual labor movement and the challenge it posed to elites in nineteenth-century America. Manual labor promised to reduce education costs and to democratize access to education for the poor, whether black or white, who would earn their way through school. Manual labor advocates hoped also to inculcate respect for physical toil and narrow the widening gulf between blue-collar and white-collar occupations that an emerging bourgeois culture had made one of the critical distinctions in the new, emerging system of social stratification. The manual labor movement also challenged conventional notions of manliness and femininity, defining them not in terms that produced "success" in the marketplace or in the home, but in terms of moral character vital in the struggle to sustain a Christian republic. And critics who perceived a link to immediatism and abolitionism were correct. The manual labor movement nurtured a matrix of ideas and experiences that helped transform mere saints into abolitionists.

Jocelyn singled out New Haven's elites for blame for the rejection of the manual labor school. The fear that Yale's white students would "abuse colored youth," like the equally "ridiculous" fear of "amalgamation," was largely the result of the "feelings of men of riper years."[10] There was no reason to fear free blacks. The numbers of "vicious and abandoned" in New Haven had declined, while "many have become pious and industrious, and those who come to our city are usually virtuous and respectable."[11] Why had some whites privately encouraged a school that in public they now execrated, Jocelyn asked? "Simply because" by welcoming a manual labor college, New Haven would have "declared more than could have been written in a hundred pages, our assurance of the equal right to literature, in common with other citizens." In short, the manual labor college would strike a blow against the cardinal assumption of African colonization. In New Haven, Jocelyn concluded, "we have unwitting touched the hidden springs of prejudice and oppression *by a word*." Now the friends of African Americans knew what they faced: "the spirit which trifles with the interest of the oppressed," the "weaknesses of the great," and "the spirit of the unthinking." Among professed Christians there was in fact "a vast amount of unsanctified nature in us all, which must be purified before we gain the celestial city."[12] In 1834, Jocelyn abandoned services at his black church, no longer able to contend with continued disturbances to the peace and security, and transferred his energies to the cause of immediate abolitionism in New York City.[13]

The New Haven debacle occurred at a time of intense racial anxiety in both the North and the South. Nat Turner's rebellion made colonizationists more certain than ever that time was running out and that rapid action was necessary to finance large-scale removals. Southern anticolonizationists drew the opposite conclusions: that any agitation of the slavery question, even by philanthropically minded slaveholding colonizationists, unsettled both the free and the enslaved blacks in the South. Meanwhile, in the North, an antiblack riot in Providence, Rhode Island, in 1831 that lasted several days and left several dead was just the beginning of a new series of racial disturbances. It was followed by riots in Hartford and New York in 1834 that confirmed the intensity of prejudice against black advances.

Reflecting on the events in New Haven, Benjamin Silliman, a Yale professor of geology who had participated in the New Haven circle that in the 1820s had encouraged Jocelyn and black uplift, reaffirmed his commitment to African colonization as the best hope. Addressing Bacon's Center Church on the Fourth of July in 1832, Professor Silliman praised the neat, industrious, and sober blacks who followed Jocelyn, but declared the founding of a manual labor college to be premature and

something that tended to discourage black emigration. While supporting education primarily to train blacks for Africa, Silliman thought it visionary to attempt suddenly to elevate them in the United States. Though
he hoped most free blacks could be persuaded to leave and acknowledged
that those who wished to remain deserved proper education to prepare
them to become laborers, mechanics, farmers, and seamen, he declared
that they would remain "during this generation and perhaps forever" excluded from social equality and political life.[14] Silliman warned the white
friends of free blacks not to discourage voluntary emigration out of a
misguided commitment to immediatism and racial equality.

The attempt to found a black manual labor college in New Haven revealed as no previous event had the depths of white prejudice. The New
Haven *Religious Intelligencer* thought the city's actions had humiliat-
ingly exposed "the unrighteous prejudices of the country . . . to deny the
poor blacks a place of education." Prejudice was "the fruit of our own
cruelty and crime" and led men to "cut off a portion of our fellow being from knowledge and the blessings which follow in the train of those
gifts." Even worse, it was not the rabble, but those who "rank high or-
dinarily for wisdom and discretion" who led the unthinking multitude.[15]
The Baptist *Vermont Telegraph* expressed astonishment "that there
could be found in our own free and happy New England a city, town or
village, which would not be proud" to welcome a college for "a degraded
and injured race."[16] "Men complain of the ignorance and vice of the colored population," pointed out the New York *Journal of Commerce*—a
voice of Presbyterian commercialism, once sponsored by the Tappan
brothers, Arthur and Lewis—"and yet when a project is presented to rescue them . . . from their deep degradation, the same men are roused at
once to the highest pitch of indignation." And from Boston came denunciations of the "vulgar and unmanly prejudice" of New Haven, suggesting that Boston seize the "the glory" of establishing the first seminary "for the instruction of a much wronged race of men."[17] "I scorn
the men who fear that the blacks, if educated, might become our rivals
and associates," another wrote. "Is our respectability so fragile and factitious as to be destroyed by such intercourse? Is it superficial as the distinction of color? Will such narrow and unreasoning aristocracy be allowed here to raise its voice against one of the great rights of humanity,"
the right to an education?[18] "The friends of the college will do well to
look to Virginia or Kentucky for a location," sarcastically advised
William Goodell in the New York *Genius of Temperance*.[19]

The reaction of African Americans to the outcry in New Haven was surprise. Samuel Cornish declared that while blacks were accustomed to being abused by the rabble, "and they only," the leading role played by the gentlemen of property and standing in New Haven came as a shock. He assured whites that in endorsing the manual labor college, the National Negro Convention had no intention of interfering with slavery, but he also insisted that it would not abandon the college. Unwelcome in New Haven, African Americans would seek another more hospitable site, but, Cornish added, "we think the dignitaries of this *seat of science* have descended below themselves. It is beneath the gentleman, the patriot, or the Christian to endeavor to crush a feeble institution."[20]

The failure at New Haven did not kill the idea of a manual labor college. The National Negro Convention in 1832 reaffirmed its commitment. Securing funds for such an institution somewhere else became one of the objectives of William Lloyd Garrison's first trip to Britain in 1833, financed in part by blacks. But the defeat at New Haven was harbinger of more to come.

In 1833, Prudence Crandall's efforts to operate a female academy at Canterbury, Connecticut, at first open to members of both races, and then run exclusively for young African-American females, met the same fate as the manual labor college at New Haven.[21] Invited by the town's elite to establish a school for their daughters, Crandall, a Quaker educated at the Friends' school in Providence, Rhode Island, arrived in Canterbury in 1831 with no intentions of challenging racial hierarchy. She employed a young black woman, Marcia, however, who was slated to marry the son of a respectable black farmer, William Harris, the local agent for the *Liberator*. Marcia lent Crandall a copy of the paper, which awakened her to the "the double-dealing and manifest deception of the Colonization Society." When Sarah Harris, William's daughter, asked to attend the school, Prudence could not deny such a reasonable request, especially since Sarah was an exemplary person, a born-again Christian member of the Canterbury Congregationalist Church. "My feelings began to awaken," she recalled. Perhaps influenced by the events in New Haven, she "saw the prejudice of whites against color was deep and inveterate," and concluded that it was "the only chain that bound those heavy burdens on the wretched slaves."[22] Crandall could not foresee the storm her decision produced.

The Canterbury parents withdrew their daughters, and the town meeting declared inveterate opposition to Crandall's subsequent plan for an all-black school. In March 1833, the *Liberator* ran an advertisement for students, and young black women from Boston, Providence, New York, and elsewhere headed for Canterbury. "If possible Miss Crandall must be sustained at all hazards," Garrison wrote, for "the New Haven excitement has furnished a bad precedent," and "a second must not be given, or I know not what we can do to raise up the colored population, in a manner which their intellectual and moral necessities demand."[23]

Leading the town's opposition, Andrew T. Judson, a Democratic politician and colonizationist, warned that "once open the door, and New England will become the Liberia of America," subverting the entire colonizationist scheme. "The colored people can never rise from their menial condition in our country," Judson argued, and "they ought not to be permitted to rise here." "Let the niggers and their descendants be sent back to their fatherland, and there improve themselves if they can," Judson blustered. The *Norwich Republican* agreed: the school threatened "to break down the barriers which God has placed between blacks and whites—to manufacture '*Young Ladies of color*'" who would go forth to entice "our white bachelors." From this perspective, Prudence Crandall's scheme was really a plot "to force the two races to amalgamate."[24] Prosecuted for violating Connecticut's new "Black Law," hastily passed legislation that forbade anyone from operating a school for out-of-state blacks without permission of the local community, an exhausted Crandall gave up after the Supreme Court of Errors reversed her conviction on a technicality.

The law now formalized the hidden springs of prejudice that had surfaced earlier at New Haven. "It strengthens the unreasonable prejudice already pervading the community against blacks," Crandall's lawyer told the Court of Errors.[25] The Black Law merely codified community sentiment that went back to the birth of the Federal Union, Judson answered. Free blacks never had been citizens of the United States and therefore they had no right to move freely from one state to another. "The distinction of colour so far from being novel, is marked in numerous ways in our political system," Judson argued. The principle at stake was momentous and could "destroy the government and this *American* nation—blotting out this nation of white men, and substituting one from the *African* race."[26] Judson's hysteria, no less than his vulgar rhetoric, suggests how sharply Crandall's modest efforts to help free blacks stung white consciences. First at New Haven and now at Canterbury, the prospect of offering educational opportunity for African Americans threatened the very existence of the Union, in the eyes of some. They believed the time had come to make clear the nature of the United States as a *Herrenvolk* republic, for whites only.

In 1835, white pressure was brought to bear against the Baptist academy at New Canaan, New Hampshire, which was torn down after it opened its doors to African Americans. In New Hampshire, as in Connecticut, leading men and prominent colonizationists manned the barricades against black uplift. The events not only revealed more clearly the depths of "the hidden springs of prejudice" in the United States, but also revealed the extent to which the prejudiced typically do not recognize their prejudice. But now white prejudice faced a challenge. Blacks had led some whites to question colonization, to affirm the possibilities of black advance in their native land, and to recognize the pervasiveness of racial prejudice in American society. Garrison, Jocelyn, Crandall, and their black allies learned at New Haven, Canterbury, and New Canaan that they faced far more formidable opposition than any had anticipated. There was no choice now but to launch a frontal assault on the assumptions of prejudice.

The Assault on Racial
Prejudice, 1831–1837

In June 1831, full of optimism, William Lloyd Garrison made a tour of urban black communities, including New York City and Philadelphia, to speak directly with those who provided the *Liberator* with the bulk of its support. Garrison hoped to win additional black subscribers for the *Liberator,* now his mainstay. During the tour, he certainly won the personal devotion of many African Americans. Never before had they heard a white man vindicate the race so boldly, with a promise of full equality in the near term. Garrison had to rely on black leaders to organize these meetings, and for their part, they employed the tour as one element of a continuing nationwide effort to arouse black consciousness, militancy, and opposition to colonization. At the request of his "colored brethren, in the various cities," Garrison published his extraordinary *Address Delivered before the Free People of Color,* which went through three editions in two years.

Garrison's tour occurred at a critical time. Blacks increasingly were speaking out against colonization, and the testimony of black voices contributed a crucial element to the effort to combat white racial prejudice and to convert white citizens from gradualism to immediatism and from colonization to emancipation. A year after his address and tour, thanks to the new activism among blacks that it helped fuel, Garrison was able to publish his most important literary contribution to the cause of abolitionism and racial equality, *Thoughts on African Colonization.* Through it, for the first time, blacks gained access to a significant sector of white opinion; in turn, whites learned firsthand the views of African Americans on colonization. Just as Garrison's address helped energize the black movement, the black movement contributed the energy that began to make it possible for abolitionists to expose and attack white racial prejudice.

Blacks probably provided most of the readers who snapped up copies of Garrison's address, as they did two years earlier, when David Walker's apocalyptic voice thrilled them. Now a white man, converted by blacks to the struggle for immediate emancipation and racial equality, stirred them as they never had been stirred before. His color was the great surprise. Before Garrison met the British antislavery leader Thomas F. Buxton during his first trip to Britain in 1833, Buxton had assumed that he was black.[1] To American blacks, it was just as astonishing that a white man expressed the views hundreds heard during this tour.

Garrison began his address with a confession of guilt, of shame for those "of my own color . . . who have done you so much injustice." To atone for his own past sins—his indifference and his support for colonization—he pledged his "health and strength, and life . . . to work for your social, intellectual, political and spiritual advancement." Addressing his audience as "Countrymen and Friends," Garrison predicted "glorious and sudden changes" would unshackle the slave and secure to free blacks "the same rights in this country as other citizens." For that to happen, blacks themselves had an important role to play. Praising the self-help virtues, Garrison argued that industriousness, orderliness, piety, and temperance would confound the libelers of the race, while the new college at New Haven would allow black youth for the first time to "enter into competition with whites, on equal grounds" and thereby disprove at last that "they are of inferior capacity." The graduates of the college, he confidently predicted, would silence "your incredulous traducers, and finish the controversy which has so long divided public opinion." Someday, he was certain, the college would send forth black Websters and Clays, Dwights and Edwardses, "Judges, and Representatives, and Rulers of the people." The college, he believed, would evaporate "the mists of prejudice."[2]

Finally, Garrison turned his guns on the American Colonization Society. "Abandon all thought of colonizing yourselves, as a people, in Africa, Hayti, Upper Canada, or elsewhere," he insisted. America was the African Americans' "only home." The way to "destroy the Colonization Society" was to "refuse to go." Whites would then "feel necessitated to admit you to the rank of citizen" to enjoy "liberty—equality—every republican privilege." Two months before the collapse of the New Haven college plan, Garrison predicted that "the victory is half won—the tide of public sentiment is turning in your favor, and your deliverance is sure."[3]

To destroy the Colonization Society, Garrison argued, "you must hold an active correspondence on the subject with your brethren, all over the country, and conjure them all to stand firm."[4] That already was happening. In January 1831, beginning in New York, five months before Garrison's tour, black citizens had met to reject colonization as an "unholy crusade against the colored population of this country . . . totally at variance with true Christian principles."[5] Similar meetings occurred at Boston and Baltimore in March, at Washington, D.C., in May, at Brooklyn in June, at Hartford in July, at New Haven, Nantucket, and Columbia, Pennsylvania, in August, at Pittsburgh in September, at Harrisburg and Rochester in October, at Providence and Trenton in November, and at Lyme, Connecticut, Lewistown, Pennsylvania, and New Bedford, Massachusetts, in January 1832. Coming on top of the assault on colonization in *Freedom's Journal* between 1827 and 1829, and on top of David Walker's attack and the rejection of colonization by the first national Negro convention, these meetings demonstrate that blacks were mobilizing as never before in the struggle for equality. But whereas in the past their views had gone largely unnoticed in the white community, this time, the depth and intensity of black hatred for colonization and belief in the idea of racial equality reached a much wider white public.

Garrison decided to reprint all the black protests cited above as part 2 of *Thoughts on African Colonization,* published in June 1832. *Thoughts on African Colonization* was "the greatest blow of his life— or any man's life," said Elizur Wright Jr., one of Garrison's first important converts.[6] Selling three thousand copies in nine months and purchased in bulk by Arthur Tappan for personal distribution, *Thoughts* was the major fruit of Garrison's own education by blacks, who had supplied him with the arguments and with back issues of *The African Repository,* the ACS's monthly, from which Garrison documented his thesis that colonization strengthened slavery while defaming and degrading free blacks. Garrison filled most of the pamphlet with block quotations from colonizationist sources, overwhelming readers with proof to buttress each of his main contentions: that the ACS "is pledged not to oppose the system of slavery," that it "apologizes for slavery and slaveholders," that it was "nourished by fear and selfishness," and that it aimed "at the utter expulsion of the blacks" by disparaging free blacks and denying "the possibility of elevating the blacks in this country." Throughout, he sounded the note of the prophetic scourge of sin. It was Garrison as Jeremiah.

Thoughts on African Colonization achieved two strategic objectives. It converted a crucial core of early white abolitionist leaders and rank and file, more than any other work, and it triggered an extensive debate between partisans of the ACS and abolitionists that shortly sidetracked colonization as a popular movement. By 1834, following a series of debates in cities and towns of the Northeast and in the press, colonization had lost credibility among the broader public, even those not ready to embrace abolitionism, while immediatism gained momentum. White immediatism was thus forged in the battle against African colonization. Rejection of colonization led some also to a commitment to racial equality, which was Garrison's own personal trajectory.

Part 2, the most striking feature of *Thoughts on African Colonization,* nearly one-third of the total number of pages, reprinted the "Sentiments of the People of Color" as expressed in anticolonization meetings held from Boston to Baltimore. Garrison's radical assumption in devoting so much space to black voices was that their opinions counted, or should count. "Their desire ought to be tenderly regarded," he pleaded.[7] The eloquence, sincerity, and depth of conviction, together with the command of logic and historical evidence with which African Americans made their case, were eye-opening to whites. Few whites had ever encountered such a display of black intellect and such moral intensity. Black testimony undermined colonizationist defamation of black intelligence and provided the crowning proof that Garrison was correct in contending that the American Colonization Society "deceives and misleads the nation."[8] "For the first time," wrote Oliver Johnson, Garrison's sometime collaborator at the *Liberator,* these "down-trodden people" received "a hearing before the American people" allowing "them to speak in their own language."[9]

In the half-dozen years following the publication of *Thoughts on African Colonization,* white abolitionists, in the course of producing the founding texts of the movement, developed the most extensive defense of racial equality in American history. From Lydia Maria Child's book-length *Appeal in Favor of That Class of Americans Called Africans* (1833), to a fifteen-page pamphlet, *Prejudice against Color* (no date), published by the American Antislavery Society, to Richard Hildreth's powerful first antislavery novel, *The Slave, The Memoir of Archy Moore*

(1836), abolitionists addressed the issue of prejudice and argued for immediate emancipation. Believing that racial prejudice underpinned slavery, abolitionists committed themselves not just to emancipation, but, in the words of Article 2 of the New England Antislavery Society's constitution in January 1832, "to improve the character and condition of the free people of color, to inform and correct public opinion in relation to their situation and rights and obtain for them equal civil and political rights and privileges with the whites."[10]

Correcting public opinion was no mean task. "Our prejudice against the blacks is founded in sheer pride; and it originates in the circumstance that people of their color only, are universally allowed to be slaves," Child argued. "We made slavery, and slavery makes the prejudice."[11] Color phobia, abolitionists contended, is irrational, wicked, preposterous, and unmanly. It is contrary to natural rights and Christian teaching, which recognizes no distinctions based on color.[12] Race prejudice, Elizur Wright Jr. exploded, is "a narrow, bitter, selfish, swinish absurdity."[13]

Believing racial prejudice to be irrational, but believing people capable of reasoning their way to self-improvement, white abolitionists marshaled an impressive array of arguments against those still in its thrall. Rarely did the scientific argument that informed so much of the debate over race in the late eighteenth and early nineteenth centuries figure in abolitionist thinking, however. Abolitionists accepted the prevailing view of Enlightenment science that blacks and whites belong to the same species and that physiological differences do not correlate with mental and moral qualities, which, they believed, are the result of environmental circumstance. Abolitionist environmentalism never wavered, but the underpinning of their views was Christian faith in the unity of mankind: "God hath created of one blood all nations of men for to dwell on the face of the earth." To elevate one race over another because of color, hair texture, lip thickness, or nose shape introduced arbitrary and invidious man-made distinctions into God's creation. Such prejudice was tantamount to blasphemy, they argued, for it degraded part of God's creation for selfish, prideful, exploitative purposes. "I would as soon deny the existence of my Creator," Garrison thundered, "as quarrel with the workmanship of his hands." That workmanship is all the more wonderful for its "gorgeous multifarious productions of Nature."[14] Abolitionists challenged white racists to confront God: "Will you look your Maker in the face and tell him you find a natural 'instinct' in your bosom, which He has implanted there—and which forbids you to love any of his equal children, except the *white* man?"[15]

To make their case, abolitionists appealed to history, and here they received unwitting support from the colonizationists. They had argued that the achievements of Africans in antiquity, as founders of civilizations and teachers of the Greeks and Romans, demonstrated that black intellect could not be inherently inferior. Past black achievements proved that once restored to their natal continent, freed from the debilitating influence of slavery and white prejudice, blacks would thrive. Colonizationists thus boosted the achievements of the Egyptian, Ethiopian, and Carthaginian civilizations in antiquity to counter the apprehension that left to themselves, without the benign, patriarchal oversight of whites, repatriated African Americans never could flourish and might even perish.[16]

Abolitionists seized on this historical argument and turned it to their own purpose: if white prejudice relented in the United States, blacks would progress even more rapidly than free blacks already had. History proved that it was enslavement and prejudice that stunted black achievement, not inherent limitations of black intelligence or morals. The glory that was Ethiopia and the grandeur that was Egypt were proof of that, they thought. In more recent times, however, "Ethiopians of the whole civilized world, are become an inferior race," and people have forgotten the skin color of Cyprian, Cyril, Athanasius, and St. Augustine.[17] When blacks led the world in civilization, "there was no prejudice amongst the whites against their color."[18] The decline of the ancient black civilizations was no more proof of black inferiority than the sad condition of modern Greece, a land once inhabited by Homer and now by ignorant pirates, was proof of white inferiority.[19]

More contemporary evidence, especially the biographies of notable modern African achievers, bolstered the historical argument. European travel accounts revealed that Africa was no Dark Continent, but a land of impressive rulers, industrious peoples, and productive economies. A black professor at Wittenberg University in Germany, several talented mulatto and black military men who commanded the respect of Europeans, a black druggist and mathematician in England, and the poet Phillis Wheatley in America were cited as a few examples among many of the triumph of gifted blacks over prejudice. Thomas Jefferson had denied that Phillis Wheatley's "poems have any merit," but Lydia Maria Child thought he would have "judged differently, had he been perfectly unprejudiced."[20] "If we are willing to see and believe, we have full opportunity to convince ourselves that the colored population are highly susceptible of cultivation," Child argued. That many remained ignorant,

even after emancipation, she insisted, was the result of "the cruel prejudice, under which colored people labor,"[21] as the recent events at New
Haven made evident. "Tyranny always dwarfs the intellect."[22]

Racial prejudice, abolitionists pointed out, was stronger in the United
States than in any other country. "No other people on earth indulge
so strong a prejudice with regard to color as we do," Child argued.
In Europe and Latin America, blacks faced much less prejudice and
hostility. Although "the Hollanders are somewhat whiter than the
Americans," abolitionists pointed out, they treated blacks with respect,
as did the British. In Brazil, Child reported, enslaved blacks were "far
lower than either animals of burden," but those who were citizens were
"remarkable for the respectability of . . . appearance."[23] Nor was color
phobia implanted by God in man. Look at children, William Jay urged,
whose prejudices derived entirely from adult example and instruction.[24]

At bottom, abolitionists argued, racial prejudice rested above all on
an ignorance of the deforming consequences of white prejudice. Few
whites were "really aware of how oppressive the influence of society is
made to bear upon blacks," Child pointed out. In the churches, whites
confined them to "nigger pews" and excluded them from the schools
that white children attended. Whites would not sell them a decent seat
in the theater, or ride with them on stagecoaches or on steamboats,
or allow them to hold any jobs except as barbers, shoe blacks, sailors,
domestics, and waiters. None of this was news to Child's white readers,
as she knew, but she believed discrimination to be unthinking, taken
for granted without reasoned examination. White Americans did not
suffer from a lack of "kind feelings and liberal sentiments," but rather
from ignorance; "they have not *thought* upon this subject."[25] The
abolitionists were determined to make them think.

Whites were simply ignorant of the character of the free black community. Northern blacks "are more temperate and more industrious"
than whites in similarly "indigent circumstances," especially the "foreign emigrants who are crowding to our shores." Black "advancement
in intelligence, in wealth, and in morality, considering the numberless
and almost insurmountable difficulties under which they have labored,
has been remarkable," Garrison argued. Whereas thirty years ago
Philadelphia blacks owned hardly any property, today they possessed
hundreds of thousands of dollars worth, saving small sums accumulated
from "shaving the beards, cleaning the boots and clothes, and being the
servants of their white contemners." In Baltimore, Philadelphia, and
New York, several blacks had accumulated between ten thousand and

one hundred thousand dollars in property. Nearly fifty black associations formed for benevolent, political, educational, and moral purposes in Philadelphia alone testified to the "good sense, sterling piety, moral honesty, virtuous pride of character, and domestic enjoyments which exists among this class."[26]

Once whites understood that blacks had contributed much to civilization, that enslavement and prejudice had kept African Americans from realizing their potential, that even despite fearsome obstacles some had surmounted the barriers to achievement, and that color phobia was irrational, antirepublican, and blasphemous, radical change in white behavior and black fortunes became possible. The practical way to begin, Child advised, was "to speak kindly and respectfully of colored people on all occasions," "repeat to our children such traits as are honorable in their character and history," and "avoid making odious caricatures of negroes."[27] Quoting David Walker, Garrison called on white Americans to "throw away your fears and prejudices then, and enlighten us and treat us like men, and we will like you more than we now hate you." The true policy, Garrison argued, "is to meliorate their condition, invigorate their hopes, instruct their ignorant minds, admit them to an equality in privileges with our selves, nourish and patronize their genius."[28]

American republicans, above all people, should be wary of the argument that regarding a class of people as inherently inferior justified their permanent subordination, for that was the argument aristocrats everywhere employed to deny the poor their natural rights. Throughout history, elites imposed oppressive laws to degrade the many, fastening on them poverty and ignorance and then using the consequences of an artificially contrived inequality to depict its victims as inherently inferior. The American Colonization Society, led by the likes of Clay and Monroe and the princes of the church, was no different. Like poor whites, all poor blacks needed "to manifest a perfect equality, is an equality of rights and knowledge." The notion that blacks were created naturally inferior was mere "moonshine."[29]

Because the United States was founded on the principles of the Declaration of Independence and on the principles of the Gospel, Garrison refused "to despair for the social and political elevation of my sable countrymen."[30] The country now had to face the contradiction between republican principles of equality "and that aristocracy of color which has become hereditary among us," Samuel May explained. That conflict was "the *greatest* question our nation is now called upon to decide, whether our immense colored population shall henceforth be permitted to rise among us, *as they may be able,* in intellectual and moral worth."[31]

Yet none of the white abolitionists' arguments could match the impact of the black testimony Garrison reprinted in *Thoughts on African Colonization.* "It is too late now to brand with inferiority any one of the races of mankind," New York African Americans thundered. "We ask for proof." The colonizationists, so adept at defaming blacks, spoke out of ignorance. "We ask them to visit the dwellings of the respectable part of our people." Over and over, as always, African Americans affirmed their Americanness, their determination to struggle, and their optimistic hopes for the future. "This is our home, and this our country," the New Yorkers pledged.[32] And from Brooklyn blacks: "We pray the Lord to hasten the day, when prejudice, inferiority, degradation and oppression shall be done away, and the kingdom of this world become the kingdom of our God and his Christ."[33]

White abolitionists did not overlook or underplay the shortcomings of the black masses, but they never wavered in their belief in equality. "Amidst all their faults there are redeeming qualities, which must put to shame every white man," Elizur Wright argued. "No field in the world is richer in instances of stern moral courage, unbending decision of character, exact integrity, unassailable fidelity, self-sacrificing patriotism, ardent thirst for knowledge, disinterested benevolence and unfeigned piety, than the history of our free colored brethren."[34] "The primary difference between the Abolitionists and their opponents lay in the fact that the former asserted, while the latter denied, the perfect humanity of the Negro," Oliver Johnson declared in his biography of Garrison. "It was this that made them so dangerous in the eyes of the slaveholders."[35]

The colonizationists soon began to mount counterarguments, often with considerable uneasiness over the issues that the abolitionists had raised. Rev. Leonard Bacon, editor of the *Christian Spectator,* the organ of Taylorite, evangelical Congregationalism in New Haven, for example, watched the emergence of immediatism with alarm. Critically reviewing *Thoughts* in the journal, he recognized that Garrison represented a threat to colonization, white supremacy, and elite authority, including that of the clergy. As a leading clerical colonizationist, Bacon had good reason to take alarm. Bacon warned the annual meeting of the ACS of the danger that free blacks might fall into the hands of demagogues who knew exactly "how to move on these people in the line of their prejudices. 'This country,' they tell them, 'is your country; here you were born, and here you have a right to stay.'"[36] Although it was black abolitionists who had converted white abolitionists, from Bacon's blinkered perspective and that of other colonizationists, only white agitators could threaten colonization's bright future.

Bacon singled out Garrison's advocacy of racial equality as especially dangerous. He denied that Christians "generally treat the people of color with 'utter dislike,'" notwithstanding the recent events in New Haven. Garrison's attack on white prejudice, he argued, dangerously aroused blacks against whites by tending to "irritate [blacks] and strengthen every prejudice, every unkind, angry feeling in their bosoms," threatening even to arouse "the wild beasts of the forests." When Garrison preached self-help, Bacon approved, but he thought Garrison went too far. In advocating a manual labor college at New Haven, in predicting that some day the school would turn out black Hamiltons and Clays, in urging blacks to vote only for black candidates or white friends, in demanding equal treatment in white churches, in urging that blacks buy from one another, not where it was cheapest, and in advocating that they sue in federal courts to overthrow discriminatory state laws as violations of the federal constitution, Garrison brazenly encouraged vanity and militancy, instead of soothing and counseling blacks to subdue their feelings. Discriminatory laws were not the cause of inferiority among blacks, Bacon argued. Rather, the blacks' own lack of self-esteem was to blame. The way for them to gain respect was not by insisting on rights and demanding acceptance, but by quietly and humbly demonstrating usefulness. "They must vanquish prejudice, not by contention, but by their merits . . . by the law of love."[37] By contrast, Garrison was a "willful incendiary" who aroused in African Americans "the lust of possessions and the desire of recompense for wrong."[38]

Bacon never wavered in his commitment to black uplift and repatriation. Yet while criticizing discriminatory laws, he rejected a racially egalitarian society. Few Northern evangelicals wrestled so painfully with the question of slavery and race as Bacon. The rise of abolitionism placed him on the defensive, yet he retained faith in colonization while admitting that blacks could advance without removal, though he remained reluctant to attack white prejudice or promote racial equality.

Bacon spoke for a major spectrum of northern Christian opinion. Although abolitionists from the start appealed to Christian conscience, most denominations remained stolidly resistant. Before the struggle between abolition and the churches came fully into the open, Garrison voiced scattered criticisms of the role the churches had played in the slavery question. In his earliest major addresses, he denied any claim to clerical authority, yet in assuming the mantle of an Old Testament Jeremiah, he unavoidably adopted a clerical persona, and he trod on the clergy's jurisdiction as moral overseers when he criticized the white churches for failing to honor the black portion of God's creation. His rhetoric, no less than his arguments, amounted to a challenge to religious authority and sincerity, for he infused into his speeches and writings endless allusions to the Bible, direct quotes and extended pastiches inspired by Scripture, as well as by moralistic sentiment drawn from English literature. "Glory to God in the highest, for the prospect which he holds out to our visions," he told his black audiences. "Make the Lord Jesus Christ your refuge and exemplar . . . that through Christ . . . you may do all things."[39]

At bottom, as we have seen, abolitionist belief in immediatism and racial equality rested on Christian faith. African Americans had awakened a few whites, like Garrison and Jocelyn, to the contradictions between that faith and racial beliefs and practice in the North. The burden now fell on these initial white converts to convert others. Because so many Americans professed to share with the white abolitionist founders a belief in a republic rooted in Christian virtue, that burden seemed reasonable. "Let four hundred worthy ministers and four thousand schoolmasters, in this land, rise up and assert the rights of colored men, and devote themselves, in a gospel way to their interests, and whatever prevents their elevation here, would be like the mists of the morning," Elizur Wright Jr. affirmed in 1833.[40] Rev. Leonard Bacon's attack on Garrisonian immediatism at its inception, however, was a harbinger of trouble ahead.

PART 2

Social Sources of a Mass Movement, 1831–1840

In 1837, *The American Anti-Slavery Almanac* recalled that in 1817, "more than 3,000 free people of color assembled in Philadelphia" unanimously responded to the call for African colonization "with *one long, loud, TREMENDOUS NO.*" Meetings of black people followed "in most of the cities and large towns in the northern states, and it was their unyielding opposition to the cruel scheme of expulsion that first induced Mr. Garrison and his friends to oppose it."[1]

The first handful of whites who, with Garrison, rejected colonization for racial equality and abandoned gradualism for immediate abolition had no idea how arduous a struggle they faced. At first, Garrison, having seen the light, instinctively shared it with Daniel Webster, Lyman Beecher, William Ellery Channing, and other leading New Englanders, hoping that they might embrace the cause. Throughout his career he had benefited from elite sponsorship, but now he met only flat rejection or stunned silence. As he took the lead to instruct the mighty, he learned that change never could come from the top down, confirming his sense of isolation from men of power. His imprisonment for attacking a respectable Newburyport businessman as complicit in the sin of enslavement was a foreshadowing of how the law served the mighty.

Garrison had few friends at the time he launched the *Liberator*, in January 1831, and more of them were blacks than whites. At about the same time, Jocelyn, Arthur and Lewis Tappan, and a few others opted for immediatism and made converts in their circles. The immediatist cause developed with remarkable rapidity, however, considering the obstacles it faced organizationally and conceptually. A handful of pamphlets and dozens of speeches and private conversations converted the first cadre between 1831 and 1834. These in turn converted others who, inspired by their own conversions, multiplied the propaganda. By 1835, a small library of classic immediatist tracts could claim credit for the conversion of thousands by means of arguments that were spread orally at first by a small group of proselytizers and then by a small army of full-time agents. From these beginnings, organized abolition mushroomed into a mass social movement that, as the result of a flood of print propaganda and tours by agents, numbered by 1838 nearly thirteen hundred and fifty societies spread from Maine to Illinois, with some one hundred and forty thousand members.

No social movement of similar character had ever existed in the United States. Whereas some benevolent, philanthropic, religious, and fraternal associations could boast large numbers by the 1830s, none faced such formidable hostility from elite opinion, nor did any embrace such radical doctrines as immediatism and racial equality. The temperance movement, for example, to which many abolitionists mistakenly compared their own efforts, begun in the late 1820s with modest temperance, not teetotaling, had extensive elite support, and did not at first elicit the intense opposition that later "ultra" teetotalism and prohibitionism generated. Not until 1836, a decade after it had come into existence, did the evangelically controlled American Temperance Society adopt the teetotal pledge, and even then it did so on a voluntary basis. Churches remained loath to make teetotaling a test of faith, and politicians, secular and ecclesiastical, were wary of entangling the liquor question with electoral politics. Abolitionism grew, by contrast, in the teeth of elite hostility, intense popular prejudice, and physical violence, and it required an exceptional organizational and ideological commitment.

People joined by signing the constitution of their local society, typically committing themselves to work for the immediate end of slavery and the elevation of free blacks to a position of equality. They paid dues periodically, subscribed to antislavery publications, circulated petitions, queried candidates for public office, and attended monthly or more frequent meetings, where they planned activities, engaged in intense self-education and discussion, and elected officers. Few could sustain such activities for very long, but for nearly a decade, tens of thousands of men, women, and children joined and participated in the most controversial mass movement of their age.

As we have seen, the decisive factor in the conversion of early abolitionists such as Garrison and Jocelyn was the influence of the free black
community in the North and its opposition to African colonization. But
as we have seen as well, the early converts, like those who followed them,
were remarkably more open to such influences than others around them.
The founders first gravitated to immediatism from different backgrounds, yet when these are examined comparatively and probed deeply,
it becomes clear that they shared underlying religious and social characteristics that distinguish them from other members of their generation—the first generation compelled to assimilate morally and behav-
iorally the implications of the market revolution. The three parts of the
book that follow anatomize the social sources of abolitionism by examining in depth the characteristics that participants in this mass movement
shared. And it was indeed a mass movement; unlike colonizationism, its
impetus came from men of all walks of life, not just from elites, and for
the first time in the United States on a large scale, from women as well.

As we already have seen, religious commitment was important to those
recruited to the abolitionist cause. Some were deeply devoted to the new
evangelical Protestantism spawned in New York and the Midwest by
Finneyite evangelism and in New England by the Yale New Light libera-
tion of Calvinism from determinism, optimistic movements that fit in well
with an age in which people demonstrated to an unprecedented extent
their capacity to transform the earthly world. Others rejected the New
Measures of New York's Finney and the Arminianism of New England's
Lyman Beecher and Nathaniel W. Taylor and adhered to a sterner,
Edwardean Calvinist morality. Abolitionism reawakened their intense
sense of human sin, focusing it on slavery and racial domination as the
most timely expressions of selfishness and depravity. Still others grew up
in families that shared neither the old nor the new evangelical religious
cultures. However different they were from the evangelicals, Unitarians,
Quakers, and Episcopalians, even "Nothingarians," were equally in
search of a moral anchor in a turbulent, seemingly amoral world.

The religious wellsprings of immediatism pose formidable explanatory problems for anyone seeking to understand its social origins. While
most antislavery men and women regarded slavery as a violation of
Christian teaching, most Christians did not accept the fundamental immediatist doctrine that slavery and racial inequality are sin. The abolitionists, in their turn, were so blinded by the assumption that they shared
with fellow Americans a common Christian culture, as rich in the
South as in the North, that they were convinced that conversion of the

country lay immediately ahead. That Christian culture, however, was immensely complex and diverse. Although all Christians shared the basic teachings of the faith, differences in history, experience, and interest generated conflicting doctrinal variants with conflicting social implications. Why some Christians embraced the immediatist message of racial equality whereas most rejected it requires probing into the lived experiences that set them apart and prepared their distinctive response to the immediatist message.

William Goodell and the Market Revolution

The experiences and influences that brought nineteenth-century Americans into the abolitionist fold are epitomized in the life of William Goodell. In 1836, William Lloyd Garrison told Goodell that "without your early cooperation the anti-slavery cause would have dragged heavily."[1] Goodell was set on the path toward abolitionism by the strong religious and moral influences he absorbed from his family at home. Once on his own, he found himself at sea in a world being transformed by the forces of the market revolution, and he struggled to find a career in that world. He found that career as a reformer. Goodell took his place among many contemporaries who, working from the ground up as part of a popular movement for reform, sought to give order and stability to a society in which they perceived the old standards of morality and behavior being swept away by market forces that undermined republican virtue and sent Americans in pursuit of the chimeras of wealth, luxury, and aristocracy. But Goodell's extreme views on reform set him apart from many contemporary reformers and helped him see abolition as the ultimate reform. His evolution toward immediatism illuminates how one man's crusade on behalf of social reform, triggered by the spread of the market revolution, prepared him for the greatest struggle of his life, the struggle for racial equality

Born in 1792, Goodell lost both parents by the time he was fourteen and grew up in the household of his Connecticut grandmother, a woman of powerful intellect and strong character, steeped in the knowledge of history and literature. Goodell remembered her as "one of the strong-minded women of her times."[2] Converted by George Whitefield during the First Great Awakening, the grandmother had heard Jonathan Edwards preach and transmitted to Goodell her evangelical faith. Through his long career, Goodell remained faithful to an orthodox Christian theology rooted in Puritan, Calvinist tradition.

Meager resources prevented Goodell from going to college, so he worked first as a clerk and then went into business on his own as a merchant. His failure in this venture was one of a succession of financial failures that dogged him over a period of about ten years. In 1816, he gained experience as supercargo for a well-known Providence firm engaged in the China trade and then went to work for another that plied the coast. Stationed in Wilmington, Delaware, in 1819, he first encountered both slavery and the impressive skills of black carpenters and craftsmen. He then went into business in Alexandria, Virginia, partner in a firm engaged in the flour trade, but in 1824, Goodell failed again. Moving to New York City, he found work as a bookkeeper in a wholesale metals-importing firm, but in 1827, Goodell abandoned business for journalism and moved to Providence to edit the *Investigator and General Intelligencer.*

"Cultivate political knowledge and virtue; preserve equality and freedom, but avoid licentiousness" was the motto of the new journal.[3] Goodell's weekly was one of hundreds of new publications appearing in the 1820s; his experience was the seedbed that nurtured a career in reform. Looking back on this period from the 1850s, Goodell recalled the ferment of evangelical culture, full of enthusiasm for new organizations devoted to missionary work, to Bible, tract, and educational societies, inspired with the millennial hopes generated by a renewed wave of revivals that revitalized American Christianity. Goodell thought much of the credit belonged to the new preaching, which built on the work of Jonathan Edwards and Samuel Hopkins. The Finneyite revival in western New York especially impressed him because it nurtured a broad range of moral reforms. The result was "an increasing spirit of inquiry in respect to Christian ethics, and the bearing of religious principles upon the social relations and political duties of man." This, he believed, was what had inspired peace and temperance societies, the Antimasonic movement, campaigns against gambling, theaters, fashion, Sabbath breaking, and the mistreatment of Native Americans. It was what eventually had led to abolitionism. "In short," he wrote, "it was a period of unwonted if not unprecedented moral and political inquiry."[4]

At the same time, a new democratic culture took shape. Moral leadership was no longer the province of a few drawn from elites; ideas now circulated not just from the top down, but also from the bottom up. Newspapers no longer confined themselves to politics and business, nor were they read by just a handful. Religious and other weeklies proliferated and reached wide audiences, including women. Lecturers and agents roamed the land, denouncing moral evils and pointing to the paths of reform. People acquired a new sense of their right to participate in the formation of public opinion, for the new agencies of mass communication solicited public support and thereby acknowledged its plasticity and sovereignty. Typically, traveling lecturers received immediate feedback from their audiences. Abolitionists, for example, often took votes at the end of meetings on resolutions that endorsed either immediatism or colonization, thereby crystallizing the opinion of the meeting, rather than permitting it to dissipate. Where support was strong enough, an anti-slavery society was established.

To start a publication did not require much capital or organizational backing. James G. Bennett established the *New York Herald* with only $500; Garrison, acting alone, must have begun the *Liberator* with much less. First in Providence, then in Boston and New York, Goodell boldly set himself up as moral arbiter in a succession of journals. "Whoever pleased might become an editor of a newspaper," he recalled, "and whoever chose to subscribe for it, at a trifling, was introduced into the 're-public of letters.'" The print explosion helped to make the United States a reading nation, and many readers insisted on expressing their own opinions by writing letters and unsigned articles, which became a staple of the press. Now, even "the most dependent could stand here on a level with the most powerful," Goodell noted. "Farmers and mechanics, journeymen and apprentices, merchants and clerks—females as well as males—participated in the privilege." From all over the land, "from the counting-house, from the anvil, from the loom . . . from the parlor, perhaps from the kitchen, there came paragraphs." One could not understand the social ferment of the 1820s and 1830s without taking "into account the new power and changed direction of the public press, constituting a new era in human history," Goodell concluded. Inevitably "the morality of unpaid and forced labor" would come under critical scrutiny in an era "when laborers of almost all classes were giving free utterances to their thought."[5]

Goodell's weeklies expressed the distinctive voice of nonsectarian, evangelical moralism, his own and the like-minded, whom he printed or reprinted from other journals. The prospectus of his first paper, the *Investigator,* set the tone and prefigured the message: "Considering as we do, that political science should be based on moral principles; and that no scheme of morals has ever appeared among men, so pure, so salutary, so mild, or so efficient as that furnished by Christianity, we shall endeavor to conform our political maxims to its precepts." Goodell did not advocate formation of a Christian party in politics, and he explicitly disdained any union of church and state, but he insisted that candidates for office and public measures conform to the standards of Christian virtue.[6]

Unprecedentedly rapid social change had played havoc with the older moral standards that had governed social relations. In Rhode Island, especially, textile factories harnessing water power were transforming the countryside morally as well as physically. "Arcadian seclusion and rural simplicity are passing away," Goodell noted, as farmers gave way to weavers and spinners. He regarded economic development as a triumph for "science, industry and art," yet believed it also posed grave dangers unless advances in intelligence and virtue accompanied advances in wealth.[7]

Goodell saw signs of moral decay everywhere, the sure sign of trouble for a republic dependent on public virtue. The ascendancy of Andrew Jackson in 1828 exemplified in Goodell's mind the corruption of public life that tolerated dueling, Sabbath breaking, intemperance, and licentiousness.[8]

Moral decay was just as evident in business as in politics. Older ethical standards gave way to fraud, dishonesty, and wild speculation. A man now could be defrauded out of his entire estate while the guilty went free. Community opinion provided no protection, whereas forty years earlier, dishonest traders suffered ostracism. In the new order of the market revolution, swindlers, especially those who practiced "refined knavery," won high regard as clever businessmen. New York City, in particular, had become the favored refuge and playing field for conspirators and cheats.[9] How could the country secure political stability, Goodell wondered, when it permitted "every species of legal and illegal swindling by which aristocratic rapacity and professional dexterity can contrive to rob, with impunity, the widow and the fatherless," and when employers were "permitted to plunder the poor with impunity"? Gambling had become respectable by means of lotteries and card playing, banks, insurance offices, and stock jobbing.[10] The recent surge in the price of flour illustrated how wild speculation, not actual shortages, put consumers at the mercy of greed.

> Plain dealing once bore sway, that virtue fled
> A game of chance suspends a nation's bread.[11]

Such developments explained why foreign radicals such as Robert D. Owen Jr. and Frances (Fanny) Wright found an audience for an attack on private property. Intemperance and debauchery among the lower classes and rapacity and licentiousness among the higher orders made people more receptive to radical nostrums. The propertied classes in the large cities, Goodell argued, were "always . . . among the *last* to lift their fingers for the preservation of those virtuous principles and habits, without which, their hoarded heaps and deeds of warranty are like chaff in the whirlwind." Since their wealth rested on swindle and theft, or at best on dubious scheming, they were incapable of reform: "If our city capitalists escape the wreck of revolution," he predicted, "it must be by the instrumentality of the more humble, and better informed middling classes of the interior. They alone can be depended on."[12]

New fortunes generated class snobbery among those who were most successful in the marketplace, threatening the "middling classes" with a newly minted monied aristocracy that judged people's worth by their fortunes, not their character. The spirit of creeping aristocracy had infiltrated business, politics, and even the churches. "Preserve equality and freedom but avoid licentiousness," Goodell pleaded. "Get the wealth from your fertile soil; but dash the chalice of luxury from your lips."[13]

Yet not even the "middling classes" escaped the corrupting influence of the market. The allure of acquisitiveness, consumerism, and debt tempted all. A new system of "artificial respectability" held butchers superior to bakers, shoemakers to cobblers, hatters to tailors, grocers to sellers of dry goods. Honest industry entitled people, whatever their calling, to respectability, but instead a factitious standard was taking its place.[14] Goodell reprinted the cautionary tale of "Fritz Pigiron," a blacksmith, who started with just an old anvil and few tools, but by dint of economy, skill, industry, and a frugal wife, became prosperous and respected. Not content with a moderate-sized house, he built a larger one and filled it with expensive furniture until no other house in the village could match it. Then he began to give parties to show off the accumulations. Having set up as a gentleman, Fritz tore down his shop and abandoned his leather apron. High living and debt, however, plunged him into bankruptcy. After the house was sold, Fritz was found dead in an upper story, his head strangled by a leather apron, as "if the badge of his early prosperity, when cast off, should still continue in existence only to become the instrument of his death."[15]

Still, Goodell remained confident that "through the instrumentality of the industrious middle classes—the hardy yeomanry and mechanics of the country," the republic might be saved.[16] This required mobilizing people behind a range of issues that constituted Goodell's broad notion of "moral reform." "Freedom and equality can never be maintained," he preached, "without sobriety and virtue. Patriarchs of the Revolution knew this. . . . But times have altered since 1776. . . . Of what use is the *theory* of freedom to a people bent on becoming *practically* the slaves of voluptuousness?"[17] Goodell displayed special sympathy for the plight of wage earners. He opened his pages to advocates of suffrage reform in Rhode Island, where a property qualification disenfranchised the growing factory population. In a republic, all men, regardless of wealth, had the right to vote, he argued. It was dangerous to deny a growing segment of the citizenry the opportunity to participate.

Goodell also printed attacks on the exploitation of child labor and of seamstresses who were paid starvation wages.[18] In the pursuit of private gain, people ignored the claims of the common good. "*Is it safe for a Commonwealth to compromise moral principle for the sake of a pecuniary advantage?*" Goodell wondered. Even "the best citizens" abandoned the public arena, not bothering to vote, so preoccupied were they in the pursuit of private enterprise. Citizens, for example, pleaded for tariff protection to aid the manufacturing industry, but took no interest "in the cause of the operative *manufacturers*," caring more about increasing the production of cloth and profits than about "elevating the moral and political condition of the human beings who are to fabricate or consume them."[19] Goodell printed a letter from Pawtucket, a center of textile manufactures, protesting that mill operatives, including children, had to labor fourteen to fifteen hours a day, stunting mind and body.

Hypocritical employers came under withering criticism for advocating strict temperance for their employees, thereby saving the cost of providing the customary drams, but refusing to give up alcohol themselves. Goodell preached the temperance message to all classes. He also sought to persuade workers that strict observance of the Sabbath prevented the enslavement "of the apprentice, the laborer, the dependent, and the needy." Forced labor on the Lord's day "would in effect, wrest from a large portion of the people their only leisure for moral and intellectual improvement." Goodell's argument explains why hundreds of New York City working people supported the Sabbatarian movement and signed petitions to Congress to close the post office on Sundays. Respecting the Sabbath inhibited an amoral bourgeoisie from carrying on business seven days a week. The Sabbath had suffered desecration because "the *profitable* has become everything with us," Goodell lamented. The drive "to become rich" had "caused everything to be prized according to its value *in the market.*"[20]

When Goodell moved the *Genius of Temperance* to New York, he established a special column on the front page called "The People's Advocate" that reprinted material from the workingmen's press. He displayed sympathy for the New York City Workingmen's Party, especially after the majority repudiated the radicalism of Owen and Wright.[21] While Goodell believed that personal reform was a key to ending the suffering of the poor, he also argued that just and equitable laws were necessary to "give to every man an opportunity of accumulating wealth by fair and honorable means" and to promote an equalization in "the possession of property in the community."[22]

Goodell also paid attention to the problems of women, devoting part of the back pages to "the Ladies." Goodell viewed women as upholders of morality and Christian culture, and while not challenging explicitly the restricting view that a woman's place was in the home, Goodell printed articles that tended to enlarge the sphere of women. A defense of female education insisted that women never could achieve their potential without fully developing their minds. Beauty might give women influence over men, but it is transient; the influences of intellect and virtue, he argued, are enduring.[23] As mothers, women could encourage or resist the spread of consumerist display and class snobbery among children. Some, for example, allowed girls to read trashy novels and sent them to fashionable boarding schools to learn music, French, and embroidery, as well as how to curtsey and dance waltzes, from which they emerged as proud, vain "Dandyettes," likely to snare in marriage a worthless "Dandy."[24] While some mothers encouraged consumerism, others struggled on behalf of moral reform and temperance.[25]

Popular culture played an important role in shaping the character of women and men. The reason that so many women had turned out to hear Fanny Wright, Goodell declared, was that their minds already were seduced by romantic novels to think of Fanny Wright as a glamorous, heroic personality.[26] Fiction and theater subvert morality, he argued, singling out the Waverley novels of Sir Walter Scott. He attributed

Andrew Jackson's election as president to "the Waverley influence," which favored military heroes, aristocratic splendor, and talented libertinism.[27] The Waverley influence explained the ascendancy of selfish faction and military characters over men whose education, culture, and morals better fitted them to hold office.[28]

Since American republicans naturally would not tolerate an open defense of monarchy and aristocracy, Scott's seemingly harmless romances were especially dangerous. American readers sought amusement, unaware that Scott's novels advanced views subversive of republicanism.[29] Young Waverley, educated by a Tory uncle in mid-eighteenth-century Britain, is imprisoned by the Whigs, who mistakenly think he has deserted to the Jacobite cause. Rescued by Scottish Highlanders, Waverley joins the forces of the Stuart Pretender. After the Jacobite invasion of England fails and the rebellion is put down, Waverley wins a pardon and marries a rebel's daughter.[30] Hostile to Whigs and flattering to Tories, Scott's novels exemplified for Goodell the pernicious influence of "the *literature of Bacchanalianism*" against which moral reform had to struggle.[31]

Though Goodell defined "moral reform" to cover a broad range of social problems, from Sabbath breaking to the exploitation of labor, his top priority remained temperance. Goodell echoed the standard indictment of alcohol: it wasted the body, deranged the mind, and was responsible for more of the crime, poverty, and suffering in the country than any other cause. But as a staunch advocate of teetotalism and an opponent of all forms of alcohol, including wine and medicines containing liquor, Goodell occupied an ultraist position that was not yet acceptable to the mainstream of the organized temperance movement. As a result, Goodell came into sharp conflict with it in both Massachusetts and New York, and fell out with the American Temperance Society, organized by evangelicals in Massachusetts in 1826 to compete with an older temperance society under Unitarian control. The ATS did not require teetotalism until 1836, a decade after the *National Philanthropist* insisted that nothing less would achieve sobriety. Goodell also criticized evangelical leaders who temporized in deference to public opposition and in fear of confronting wealthy opponents of teetotalism, including liquor dealers, within the churches. After the ATS established its own weekly in Massachusetts, the *Journal of Humanity,* Goodell lost readership, which led him to relocate to New York City. In New York, he again came into conflict with the organized temperance movement for similar reasons. Many regarded teetotalism and a ban on wine as extreme, certain to antagonize influential laity and to split the churches. Goodell further alienated evangelical temperance leaders because of his support for the antiprostitution movement. Once again, Goodell found that hypocrisy and timidity among evangelical leaders tolerated low moral standards within the churches. In advocating a strict temperance standard that alienated him from organized temperance and its evangelical leadership, Goodell displayed an antinomian impulse that soon carried over to the question of slavery and racial hierarchy.

The Missouri debates had made Goodell think about the slavery question, resulting in an article in the *Providence Gazette* in 1820 attacking bondage as a violation of Christian teaching and natural rights.[32] From the establishment of the *Investigator* in 1827 onward, Goodell displayed a mild interest in slavery, sympathetically reporting Benjamin Lundy's visit to Providence in the late 1820s and publishing the text of Garrison's Park Street Church Address in 1829, which he praised. Garrison briefly worked on Goodell's newspaper. He and Goodell socialized and shared a growing concern over slavery just before Garrison moved to Baltimore to join Lundy. Though most religious weeklies closed their pages to immediatist attacks on colonization, Goodell opened his columns to both sides. Like other abolitionists, he had endorsed the American Colonization Society, and though Garrison's arguments in *Thoughts on African Colonization* impressed him, he persisted in thinking that the two approaches were compatible.

Fearing that Goodell might defect to the Garrisonians, the ACS's Robert Finley visited Goodell to bolster his support for colonization, but by the summer of 1833, the die was cast. Nat Turner's insurrection had persuaded Goodell that the ACS simply wished to remove troublesome blacks. When the ACS refused to oppose forced expulsion of free blacks, his confidence further weakened. The Crandall case in Canterbury, Connecticut, completed his conversion, for it made clearer than ever "the hidden springs of prejudice" that coiled within the movement for African colonization and among its Northern supporters.

"Degradation of the men of color is a deep blot on our country's fair fame," Goodell now asserted.[33] To gain better knowledge of free blacks, he visited Newton, Pennsylvania, where he observed an intelligent and prosperous black community. A visit to the African Free School in New York City further confirmed his view of black achievement.[34] Like other early converts, Goodell realized that prejudice underlay the argument for colonization and thwarted any hope of abolition, gradual or immediate. The decision for immediatism was, therefore, a decision for racial

equality. Looking back from 1853, Goodell concluded that "were it
not for this stupid prejudice against color, the scepter of the slaveholding oligarchy would drop powerless at once and the nation would be
disenthralled."[35]

From 1833 on, Goodell threw himself wholeheartedly into the immediatist cause. He joined the Tappans as a founder of the New York
City Antislavery Society in October and attended the founding convention of the American Antislavery Society in December. He edited the
Emancipationist (1834–36), the weekly published by the American
Antislavery Society, and then moved to Utica to edit the *Friend of Man*
(1836–42), sponsored by the New York State Antislavery Society. In the
late 1830s, he became one of the architects of political abolitionism, a
founder of the Liberty Party who advocated broadening its program
beyond one idea—abolition—to include a platform of economic reforms
aimed at recruiting wage earners and small producers. These reforms
included free trade, free public land, inalienable homesteads, and
government retrenchment.[36]

Goodell grounded his understanding of the struggle for equality in a
historical exploration of the origins of democracy and the conflict between democracy and its enemies. In a two-volume work, *The
Democracy of Christianity* (1849–52), Goodell synthesized the efforts
of a lifetime to reconcile political economy and bourgeois social relations with Christian teaching.

"Whoever would understand and sustain free institutions should
study the commonwealth of the Hebrews," Goodell argued.[37] God created all human beings equal; the unity and equality of humanity were central and unique to Jewish and Christian teaching, whereas heathenism
artificially divided people into distinct races, some of which pretended
to more exalted origins and worth than others. When Cain violated "the
law of equal and impartial love," he made war against the God-given
principle of "human brotherhood" and introduced ambition and pride,
the enemies of egalitarian democracy, into the human condition. The history of the Jews exemplified the eternal struggle between democracy and
aristocracy. Democratic habits and moral virtue flourished as long as the
Hebrews were a simple, pastoral people. The emergence of rich and populous cities, however, like Sodom or the cities of Goodell's own day,
brought with it "modern monuments of aristocratic distinction, splendor, luxury, effeminacy, and pride," dominated by the idle who inhabited mansions and devoured "the hard earnings of the poor" (1:54).
Punished by exile to Egypt, the Hebrews suffered oppression in a land

where "the democratic principle of human equality and equity had been supplanted . . . by the opposite principle of aristocracy, monopoly, class legislation, and injustice" (1:64).

The Exodus liberated the Jews from servitude to live under the Mosaic code, "the teacher of all subsequent ages in the science of liberty and law," the ultimate source of the English common law and the Declaration of Independence (1:113). Mosaic democracy was social democracy, in Goodell's view: "The mischief of the monopoly of the soil, so affectingly manifest in Egypt, and so closely connected with the bondage and oppression of the Hebrews in that country, were to be guarded against in the most effectual manner." Jewish law secured "the equal division of the lands" and prevented "their permanent alienation," placed limitations on the collection of debts and banned usury, "chartered monopolies" and "commercial restrictions" in order to prevent "a very unequal distribution of property"(1:333–35). By contrast, Goodell complained, "modern legislation, instead of protecting the poor from oppression is chiefly or at least constantly occupied in assisting oppressors to do their work the more effectually." In the commonwealth period of Jewish history, there was no "class legislation" such as the "legalized monopolies, exclusive privileges and inequalities" of modern nations, including Jacksonian America. Taxes were directly proportioned to income, government spending was modest, and there was no standing army or navy (1:165). Through Israel, God had hoped to teach mankind the lessons of equality, brotherhood, and democracy (1:237).[38]

In time, however, the influence of surrounding monarchies and human corruption produced distaste for democratic institutions and clamors for a king and empire. "Man ceases to be a worshipper of God only because he has become a worshipper of himself," Goodell explained. "Estranged from God he finds no nobler object of worship than the strongest man" (1:257). The Hebrew prophets preached against "princely rapacity, oppressive exactions, fat salaries, extortion, monopolies, class legislation, inadequate or withheld wages," but without long-term success (1:322).

God then sent the Jews a new messenger, "the carpenter of Nazareth," but "the mass of the Jewish people . . . bowed down before the emperors . . . and priesthoods, and kings, as for centuries their fathers had been accustomed to do, in utter forgetfulness of the simple democracy God had provided for them" (1:343). Jesus taught that a "God of Love and Mercy never created the masses of men to be the serfs of a select few" (2:39). Goodell contrasted "class legislation," which enabled a handful to amass capital and control labor, with God's "laws of healthful and legitimate human industry and brotherly intercourse in the production and free interchange of the fruits of the earth" (2:47). Christ preached anew the brotherhood of mankind, that God is no respecter of persons or of those privileges—wealth, fashion, birth, and nobility—on which aristocracy rested (2:174). That message never was more relevant, Goodell insisted, than in the nineteenth century, "this Mammon age," in which an aristocracy of wealth, "the most sordid and yet the most potent of all aristocracies," arrogantly lorded over "starving operatives," opposed "guaranteed homesteads for the poor, except the workhouse," and resisted a ten-hour workday that provided time for leisure, rest, and recreation essential for "the spiritual health of human beings" (2:197, 2:204, 2:217, 2:265, 2:266).

At the heart of aristocracy lay a contempt for manual toil. Christianity condemned the "absurd pride and detestable sloth that dread and despise useful labor," that looked "down with contempt and disgust upon the humble tasks demanded by human welfare." Monopoly, caste, class, and legislation were just "aristocratic devices by which some aimed to live without honest labor" (2:256).[39] And so was the slave system that afflicted the nation.

After finding himself adrift in the world that the market revolution had created, William Goodell discovered both a career and the secular equivalent of a religious calling in the service of moral reform. Even then, his ultraist views caused him problems. They also drove him to embrace the abolitionist cause as part of an overall effort to rescue the republic from the dangers that seemed to threaten it. By the 1840s, Goodell had consolidated a broad-based egalitarian position, insisting that abolitionism could not rely on appeals to conscience alone, but must harness the self-interest of free labor and small producers by engaging in their struggles for "universal equality and impartial justice to all."[40]

Anatomy of White Abolitionism

The most salient experiences that underlay the religious sources of abolitionism as a mass movement were critical responses to the market revolution and the new bourgeois social order it spawned. The first abolitionists characteristically were members of the generation that made the transit from the agrarian and commercial republic of the Revolutionary era to the incipient industrializing republic of the Jacksonian era. "We must have the younger generation; the older is hopeless," wrote one antislavery leader.[1] Yet youth alone did not lead to antislavery, since only a minority of the generation born in the midst of the market revolution opted for racial justice. For that minority, the search for a meaningful career worthy of their talents, values, and aspirations proved to be both defining and difficult, once they rejected or expressed doubts about the conventional career choice of making money and achieving "success" by the world's common standard. As we have seen in the case of William Goodell, these activists came to antislavery through a search for how to sacralize everyday life, seeking moral purpose in their careers and a way to impose moral order on social order. In a variety of different ways, the pattern of experiences and influences that were central to Goodell's conversion to abolitionism was present in the lives of other abolitionists as well.

The search for moral purpose and moral order began in childhood, shaped by values and ambitions nurtured by parents. "Set your face against every sin especially pride," advised Elizur Wright Jr.'s parents.

This was no ritualistic admonition by pietistic forbears. Wright's family had moved from Connecticut to Ohio's Western Reserve and had brought their Puritanism with them. They closely followed the moral development of their son, especially from the time he left for Yale until he finally returned home to a professorship at Western Reserve College, where Garrison's *Thoughts* found one of its first and most important early converts. Wright served in the 1830s as executive secretary of the American Antislavery Society and as editor at the movement's quarterly.[2]

For years, Wright had searched for an appropriately holy vocation. Converted during a revival in 1820, Wright remained restless, unable to accept Calvinist orthodoxy, yet troubled by the luxury-loving arrogance of the Southern students (they mocked the homespun he wore) and the questionable piety of the Yankee students. Attracted by Taylorism, Wright hesitated before pursuing a career in the ministry. After a bout of teaching school, he drifted to western Pennsylvania, where he distributed religious tracts. Trudging from place to place to spread the Word, Wright once again encountered disillusionment. In Pittsburgh, he reported, "Men are too much engaged for themselves, to mind the welfare of others." "Every man here seems to be straining every nerve to get rich," he wrote his sister, "with the hope of spending his money some day or other in a place that is *cleaner.*" Wright never had seen people so wrapped up in business "that they do not mind washing their faces."[3] From Yale to Pittsburgh, Wright pondered how to arouse conscience. His 1833 pamphlet attacking tobacco, published just at the time he embraced immediatism, targeted temptation that indulged "an inordinate sensual appetite." Wright believed that subduing appetite was a necessary precondition for confronting sin, and earlier he had embraced temperance at Yale. Like many on the road to abolitionism, Wright tended toward extreme moral commitments.[4]

When Wright read Garrison, however, he discovered the ultimate, most demanding of Christian commitments, a "revolution of the soul." Immediatism involved the supreme test, subordinating racial pride, applying the Golden Rule to the most despised. People had been "blinded by a strange prejudice," he recalled.[5] Repudiation of irrational, anti-Christian prejudice thus was the key. "What's the good of a revival," Wright once taunted Finney, "if white Christians will not sit next to 'Niggers'?"[6] Garrison's *Thoughts on African Colonization* had exposed the hidden prejudices of white Christians. In 1833, still at Western Reserve, Wright had listened to a speaker from the Seamen's Friend Society plead the cause of sailors, yet neither the minister nor the audience imagined that the Golden Rule applied to the slave. Hypocrisy and insincerity governed when it came to colored peoples. No other human beings had been so shockingly neglected by the pious, Wright observed, except the prostitutes. If racial prejudice was irremediable, as colonizationists insisted, then sin was irremediable. Before leaving Western Reserve, Wright boldly defied racial prejudice. He brought John Vashon, a black gentleman from Pittsburgh, to march proudly with him in the graduation procession, shocking the college's smug Yankee faithful.

By 1837, Wright, like many other of the original immediatists, had drifted away from Christian orthodoxy: "I am sick of selfish, luxurious, good for nothing religion," he confessed, "eternally a wondering if one is damned, what will become of me." Such self-absorbed people were "more concerned about escaping hell than doing right."[7] Wright's drift toward apostasy had its roots in the same search for Christian truth and sincerity in a world of self-interest, greed, and luxury that had led him to immediatism.

Beriah Green came to immediatism and abolitionism by a similar trajectory. Green learned from his father in his humble Vermont cabinet shop never to forget the ennobling lessons of manual toil. It taught self-reliance, resistance to snobbery, and respect for all manner of humanity, whatever their occupations. Green, an orthodox Calvinist inspired by Hopkins and Nathanael Emmons, preached to several congregations before joining the faculty at Western Reserve. Like his colleague Wright, he became one of Garrison's earliest converts. In 1833, he gave the keynote address at the founding of the American Antislavery Society. At about the same time, he took over the leadership of Oneida Institute, the country's leading institution of the manual labor movement, devoted to integrating manual and mental labor while affording education to those with little money.

This conjunction of the antislavery and manual labor movements was not fortuitous.[8] The manual labor movement emerged from a distinctive strain of evangelical sensibility troubled by the emerging capitalist order. The movement was no frontal assault on capitalist social relations. Rather, it registered disquiet with aspects of market culture that put a cash value on human relationships. Slavery, as seen from the point of view of the manual labor movement, was just the starkest example of the way market calculation demeaned humanity. At the leading white manual labor schools, such as Oneida Institute and Oberlin, manual labor, abolitionism, and racial integration were each expressions of a communitarian, egalitarian ethos at odds with the dominant strain of competitive individualism, an effort to balance moral values against market values. Many troubled young men searching for a career in the changing world of the early nineteenth century found in manual labor and then in abolitionism an antidote to moral anxieties generated by the market revolution.

Green embraced manual labor because he was no respecter of persons, whether the measure was a person's purse or a person's color. Green had been a colonizationist in the 1820s, but as it had for Wright, Garrison's exposé of the anti-Christian racial prejudice behind the movement marked a turning point for Green. When at an early public meeting in defense of his newfound immediatist commitment someone challenged the sincerity of any white person who advocated racial equality, Green realized how fully hatred of Negroes had penetrated Christian culture. From that time forward, he became an uncompromising champion of racial equality, now for him a litmus test of genuine Christian belief. He fought successfully to open Oneida Institute to blacks, which then trained a number and won notoriety as "the nigger school." In the process, he lost support from New York State's hostile Democratic legislature. His understanding of Christian teaching remained firmly rooted in the universal application of the Golden Rule, with no exceptions. "If we despise the meanest of our species," Green preached, "we despise our Judge." One can be a Christian only by embracing the brotherhood of mankind: "the regard which we manifest for man," whatever his circumstance, "is a fair test and just measure, of our regard for God."[9] Class snobbery and racial prejudice went together; at Oneida Institute, Green struggled against both.

The impulse to find a career with a high moral purpose and to impose moral order on society was not confined to the North. Growing up in one of Kentucky's first families, which always had regarded slavery as wrong, even as it owned slaves, James G. Birney inherited the legacy of a clan that had fought to make Kentucky a free state. Symptomatic of a patriarch's moral sensibilities in the age of the market revolution, Birney's father charged no rent to poor families, forbade the whipping or sale of slaves, and pursued the most conservative personal financial practices, rarely lending money to make money. Young Birney's mighty Scottish Aunt Dugle went further and refused to own bondsmen. While a student at Princeton, Birney become acquainted with the extraordinary black businessman James Forten of Philadelphia. His respect and admiration for Forten spilled over to shape his views of the potential of all humanity.[10]

Birney brought his family's antislavery legacy to the Alabama frontier in 1819, hardly a hospitable place for it during the emergence of the Cotton Kingdom. There he sought to restrain the rapid growth of the peculiar institution by restricting slave imports for sale. More powerful contrary economic and demographic pressures prevailed, abetted by proslavery Jacksonian politicians. Disappointment and guilt led Birney to contemplate shifting careers and becoming a minister, but soon he found it was not necessary to change occupations to soothe a conscience troubled by worldly success.

In 1826, by then northern Alabama's richest lawyer, Birney experienced conversion to the Presbyterian Church and promptly took up the cause of the Cherokees, who stood in the way of the Cotton Kingdom's advance. Despairing over Alabama's development and deeply anxious that a slave society was no place in which to rear Christian sons and daughters, Birney made one last stand, as agent of the American Colonization Society. He believed if he could convert the elites in the Deep South legislatures to colonization, the slaveholders would follow with rounds of emancipation. But white indifference and opposition, together with black resistance, eventually shattered Birney's colonizationist faith.

Sensing from at least 1828 onward that the political tide moved against him—the Jacksonians in power in Alabama repealed in 1829 the limit on slave importation that Birney had sponsored in 1827—his thoughts turned to moving North. He went first to Illinois and then, in 1833, to Kentucky, where he imagined the state's old antislavery tradition offered a more promising environment for launching a new campaign for gradual emancipation. However, Birney found that most of his old neighbors, even his fellow Presbyterians, were not much more hospitable than the citizens of Alabama. Even in the Bluegrass State, a secret society had been formed to suppress antislavery dissent. Nor was Birney encouraged by Kentucky's leading politician, Henry Clay.

A former supporter of President John Quincy Adams, Birney sought two interviews with Clay, Adams's National Republican successor, first in 1830 and then in 1834, to gauge where Clay stood. These interviews only deepened Birney's disillusionment with politics and colonization. He concluded that for Clay, colonization was a political ploy allowing him to pretend to an antislavery sensibility in the North while reassuring slaveholders in the South. An ambitious, amoral character who had sided with the proslavery Jeffersonian republican faction as far back as Kentucky's constitutional convention in 1799, Clay epitomized for

Birney the trouble with the African colonization movement: it sapped all
moral energy by taking people's minds off the sinfulness of slavery. As
for Clay's rivals, the Jacksonians, they were, if anything, worse, standing in the forefront of slavery's expansion throughout the West from
Missouri to Texas. Jackson's election in 1828 only emboldened the
proslavery extremists to launch a final assault on the barriers to the extension of slavery in the West, accelerating the removal of Native
Americans while attacking the tariff and suppressing dissent at home.

Despairing of Kentucky, let alone the rest of the South, in 1834 Birney
visited Cincinnati, where Weld and the students at Lane Theological
Seminary were debating colonization versus immediatism. There he completed his conversion. Like the young seminarians, he concluded that
"there is not in colonization any principle, or quality, or consistent substance fitted so to tell upon the hearts and minds of men as to ensure
continued and persevering action." Colonizationist persecution of free
blacks, notable in Ohio's "Black Laws," meant that it was above all a
system for "the refinement of inhumanity," at once "cruel and unmanly."[11] Birney's final conversion to immediatism was the logical consequence of a career faithful to family tradition and to values that imposed moral restraint on ambition. These forced him to abandon a career
based on the struggle for the slave in the South in order to carry on that
struggle where it might prosper, in the North, in the hope of some day
transforming his native region.

Like Birney, William Jay, son of the Revolutionary generation's New
York emancipationist leader, Federalist John Jay, inherited more than
property and social standing. For all his privileges by birth, young Jay
remembered that others were less fortunate: at Yale, he joined the
Brothers in Unity, a debating society founded to oppose "the senseless
class distinctions and degrading servility" that conventional notions of
hierarchy justified. Intending a career in law, he naively saw himself as
devoted to a calling through which he could "protect the weak from the
power of the strong" and "shield the poor from the oppression of the
rich." But Jay was like others intending legal careers—among them
Edmund Quincy, Charles G. Finney, Charles Sumner, and Wendell
Phillips. The bar failed to satisfy his longings and sent him in search of
a more morally satisfying career. "I cannot study Blackstone in order to
collect debts when so many are deprived of their liberty," confessed a
friend of Elizur Wright Jr.'s. In any event, poor eyesight, if not distaste
for the acquisitiveness of lawyering, led Jay to take up estate management, which left more time to pursue moral and benevolent causes.[12]

Though Jay was born into the Episcopal Church, his faith was that of a Low Churchman with pronounced evangelical tendencies. Moral issues galvanized his energies: he wrote an essay against dueling, opposed idle ceremony and pretentious ritual in High Church Episcopalianism, and conducted morning and evening prayers for all members of his household, including blacks. In 1829, he defended the Sabbath against desecration, especially by those operating boats and trains. For Squire Jay, "a workless faith" was "a worthless faith."[13]

That faith shaped his views of the engulfing marketplace. The estate he managed in Westchester County was not far from the country's commercial metropolis, but celebration of the market revolution was not for him. He preferred the rural life to the urban scramble, living within his means, sustaining a simple lifestyle for a man of his class, and rejecting the consumer display of luxury and foreign fashions. He believed in the ennobling influence of manual toil, hated the theater, and despised buying and selling on credit. When the great crash came in 1837, Jay blamed speculation, credit, and living beyond one's means.

The path that Jay took to immediatism and abolitionism was somewhat different from those already examined. Although he was influenced by his Low Church and evangelical beliefs, Jay grew up in a family with an old antislavery pedigree. Jay traced his conversion to immediatism to the writings of Elizabeth Heyrick, the English pioneer advocate of immediatism who published her influential tract, *Immediate, Not Gradual Abolition*, in 1825. His father's long defense of black rights immunized Jay against colonizationism; his brother had defended free black voting rights at the 1821 New York State constitutional convention, and in 1826 he worked to liberate a local free black kidnapped as a runaway and imprisoned in the slave pens of the nation's capital, one of the busiest slave markets. In the late 1820s, before Garrison took up the cause, Jay and others in New York and Pennsylvania launched a petition campaign to abolish slavery in the District of Columbia. Jay's hostility to the ACS gathered force after the suppression of Prudence Crandall's school. Judging himself a "Christian and republican," he explained that "antislavery is part of my religion. . . . I cannot be indifferent to it, and yet love my neighbor. . . . The subject involves the integrity of Christianity and the purity of the church."[14] In the 1830s, William Jay's respectability made him a powerful voice for immediatism among the thousands put off by the intensity and quirks of other antislavery leaders.[15]

Like many abolitionists, Joshua Leavitt was instructed by his upbringing in the intense moral concerns that eventually brought him to the cause. Heath, Massachusetts, where he grew up, was a homogeneous small town populated mostly by Federalists and Congregationalists. From his parents—his father was an unostentatious businessman, deacon, and militia colonel—he had learned to sympathize with those less fortunate and to accept responsibility for promoting the general welfare. As early as 1800, his father had embraced the cause of temperance, and at the age of fifty, bothered by a troubled conscience, underwent a second conversion that led him to abandon making money and to devote himself to benevolent work. At Yale, the son became a founder of the Benevolent Society, an organization fashioned to help poor young men attend college. In 1823, young Leavitt, expressing personal values similar to his father's, abandoned a career in law and entered Yale Divinity School, emerging as a minister and manager of the Connecticut Sunday School Union.

As early as 1826, Leavitt expressed moral unease with slavery in the pages of New Haven's procolonizationist organ, the *Quarterly Christian Spectator*. While he accepted colonization, he remained skeptical, for it failed to grapple with the evil of slavery. He also did not share the common view of blacks as a hopelessly degraded race. Even his cautious criticism of slavery did not spare him from Southern attack. In the late 1820s, Leavitt's belief in disinterested benevolence led him to accept leadership of the Seamen's Friend Society and then a commission as a temperance agent. He worked with the Tappans in distributing tracts, and together they welcomed Finney to New York City, where resistance to the great revivalist among conservative evangelicals remained strong. The Tappanites established the first of several free churches, aiming to breach the barriers that discouraged wage earners from joining because they could not afford a pew. When organized workingmen such as the printers repudiated the agnosticism that had tarnished the cause of the Workingmen's Party, Leavitt reached out to them, believing that Christian faith must manifest itself in everyday life and must appeal to all strata of society. Although other religious editors and evangelical leaders drew the line at such ultra measures as teetotalism, the crusade against prostitution, and Finney's radical New Measures in the early 1830s, Leavitt, like many ripe for conversion to abolitionism, embraced them all with enthusiasm.

By 1831, he had come to regard slavery as sinful, although he still clung to the ACS and gave priority to the Finneyite revival. But by 1833, with the fires of the religious awakening receding, his doubts about colonization swelled, and in that year, influenced by the Tappans, he converted to immediatism as a matter of "a religious duty."[16] Thereafter he threw himself into the cause for racial equality, working with Lewis Tappan and the African-American minister Samuel Cornish to advance black education through the Phoenix Society, a biracial organization. He also opposed segregation in the New York City revival churches, though Finney insisted on it so as not to jeopardize success in converting white sinners. In the 1830s, Joshua Leavitt became the Finneyite revival's greatest journalistic champion, editor of one of the country's most widely read evangelical newspapers, the *New York Evangelist,* which, unlike most others, opened its pages to abolitionism. The paper lost one-third of its subscription list in 1834 because of his abolitionist sympathies. By printing Finney's *Lectures on Revivalism,* the bible of the New Measurites, he revived his fortunes.[17] Looking back from such a varied career in the 1830s, Leavitt could well imagine that the path from Heath and home seemed tortuous, yet traced a straight line.

When abolitionism swept through Lane Theological Seminary in 1834, students crowded into Asa Mahan's Sixth Presbyterian Church, for he alone among the clergy supported immediatism and racial equality. Mahan thereupon became persona non grata among other Cincinnati Presbyterians, including Lyman Beecher, but the Laneites found him the perfect person to head the new manual labor antislavery school established at Oberlin with Tappanite funds and Finneyite blessings.[18]

Like other early immediatists, the young Mahan grappled with the state of his soul with a seriousness and precocity that marked him as special. His mother was an enthusiastic follower of Edwards and Emmons. Under such influence, the son became deeply fearful of damnation and immersed himself in religious contemplation. By seventeen, Mahan had undergone conversion and had started to preach. He moved away from Edwardean theology toward embracing free will, yet he feared betraying his mother and her love for Nathanael Emmons's brand of Calvinism. Still, he believed that the doctrine of determinism paralyzes the will, inhibiting conversions. At Andover Theological Seminary, he found determinism still strongly entrenched, but piety low. Doctrinal discussion edged out vital godliness; students preferred preaching that drew abstract, mechanical formulas. Andover, he concluded, was the least morally and spiritually vital place he had ever known. Even the professors were wanting in faith.

Finney became his model, but when he spoke out in ultra tones against alcohol during Finney's Rochester revival in 1831, Mahan lost his suburban pulpit. As it did for other Finneyites in western New York,

Mahan's path led to Cincinnati, where there were Presbyterians ready both for the New Measures and the social action they inspired.

Whereas only a minority among evangelicals followed the trajectories of men like Wright, Green, Birney, Leavitt, and Mahan, abolitionism was even rarer among nonevangelicals such as the Unitarian Samuel J. May. He was son of a Boston merchant who abandoned Congregationalism for Boston's Episcopalian King's Chapel, where he served as warden for thirty-six years. His father stood as living proof that wealth and fashion "are not essential to the highest respectability."[19]

May learned to internalize the acute sense of personal virtue and civic responsibility his father stressed. As a youth, he admired a black schoolmate as one of the ablest in the class and he embraced a Boston Jewish family whom his father had befriended. At Harvard Divinity School, May's sense of social responsibility received further strengthening from the Unitarian emphasis on the ethical teachings of Jesus, not on dogma. Throughout his life, the religion of the heart, the God of Love, and the imperatives of good works distinguished May's faith. Forgoing an opportunity to lead a fashionable urban Unitarian church, May displayed his distinctive mettle and his own brand of ultraism by opting for missionary work, hardly a Unitarian minister's typical calling.

Unitarianism emerged in the early nineteenth century as the preference of a rationalist, educated, materially comfortable, small upper stratum concentrated especially around Boston and eastern Massachusetts, where the theological Liberals had captured Harvard. In an age of explosive denominational growth, when new faiths such as the Disciples of Christ, Mormons, and Free Will Baptists appeared on the scene and older ones such as the Baptists and Methodists emerged as numerically dominant, Unitarianism neither evangelized nor spread. Against the advice of his parents, in 1822 May chose to try to carry the Unitarian word to Brooklyn, Connecticut, a small town in the eastern part of a state where most of the better-off were Congregationalists. May's church did not prosper, though it did gain support from the Bensons, an old Rhode Island pioneering antislavery family whose patriarch, George Benson Sr., retired from business in Providence to the nearby Connecticut countryside.

Central to May's missionary strategy was his enthusiasm for reform, which was generally lacking among Unitarians, who considered enthusiasm of any sort bad form. He became a teetotaler in the 1820s and a temperance activist, and helped dry up much of the town. He also took up educational and peace reform and the lyceum, and he organized a branch of the American Colonization Society in 1829.

Equally telling were May's efforts to make Unitarianism popular. He published a short-lived denominational newspaper in Brooklyn beginning in 1831 and upheld the Unitarian cause in debates with Hartford's Congregationalist eminence, Rev. Joel Hawes. More important, he sought to humanize religion: he reconceived the Sabbath from a sober and gloomy day, repulsive to the young, to a day of joy, even play. He doffed his somber ministerial gown because it erected a barrier between him and his people. He opened Communion to others besides the members of the church and replaced the Friday afternoon lecture before Communion with a weekly meeting for religious improvement that aimed "to help one another to live, as well as speak the praise of God, and make life itself a continual prayer."[20] When a call came from a new Unitarian church in Providence in 1828, which would have meant an advance in worldly fortunes, May remained in Brooklyn, unwilling to abandon his poorer and more difficult flock. Earlier he had revealed his goals. "My zeal is not to spread Unitarian doctrines but the idea that religion is something practical," he confessed.[21] When his people wished to attend a revival in 1833, he did not discourage them, even if he lost members. "I am not so anxious to have my Society grow as that true religion increases among us."[22]

True religion made him stir during the great debates over slavery in Missouri. He gave one of his early sermons on slavery, read John Rankin's pioneer abolitionist tract in 1825, and received a visit from Benjamin Lundy on tour in 1828, who lectured at George Benson's home in favor of colonizing blacks in Texas.[23] May was a man wrestling with the moral dilemmas of the age.

When he read in the paper that an obscure young man, William Lloyd Garrison, was lecturing on slavery in Boston in 1830, he had to hear him. He quickly fell under Garrison's spell. At first he resisted Garrison's contention that abolition and colonization were incompatible, but as the logic of Garrison's argument for racial equality sank in, May realized that he had been deceived by colonization, that there was no way to reconcile its contempt for Negroes with God's love for mankind. On first encountering him, Garrison's most astonishing quality seemed his utter lack of racial prejudice, for May had never met anyone who regarded blacks as brothers. Garrison alone understood "that the outrages perpetrated upon Africans were wrongs done to our common humanity."[24]

Before 1830, May recalled, the common view of blacks was as a stupid but kindly and jolly folk not worse off in slavery than some poor white laborers in freedom. Prejudice was universal among educated and uneducated whites alike. When May denounced slavery as rooted in prejudice in a guest sermon in Boston in 1833, he caused a stir. White prejudice, not black inferiority, was responsible for the tolerance of slavery and the shortfalls of free African Americans, he preached: "It is our *prejudice* against the color of these poor people that makes us consent to the tremendous wrong they are suffering." Were the slaves white, Northerners would not remain silent. "Will our *prejudice* be accepted by the Almighty?" he asked.[25] Such words could not be published under Unitarian auspices, so when his sermon reached the printed page, the offending passages were struck out. His father warned him that if he persisted, he would ruin his career, but a woman who had heard him that Sunday had burst into tears. She never before had heard a minister plead for the slaves from the pulpit. May knew then that he had struck some hearts and consciences.

For May, this was the beginning. In Brooklyn, he banished "the nigger pew," not without protest. When Prudence Crandall's school in nearby Canterbury became the focus of white bigotry, he became her staunchest ally, visiting the town to appeal to reason, and when that failed, writing a pamphlet on her behalf, earning his reward shortly thereafter in the dedication by Lydia Maria Child in her *Appeal in Favor of Americans Called Africans:* "for his earnest and disinterested efforts in an unpopular but most righteous cause." The events in Canterbury, which dramatized the Negro-despising convictions of the colonizationists, completed his conversion.

In the end, May's antislavery activity was too much for his church, and he lost his pulpit in Brooklyn. When May moved to South Scituate, Massachusetts, in 1836, he continued to preach against segregation in the church, and again faced grumbling. A year before, he had told Ralph Waldo Emerson that the issue between immediatism and colonization was "whether you should remove them [blacks] from prejudice or the prejudice from them."[26] Black removal now meant for him acquiescing in white sin. Removing prejudice, he learned in Brooklyn, Canterbury, and Boston, was as difficult as any task he would ever face.

In 1834, a friend of his father's tried to dissuade May from his course. The friend agreed "that negroes deserved humane treatment," but remained adamant that "they could never be elevated to equality" because they were "an inferior race intended to be servants." May stuck to his guns:

Sir, we Abolitionists are not so foolish as to require or wish that ignorant negroes should be considered wise men, or that vicious negroes should be considered virtuous men, or poor negroes should be considered rich men. All we
demand for them is that negroes shall be permitted, encouraged, assisted to
become as wise, as virtuous, and as rich as they can be and acknowledged to
be just what they have become, and be treated accordingly.

But that did not satisfy his critic: "If you should bring me negroes who
had become the wisest of the wise, the best of the good, the richest of
the rich I would not acknowledge them to be my equal." May had
plumbed the depths where reason, common sense, and decency could
not contend against "the insanity of prejudice."[27]

May's abhorrence of elitism and caste did not stop with color prejudice. He had no use for the pretensions of bourgeois, consumerist display or for the use of the titles "esquire," "reverend," and "doctor"
that most members of his class insisted on to remind others of their social superiority. He insisted that all in his household treat laboring folk
with respect and not indulge in the common practice of calling grown
working men and women by their common names, but address them
as "Mr." and "Mrs."

In the 1830s, May became deeply immersed in antislavery work and
a leader in the American Antislavery Society, to the annoyance of the
Tappan brothers, the organization's financial angels. To these orthodox,
evangelical Finneyites, the presence of a Unitarian in the front ranks rankled in a cause so steeped in faith, especially since Lewis Tappan himself
had abandoned orthodoxy for Unitarianism in the 1820s before returning to evangelical Christianity. Yet the Tappans and May shared more
than they may have realized: all sought to elevate morals above markets.
May recalled in his memoirs that in 1830 the churches were second
only to the making of money in popular influence. Whatever their
theological and temperamental differences, May and the Tappans aimed
to give morals primacy.

Rarely have successful businessmen struggled so arduously and left
such a rich record testifying to their efforts to reconcile commerce and
culture, business and benevolence as Arthur and Lewis Tappan, opera-
tors of the largest silk-importing firm in New York City in the 1820s and
1830s. The struggle began in Northampton, Massachusetts, in the home
of their father, who was a goldsmith, pious and respectable, but without
ambition, which puzzled Lewis. As in the case of many other early abolitionists, the moral influences they received at home set them on the path

they eventually followed. The Tappans' mother was a powerful moral and intellectual figure. Steeped in Edwardean Calvinism, she taught the sons that holiness required active work to carry out God's will on earth, a central strategy in the struggle against one's own sinfulness.

Lewis became a merchant's apprentice in Boston, a city that his mother warned against, with its theaters, lewd women, and venereal disease and that Lewis agreed presented "a picture of dissipation and laxness."[28] Lewis then went into the hardware business and prospered during the War of 1812. He joined a circle of rising businessmen and professionals and abandoned his mother's faith for fashionable Unitarianism, made all the more attractive by William Ellery Channing's compelling preaching. His mother labored to reclaim the wayward son, but to no avail. But then, in the mid-1820s, his business suffered some troubles, and Lewis reexamined his views, influenced by the arrival in Boston of Lyman Beecher, who led the revival of evangelical orthodoxy in the Hub. In 1827, Lewis made public his reconversion to evangelical Christianity by publishing an attack on Unitarianism, affirming the superior virtues of Trinitarian orthodoxy. For years, he declared, he had observed which brand of Christian faith made sinners better men and women, judged by their deeds of holiness in everyday dealings. The Liberals he found more worldly and self-absorbed, the orthodox he judged more selfless and God-absorbed.

He joined his brother Arthur, who never had abandoned orthodoxy, in his New York firm, and the two together poured their formidable money and energies into the work of religious benevolence. They circulated tracts and Bibles, and they worked for the Sunday School movement, the temperance cause, the peace movement, the Sabbatarian campaign, seamen's betterment, the crusade against prostitution, and the manual labor crusade, giving aid to Oneida, Lane, and later to Oberlin. They provided much of the leadership that brought the Finneyite revival to New York City, promoting the organization of a series of free churches.

Beyond this dizzying commitment to evangelical benevolence, they worked assiduously to bring Christ into the countinghouse and warehouse. Their clerks had to attend church weekly and live in pious, preferably temperance, boardinghouses. The more obedient and promising received help in starting independent careers. The Tappans sold merchandise for cash and short credit at fixed prices, appealing to country traders, often from New England stock like themselves, who felt assured that all customers received the same fair prices and terms of trade, even when ordering by mail. By limiting credit sales—they later wished they had granted none—they hoped to discourage speculation, greed, and neglect of domestic duty. In all these ways they hoped to do business the Christian way. To protect businessmen from those who did not, they established a credit agency to rate risks by providing information about the probity, morals, efficiency, and success of prospective borrowers.

Lewis dated his conversion to immediatism from 1833. The nullification crisis, a clerical friend instructed him, was the opening battle over slavery: "The scorpion whip of South Carolina dripping with the blood of the slave was shaken over Congress with mighty effect!" The crisis was designed to forestall all future agitation of the slavery question by raising the specter of disunionism. In reality, however, Lewis and his brother had been drifting toward immediatism for some time.[29]

Like others, they came to immediatism from colonization, but they were among the first to realize their error. Their absorbing obsession with sacralizing everyday life made them more sensitive to their own faults, more critical of conventional wisdom and of social convention, more alert to Christian hypocrisy. Garrison's message played a part in their shift; but the claims of African Americans to equality proved central to the maturation of their Christian benevolent worldview. In Boston in the early 1820s, Lewis had observed with admiration the performance of black children in a colored school; six months later, he heard a Cherokee preach at Park Street Church in nearly perfect English, fulfilling scriptural prophecy, he claimed.[30] When blacks sought white support to establish a manual labor institution in New Haven, the Tappans proved receptive. They were especially vulnerable to the argument that slavery was sin, the sin of pride and selfishness. Lewis attributed popular indifference toward slavery to "the eagerness of men to accumulate and hoard money, to require service for inadequate compensation, to lord it over the dependent and poor, to widen the distance between the labor and affluent portions of the community, and to establish unchristian and antirepublican aristocracy."[31] In all their earlier works of religious benevolence, they had struggled against the perils of acquisitiveness in themselves and others. In slavery, they discovered its darkest fruits.

While they poured thousands of dollars into changing Southern opinion through mail campaigns and in efforts at diffusion of abolitionist propaganda, they struggled equally hard and with equal frustration against racial prejudice at home. They demanded that Finney abolish segregation in the Chatham Street Church. In the course of a struggle to integrate the Presbyterian churches of New York City, Lewis suffered excommunication. And they insisted that black speakers be placed on the program at antislavery events. In discovering the sin of prejudice, the Tappans discovered a new measure of who was a genuine Christian, a test not many churchgoers passed. The opposition to black self-help in New Haven, backed by colonizationist leaders and some of Congregationalism's most important evangelical figures, together with the subsequent discovery that the ACS relied on the sale of rum to do business with the natives in Africa, completed the process by which the Tappans saw through the facade of colonizationist piety.

Central to their understanding of Christian faith was a loathing of caste. Arthur, brother Lewis explained, regarded "all men without distinction of complexion or condition." Parents had an obligation to train children to act kindly toward the less fortunate. The rich had a special burden to display sympathy toward the poor and "the laboring classes toward each other, irrespective of condition or complexion." In a Christian republic, Arthur believed, if children from all backgrounds did not mix and behave kindly toward one another "how, as men will they be able to meet at the polls, sit on juries, attend political meetings . . . and mingle with their fellow men in all the various walks of life, on equal terms, as the religion of Jesus, and the laws of the land require?"[32] Even in retirement, Lewis remained obsessed with the question that had haunted him throughout his career: "Is it right to be rich?" The conventional answer was that the rich deserved their good fortune, the fruit of intelligence, hard work, shrewdness, and God's favor. The Tappans, struggling with guilt, knew better and spent their lives proving it.[33]

Like the Tappans, Wendell Phillips was set on the path to abolitionism by the teachings of his parents. Born to privilege and growing up in a mansion in a newly constructed Boston Brahmin enclave on Beacon Hill, Phillips was the son of a Federalist lawyer and judge who was a member of the Harvard Corporation, and Boston's mayor. His parents did not abandon orthodox Congregationalism for either Unitarianism or Episcopalianism, however. There was something old-fashioned, too, in the way they reared their children. Each learned a manual skill. Wendell became an expert carpenter, and together the children were responsible for daily household maintenance. "Never ask another to do for you what you can do for yourself," the parents exhorted, in an age with no shortage of domestic servants for people of their means.[34] Phillips's parents impressed on him the importance of self-discipline and of serving some higher purpose than personal achievement, a legacy from the Revolutionary generation's belief in the duty of civic virtue. By the time Phillips was a student at Harvard, he displayed both self-confidence

and self-control and now was ready to exhort others as he had been exhorted: "Passion must be controlled at all cost, for unrestrained passion
could cause personal debasement and endless social destruction, creating the worst imaginable forms of enslavement for individuals and nations."[35] After he graduated from Harvard, Phillips carried with him "a
powerful republican ideology distrustful of unchecked power, privileged
hierarchy, social disorder, and popular licentiousness."[36]

Yet Phillips could find no place for himself. He tried practicing law,
first in Lowell, and then in Boston, but by 1834 was contemplating quit-
ting. Immersion in family history and genealogy provided an escape from
the boredom and sordidness of the law, which he regarded as little more
than a branch of business. Two experiences changed his life. First, a
Boston mob threatened Garrison and a group of female abolitionists in
1835, and then another mob murdered Elijah Lovejoy in Alton, Illinois.
When respectable members of his own class, such as the state's attorney
general, rationalized mob violence in defense of the Union, Phillips
sensed that slavery threatened everyone's freedom and was perverting
the character of the republic. That the mobs would attack women made
that perversion the more evident.

Among Boston's active antislavery women was Ann Terry Green, a
cousin of Garrison's most important female ally in Boston, Maria Weston
Chapman, leader of the Boston Female Antislavery Society. Through
Green, Phillips gained access to the world of antislavery men and women.
They came from all classes and mixed as equals, deferring to one another
on merit, their lives overflowing with moral purpose. Here were powerful women, like Chapman, who dominated her financier husband. By convention, they were supposed to be confined to the domestic sphere, but
they had burst the artificial division between private and public and had
found inspiring, prophetic meaning in their lives. Compared with them,
Phillips, with every advantage of class and gender, had wandered into
early adulthood without purpose. "Which of us ever dreamed . . . what
selfish lives we were leading 'till the slave plucked the bandage from our
eyes—& showed us our feet resting on his neck?" he later asked.[37] Love
and calling now joined in holy union. Defying his mother, Phillips married Ann Green, though she remained an invalid for the rest of their life
together. As he traveled the country as abolitionism's most gifted orator,
Phillips carried the invalid's battle to the far corners of the republic.

Garrison described Phillips's conversion as the "abandonment of
legitimate ambition," but that ambition had found no worthy purpose
until Phillips discovered in abolition an alternative to the ennui of

everyday drudgery, with "its rising, eating, lying down," an escape
also from life's "dull and rotting weeds."[38] The antislavery cause had
"revealed to us the joy of self-devotion—taught us how to intensify life
by laying it as a willing offering on the altar of some great cause."[39] The
struggle against slavery, a public crusade, was also a private struggle over
"pride, over self-interest, over avarice, over lust, over all the prejudices
and bad passions of the human breast."[40]

Edmund Quincy, another of Garrison's Boston faithful, made that
same discovery. Like Phillips, Quincy carried a heavy family legacy. His
father, too, had been a distinguished public man, also mayor of Boston,
and like Phillips, he was repelled by the prospect of practicing law, though
he studied for a career at the bar. The new Boston disgusted him. The
market revolution soiled whatever it touched. His father would not invest in the new manufacturing companies because he disliked industrial-
ism, especially the exploitation of child labor. An old, unreconstructed
Federalist, the elder Quincy thought the republic cursed by slavery from
its founding. The slaveholders, he believed from firsthand observation,
were "violent, overbearing, and insolent" and undeviatingly had pursued
"the extension of slavery . . . from the days of Jefferson."[41]

Edmund preferred the old Boston to the Boston of tenement houses,
those "meaningless soulless masses of matter."[42] And he agreed with his
father that politics was "a bubbling mass of corrupt matter." Just as
Phillips escaped into family history, Quincy immersed himself in literature.[43] "Life without literature is death," he confessed. Long walking
tours in the New England countryside allowed him temporarily to shut
out "the sordid world of Boston in the 1830s." Emerson caught the
essence of the new order that so alienated Quincy: "a system of distrust,
of concealment, of superior keenness, not of giving but of taking advantage" that poisoned and corrupted human relationships. Quincy
would have none of it. He remained aloof from politics and refused to
invest in manufactures.[44]

Ten years after graduating from Harvard he still had found no compass. Then, in October 1836, he met Richard Hildreth, an antislavery
journalist and the author of *Archy Moore,* the first antislavery novel.
Hildreth taught him that a deadly struggle between freedom and slavery
would shape the future and that slavery alone prevented the country
from fulfilling its promise. The abolitionist mobbings also proved decisive, as they had for Phillips. Slavery was destroying free expression,
elevating the principle of aristocracy over republican equality, and
encouraging a sordid selfishness that led country folk to abandon

productive labor on farms for "the thick atmosphere & at best dubious pursuits of the city."[45] At Harvard, too, students learned "the gospel according to Wall St.," which they summarized in the catchpenny slogan, "Make all the money you can."[46]

One thing that emerges clearly from the influences and experiences that brought these abolitionists to the cause is that becoming a man in the new bourgeois order had become more problematic than it had been in the past. This obsession with "manliness" is a leitmotif that runs through the report that Theodore Dwight Weld composed for the Manual Labor Society in New York City prior to enrolling in Lane Theological Seminary in Cincinnati and eventually departing for his most important life's work, as a paid agent of the American Antislavery Society. Weld was one of those ultraists who came to abolitionism via conversion in the Finneyite revival and, like Beriah Green, via the attractions of the manual labor movement.

Growing disdain for physical labor, Weld argued, was producing a race of "sickly and effeminate" males, the inevitable result of "inactivity, idleness, and dependence." As the country underwent economic transformation, conceptions of gender also underwent change. "In the modern market," Weld claimed, there was a short supply of "*manhood, full grown manhood.*" Weld believed that modern men were wanting in "firmness, decisiveness, perseverance, courage and constancy, and generous self-sacrifice." The new consumerism was producing a "generation of dandies," whereas "real" men were "careless of their appearance, slovenly in their dress," a good description of Weld himself.[47]

In manual labor schools, Weld promised, hard toil would toughen their bodies and simple living would insulate them from consumerist display. Manual labor therefore would graduate youth "whose firm set frames and brawny muscles *indicate their sex.*" Other schools graduated "*dessicated* mincing things of powder and perfumery, noxious specimens of *diluted* manhood, scribbling sentimentally in albums, and lisping insipidity," or as he scathingly described them, "knights of the reticule, valorous in onset upon cologne bottles, and prodigies of prowess among sprigs of rosemary." Above all manual labor built character. A student might wear homespun, as at Oneida Institute, but he possessed "overmastering intellect and lofty daring," just what the country needed. He was a man who would "dare and endure . . . expand his views, and elevate his aims . . . ennoble his purposes . . . giving him an onward momentum over everything but impossibility." Here were precisely the qualities needed by those who took up the cross of abolition.[48]

Underlying Weld's sensitivity about "manliness," "dandies," and effeminacy lay a diffuse anxiety over gender roles common among men who opted not to compete in the marketplace. In a pre-industrial order of self-sufficient households, sons followed in a father's footsteps because occupational choices remained limited. By the early nineteenth century, young men, forced to become self-fashioners, faced a bewildering array of career paths. Weld himself and a large fraction of the students at Lane were over twenty-five, some in their thirties, yet still unsettled.

Weld had thrashed around for years, ambivalent about becoming a minister, like his father, who seemed a failure. Finney offered a role model, but Finney had transformed the pulpit in ways that dismayed Weld's father. Weld in the end chose Finney, but not the ministry. Instead, he became a new social type, the professional reformer, an agitator as deeply moved by Christian impulse as any revivalist. The first great test of Weld's "manliness" occurred at Lane, where Weld's ministerial ambitions suffered derailment when he ran into roadblocks to acting on Christian belief. For Weld, the core of manliness was possessing the moral character to act on conviction. Doing so led him and others at Lane and elsewhere to immediatism.[49]

Changes in the ministry conflicted with Weld's conception of manliness. Ministers had become employees, serving short tenures, no longer devoting a lifetime as shepherds to one or two flocks, as in the colonial period. Clergymen were hardly the powerful figures of authority they once had been, for now they held precarious tenure at the grace of governing boards, usually successful businessmen, no more inclined to tolerate antinomian opinion than the trustees of Lane. Finney's troubles with the clerical establishment in the late 1820s revealed how even the most gifted revivalist of the age had to trim his sails to appease the powerful. In the 1830s, ministers discovered that preaching teetotalism or abolition could cost them their pulpits. For ministers as for other men, "success" in the marketplace became the conventional measure of manly accomplishment.

By insisting on the manliness of simple living, physical labor, and the moral courage involved in advocating ultraist views in the teeth of popular opinion, Weld refused to measure a person's worth by conventional standards of success that sacrificed independence for social position.[50] Weld, like the great writers of the American Renaissance, "felt self-consciously deviant from prevailing norms of manly behavior." For Ralph Waldo Emerson, "becoming a man . . . meant escaping conformity either to the rivalries of the marketplace, where men became things, or to the suffocations of domestic gentility, where men became women."[51]

Compounding the problems of male identity was the feminization of religion in a gender regime that sharply differentiated between men's and women's spheres. As Finney's disciple, Weld understood that the fate of the revival rested largely on the shoulders of women, who dominated church membership and who gave the revival its energy. Finney's defense of women's role in the New Measures, praying publicly and by name for fallen males, proved to be the thorniest issue between him and his critics. As Weld and other young men contemplated a career in the clergy, they could expect to be lionized by women, but their manliness would remain suspect as long as their work remained centered in the women's sphere, particularly as long as they spoke for the "women's" position on the personal imperative of conversion, which few men experienced, and in the debates over child rearing, membership in secret all-male societies such as the Freemasons, temperance, antislavery, the abolition of prostitution.[52]

Five years after proselytizing for manual labor and converting to immediatism, Weld married Angelina Grimké, a pioneer in abolitionist-inspired feminism. In linking his life with a woman like Grimké, the feminist implications of his manual labor beliefs and then of abolitionism bore fruit. By appropriating religiosity and moral leadership as fundamental to true manhood, Weld claimed for men qualities claimed by conservative opinion to be preeminently feminine.[53]

Weld's evolution as an abolitionist had come slowly. When he started on his national tour for manual labor, he had not yet committed himself. Garrison was not widely known in 1831–32, and while Weld alternated his lectures on manual labor with others on temperance and female education, he remained publicly silent on slavery. His older friend and fellow Oneida County evangelist Charles Stuart, who was also converted in the Finney revival in western New York, had embraced immediatism in 1831 before sailing for Ireland to press the cause in the United Kingdom and knew that his younger friend was pondering the problem of slavery. Stuart sent Weld a copy of his important early immediatist pamphlet, which had been published in Britain. Weld also discussed the slavery question on his manual labor tour of the South with Alabama planters and colonizationists James G. Birney and Rev. William Allan. A visit to Western Reserve College in Hudson, Ohio, was especially important because key faculty members, including

Elizur Wright Jr. and Beriah Green, had just read Garrison's *Thoughts on African Colonization*. At about the same time that Weld left for Lane, two of the major sponsors of the Manual Labor Society, the Tappan brothers, also were moving toward abolitionism. In committing substantial funds to Lane, they hoped that its graduates would spread abolition along with the Gospel, which in their minds had become inextricably linked.[54] This nexus—the manual labor movement, revival-inspired ultraism, and the testimony of black anticolonizationists—helped convert to the cause the man who himself converted more Americans than anyone except Garrison himself.

Nothing is harder to discern precisely in history than motives, and those of the founding figures of the abolitionist movement are no exception. Yet for all the opacities of historical reconstruction and the diversity of experience among the careers reviewed here, a common element emerges. Some were more shaped by republican political culture—Phillips and Quincy, for example—than by the religious culture so formative in May's liberalism or the Tappans' orthodoxy, but whatever the precise trajectory of their conversion to immediatism, their unease with the new world of social relations created by the market revolution distinguished them from most contemporaries.

God, the Churches, and Slavery

"Let us see, Sir, whether our cause has given us any evidence that it is of God," Garrison proclaimed at the second annual meeting of the New England Antislavery Society.[1] "Religious principle is the only lever, and public opinion the fulcrum by which the great mountain of oppression is to be removed," predicted Arnold Buffum, president of the society and an early antislavery traveling agent: "We must address ourselves to the religious sentiment and feeling of the people."[2] "Let us, Christian brethren," Elizur Wright Jr. urged, "for I will not waste an appeal upon those who do not acknowledge the authority of the Gospel, dispassionately, and in the fear of God," inquire as to whether the colonization society is *"doing what the Gospel requires to be done for the removal of slavery and its concomitant sins."*[3]

Colonization, and even slavery itself, still could marshal prominent advocates and well-received arguments to contest abolitionist claims, however, and as certain as early immediatists were that their cause enjoyed God's blessing, the apathy, indifference, and hostility they faced among most Christians posed formidable obstacles as well. If, as abolitionists believed, God was on their side, they knew they could not say the same about His churches. As it frequently did when applied to other reform causes, the ultraism of the abolitionists provoked resistance from denominational leaders and other defenders of the status quo. Yet it also served as a mode of appeal to others in those same denominations, those who felt equally disturbed—and marginalized—by developments stemming from the market revolution.

Most religious weeklies, reflecting the endorsement of denominational leaders, embraced colonization and either ignored or were hostile to the immediatist message. The Garrisonians recognized from the beginning that neither the *Liberator* nor other publications could penetrate the mass of Christian indifference or puncture the sanctimony of colonizationist piety. They decided, therefore, to carry the immediatist message directly to the countryside through traveling agents and debates in towns and cities. These piqued the curiosity of the populace, some of whom had few other diversions, to come out and listen to a strange new message. During one of his earliest forays into the hinterlands as an agent of the antislavery society, Buffum, a Quaker hatter, reported mixed results. In the fall of 1833, in Northampton, Massachusetts, and Troy, New York, no church opened its doors. Where ministers and church boards were tolerant and open-minded, agents made inroads, but they never could count on the churches, whatever the denomination. As late as 1836, when New England abolitionists met in Boston, not a single church would provide meeting space.

When Lane Theological Seminary's governing board, made up of businessmen, lawyers, and clergymen, swiftly suppressed the enthusiasm for immediatism that followed the historic debate there between Garrisonian abolitionism and colonizationism, it was no isolated event. In the months before the upheaval in Cincinnati, college presidents, typically leading figures in their denominations and also, typically, colonizationists, had gathered at the annual meetings of religious and benevolent societies in New York City and agreed to arrest the immediatist danger, sensing that naive, pious young men, many intent on careers in the ministry, were especially vulnerable.[4] The Lane trustees simply pursued a national strategy that Amherst College, Andover Theological Seminary, and Wesleyan also followed.

Efforts to establish an antislavery society at Andover, for example, a chief producer of Congregationalist ministers, made little headway until 1835, when the charismatic English abolitionist George Thompson, traveling in New England, addressed students at the Andover Methodist Church. Nearly half were swept away, and these, ready to abandon colonization, invited him to the seminary chapel. But the faculty moved quickly to halt the infection. Formation of an immediatist society would split the students, divert them from piety and study, jeopardize their chances of securing pulpits upon graduation, and alienate vital support from the wealthy donors and beneficent churches on which Andover depended. The faculty thereupon secured dissolution of both colonizationist and immediatist societies and obtained from the trustees authority to approve the existence of any student organization.

Andover conservatives had learned well the lessons of Lane, but they also benefited from the differences between the Lane and Andover students. The Lane students were exceptionally mature, and a large number came from Oneida, where Finneyite evangelicalism and manual labor egalitarianism already had forged them into a powerful, self-confident body, aggressively questioning colonizationist piety and disinclined to defer to elders. The Andover students were more disparate, conventional, and deferential. The contrast reveals that local contexts and particular experiences influenced whether religious impulse yielded to immediatist enthusiasm.

Andover's stance was symptomatic, however. Throughout the 1830s, the leaders of the Baptists, Methodists, Congregationalists, Presbyterians, and other denominations regularly put down immediatist challenges at regional and national meetings, and most of the denominational press remained unmovably hostile to abolition. By the late 1830s, frustrated abolitionists identified the Northern churches as the chief bulwarks of slavery.

Yet Garrison's and Buffum's belief that "religious principle is the only lever" was not misplaced. After half a dozen years of agitation, immediatists had made strong inroads in religious communities, even though they failed to conquer the majority, the doctors of divinity, the seminaries, and the prestigious urban pulpits. Antislavery organizations also derived the bulk of their leadership from people affiliated with the churches, most notably the Congregationalists and Quakers, but also others from a wide variety of sects.[5] In western New York and in Ohio, the Finneyite revival ploughed fertile fields for the subsequent spread of the antislavery message by dozens of young men such as Weld and the Lane graduates hired to proselytize by the American Antislavery Society in the mid-1830s. The nationwide speaking campaigns fulfilled the promise of the founders of the American Antislavery Society in December 1833, targeting Christian leaders and the rank and file: "With entire confidence in the overruling justice of God, we plant ourselves upon the Declaration of our Independence, and upon the truths of Divine Revelation, as upon the EVERLASTING ROCK. . . . We shall enlist the PULPIT and the PRESS in the cause of the suffering and the dumb. We shall aim at a purification of the churches from all participation in the guilt of slavery."[6]

Overcoming resistance in the churches proved far more formidable than the early Garrisonians and Weldites had anticipated. They discovered that people's understanding of what it meant to be a Christian when applied to the slavery question varied enormously, even within the same denomination, theological tradition, or meetinghouse. Most had never given much thought to slavery. The minority that had, like many of the original immediatists, had gravitated toward colonizationism. The commitment by leading denominations and church leaders to colonization rested on solid foundations, including its compatibility with sectional harmony, political expediency, seeming practicality, and deep-seated racial prejudice among white Northern Christians. The immediatist assault on colonization, therefore, challenged not only colonization's moral principles and utility, but the authority of the country's religious leadership and the harmony of the churches.

What was even more disturbing, immediatism challenged the hitherto unquestioned assumption that all the North was antislavery in principle by denigrating as "hollow sympathy" Northern opinion that acquiesced in slavery's vast expansion into the Cotton Kingdom. "Unaccompanied by philanthropic action," such professions of antislavery were "from a moral point of view worthless,—a thing without vitality—sightless—soulless—dead."[7] The differences between genuine and spurious antislavery sentiment were profound.

Immediatists declared slavery to be a personal sin; conservatives held it to be either sanctioned by the Bible or, at worst, a national evil, deserving of eventual destruction, but not requiring immediate social upheaval or radical personal action. Immediatists depicted slavery as "man-stealing," the reduction of human beings to things, the crime of crimes in a Christian republic. Conservatives recognized circumstances under which conscientious, paternalistic Christians acquired slaves, such as through inheritance, and believed they could not abandon their flesh-and-blood property without abandoning Christian duty to care for the weak, provide for their religious education, assure their kind treatment, and prepare them eventually for a better future. In this view, mere ownership did not necessarily reduce people to property; between the Christian master and other masters lay an awesome gulf. Both immediatists and mainstream Christians relied on suasion and appeal to the master's conscience to effect change, but whereas abolitionists thought it necessary to prick Southern consciences directly by censuring slavery as evil and indirectly by arousing Northern sentiment against it, conservatives insisted that only tender regard for Southern sensibilities ever could persuade. Immediatists retorted that half a century of such tender regard had allowed many slaveholders to profess that they, too, deemed slavery an evil that time someday would remedy, while bondage expanded, conscience reposed, and the Southern and national stake in chattel labor grew ever larger. Slaveholder tolerance of antislavery sentiment before 1830 proved how little antislavery sentiment mattered.

Furthermore, immediatists refused to wait the decades or the century that conservative gradualists were prepared to endure before slavery passed away. Masters had to renounce forthwith ownership in man, pay wages to their laborers, abandon corporal punishment, respect family integrity, and thereby begin the transformative process by which slave labor became free labor.

Immediatists believed all Americans, including the citizens of the North, shared in the guilt of enslavement; mainstream Christians regarded slavery as an intractable Southern problem requiring Northern patience and sympathy. Finally, immediatists deemed the abandonment of racial prejudice and colonization to be indispensable, since without equal opportunity there was no prospect that the two races could live peacefully and productively side by side. As long as Northern Christians believed that free African Americans belonged in Africa, they could not expect white Southerners to free their slaves, since the colonization of two million was a chimera, impractical because of cost and the indispensability of black labor to the production of wealth and cruel in the face of black resistance and the tragic fate that had met hundreds of American blacks already buried in Liberia. The inveterate, nearly universal prejudice of Northern Christians toward the free African Americans, therefore, brought the issue of slavery to the door of every Northern church and into the midst of every community, since abolitionists contended that slavery rested on prejudice and prejudice formed the rock upon which both emancipation and American Christianity foundered. In linking immediatism with racial equality, the early abolitionists squarely challenged the nearly universal evangelical conception of the American millennium as for whites only. The logic of immediatism thus challenged mainstream Christian opinion at every turn.

In 1834, the young pastor of Boston's Pine Street Congregational Church, Amos A. Phelps, published *Lectures on Slavery and Its Remedy,* an early compendium of immediatist arguments derived from his own recent conversion. Dedicating them "to the Ministers of the Gospel of every Denomination of Christians," Phelps solicited endorsements of his views less "to swell the number" than "to make the impression at the outset that" antislavery, "like the cause of Temperance, is a common cause—a common work."[8] One hundred and twenty-four clergymen responded: nearly two-thirds hailed from Maine and Massachusetts, which alone accounted for 40 percent, and New York and Ohio accounted for nearly 25 percent. Congregationalists and Presbyterians dominated, providing 70 percent, while Baptists provided 12 percent. Phelps claimed no representativeness for the sample of respondents; undoubtedly there were others he never reached or who had chosen not to respond, yet who adhered to immediatism.[9]

Phelps's target was the large mass of uncommitted. Though "slavery in our land is a great and threatening NATIONAL evil," he exhorted, those expert in preaching against sin had "woefully and criminally overlooked" this subject. Even indifference, silence, and neutrality abetted sin and involved Christians "in personal guilt," for as *the HINGES of public sentiment in respect to all prevailing sins,*" the clergy possessed the power to revolutionize popular opinion unless they faltered because of fear and self-interest, including the loss *"of a good living."* Since prevailing sins such as intemperance, prostitution, and slavery were "sanctioned and made popular . . . by the practices of large classes of the community," Phelps deemed it "the grand and special business of the ministry—their *professional* business—" to assault such *"strong holds of Satan."* This required that preachers "ought ever to be ahead of public sentiment," as risky as that might be.[10]

Born in Connecticut, the son of pious parents, Phelps had been raised by a widowed mother left with an insolvent estate whose debts she somehow managed to pay. Equal determination drove her desire to give Amos an education. In 1821, Phelps underwent a conversion and later attended Yale, where he enthusiastically imbibed Taylorite teaching, settling as junior colleague at the Congregational Church in Hopkinton, Massachusetts. Then trouble struck. His temperance principles alienated members of the congregation, who secured his dismissal. Boston then beckoned, where he settled at the Pine Street Church in 1832, benefiting from the support of Lyman Beecher and others eager to advance Taylorites in the local pulpits.[11]

By the summer of 1833, Phelps had become an immediatist activist, delivering a sermon before the New England Antislavery Society, giving lectures in Boston and elsewhere, and heading up the newly formed Young Men's Antislavery Society in the metropolis. At the annual meeting of Massachusetts Congregationalist ministers in the summer of 1834,

Phelps appealed for endorsement of immediatism, but the delegates' preference lay with colonization and with vague expressions of support for the slave.[12]

As with so many others, Phelps's path to immediatism lay through colonization, first its embrace, then the discovery of its deception of the benevolent, and finally recognition of its tendency to deflate conscience and deny the claims of black humanity to equality. Substantively, there were no new arguments or fresh logic in Phelps's abolitionist lectures. Rather, he refined the ideas of Garrison, Wright, Beriah Green, Lydia Maria Child, John Greenleaf Whittier, and other founding figures, avoiding polemics and coolly and systematically answering all the common objections that the immediatist case elicited. The mildness of the language and the careful, logical progression of the argument especially aimed to appeal to sober clergymen.

In several respects, however, Phelps's lectures touched clergymen and other Christians to the quick. At the outset, he renounced colonization and declared "that the time has now come when the friends of God and man ought to take a higher stand."[13] In an appendix devoted to discrediting colonization, he confessed his own error. "It is a scheme, in which I was once deeply interested," he admitted. He had preached, written, and raised money on its behalf, but he "did not then understand the real nature and tendency of the scheme." The Garrisonians had undeceived him, as they had others. Phelps now saw "my error and my sin; and though it was a sin of ignorance, still I desire to repent of it, and send out this little book, to speak for the oppressed . . . that I may thereby do something, to make reparation for the injury done by former neglect and error."[14] This extraordinary public confession appeared at the height of the struggle between colonization and immediatism, a struggle in which leading clergymen manned the colonizationist barricades, including Lyman Beecher, Nathaniel W. Taylor, Leonard Bacon, and other luminaries of the obscure Phelps's denomination. Phelps's abject confession aimed to trigger pangs of guilt in others similarly led astray.

At the same time, Phelps denounced racial prejudice. Slavery, not color, unfitted people for freedom, robbing them of incentive and self-respect; emancipation would restore both and assure that the ex-slaves would be competent to assume the burdens of citizenship. "Mind is mind, man is man, whatever his complexion or the circumstances of his existence," Phelps averred.[15] Enslave whites and they, too, would appear servile and lazy, abject and brutish. The cry that black freedom would lead to racial mixture was "entirely groundless—the offspring of a most cruel and wicked prejudice," which merited "only pity or contempt." Such prejudice savored not of heaven, but of hell. "Professing Christians," Phelps thundered, "there is a *God* who is no respecter of persons. Look well to thine heart then."[16]

In summoning the guilty to repent, Phelps was logically applying to slavery the doctrines of immediate repentance and the necessary appeal to free will that echoed from the Yale Divinity School and from Taylorite and Beecherite New Light preaching. Finneyite revivalism left Weld and others susceptible to the radical social implications of the immediatist message; Phelps exemplified another, related sort of convert—the youth carried away by the applicability of theory to practice. The opposition of the Christian mainstream to antislavery immediatism struck Phelps as inconsistent. "Indeed, the doctrine of immediate emancipation is nothing more or less than that of immediate repentance, applied to this particular sin."[17] Those who distinguished slavery by declaring it a political, not a moral or religious, question were self-contradictory, since they did not hesitate to intervene in the public sphere against intemperance and Cherokee despoliation and in favor of strict Sabbath observation by the post office. The contradiction between the demands that evangelical leaders made for immediate and total renunciation of alcohol while exhibiting tolerance for slavery especially bothered Phelps.[18]

Yet Phelps himself had gotten into trouble over temperance, which should have served as a warning that the consistent application of principle could be dangerous. In the eyes of the mainstream, it bespoke ultraism, the immediate eradication of all social sins, regardless of the consequences. As we have seen, such ultraism was a hallmark of the antislavery religious temperament, which demanded an unbending consistency in the face of Christian duty. Anything less was viewed by people like Phelps as crass expediency, subversive of Christian principle and of the ministry's moral authority.

Phelps mentioned not only teetotalism, but "moral reform" as an example of the objectives demanding immediatist attention. And just as Goodell's teetotalism caused difficulty with the clerical mainstream, so did uncompromising "moral reform." In New York City, a center of prostitution—ten thousand women of easy virtue were said to sell their services in the early 1830s—Rev. John McDowell, leader of the Moral Reform Society, was put on trial and driven to his grave by the prim and proper Presbyterians who regarded the antivice crusade as pandering to prurient interests, bringing into the open what must be left hid-

den. As respectable evangelicals sought to suppress the moral reformers, abolitionists stood up as their staunchest champions. The leadership of the American Society for the Observance of the Seventh
Commandment ("Thou shall not commit adultery") included Beriah
Green, Lewis Tappan, Theodore Weld, Joshua Leavitt, and other leading immediatists.[19]

As with teetotalism and the crusade against prostitution, abolitionists displayed a penchant for ultraism that scandalized the sophisticated.
That same ultraist tendency had attracted many Christians and a high
proportion of prominent abolitionists to Antimasonry. They became
convinced that Freemasonry subverted Christian faith with a fuzzy-
minded, nonsectarian liberalism, erected factitious barriers between
Masons and non-Masons that rewarded men not for moral worth but
for membership in a secret society, and threatened the authority and discipline of the churches. Garrison, a delegate to the 1832 Massachusetts
Antimasonic convention, spoke for many antislavery proponents when
he proclaimed, "I go for the immediate, unconditional and total abolition of Freemasonry."[20]

In each case—teetotalism, "moral reform," antislavery, and Antimasonry—ultraists sought to establish new standards by which to judge
Christian behavior. To avoid the dangers of ultraism in causing splits and
convulsions, it seemed therefore necessary to curb the ultraist impulse
before it wreaked havoc. Antislavery immediatism was seen as the most
dangerous of all the extremist currents by those who opposed them,
for it threatened not just to divide Christians over colonization, racial
equality, and slavery, but to break up not just entire denominations, but
the Union itself.[21]

Phelps, however, believed that "expediency"—whether the issue was
teetotalism, prostitution, Antimasonry, or slavery—betrayed the doctrine of immediate repentance that he had been taught and that he
preached. The expedient said: "What! you would have *all men, every
where,* repent—no matter who or what they are, or how they are situ-
ated—rum drinkers, rum-sellers, harlots, and sinners of every class and
character, even to the slave-trader and slaveholder &c. &c.—you would
have them all repent at once!" Some were afraid that were the doctrine
of immediate repentance enforced by the churches, "it would turn the
world upside down" and set the whole city of Boston in an uproar,
throwing out of business "the distilleries and dram-shops, and lottery
offices, and brothels, and theaters," turning thousands into paupers,
ruining even "respectable men," and expelling Christians from the

churches just because "they winked at some little sin."[22] Yet to doubt
the efficacy of the call for immediate repentance was to doubt the powers of the Gospel, and to do so mainly out of fear of popular displeasure,
Phelps believed. Christianity never had feared the multitude and always
had confronted unpopularity, Phelps argued. Immediate repentance, as
both a theological doctrine and a social teaching, Phelps concluded, was
in perfect accord with the plan of Christianity "in respect to all sin, slavery not excepted. . . . It is simply the application of his plan to the abolition of every sin to the abolition of this particular one."[23]

The 1820s and 1830s were a watershed in the struggle between ultraist and mainstream Christianity in the United States.[24] Like other re-
ligiously inspired social reform movements that attacked theaters, novels, prostitution, Sabbath breaking, fashionable dress, the consumption
of alcohol, and unhealthy diets, abolitionism envisioned itself as mani-
festly doing the Lord's work. The collapse of revivalism by the early
1830s, however, was the beginning of a sea change. Those living through
the decades of the Second Great Awakening (1800–1831) could not
know that this was a unique period in American history and that thereafter the balance between the secular and religious would shift steadily
in favor of the former. Nor could they fully appreciate the extent to which
the dichotomy between the secular and the religious would blur because
of the service the churches performed in facilitating and legitimating the
market revolution by blessing individualism, acquisitiveness, bourgeois
self-discipline, and social striving.

Some, however, could not ignore the contradictions between Christian
professions and Christian behavior. An attack on selfishness, the chief
obstacle to the sinner's conversion, was a major motif of antislavery discourse, especially in its religious versions. Selfishness explained, too, why
"money, power and popularity have had the control, not only of the principal political, but also religious newspapers of the country."[25] It explained why churches sheltered factitious distinctions based on color,
wealth, and social status, whereas "God's holy government" was no respecter of persons.[26] The panoply of ultraist reforms became tests for purifying the churches and for evaluating the sincerity of professing
Christians. In a world of hypocrites, as the ultraists saw it, such tests
were unavoidable.

With some cause, abolitionists saw themselves as the most zealous, consistent, disinterested Christians, in the forefront of every movement for
human betterment. "Opposed to theatres, expensive pomps and parade

of every kind," James G. Birney's newspaper explained, "such of them as are engaged in profitable pursuits would soon grow rich, were it not that they gave so much of their money . . . to the benevolent causes."[27]

Phelps's assault on expediency fell with special resonance on several of the 124 ministers who responded to his call for endorsements of his *Lectures on Slavery*. Many of these men tended to be at odds with popular religious innovations, adherents of an older tradition of the ministry in which clergy served nearly a lifetime in one place as faithful shepherds of communities where one church held sway. Such men paid little regard to popular enthusiasms. They were not attuned to the strategic thinking of leaders of their own denomination, such as the Congregationalists Lyman Beecher and Nathaniel W. Taylor, who were seeking to compete with Methodists, Baptists, and other sects whose doctrines, worship styles, and revival methods attracted the multitudes. They looked back instead to the Puritan past and lamented declension in the old Bible commonwealths.

Examining the sermons they preached and the history of the churches over which they presided, one finds sharp discomfort with the way economic and social changes, especially the subordination of spiritual to secular interests, the spread of religious pluralism, and the rise of popular Christianity, were transforming their communities. Many had participated in the 1820s in the grueling conflicts in Massachusetts between Trinitarian Congregationalists and Liberals—Unitarians, Universalists, and Nothingarians—over control of the town church before the end of established religion in the state in 1833. One telling sign of their discontent with the spread of latitudinarianism was the strength of the Antimasonic party in the towns in Massachusetts and Maine where those who wrote to endorse Phelps's *Lectures* held pulpits and where Antimasonic party activists were typically prominent laymen and deacons in conservative Congregationalist churches.

Doctrinally, those who responded to Phelps's plea tended to adhere to Calvinist tradition and thus were critical of the innovations of Finney, Taylor, and Beecher. Rev. Asa Rand of Lowell, for example, published sharp attacks on Beecher for sponsoring Finney's revival in Boston and for advancing Taylorism, which he equated with an Arminianizing of Calvinism. Finney, he complained, "has made off strangely with the doctrine of entire depravity, reducing it to a trifling matter" while instructing that "the sinner converts himself very easily, by a simple act of his own will." The result was a multitude of superficial converts, doctrinally ignorant and certain to backslide. Rand reaffirmed Calvinist orthodoxy: "We do believe in the entire depravity of the heart, and that no sinner will turn to God without special and renewing grace."[28]

Others, like David Oliphant, who served at the Third Congregational Church in Beverly from 1818 to 1834, denounced unfaithful ministers afraid of antagonizing the rich, the fashionable, and the powerful. Such pastors ignored the spread of worldliness, intemperance, lewdness, and Sabbath breaking. Some even participated "in the gayest scenes of pleasure, which earth affords."[29]

Only true piety could assure long-term national prosperity, Oliphant insisted: "And the influence of puritanical piety, with whatever contempt it may be regarded by some of the sons of the pilgrims, has been felt from their day down to the present; and although it has been in no small degree lost, it is most devoutly to be hoped that this piety is to revive, and its influence to be even more powerfully and extensively felt."[30]

By insisting on deep piety and orthodox doctrinal beliefs, the church could discriminate between authentic and spurious revivals, "real and supposed conversion, benevolent and selfish religious affections and experiences."[31] Unfortunately, though Calvinism remained "the creed of almost every nominally orthodox church in New England that has not recently changed its creed . . . yet who could fully, plainly and systematically preach those doctrines without being called Hyper-Calvinists, Ultra-Hopkinsians, Hyper-Orthodox, &c?"[32]

David T. Kimball of Ipswich's First Congregational Church (1806–59) identified the impermanence of the ministry as another betrayal of the Puritan past. "The present is a time of uneasiness and dissatisfaction, of restlessness and commotion," he lamented. "All the elements of society are changing" and "a spirit of innovation extensively prevails." New England, once the Land of Steady Habits, was now home to innovation. In the past thirty years, he noted, the ministry had lost permanency as the clergy became a profession more than a calling, a career open to the main chance, rather than a commitment to serve a single community for the bulk of one's life. Where ministers had once spent thirty years in a town, now they averaged five. Ambitious preachers moved onward and upward to better-paying, less onerous jobs, and restless congregations got tired of old preaching and traded in for a new model. The bonds between minister and people never could be close once transience replaced permanence. The mobile careerist hardly could get to know his people deeply or earn their confidence enough to risk preaching the unpopular truths. He would bend with the people's desire for novelty, yet novelty was "one of the greatest enemies of solid piety," Kimball believed.[33] Kimball wrote of the permanence of clergy in the old days from experience; he belonged to the past. At his jubilee in 1857, he was proud that for five decades his "pastoral and social visits" had not neglected any family "of whatever rank or character" and that he had presided over nearly one thousand marriages and an equal number of funerals.[34]

These themes of declension in piety, doctrine, and social relations were the hallmarks of Hopkinsian Calvinist preachers, who were particularly prominent among the Phelps endorsers in Massachusetts. The preeminent Hopkinsian was Rev. Nathanael Emmons, who for over fifty years occupied the pulpit of the Congregational Church, the only church as late as the 1830s in Franklin, Massachusetts, seventeen miles south of Boston. In 1835, the ancient Emmons, now retired, who still wore eighteenth-century clothing, journeyed to New York City to attend the annual convention of the American Antislavery Society, where the delegates invited him to take the chair. Though he was ninety-one years old, claimed the editor of the *Emancipator*, Emmons stood as a "reproof to many in the prime of manhood who either think themselves too old to learn anything new; or value their reputation and popularity too high, to hazard the support of any thing before it has enlisted the suffrages of a majority of the wise, and learned, and wealthy."[35] A visitor to Franklin later found the silver-haired ancient in his Revolutionary War costume, still an enthusiastic immediatist: "Yes, I enter deeply into the spirit of the abolition cause. It is the spirit of '76, it is the spirit of liberty and it *must go.*"[36]

For decades, Emmons, who had trained dozens of ministers in Calvinist theology, was the dominant figure in the far-flung Mendon Association, a group of Congregationalist churches that stretched through southeastern Massachusetts west toward Worcester and that refused to join the General Association of Congregationalist Churches in Massachusetts until the 1840s. For decades, too, Emmons refused to modify Calvinist doctrine to accommodate an age inflated with its sense of human ability, a sure sign of spiritual declension from a more pious, Puritan past. In 1832 Emmons electrified the Antimasonic party when he embraced the cause, and through his many disciples he helped to make southeastern Massachusetts the movement's stronghold. His affinity for abolitionism was not surprising.

Among the Mendon Hopkinsians, none became more active in public life than Phelps endorser Rev. Moses Thacher, elected to the Massachusetts Senate as an Antimason, a founder and a vice president

of the New England Antislavery Society, and one of Garrison's closest
early collaborators. Educated at Brown, trained in Hopkinsian
Calvinism by Rehoboth's Rev. Otis Thompson, who was editor of the
Hopkinsian Magazine from 1824 to 1832, Thacher settled as minister
of the Congregational Church in North Wrentham in 1823, joined the
Masonic lodge, and then, after Antimasonry became a national movement, saw the light and thereafter crusaded tirelessly to destroy the secret society.

Demanding that Freemasons in the church renounce the order,
Thacher led a split when the Masons refused. They retaliated by slan-
dering him as an adulterer. Years of public acrimony ended in a tawdry
libel trial that formally vindicated Thacher but left him with a tattered
reputation. These events forced his departure from the North Wrentham
pulpit in 1838, a sad fall since 1831, when the Antimasonic party state
convention had celebrated his name as "engraven in our hearts and . . .
destined to live in the history of our country."

In 1835, Thacher established the *New England Telegraph,* a weekly
designed to succeed where earlier Hopkinsian voices had failed. The paper steadily attacked doctrinal innovation, especially the Arminian tendencies in Taylorite-Beecherite New England Congregationalism. "I
know it to be the character of multitudes to preach *disinterested benevolence,*" but to "practice *selfishness,*" Thacher announced in the first issue. Hundreds who professed to be orthodox "would much sooner . . .
pay for a wicked, time-serving political paper . . . half filled with 'idle
tales,' buffoonery, nonsense, and even infidelity, than help support a
sound and thorough religious periodical." Should his paper fail, Thacher
would take it as proof certain of "the covetousness and delinquency of
professedly orthodox Christians."[37]

Thacher also filled the *Telegraph* with abolitionist arguments: "Unless
we are willing to place our colored brethren upon a par with ourselves,
admit them into our families, to our tables, into our schools, academies
and colleges, and to all the rights and immunities of free citizens; we are
but the abettor of slavery, and all our professions of philanthropy are
vain and hollow hearted." Prejudice was the foundation of slavery and
violated "the great law of love."[38] Slaveholders, like Masons, should be
purged from the churches, along with liquor sellers, drinkers, and
Sabbath defilers.[39]

Hopkinsian influence extended from southeastern Massachusetts into
northern Rhode Island, where another Phelps endorser, Rev. Thomas
Williams, spent most of his long career. Williams attended the annual

conventions of the American Antislavery Society in 1834 and 1836 and served as a vice president of the Rhode Island state society in 1837. Garrison described "Father" Williams as an eccentric in dress who observed the Sabbath on Saturday.[40]

Educated at Yale and Brown, Williams studied theology with Emmons before launching a long career that stretched from the early nineteenth century through the Civil War. Throughout, he remained faithful to his earliest convictions. Throughout, he also revealed an unconventional streak. After leaving college, for example, he taught black students in Boston, a job most white teachers shunned. Nor did he seek a comfortable ministry, but preferred serving as a peripatetic evangelist, first in eastern Connecticut, then in western New York, and then in Providence, Rhode Island, at the Richmond Street Congregational Church, an abolitionist stronghold. In the 1830s, he moved to the Congregational Church in Barrington, Rhode Island, another abolitionist center. Advancing age failed to alter his preference for "job work" over a permanent, more comfortable settlement.

Hopkinsian theology nourished Williams's attraction to abolitionism. "His preaching was marked with great honesty, earnestness, and scriptural authority," wrote the town historian of Barrington. In the 1850s, Williams was still affirming tradition and criticizing the Taylorite-Beecherite efforts at modernization. He linked his theory of sin to his social teaching. Unless people display "the supreme love to God and true love to man," they must lack "the true spirit of religion or of humanity."[41] Authentic Christians would reject man's selfish nature for "genuine benevolence" and "practical self-denial."[42] "Holy love" is "the essence of obedience to the Gospel," a "pure, perfect, impartial, universal, and disinterested" love that compels Christians "to do justice to the poor as well as to the rich, to the weak as well as to the strong, to the despised as well as to the honorable."[43] In reality, however, white Americans excluded "Indians, Negroes, or Mulattoes, from the just rights of men, Christians and citizens."[44]

In the aftermath of the Prudence Crandall affair, Williams visited Stonington, Connecticut, in 1834, where he encouraged a few pious women to instruct thirty black children. Once again there were strong objections, including a complaint by a Christian father: "If you educate these young blacks, they will soon know as much as our children!"[45] Once again, Williams observed the corruption of white pride feed white prejudice and reveal how far people had fallen from their Puritan roots.

At its inception, in Williams's version of history, Rhode Island had practiced "the fundamental principles of Christian and civil liberty, order and peace," but in time, people followed leaders who opposed "the true Christian principle and policy of Rhode Island Protestantism."[46] "Union with slavery and enjoyment of liberty and the practice of righteousness are forever impossible," Williams exhorted.[47] The country was in "constant danger of moral declension," he warned in 1816, for despite all the new societies that had sprung up to spread the Gospel and reform the world, Americans forgot "the poor and needy . . . in our streets"; in business, we "do not pay our debts; nor speak the truth to our creditors," while in politics, "flattery and deceit are practiced from the cabinet of the President to the caucus of the village."[48]

The corruption had spread to the churches, where "ambitious and worldly men" filled the pulpits, puffed with "proud and selfish hearts," devoted less to saving souls than to feeding "themselves and their families with worldly riches, honor, and pleasures." By exalting human will, the preachers soothed the faithful as they smugly sat cushioned on "the throne of . . . selfishness."[49] In 1855, Williams was still lamenting that "ambition and avarice" governed the country, unleashing "every abomination and transgression against God and man." Now, as in the past, this heir of Jonathan Edwards preached, "worldly policy, deceitful management, popular measures and selfish fancies are the order of the day, at the present time in New England."[50]

Williams was one of just three Rhode Island preachers who endorsed Phelps's immediatist appeal. Far to the north, in Maine, a substantial group of endorsers confirms the picture of the ultraist religious mentality that, like the Hopkinsian and other conservative Calvinists in Massachusetts, provided abolitionism with much of its earliest clerical support in New England.

Ten of the twenty-seven Maine endorsers were centered in Kennebec County, including a majority of the members of the Kennebec Association of Congregationalist Churches, established in 1816. A center of Calvinist missionary enterprise devoted to spreading Congregationalism to the pioneering towns of Maine in the early nineteenth century, the Kennebec association contained a concentration of old-fashioned, antimodernist clergy. Many of the churches of the region owed their founding to the missionary labors of tireless members of the association, who saw to the selection of orthodox men once there was sufficient support in a town for a settled minister. The towns in the association, like the ministers, showed an affinity for ultraist movements; the Antimasons, very weak in Maine overall, polled better than twice their statewide percentage in these towns, where party activists also lived.

The antislavery clergy pressed themes in their sermons similar to those found among Massachusetts abolitionists. They preached the fundamentals of the Calvinist tradition, and they denounced hypocrisy in the churches, selfishness, acquisitiveness, and formalism that failed to carry faith into work. They also deplored the weakening of ministerial authority. Some were austere, deeply pious men, like Josiah Peet. For thirty years, he rose at four in the morning and retired at midnight, and could be heard praying aloud in his house. For eighteen years, he also served throughout the region, preaching in five other towns.[51] Others, like Joseph C. Lovejoy, attacked the effort to separate morals and politics. He asked how devoted Christians could support a slaveholder, gambler, and duelist like Clay for president. How could politicians desire "that labor may receive its just reward" and still support a slaveholder like Clay?[52] Others, like Swan C. Pomroy, exposed those who professed to be Christians but were "bitterly opposed to those pure, heavenly, self-denying principles of the gospel, which alone are adapted to renovate and save the soul."[53] Why were missionaries dispatched among Native Americans and to rescue heathen in the four corners of the globe, but not to the slaves in the South, most of whom were cut off from the gospel, Pomroy wondered.[54] Without the gospel, the Union was doomed, Swan predicted in 1833: "We shall run upon those very rocks where all the republics which have gone before us, having suffered shipwreck."[55]

No one exemplified the Maine clerical abolitionist type so well as Rev. David Thurston of Winthrop, a founder of the American Antislavery Society. Educated at Dartmouth, where only two students out of a class of thirty-six were members of any church, Thurston spent the rest of his life attempting to rescue souls. He studied theology with Rev. Asa Burton, an orthodox Calvinist from Thetford, Vermont, and settled in Winthrop in 1807, serving there thirty-eight years, watching his congregation triple. When offered a professorship by the Maine Charitable School, he heeded his town's plea not to leave. He became one of the moving forces behind the organization of the Kennebec Association of Congregationalist Churches, and his reputation spread far.[56]

In Winthrop, Thurston's influence was especially formidable. He was an important figure in the intellectual and moral growth of the community. In 1815, he helped organize the Society for the Promotion of Good Morals, which was devoted to temperance and Sunday school work. Deacon Dan Carr established the first temperance hotel in the state in

1820, and in 1830, the town voted not to license the sale of alcohol. Thurston also served as a trustee of the Agricultural Society, formed in 1818 to improve husbandry, elevate the status of the yeomanry, and combat the view of the younger generation that farming was a "rather low employment," forgetting, as Thurston wrote in the town history, the words of Ecclesiastes 5:9: "The profit of the earth is for all; the king himself is served by the field." In 1833, Winthrop women formed a Female Moral Reform Society in response to the exposure of prostitution in New York City by the metropolis's moral reformers, led by John McDowell. The next year, an antislavery society formed with 107 members, led by Joseph Metcalf, a deacon of Thurston's church, and in 1837, female and juvenile societies followed. In 1838, Thurston took leave from his church to devote himself to antislavery work for a year. A deep sense of his own imperfection drove him relentlessly to embrace reform in order to purify his society and through that process to purify himself.

Because of the weakness of evangelical religion in Maine, Thurston gave missionary work very high priority. With a population of two hundred and seventy thousand and two hundred incorporated towns in 1816, there were only between one hundred and twenty and one hundred and thirty Congregationalist churches, and Congregationalism was still the state church. Many lacked ministers. Some one hundred and thirty thousand people lived without Christian preaching, Thurston estimated. The Sabbath was nearly forgotten in many places where people were "more desirous to accumulate property than to become holy." Thousands of youth went without any religious instruction and lived "on the verge of pagan darkness," not even knowing "who was their Creator."[57] If Christians cut back on unnecessary expenses and gave up tobacco and drink, Thurston calculated, huge sums would be available for missionary work to reclaim vast numbers of lost souls.

Looking back to a lost communitarian ideal, Thurston recalled that "public worship brings together the different ranks of society. The rich and the poor . . . meet in the same place. Persons of different occupations and worldly interests, who are too prone to keep at a distance and be inattentive to each other's welfare" could come together and become "harmonized in their views and feelings."[58]

From early in his career, Thurston had exposed the shortcomings of professing Christians. Many attended church, but were not "rightly affected with what they hear."[59] "In many churches," he observed, "the members are distinguished from men of the world, only by their outward profession" and remained "selfish and avaricious . . . living without praying with their families."[60] Thurston did not spare the ministry itself. Clerical education in the new seminaries neglected the cultivation of piety for instruction in theology. The minister who was himself selfish, covetous, and sought popularity could do little good.[61]

Declension from the Puritan past was a persistent and powerful theme for Thurston. The nineteenth century was an age of "unrestrained selfishness and avarice" in which children with ample means neglected the support of aged, needy parents.[62] The prevalent doctrine of expediency led men to be more concerned with acquiring wealth than with Christian duty; while in politics, Christian duty succumbed to the imperatives of party success. So lax had church discipline become that the test of Christian character had fallen until there was hardly any difference between church members and others.[63]

From Maine and Massachusetts came voices like those of Emmons, Thatcher, Williams, and Thurston, seeking to sustain in the age of the market revolution the precepts and practices of an earlier Puritan communitarian order. It was this Jeremiah-like sense of decline from an older, better, sterner time that led them to embrace immediatism and other ultraist projects aiming to impose moral order on an amoral society. The presence of these voices in the ranks of the early abolitionists reveals the complexities of evangelical culture and the inadequacy of explaining the origins of abolitionism by seeing it as rooted exclusively in the modernizing currents within that culture. Abolitionism was a complex movement that is not reducible to simple generalization, yet both Finneyites and Hopkinsians shared a critical view of the vast social changes the market revolution brought, a view that put them on common ground. In small-town backwaters like Emmons's Franklin and in new centers of the emerging industrial society such as Lowell, Massachusetts, where seven clergy endorsed Amos Phelps's immediatism, tens of thousands of Americans awoke from slumber and created a diverse, heterogeneous mass movement.

~ 10

"The Tide of Moral Power"

"The hope of the slave is in the free laboring population of the North," abolitionist leaders repeatedly affirmed,[1] but in the early 1830s, efforts to reach and persuade even a fraction of that free laboring population faced formidable obstacles. To mobilize a mass movement committed to immediatism involved nothing less than *"revolutionizing the public sentiment of the country"* and necessitated convincing Americans "of the sinfulness of slavery and of the duty and safety of its immediate abolition."[2] The difficulty of the task did not, however, faze the founders, in part because they underestimated the breadth and intensity of the opposition and overestimated the extent to which a national cultural consensus on behalf of Christianity and republicanism would smooth immediatism's path. Believing they were engaged in God's work, the early abolitionists plunged ahead with extraordinary self-confidence. In the aftermath of the Lane rebellion, Theodore Weld claimed in May 1834 that "no moral enterprise in this country has ever made such progress beyond expectation, prayer and hope as this most glorious millennial enterprize."[3]

By the end of 1834, there were only seventy-five antislavery societies in the entire country, and only ten in Ohio. Yet Weld was prescient. In the next year, the number of antislavery societies tripled, and by 1838 there were nearly thirteen hundred and fifty, with an estimated membership of over one hundred and twenty thousand, a fourfold increase since 1836. "What cause ever before in less than three years, in the face of obloquy, and a nation's opposition, was found able to organize between six and seven hundred societies comprising the most elevated piety, the warmest philanthropy, the most distinguished talents, with untiring industry?" boasted New York immediatists in 1836.[4]

The abolitionist movement spread not only because of the indefatigable efforts of those who promoted it, but also because it had true grassroots appeal among "workingmen" and "the laboring classes," terms in nineteenth-century American discourse that could include small producers, such as family farmers, self-made manufacturers, master artisans, and mechanics, as well as wage earners employed in artisanal shops and factories. In antebellum America, class affiliations, to the extent that they were consciously acknowledged, were expressed in morally weighted terms. As a growing mass movement, the abolitionist cause could position itself among the simple and virtuous who were engaged in productive labor and against the unproductive, the luxurious, and the idle—the elites in business, politics, the churches, and the schools, North and South, who defended colonization, opposed revivals, reform, and immediatism, and sought to put down efforts to purge the United States of its greatest sin.

Only the growth of a large-scale temperance movement, which claimed hundreds of thousands of members organized into local societies, offered any comparable contemporary example of a mass social movement, but abolition and temperance were not comparable in many fundamental respects. Temperance had broad-based support within the churches and among elites, which assured it extensive financial resources. It did not threaten the political system, or incite sectional conflict, or elicit mob violence and subsequent attempts at repression, and since it did not insist on teetotalism during the period of rapid growth in the late 1820s and early 1830s, it avoided the taint of ultraism, with its demands for difficult changes in personal behavior.

The formidable obstacles facing immediatism made its growth as a mass movement an extraordinary phenomenon that challenges historical explanation. Most of the early abolitionists were relatively obscure individuals with few resources. Garrison was sneered at as "a mere mechanic," Arnold Buffum as a hatter, and they depended at first on blacks for funds and subscribers. The Weldites, young men not yet launched on their careers, were dependent on the financial support of others. Even wealthy businessmen like Arthur and Lewis Tappan were mavericks within the evangelical community of New York City, their ultraist views isolating them from the mainstream.

TABLE 1   GROWTH OF ANTISLAVERY
SOCIETIES, 1832–1838

	1832	1833	1834	1835	1836	1837	1838
Maine	0	3	6	22	34	33	48
New Hampshire	0	1	9	12	42	62	79
Vermont	0	3	12	39	44	89	104
Massachusetts	2	8	23	48	87	145	246
Rhode Island	0	1	2	9	20	25	26
Connecticut	0	2	2	10	15	39	46
New York	0	6	7	42	103	274	369
New Jersey	0	0	2	3	6	10	14
Pennsylvania	1	2	2	6	32	93	126
Delaware	0	0	0	0	0	0	1
Ohio	1	6	10	34	133	213	251
Michigan Terr.	0	0	0	2	4	17	19
Indiana	0	0	0	0	1	2	6
Illinois	0	0	0	1	2	3	13
Kentucky	0	0	0	1	1	0	0
Tennessee	0	0	0	0	1	0	0
Total	4	32	75	229	525	1005	1348

NOTES AND SOURCES. No data after 1838. Data for 1832–34 come from the 1836 source, but there remain much missing data on the date of formation of antislavery societies: *Annual Report of the American Anti-Slavery Society . . . 1836–1838* (New York, 1836–38). For 1836, 89–91; for 1837, 123–140; for 1838, 129–152.

In the North, apathy and indifference toward slavery were the toughest barriers. Northerners already thought of themselves as opponents of slavery. They had abolished the institution a generation earlier, after all. Most therefore regarded slavery as a Southern institution for which Yankees had no responsibility and about which they had no further obligation to think. Nor did they believe they had any right to criticize or interfere. For most, until abolitionist agitation pricked their consciences, the peculiar institution was a distant abstraction. Northerners also were largely ignorant of the actual conditions under which slaves lived and gave almost no thought to their plight.

The federal government, from its inception, recognized the existence of slavery and constitutionally guaranteed the security of human bondage, where it existed, as a condition for national unification. Politicians sought to keep attacks on slavery from entering the national political arena and were largely successful until the mid-1830s. The adoption of a "gag resolution" in 1835 and its reenactment by the House of Representatives for the next eight years, negating the efforts of hundreds of thousands of citizens who petitioned Congress to abolish

TABLE 2   ESTIMATED ABOLITIONIST
SOCIETY MEMBERSHIP, 1836–1838

	1836	%	1837	%	1838	%
Maine	872	3	964	1.8	1342	1.8
New Hampshire	2087	7.4	3942	7.4	4208	5.8
Vermont	2524	8.9	5797	10.9	6739	9.2
Massachusetts	6020	21	8370	15.7	14692	20.2
Rhode Island	1948	7	2035	3.8	2075	2.8
Connecticut	277	1	1391	2.6	1597	2.2
New York	6652	24	15659	29.3	23237	32
New Jersey	60	.2	210	.4	382	.1
Pennsylvania	1110	4	3933	7.4	5295	7.3
Ohio	6531	7.3	10344	19.4	12290	16.9
Michigan	70	.3	638	1.2	638	.1
Indiana	0	0	35	< .1	83	< .1
Illinois	0	0	42	< .1	272	< .1
Total	28151		53360		72850	
Est. Total	53651		85610		121720	

NOTE AND SOURCES. A considerable amount of membership data is missing. Estimates are derived for each state by multiplying the number of societies for which there were no data by the average membership of all societies for which there are data in that state. For sources, see table 1.

slavery in the District of Columbia or to reject annexation of the slave Republic of Texas, effectively curtailed the right of petition guaranteed by the Bill of Rights. By refusing to consider antislavery petitions, the House of Representatives showed how far politicians were willing to go to block the spread of antislavery agitation in national politics.

The Southern campaign against the tariff in the late 1820s, culminating in South Carolina's threat to resort to force to nullify an act of Congress, dramatized the danger to the nation should slaveholders believe that the doctrine of states' rights, guarantor of their peculiar institution, was at risk. The nullification crisis grew out of slaveholders' fears in the 1820s, before immediatism emerged as a significant force. Nullification was a harbinger of the violent reaction in the South to the growth of immediatism in the North. Those who challenged slavery, therefore, were apt to appear to most citizens as sectional firebrands and threats to the Union. Immediatists had to overcome the onus of disloyalty, of being seen as enemies of the nation.

In grounding immediatism in a challenge to white prejudice against free African Americans, abolitionists further complicated their task, for most Northerners and Southerners, whether they regarded themselves as opponents or defenders of the peculiar institution, assumed that blacks either were created innately inferior to whites or would remain subordinate so long as they lived in a white society. Convincing Northerners that free blacks were the victims of prejudice and that they deserved help to realize their potential as the equals of whites defied conventional wisdom and assumptions about race that most unthinkingly took for granted, without imagining that such views were steeped in prejudice, without reasonable foundation.

The attack on abolitionists as "amalgamationists," advocates of intermarriage, was one of the most explosive and effective means of closing minds to abolitionist argument. It could arouse intense, sometimes violent public hostility. The appeal to prejudice transcended social distinctions among whites, cutting across class, ethnic, religious, and party lines. In provoking mobs against antislavery proselytizers, no allegation was so potent as the cry against amalgamation. Nor was the attack readily countered. Some abolitionists believed as matter of principle that no laws should prohibit intermarriage and advocated the repeal of miscegenation statutes; all insisted that they did not encourage racial mixture, but they could not deny that interracial mingling on a plane of equality might lead to the dreaded blood taint. And since some white abolitionists such as the Lane rebels intermingled with blacks in antislavery activities and in churches, visited and socialized in the black community, and claimed friends among black leaders in an age when the strictest separation of the races was the norm, their behavior made the charge of amalgamation plausible. Whatever their views on intermarriage, immediatists regarded the charge of promoting amalgamation as an inflammatory red herring, a diversion from the moral imperatives of freeing the slaves.

Accused of threatening the peace of the Union and the dominance of the white race, the early immediatists thus gave opponents ample justification for suppressing the movement before it spread beyond a handful. In addition, the American Colonization Society offered a superficially plausible alternative, one that promised to promote gradual emancipation without antagonizing slaveholders and without threatening either the Union or white supremacy. Confronting a solid front of hostility from the nation's religious and political leaders in command of the press, platform, and pulpit, the early abolitionists seemed hopelessly outmatched.

Few social movements in American history suffered such systematic, unrelenting misrepresentation. Opponents accused immediatists of inciting the slaves to insurrection. The outbreak of Nat Turner's rebellion in Southampton, Virginia, in August 1831, just months after Garrison began publishing, and later, in 1835, the gigantic mail campaign that flooded the Southern mails with abolitionist propaganda, made Southern fears of slave rebellion seem reasonable. Though abolitionists opposed violent resistance by the enslaved, sought change only through peaceful means, and directed their appeals to Southern whites, not slaves, critics easily convinced many that abolitionists endangered the security of life and property in the slave states.

Since the Constitution did not permit Congress to outlaw slavery in the Southern states, opponents charged abolitionists with aiming to break the social contract upon which the Union rested. The early abolitionists, however, harbored no unconstitutional designs. They understood that to end slavery, except in the territories or in the District of Columbia, over which Congress held jurisdiction, they must persuade Southerners to renounce the peculiar institution and replace it with a free labor system. Moral suasion, not federal compulsion, was the immediatist goal. The early immediatists, however, could not foresee that Southern whites would prove resistant to suasion. For generations since the American Revolution, many Southerners professed to believe that slavery was an evil. Thousands had freed their slaves in the late eighteenth century, and before 1830, most antislavery societies, advocating gradualism, were located in the South. Not until after 1830 did Southerners develop a full-blown ideological defense of the peculiar institution. As late as 1832, Virginia debated whether to adopt a plan for gradual emancipation, which went down to defeat in a close vote. As Christians and republicans, Southerners ostensibly occupied common ground with the abolitionists, who did not at first appreciate the extent to which both Christianity and republicanism could be put in service of chattel slavery and white supremacy.

Abolitionists, therefore, had reason to assume that suasion was a practical strategy. Several Southerners were among the Laneites, had played an important role in the debate, testifying from firsthand knowledge as slaveholders themselves to the evil of slavery, and had contributed to the mass conversion of the Weldites. Henry B. Stanton concluded from the debate that Southerners were as susceptible to abolitionist logic as others. Like other Lane students, most of the Southerners sealed their conversion by preaching and holding Sunday schools among Cincinnati's blacks.[5] James G. Birney's conversion a short time later offered additional hope that slaveholders were within reach of moral suasion. Abolitionists never tired of quoting the greatest of Southerners, Thomas

Jefferson, who feared racial holocaust and predicted that on Judgment Day, God would stand with the oppressed race. "We do great injustice to our Southern brethren, if we suppose that they will all be obstinately deaf to the appeals of justice and humanity," abolitionists affirmed, especially once the North abandoned "the low standard of Southern morality on the subject" of slavery.[6]

Yet while abolitionists ultimately hoped to make inroads in the South, they judged the conversion of Northerners to immediatism and racial equality the key to penetrating the South by mobilizing Northern sentiment and political power to contain the expansion of slavery and eventually to channel "the tide of moral power" into the slave states. Events shattered that confidence, but not before immediatism elicited a violent reaction in the South.

To critics, immediatism threatened a revolutionary transformation of society that seemed as dangerous as it was impractical. Colonization had won support in the upper South and throughout the rest of the Union because it proposed to relocate free blacks to another continent without disrupting the economy or the system of race relations. Abolitionists countered that colonization was a mirage, avoiding disruption because it avoided solving the problem. Moreover, they believed that immediatism offered a safe way out. The emancipated, they assumed, would remain on the land in the South, working for wages as a free labor force, still in the service of agricultural production. Abolitionists offered no detailed plans for the transition from slave to free labor, but they recognized that once masters renounced the right to own other human beings, the process of transition to a new system of free labor would take some time, since they did not envision turning loose millions of people no longer bound by chains.

The term "immediatism" was susceptible to misunderstanding by those who refused to credit abolitionist intent or to listen carefully to abolitionist reasoning. There was hardly anything revolutionary in paying laborers for their work. Only greed and selfishness, irrational fear and delusion made the payment of laborers with dark skins seem like a revolutionary and disruptive idea. The production of crops employing slave labor was highly profitable, and sustained a luxurious way of life for slaveholders. Immediatism appeared to be "fanaticism" because paying wages would redistribute wealth and because it would subvert the paternalist justification of enslaving a people assumed to be innately incapable of managing freedom. White guilt further intensified the fear of

emancipation, as those with troubled consciences projected their apprehensions of revenge onto the future behavior of their victims.

Disruption of the Union, slave insurrection, amalgamation, the subversion of racial hierarchy, Southern economic collapse, and chronic, violent disorder—in the eyes of opponents, these were the certain results
of the spread of abolitionist sentiment. In the eyes of immediatists, such
fears were fantasy. Slavery itself, more than any other issue, threatened
to disrupt the Union, they contended. Insurrection was the result of the
suppression of people's natural desire for freedom, not of abolitionist agitation, which counseled slaves to endure quietly until the day of deliverance. Periodic slave rebellions and day-in, day-out resistance to servitude were as old as the system of slavery. Emancipation would remove
the dangers of insurrection, while free labor would bring the benefits of
a more efficient and productive labor system to the South and encourage industry, frugality, and morality among both races. The emancipated
African Americans would now gain a stake in social peace and interracial harmony. Immediate emancipation, abolitionists concluded, therefore would bless both races, freeing the bodies of the victims from the
cruelties of sin, freeing the souls of the sinners from the guilt of cruelty.

To penetrate indifference and counter misrepresentation, to revolutionize Northern opinion, required organization, which in turn necessitated human and financial resources the early immediatists lacked.
Garrison believed as "a deep conviction that without the organization
of abolitionists into societies, THE CAUSE WILL BE LOST."[7] Societies
could engage in proselytizing among neighbors, spread antislavery publications, organize meetings and invite speakers, circulate petitions, and
thereby bring the cause to the grass roots, but that required converting
a critical mass in a community. "The life and usefulness of the Parent
Society must depend mainly upon the number and efficiency of its auxiliaries," whose "regular contributions to the general fund, furnish the
life-blood that gives vitality to the whole system."[8]

Since apathy, misunderstanding, and hostility limited the penetration
of immediatist publications, sending traveling agents or speakers into
communities appeared to be the most practical means of mobilizing latent support.[9] In July 1832, Garrison and Arnold Buffum, president of
the New England Antislavery Society, a grandiose name masking the
handful of people that launched the movement, started on the first tours
of three months in New England. The American Antislavery Society,
shortly after its founding, also sought to put agents in the field, but it

was hard to find suitable people willing to serve. In time, the agency system became one of the keys to the spread of abolitionist ideas, the recruitment of new local leaders and grass-roots supporters, and the establishment of new antislavery societies.

The first converts were few and, like the early abolitionists themselves, tended to be individuals who already had displayed concern over slavery by supporting colonization. Abolitionists, therefore, sought debates with colonizationist agents, who at first were leery, but eventually agreed to meet their opponents in Boston, New York, Salem and Northampton, Massachusetts, and elsewhere. Well established and enjoying elite sponsorship, the ACS unwittingly helped provide audiences and a forum for the advocates of immediatism. One thousand people turned out for the Boston debate, two thousand in Salem, many curious to learn why anyone could doubt the conventional wisdom about how best to approach the slavery question. Some of the debates turned into prolonged and dramatic verbal duels that lasted several days, and though a majority of some audiences at debate's end voted in favor of colonization, abolitionists made converts. At the New York debate, teachers in the city's black schools rose from the audience to contest the ACS speaker's claim that none of them supported immediatism.[10] In other clashes between immediatists and colonizationists, blacks in the audience asserted their inveterate opposition to removal.

Because the ACS had sought and won support primarily from among the prominent, it never had penetrated very far among the mass of citizenry. The abolitionist attack on colonization appealed over the heads of those accustomed to shape community opinion, and such a challenge to elite leadership aroused curiosity. Given an opportunity to expose the weaknesses of the ACS—the impracticality of transporting millions to Africa, the opposition of free blacks, the hidden proslavery purposes of leading architects and advocates of colonization, the mismanagement of Liberia, with wasted funds, a high mortality rate, and dependence on liquor to trade with natives—abolitionists convinced many that they had been deceived. James G. Birney's conversion to immediatism in 1834 was a crushing blow to colonization because he had served as a colonization agent until he concluded that slaveholders were impervious to conversion.

Moreover, once immediatists had a chance to counter misrepresentations and misunderstandings by explaining their commitment to peaceful change, abolitionism appeared to some as a reasonable, rather than a fanatic, movement. Just as they had been deceived by colonization, some now discovered that they had been deceived by unfounded prejudice against immediatism. Like the more than three hundred converts who formed the Uxbridge, Massachusetts, Antislavery Society in 1834, thousands of Americans were candidates for conversion, once exposed to immediatist argument. "I must cease reading, or become an abolitionist," one Uxbridge convert explained.[11]

At first, antislavery agents had only modest success. Because of its proximity to Boston, Garrison visited Providence, Rhode Island, several times in the early 1830s, winning endorsement from the venerable Quaker Moses Brown, then in his nineties, and support from the family of George Benson Sr., to whom Rev. Samuel May introduced him. Benson, formerly a partner in the Providence mercantile firm of Moses Brown and Thomas Ives, had retired in 1824 to a farm in May's town, Brooklyn, Connecticut. He was a founder of the Rhode Island Antislavery Society in the 1780s, had enjoyed close relations with Providence blacks, and never had supported colonization. In 1833, the New England Antislavery Society honored this venerable patriarch of the antislavery movement with its presidency. Benson's son, George Jr., managed the family farm and engaged in the wool trade in Providence with William M. Chace. Both fell under Garrison's spell. The younger George purchased two hundred copies of *Thoughts on African Colonization,* recognizing its polemical power to convert readers to immediatism. Garrison also won over another Benson son, Henry, who became Providence agent for the *Liberator* and worked in the Boston office when Garrison was away. In September 1834, Garrison sealed his connection to the Benson family by marrying Helen Benson.

From the beginning, Garrison was active among Providence blacks. In August 1831, he urged them to hold a public meeting, which took place in November 1831, to repudiate colonization. "We will not leave our homes, nor the graves of our fathers, and this boasted land of liberty and Christian philosophy," they proclaimed.[12] Henry Benson introduced Garrison to Alfred Niger, a black barber, who also became an agent for the *Liberator* in Newport.[13] Seeking subscriptions from among Providence blacks, Garrison sent Benson fifty copies of his *Address to the Free People of Color,* counting on Benson family influence among the city's blacks and his own vindication of blacks to help him secure new readers: "If your colored population feel a signal spark of enthusiasm which is felt by their brethren elsewhere, in regard to *The Liberator,* they will subscribe with avidity."[14] In May 1832, Garrison urged Benson to encourage his black friends to be represented at the General

Convention of Colored Delegates: "A remissness on their part, to send a delegate at this important crisis, would hardly be excusable."[15]

Paralleling Garrison's work, Arnold Buffum, a hat manufacturer of Quaker origins from Smithfield, Rhode Island, made his early forays in 1832 as agent in New Bedford, Massachusetts, and Newport, Bristol, Warren, Pawtucket, and Providence, Rhode Island. In the state capital, he gave three addresses, including one at a crowded black church and another at a conservative Baptist church.[16] Eventually the work of Garrison and Buffum paid off. In July 1832, two Providence businessmen, John Prentice, a merchant tailor, and Wyllis Ames, a temperance storekeeper, renounced colonization. "I never had all the *prejudice* against the colored population in this city and vicinity, as many colonizationists," Prentice explained, revealing the central role the affirmation of racial equality played in conversion to immediatism.[17] Reflecting on his labors in Pawtucket, Providence, and elsewhere, Buffum reported that colonization encouraged many good men to adhere to a common view that "a Nigger is Nigger, and will be a Nigger, do what you will for him." Challenging that view was key to winning converts.[18]

In July 1832, Garrison pressed Henry Benson to organize an antislavery society in Providence, even though only a few were willing to associate. "You need no more *to begin with*. Four men may revolutionize the world."[19] In October 1832, Providence abolitionists issued an appeal: "Men, Brethren, and Fathers! Women, Sisters, and Mothers!! The clouds of divine wrath hang over us." Slavery violated the natural rights of man and the principle of Christian love and brotherhood. Genuine piety required that whites treat blacks as children of God and accept as "true and solid principles" the views blacks themselves expressed "in their recent conventions, resolutions, and addresses."[20]

Finally, in June 1833, a society was formed, the ninth established nationally in the past five months. "We believe, and would do all in our power to convince others, that 'God hath made of *one blood* all nations of men for to dwell on all the face of the earth,'" the founders affirmed. Acknowledging the diversity of the human race physically, intellectually, and morally, Providence abolitionists insisted that racial differences are "incidental, not originally inherent." God is "no respecter of persons" but values only "righteousness," and American men therefore should not place "undue estimation . . . upon the possession of wealth, of beauty, of elegant accomplishments, and upon the color of the skin." God had created all men free and equal, as the Declaration of Independence said, yet "there is not a nation in the world that has so grossly violated the

rights of man as we have done." Rejecting the right of property in human beings and declaring slavery "as an atrocious national sin,"
Providence immediatists insisted "that the colored inhabitants of our
land have as good a right to the privilege and immunities of American
citizens, as any other class of our inhabitants." Exiling them to Africa
was "heinous wickedness . . . cruel persecution," for "they are no more
Africans, than we are Europeans." The new society pledged "to send out
living agents to cry aloud and spare not . . . and show this people their
great transgressions." They held their first public meeting on the Fourth
of July to hear an address by Rev. Thomas Williams, who repeated it at
Pawtucket. The society also purchased and distributed hundreds of
copies of abolitionist tracts. By July 1835, between fifty and sixty men
had joined, not many in a city of twenty thousand.[21] The following year,
women formed a society that claimed 101 members by 1836.[22]

Finding men to serve as agents to agitate in other communities, as
Garrison and Buffum had in Providence, proved difficult. The clergy offered the most important pool, but not every prospective agent was willing to give up other activities, and not every agent who was willing to
do so was effective on the stump. The successes of a few gifted early
agents, however, such as Theodore Weld, whose campaign after leaving
Lane converted hundreds and stimulated the formation of dozens of societies in Ohio, convinced abolitionist leaders that developing an agency
system was as important as their publication program.

The emergence of abolitionism as a mass movement strongly corre-
lated with its ability to spread its message by means of agents. From its
inception, the American Antislavery Society established an Agency
Committee under direction of the Executive Committee in New York
City. The agency system reached its peak in 1837, when the American
Antislavery Society sought to put seventy in the field and devoted half its
expenditures for this purpose, including a training program that brought
new agents to New York City for intensive training and indoctrination
led by Weld, the most experienced and successful antislavery agent.

The formation of hundreds of societies in New York and Ohio resulted from the concentration of resources in those states. When agents
poured into Rhode Island, the expansion of antislavery sentiment, which
had been lagging there, took off, and societies sprang up in a majority
of towns, from which over eight hundred and fifty men endorsed the call
for formation of a state society in 1836.[23] "There has been no single burst
like it in any other cause," Garrison told the Rhode Island Antislavery
Society convention: "Let Rhode Island have the palm—for, of all her

competitors, she is now foremost in the race of freedom." From New York, where half that number had issued that state's founding convention call, the master agent, Theodore Weld, echoed Garrison in prophetic greeting: "I shout to you my fraternal 'All Hail!' . . . Let us sing unto the Lord, for He hath triumphed gloriously" in Rhode Island.[24] As in Rhode Island, in Pennsylvania antislavery membership grew very slowly until the movement invested money and agents, with telling results.[25]

"How can you stand fourteen such lectures as you give in succession?" Elizur Wright Jr., secretary of the American Antislavery Society, asked Weld, who was touring Ohio in March 1835. That month, Weld had lectured at Concord five times. At Oldtown, he debated a doctor and Baptist deacon, and though he found only one abolitionist in town, after his fifth lecture, the entire audience pledged themselves to immediatism. At Circleville, the Presbyterian minister refused use of the church, forcing Weld to debate a lawyer at the Episcopal vestry.[26] From Springfield, Weld learned of a dramatic shift in public opinion. "It is now rare to hear people say that the Fanatics will not be able to convince people to give up their prejudices," wrote Samuel Galloway, because increasing numbers of church leaders embraced the cause.[27] From Rochester, New York, Weld reported in April 1836 that abolitionist meetings had swelled the membership of the local society from one hundred and fifty to eight hundred and fifty.[28]

In a report to the Young Men's Antislavery Society of New York City, which paid his salary, Weld described his mode of operation in the summer of 1836. In most places, he usually lectured from half a dozen to a dozen times, though sometimes as many as sixteen, twenty, and twenty-five times, and once as many as thirty times. Such intensive proselytizing in a single place aimed to make sure that converts fully comprehended and thoroughly absorbed immediatist principles and were well armed to carry on the debate and convert others after Weld left. Here was an unprecedented grass-roots campaign of mass persuasion, seeking to transform public opinion mired in misrepresentation and prejudice. Only the most intrepid, persistent religious revivalists representing unpopular denominations could begin to match the antislavery campaigners.

Weld insisted that the abolition movement wanted supporters ready to give their hearts as well as their heads to the cause. He appealed to conscience, rather than to humanitarian sympathy. "I have aimed to produce an abiding, inwrought, thoroughly intelligent feeling, based on principle, and acting out with the energy and high intensity of passion, but with none of its irregularity and impulsiveness," he explained. He did not dwell on the cruelty of slavery, since hard masters always could be explained away as exceptions. Rather, he insisted on slavery's inherent violation of conscience and human personality, even under the kindest of masters.[29]

The success of Weld and the dozens of other abolitionist agents came in the face of unprecedented resistance from leading businessmen, editors, politicians, public officials, and churchmen. As early as 1833, before the antislavery movement had attracted a mass following, a New York City mob incited by newspaper editors tried to snuff out the first flames of immediatism in the nation's leading metropolis. The jailing of Garrison in Baltimore, of Prudence Crandall in Connecticut, and the resistance to the manual labor school for African Americans in New Haven were harbingers of the intense hostility abolitionism would face. Riots in Boston, Cincinnati, Utica, and New York City aimed to suppress abolitionism by force. Like the riots, the numerous physical attacks on agents, their jailing as vagrants, the disruption of meetings, the destruction of the Noyes Academy, an interracial school sponsored by abolitionists in Canaan, New Hampshire, the burning of Pennsylvania Hall in Philadelphia in 1838, and the murder of Elijah P. Lovejoy, editor of an antislavery paper in Alton, Illinois, had no precedent in American history. The suppression of student antislavery societies in colleges and the refusal by ministers and prominent laymen to allow abolitionist meetings in churches revealed that ecclesiastical, no less than secular, leaders aimed to suppress the spread of immediatism.

Violent slaveholder intolerance became evident early in the history of the antislavery movement when governments in the Southern states put a price on the head of Garrison, Amos Phelps, and the Tappan brothers. In 1835, the governor of South Carolina, echoed by other Southern political leaders, demanded that the free states criminalize abolitionist agitation. In New York, Massachusetts, and Rhode Island, political leaders responded sympathetically to these demands, but public revulsion against the denial of civil liberty blocked the movement for legally sanctioned repression. The failure to suppress abolition by law, however, led to extralegal modes of repression, such as the mobbings and riots.

Northern "gentlemen of property and standing" from Boston to Cincinnati took the lead in these efforts to suppress abolitionism. They feared that abolitionism could grow into a formidable force and threaten their power, which rested on willingness to accommodate the interests of slaveholders. Northern businessmen who traded with the South, Northern politicians who participated in party coalitions relying on

Southern votes, and religious leaders whose denominations had spread into all regions all acted to protect their vital interests by attempting to suppress the spread of abolitionism. Abolition posed a peculiar danger and elicited from its enemies a unique response. It challenged the moral legitimacy and political power of Northern leaders by aiming to build a popular movement from below. The resort to misrepresentation and repression stemmed from fear that immediatism would become popular once citizens had a chance to hear and reflect on the case for abolition. The mushrooming number and size of antislavery societies by 1835 suggests that elite apprehensions were realistic. No one could tell how far immediatism would spread, given its dynamic growth in just a few years.

PART 3

"The Bone and Muscle of Society"

The struggle against repression educated abolitionists in the realities of class relations in the United States. They came to identify themselves with "the bone and muscle of society," characterizing their opponents as "a coalition of northern and southern aristocrats" who despised the common people.[1] In the countryside, among farmers, mechanics, and small producers, they typically encountered tolerance and open minds, a willingness to hear the case for abolition. In the cities, they faced mobs organized by leading citizens who plied "the rabble" with liquor and fired them up with diatribes against abolitionists as enemies of the Union and advocates of racial amalgamation. "We are now contending, not so much with the slaveholders of the South about human rights, as with the political and commercial aristocracy of the North, for the liberty of speech, of the press and of conscience," William Jay informed the delegates to the 1836 New York State Antislavery convention. While politicians sold out the Constitution and laws for Southern votes, "our great capitalists are speculating, not merely in funds and banks, but also in the liberties of the people." Here was something new in history: wealthy elites, normally fearful of mobs, had become the "Jacobins" of the day, "striving to introduce anarchy and violence on a calculation of profit, making merchandise of peace and good order!" In Cincinnati, Jay argued, "rich and honorable men . . . proclaimed lynch law," while in Utica, the mob proclaimed themselves "good and reputable citizens."[2] Behind the mobs stood men from "all the highest vocations," including "manufactures and merchants—holders of real estate—gentlemen-speculators in stock and property of every description—lawyers and lecturers on law—officers of the government, postmasters, and land-office receivers, and ministers."[3]

As these statements suggest, abolitionists saw class relations in somewhat different terms than we are inclined to use today. Today's analysts anachronistically have exaggerated the distinctiveness of both objective class divisions and subjective class consciousness in early nineteenth-century America. Antebellum Americans resisted the overly specific social categories favored by such analysts. Instead, they were more inclined to think in terms of the producers of wealth versus speculators and non-producers, of aristocratic elites versus the democratic mass. They conceived of social class in terms of a nexus of morally charged oppositions that stretched back through the American Revolution to the language of Old Whig opponents of tyranny: virtue versus vice, rural versus urban, productivity versus idleness, yeomanry versus aristocracy, freedom versus slavery.

Today's analysts also fail to comprehend the diversity of wage-earner experience in antebellum America, for there was no working class as a single, fully formed, homogeneous, stable entity. If class is the product of experience, and especially of struggle, rather than a reified analytical category, the diverse experiences of antebellum wage earners made group stratification, cohesion, and consciousness shifting evanescent at best. Workers migrated from one market, occupation, and technological process to another, moving up, down, and sideways socially, ever in transit from one community to another, subject to varying ethnic, racial, cultural, and religious influences, encountering diverse groups of people from the countryside and from Europe.

The social characteristics of antislavery as a mass movement reflected these conceptions and circumstances. Analysis of the occupations and wealth of the antislavery rank and file confirms the self-image abolitionists had of themselves as drawn from the broad mass of middling and working people: farmers, wage earners, small proprietors, and some professional men. It confirms, too, the abolitionist belief that "aristocrats," political, social, and economic elites, together with the town and urban "mob," those lumpen elements that elites conveniently mobilized for violent purposes, stood forth as immediatism's prime foes. Precisely who flocked to abolitionist ranks, and to what extent abolitionism was a popular movement, becomes clearer from a closer scrutiny of the class rhetoric employed by the abolitionist movement and the social and economic circumstances of the antislavery leadership and its rank and file.

Abolitionists versus Aristocrats

The abolitionists' rhetoric of class relations in the United States became more fully articulated as they traveled through the country and encountered fierce resistance from "gentlemen of property and standing." They concluded that the countryside was the place where they could win the hearts and minds of Americans, that the cities were nearly hopeless, too dominated by the upper classes. The metropolises would have to be surrounded by a converted hinterland and then transformed. The "bacchanalian mobs" that assaulted abolition, they insisted, were not representative of the laboring classes because elites recruited rowdies from lumpen elements, "*the lowest dregs* of society," in order to intimidate "the *industrious farmers and mechanics.*"[1]

In July 1836, William Goodell explored the question "Why Do the Aristocratic Encourage Mobs" in the *New York Emancipator.* There was no instance of a mob, Goodell contended, that was not gotten "up by the secret or open influence of the aristocracy." Goodell believed that American elites were like aristocrats everywhere: they "love to trample upon the laboring classes" and "grind the faces of the poor." Northern aristocrats sympathized with Southern slaveholders because they shared common interests, he argued: they hated equality and republicanism, and abolitionism was "the only real and efficient Bible republicanism on the earth!"

"Aristocracy" was not so much a matter of social or economic class, although these contributed to it, but an attitude toward others. It was a moral category. Goodell did not regard wealth, station, or refinement alone as emblems of aristocracy. The real test was whether the privileged were filled with a pride that despised the poor. Northern "aristocrats" no less than Southern "aristocrats" held in contempt the principle of equal rights asserted in the Declaration of Independence.

Abolitionism, in opposition to that attitude, stood for the rights of others and thereby threatened the political power of both Northern and Southern elites. "Between the rival aristocracies of the North and South, the laboring people of the North *alone*," Goodell argued, "have constituted the only *real* democracy in our republic." For the entire history of the United States, "true republicanism" had "never effectually ruled" because free laborers had "allowed themselves to be made sport of by northern or southern aristocrats." Abolitionism finally was opening the eyes of Americans to understand that "true republicanism" never could never exist "so long as a portion of the laboring population remains enslaved."

Edmund Quincy explained to the Massachusetts Antislavery Society the grounds of the Northern elite's hostility, again in terms that yoked the economic and the moral: "It is the idea that the abolitionists are attacking property, that arouses every thing that is sordid and selfish in human nature to oppose our efforts." The businessmen of the large Northern cities aroused the mobs in defense of slavery because they were bereft of moral principles: "the eager competitions of trade leave but little time for reflection on the eternal principles of Truth and Justice."[2] That same amorality governed the attitudes of Northern aristocrats toward the democratic mass, the free laboring population.

Abolition, by contrast, was a struggle to impose on social and economic relations moral principles that were rooted in Christian teaching: "If abolitionists succeed, the principles of Christian democracy, armed with religion, sustained by law, and supported by order and equality, will prove fatal, at once to the ambition of the northern aristocrats, and the supremacy of and slaveholding of those in the South!"[3]

Advocates of Southern rights in the mid-1830s, such as Senator John C. Calhoun and Governor George McDuffie of South Carolina, defended slavery on the "mudsill" theory of social organization. This posited the inevitability of a debased, laboring class in every civilized society, whether slave or ostensibly free. Better, they argued, that the dangerous class be stripped of all power, as in the South, than perilously allowed the right to strike and vote as in the North.[4] Even if Northern aristocrats held "no fondness for the form of slavery that exists at the

South," Goodell argued, there was thus "a natural sympathy between
the Southern Slave-master and the northern Aristocrat," who liked "to
hear and say that the working-men of the North are on a level with the
slaves of the South." "Their ethics are essentially slaveholding ethics."[5]
In the South, planter-aristocrats had masqueraded as republicans for
decades, defining republicanism as for whites only and thereby seducing
those who did not own slaves into believing that slavery guaranteed
whites equality before the law, though in reality it guaranteed rule by the
white aristocracy. Whether it came from the North or the South, however, such spurious "republicanism" was deformed because it denied human rights.[6]

The moralized rhetoric of class differences thoroughly informed the
ways that abolitionists represented themselves to themselves and others.
Abolitionists made a virtue of the scorn heaped on the obscurity of their
leaders' origins, especially compared with the pedigree of the prestigious
clerics, politicians, and businessmen who endorsed colonization. His opponents condescended to Garrison as "an obscure mechanic," one of
"the working class [who] came among us," while Arnold Buffum was
dismissed as a mere hatter. But immediatists could boast that they walked
in the footsteps of other heroic artisan republican leaders in American
history, such as Benjamin Franklin.[7] Reformers always have been men
of humble origins, Massachusetts abolitionist Amasa Walker explained,
and like the founders of Christianity, they always are persecuted by government, church, and popular opinion.

And for the abolitionists, as for the early Christians, the most violent
and cruel persecution occurred in the cities and large towns, whereas the
common people in the countryside, less under the thumb of the powerful, were freer to think for themselves.[8] "The agricultural populations,
that is the heart and nerve of the People," argued Charles Stuart, "seem
only to need information, to be with us."[9] James G. Birney agreed: the
yeomanry and "the working class" never would agree with elites that
they constituted "a dangerous element in the community" or that "the
employer ought to *own* the employed." Among these laboring classes,
Birney believed, lay "the hope of the republic."[10] The colonizationist
functionary Rev. Ralph Gurley observed that while Garrison's views
failed to make inroads among "a *large* portion of the *enlightened* and
influential, yet I believe those opinions are gaining strength among the
middle and lower classes."[11]

So sensitive were abolitionists to their egalitarian claims and self-image that some, like Rev. Moses Thatcher at the founding of the Rhode

Island Antislavery Society, urged the delegates to omit all personal titles from the proceedings of the convention, a course also followed by the Pennsylvania abolitionists. The ministers and lawyers deserved no polite deference as "reverends" and "esquires"; they were mere citizens, plain "misters," like the farmers and mechanics.[12] Yet at the same convention, one of the delegates, Ray Potter, a poorly educated, self-made preacher running his own independent church in the factory town of Pawtucket, complained that the *"plain, common sense yeomanry delegates"* were ignored in favor "of the more loquacious brethren." To recognize the debt that abolition owed to the silent majority, Potter pushed through a resolution affirming "that the arduous labors and exertions of individuals in the ordinary and private walks of life in the cause of abolition, are by this society duly appreciated, and that the ultimate cause in no small degree depends on their unremitting and untiring exertion."[13] When Pennsylvania abolitionists built a hall in 1838 that would guarantee them a place to meet, subscription dollars for the building flowed in from mechanics, workmen, and women.[14]

We need not accept the abolitionist self-image as "the bone and muscle of society"—a cliché of the age—at face value, for they have left us with the names of hundreds in the rank and file, published in their newspapers and appearing in scattered manuscript records of local antislavery societies, such as a small one in obscure Waitsfield, Vermont, and a large society in Lynn, Massachusetts, the shoe-manufacturing capital of antebellum America. Tracing the demographic characteristics of hundreds of abolitionists may seem something akin to a scientific enterprise, since the end result is numbers—quantitative history—but it would be more prudent to look at these findings as suggestive, since insoluble problems in the data and methodology make them doubtful candidates for "scientific" status. Still, they tell us something, though less than we would like.

One thing they tell us is that on the whole, the abolitionists belonged to the anxious generation that came of age as the guiding hands of the Founding Fathers were falling from the helm of state. In 1838, Thomas W. Dorr, a Rhode Island Whig politician, abolitionist, and later leader of the Dorr Rebellion (1841), which took up arms on behalf of universal, native-born white male suffrage, told the "Young Men's Convention" of immediatists meeting in Worcester, Massachusetts, that the hope of the movement lay with the younger generation. Where slavery and race were concerned, abolitionists saw themselves as the true heirs of the American Revolution, for their fathers' generation had suc-

cumbed to the view that a system of "republican slavery" was a necessary evil.[15] Abolitionists believed that they inherited an obligation to
complete the unfinished work of the Revolution. Abolitionists also
shared with other social critics—Antimasons, artisan republicans, and
other Jacksonian reformers—a sense that social changes brought about
by the market revolution had subverted the political revolution by corrupting personal and civic virtue and undermining the rough, egalitarian social relations upon which a republican order rested. Coming of age
in the 1820s as the market revolution gained momentum, many abolitionists had become increasingly anxious about the social tendencies that
also concerned William Goodell, Theodore Weld, the proponents of
manual labor, and the conservative Calvinist New England endorsers of
Amos Phelps's appeal for immediatism. The nearly simultaneous deaths
of Thomas Jefferson and John Adams in the summer of 1826 at the same
time that fears erupted of a conspiracy by Freemasonry—master symbol
of dangerous forces unleashed by the market revolution—dramatized the
passing of the Revolutionary generation.

Age data for hundreds of abolitionists traced to the census in four
New England states suggest that the movement recruited most heavily
among members of the younger middle-aged group, those between thirty
and forty-five, and drew somewhat more heavily from the older middle-
aged group, those between forty-six and sixty, when compared with the
entire white male population over eighteen. In every state, the proportion of abolitionists in the youngest group, between eighteen and thirty,
fell well short of the percentage that group accounts for in the adult white
male population. Likewise, abolitionists recruited relatively less well
among members of the oldest group, those sixty-one and older. Thomas
Dorr, when he attended antislavery meetings and looked out over the
crowd or reflected on the abolitionists he knew, saw a sea of younger
faces, reflecting the age distribution of the population. In Rhode Island
74 percent of the abolitionists were forty-five or under; in Massachusetts
it was 70 percent, and in Vermont 65 percent, proportions not a great
deal different from the combined two younger groups in the entire adult
male population. So while abolitionists did tend to draw from the
younger half of the adult population, they attracted their greatest relative support from the younger middle-aged, among whom the market
revolution may have had the greatest impact in producing the immediatist, ultraist mentality.[16]

Abolitionists saw their movement as an eruption of elements of the
middling classes against elites, but the contemporary usage of the terms

"middle class" or "middling classes" is as ambiguous as the usage of the terms "laboring" or "working" classes. The occupational characteristics of abolitionists varied with the occupational opportunities in the communities in which they lived.[17] In New Hampshire and Vermont, farmers were still the dominant group in 1850, whereas in Massachusetts and Rhode Island, they had declined to under 29 percent and 20 percent of the labor force, respectively. In New Hampshire, better than two-thirds and in Vermont nearly three-quarters of the abolitionists were farmers, well above the statewide average, which was 50 percent and 52 percent, respectively, in 1850. Massachusetts farmers also were better represented in abolitionist ranks than in the labor force in 1850 by some ten percentage points, whereas in Rhode Island, they fell somewhat behind the statewide proportion of farmers in the labor force (16 percent versus 20 percent). These abolitionist farmers were predominantly owners, not tenants, claiming real estate in the census of 1850. Artisans owning $1,500 or more were classified as proprietors.

In the more industrially and commercially developed states, business proprietors and skilled manual workers formed the two dominant occupational groups. In Massachusetts, the percentage of proprietors exceeded the combined percentage for skilled and unskilled manual workers by a few points; in Rhode Island, skilled and unskilled wage earners accounted for nearly half the abolitionists, and proprietors accounted for nearly 30 percent. Still, in both states, proprietors were overrepresented compared with their likely proportions in the labor force, judging by their proportions in cities for which we have data. In both Vermont and New Hampshire, manual workers accounted for 14 percent of the sample, and proprietors accounted for 11 and 8 percent, respectively. Among proprietors in Massachusetts and Rhode Island, abolitionists were much more likely to attract master mechanics and manufacturers, who typically rose from the ranks of skilled mechanics, than to attract merchants and retailers.

The cities offer a varied picture. In Boston and Lynn, skilled manual wage earners were the most heavily represented group, accounting for better than half of the abolitionists in Boston and 70 percent in Lynn, mostly shoemakers. Still, proprietors joined in greater proportion than they probably accounted for in the labor force, over a quarter in Boston and 18 percent in Lynn, where they made up 13 percent of the occupations listed in the 1832 Lynn *City Directory*. Yet while in some communities abolitionists drew substantial strength from wage earners, in others, such as Providence, they did not.

TABLE 3   THE ABOLITIONIST RANK AND FILE

	Massachusetts		New Hampshire			Rhode Island			Vermont		
	N	% Abo. (1840)	N	% Abo.	% (1840)	N	% Abo.	% (1840)	N	% Abo.	% (1840)
Age, 1836											
18–30	200	36	31	19	39	144	36	44	22	19	41
31–45	220	39	78	49	28	152	38	29	51	45	29
46–60	116	21	42	26	20	77	19	18	32	28	19
61–24	4	9	5	12	24	6	9	10	7	12	
Occupation, 1850[a]											
Upper White Collar	40	7	8	5		9	4		3	3	
Proprietor	179	31	18	11		71	29		7	8	
Lower White Collar	26	5	3	2		13	5		0	0	
Manual Skilled	144	25	18	11		88	36		11	12	
Manual Unskilled	20	3	5	3		27	11		2	2	
Farmers	167	29	107	67		39	16		66	74	

TABLE 3 (continued)
Real Wealth, 1850

$0	27	28	17	180	51	14	15	10
1–500	28	5	14	9	15	4	9	12
501–1000	76	13	23	14	31	9	11	20
1001–2500	149	25	49	30	70	20	19	27
2500–5000	116	20	29	18	37	11	25	
5001–60	10	18	11	14	4	15	16	

^aPercentages for Massachusetts and Rhode Island exclude Boston and Providence.

SOURCES: The Massachusetts and New Hampshire abolitionists come from the list in the *Liberator*, 14 May 1836, from the following towns: *Massachusetts*: Abingdon, Ashburnham, Boylston, Bradford, Danvers, Dorchester, Hanover, Kingston, Leicster, Lowell, Mansfield, Marblehead, Marshfield, Mendon, Middleboro, Newburyport, Reading, Salem, Salisbury, Sandwich, Scituate, Shrewsbury, Uxbridge, Walpole, Westminster, Worcester, Wrentham. *New Hampshire*: Acworth, Boscawen, Bristol, Campton, Canaan, Chester, Concord, Derry, Dunbarton, Gilmanton, Goffstown, Grantham, Hebron, Milford, Orange, Pembroke, Sandown, Sandwich. The Rhode Island list comes from the *Providence Journal*, 2 February 1836. The sources for the Vermont figures are Rupert Antislavery Society MSS, Warren Antislavery Society MSS, Records of the Washington County Antislavery Society MSS, and the Chittenden County Antislavery Society MSS, all in the Vermont Historical Society. Demographic data come from the Manuscript United States Census, Population Schedules, 1850, and *The Census of 1840* (Washington, 1841).

TABLE 4   URBAN ABOLITIONISTS

	Boston		Lynn		Providence		
	N	%	N	% Abo.	% All occs.	N	%
Occupation							
Upper White Collar	8	9	7	4	2	7	4
Proprietor	23	26	34	18	13	23	69
Lower White Collar	10	11	1	0.5	0.5	5	15
Manual Skilled	49	53	130	70	74	4	13
Manual Unskilled	1	1	8	4	.2	0	0
Fisherman	0	0	0	0	4	0	0
Farmers	1	1	6	3	4	0	0

	Real		Personal	
Boston Wealth	N	%	N	%
$0	79	86	79	87
1–500	0	0	4	4
501–1000	0	0	0	0
1001–2500	3	3	3	3
2501–5000	4	4	3	3
5001	6	7	3	3
Lynn Wealth				
$0	63	34	116	62
1–3	50	27	40	22
4–10	50	27	10	10
11–20	14	8	4	2
21	9	5	7	4
Providence Wealth				
$0	15	45	10	30
1–10	9	30	12	36
11–25	3	10	4	12
26–50	2	7	5	15
51	4	5	2	6

SOURCES: Data on Boston abolitionists are from the *Liberator*, 14 May 1836; Lynn data are from the Lynn Antislavery Society MSS, Lynn Historical Society; Providence data are from the *Providence Journal*, 2 February 1836. Occupational and wealth data for Boston are from the Boston *City Directory*, 1834, 1835; City of Boston, *List of Persons, Copartnerships, and Corporations Who Were Taxed Twenty Five Dollars and Upwards, in the City of Boston in the Year 1830* (Boston, 1831); City of Boston, *List of Persons . . . Taxed . . . 1836* (Boston, 1837); data for Lynn are from The Lynn *Directory . . . 1832, 1841* (Lynn, 1832, 1841); Lynn Tax Book, 1836, MSS, Lynn City Treasurer, City Hall; data for Providence are from *The Providence City Directory . . .* (Providence, 1836) and *A List of Persons Assessed in the City Tax. . . . June 1836 . . .* (Providence, 1836). Some people listed as "not found" in tax records may have moved, inflating the percent untaxed.

The real wealth of abolitionists reflected to a considerable degree their occupational status. Rhode Island and Massachusetts, with the smallest proportion of farmers, had the highest proportions owning no real wealth in 1850. Among those owning real property, the distribution of wealth tended to center in the midrange of wealth quintiles, except in Vermont, bearing out the picture of abolitionists as men of middling fortune. In Boston, over 85 percent of the abolitionists owned little or no taxable real or personal property, whereas in Lynn, nearly two-thirds owned taxable real property, mostly in modest amounts, and nearly 40 percent owned taxable personal property. Rhode Island abolitionists were predominantly proprietors, but mostly of modest fortune: 45 percent paid no taxes on real estate and 30 percent paid none on personal property; those who did tended to own modest amounts.[18]

These demographic data etch a picture of the male abolitionist rank and file as a heterogeneous group, drawing support mostly from the younger half of the adult male population, from farmers, businessmen, and wage earners, from the propertyless and the propertied, especially from those of moderate wealth. Since other variables may be more important, such as religious affiliation, or a community's distinct political culture, such as Lynn claimed, or the antislavery movement's investment of limited resources for proselytizing in a particular area, one should not press gross demographic data too hard. Still, they provide some evidence in support of the abolitionist claim to be drawn from society's "bone and muscle"—a diverse group of native-born people from the middle ranks: farmers, skilled artisans, and businessmen, especially master mechanics and manufacturers.

A look at one abolitionist stronghold brings us closer to the grass roots for a more realistic, though more complex perspective. Organized in April 1832, the Lynn Antislavery Society boasted of being the second oldest in the country. Garrison lectured there in 1831 and again on the Fourth of July 1832 and regarded the shoe-making capital as an exemplar for the cause.[19] Before the antislavery cause emerged, Lynn had become a stronghold of the Antimasonic movement. The Antimasonic newspaper, the *Lynn Record*, its editor, Daniel Henshaw, and much of the Antimasonic party leadership provided leadership for the antislavery society, regarding slavery, like Freemasonry, as antithetical to Christian republicanism.

The 1820s and 1830s were decades of rapid economic development in Lynn as shoe manufacturing mushroomed to supply a national market. These also were decades of considerable anxiety, as citizens sought to reconcile the perils of the market revolution—the volatility of prices and wages, the discontents of wage earners, the need for a reliably disciplined labor force, the emergence of larger employers and concentrations of wealth, the temptations of excessive acquisitiveness and consumer display—with older notions of communal stability and solidarity based on shared commitments to civic and personal virtue. In Lynn and elsewhere, Masonry became synonymous with selfishness and aristocratic snobbery, as well as with contempt for women, Christian piety, and morality. In the eyes of many Antimasons, the same moral latitudinarianism that tolerated Masonry tolerated slavery and explained why so many morally dubious public figures, from Andrew Jackson to Henry Clay, were loyal to the secret, mystic order. The formation of an antislavery society in Lynn was a natural extension of the Antimasonic impulse in the struggle against national sin.[20]

The first effort to form an abolitionist society in Lynn, in January 1832, proved abortive, yet these efforts reveal the founding impulse. Influenced by Garrison's arguments against colonization and in favor of racial equality, the Lynn founders first called their organization The Colored People's Friend Society, denoting a broader purpose than emancipation. The preamble also stressed "that no *shade* or tint of color or complexion can afford just pretence" for enslaving people on grounds of "fancied superiority," language later preserved in the preamble to the constitution adopted at the successful organization in April 1832.[21]

Businessmen, especially shoe manufacturers, stood in the forefront of the antislavery society leadership, yet like the shoemaker members, they constituted just a fraction of those in their occupational group in Lynn. Many shoe bosses shunned abolition, just as they shunned Antimasonry. The antislavery leadership, like the rank and file, gave voice to a political subculture that wrestled with the disruptive changes brought by the spread of the market. The social origins of Lynn's abolitionists cut across lines of class, culture, and gender. Seven of the officers of the Journeymen Cordwainers' Society, the town's first trade union, and five leaders of the Mutual Benefit Society of Shoemakers joined the antislavery society, as did four leading businessmen who were officers of the Institute for Savings and three who were leaders in the Lynn Society for the Promotion of Industry. Two schoolteachers were among the founding members, and two of the society's most important leaders, Thomas Atwill and William Bassett, were superintendents of the town school committee. In the 1840s, two of the society's leading businessmen were influential in Lynn's Washingtonian temperance movement, an effort to spread temperance among artisans and laborers.

Not only did they draw on varied occupational groups, the Lynn abolitionists also recruited diversely from the churches. Lynn long had been a stronghold of New England Methodism, and the Methodist Rev. Shipleigh Wilson became the society's first president. Rev. Isaac Bonney and Rev. Timothy Merritt also joined, and Orange Scott, the Methodist antislavery leader, was invited to lecture in 1835 and 1836. Some thirty members of the South Methodist Church joined the society, a small minority of the town's Methodists. The Lynn Society often met in the vestry of the Baptist church and a few Baptists and Congregationialists joined, as did J. C. Waldo, a Universalist minister, and P. R. Russell, leader of the Christian Church, formed by Methodists discontented with that denomination's hierarchical, undemocratic polity. Finally, there were a notable number of Lynn abolitionists with Quaker connections, including leaders of the New Light dissenters such as businessman Jonathan Buffum and shoe manufacturer William Bassett, who became president of the society in 1839. In the late 1830s, the Lynn Antislavery Society, adhering to the Garrisonian wing of the movement, encountered increasing hostility from local Methodist and Congregationalist leadership. In Lynn, as elsewhere, abolitionists attracted ultraminded minorities from among a variety of denominations. The mainstream shunned the antislavery movement.

The daily work of the society sought to enlarge its membership and spread its doctrine. The society sponsored debates, invited lecturers to town, canvassed for new members, and gathered signatures on petitions, sometimes hiring paid agents and sometimes organizing cadres at the ward level. In June 1834, the society encouraged Lynn's women to become active in the cause, and in May 1835, women organized the Lynn Female Anti-Slavery Society to press for abolition and the removal of obstructions "to the improvement of the free colored population." Some one hundred and eighty women joined the society, and nearly one-quarter were found in the census of 1850. The occupational and wealth data of the male heads of households in which the women resided and the data for women indicate that they came predominantly from families who engaged in business (30 percent) or were headed by skilled and unskilled manual workers (42 percent). Over 40 percent of the households owned no real estate, but those that did owned modest amounts.[22] The leading officers were typically wives of male abolitionist leaders, though five of the managers elected in 1835 were unmarried.

The Lynn Female Anti-Slavery Society sometimes met at the reading room of the Young Men's Anti-Slavery Society, still another branch of the movement.[23] The reading room, which subscribed to over fifty newspapers, provided members of the antislavery subculture in Lynn with a place where the like-minded could fraternize for social, educational, and proselytizing purposes.[24] In June 1838, the Lynn Antislavery Society discussed merging the three societies, but there was still no agreement after four meetings.[25] By 1839, the society had begun to admit women, and in April 1840, two women were chosen among the officers for that year.[26]

In the late 1830s, the Lynn antislavery movement experienced discouragement. Its membership rolls had expanded considerably in 1836 and 1837, but then had grown very slowly. The split in the movement between the Garrisonians and the clerical abolitionists affected Lynn, where churches now closed their doors to antislavery agitation, as they did elsewhere under the prodding of denominational leaders. The depression of the late 1830s hit Lynn hard and caused bankruptcy among many businessmen, including some active in the antislavery cause. By decade's end, antislavery had lost its momentum in the shoemaking capital, but not before organizing a heterogeneous movement of shoe bosses and shoemakers, Methodists and antinomian Quakers, young men and women. In December 1838, the advent of the Eastern Railroad posed a new challenge to the antislavery movement in Lynn, which declared racial segregation on the trains "a barbarous inhuman act."[27]

Lynn was one of William Lloyd Garrison's favorite communities. He described it as "a proud specimen of what free, untiring, patient labor can accomplish."[28] Garrison argued that abolitionism thrived in the shoemaking capital, whereas it faced rough sledding in a crowded metropolis such as Boston, because Lynn was "the head quarters of equality." It was refreshing, he said, to escape from the extremes of wealth and poverty in Boston, where an aristocracy governed. In Lynn, people worked hard, suffered no lordly masters to rob them of their earnings, and were therefore able to care for themselves comfortably. Just as important, Lynn's citizens thought and read a great deal, patronizing the press extensively and upholding free speech. Yet it was precisely such a free laboring population, Garrison noted, whom Southern slaveholders denounced as "mudsills."[29]

Garrison's rosy view of Lynn, while exaggerated, was plausible. The tax data show a higher incidence of property ownership than in Boston or Providence, though wealth there, as elsewhere. was unequally distributed. Because most labor in shoemaking took place in the home before mechanization arrived in the 1850s, shoemakers had some control over the work process, and they also put a premium on home ownership. To an unusual degree, Lynn, despite its great growth, was an ingrown community, with few foreign-born inhabitants and an exceptionally high proportion of the population sharing one of some two dozen very common family names. "The strength of equality rested on independence within the household and mutual dependence among households," Alan Dawley found. "The *interdependence* of artisan households gave shoemakers a certain degree of independence from the forces of commerce," owing to cooperation among a "string of household workers" and partial reliance on "the cooperative work of many laboring families" to supply clothing, food, and shelter.[30] As citizens with a vote, Lynn shoemakers could claim to be the civic equals of the shoe bosses. Their participation in the Lynn Antislavery Society confirmed a sense of civic inclusion. Only a fraction of wage earners anywhere responded to the antislavery appeal, but Lynn's abolitionist shoemakers were not alone. Some thirty-seven shoemakers (and twenty shoe manufacturers) were among abolitionists traced in other towns in Massachusetts and New Hampshire.[31]

The antislavery movement also attracted support in Lowell, the state's leading factory town, from small proprietors and artisans and from factory operatives, both men and women. As early as 1834, eight clergymen, Congregationalist, Baptist, and Methodist, endorsed immediatism.[32] In that year, the *Lowell Observer,* defying opposition from leading lay and clerical figures, embraced the cause: "We are confident that our views are the views of all those whose prejudices are not inveterate against people of color. The men of this town who *work* for a living, and who constitute a large proportion of this population, *will be with us.*" Those who toil for their bread "always will frown upon a system by which one man makes use of another's labor without paying an equivalent." And the "ladies" too, the *Observer* predicted, will join the cause to relieve "the afflicted and oppressed."[33] After suffering disruption of their first organizing meeting in January 1834, the Lowell male abolitionists formed a society in March 1834, followed in December by the women, which together with the Young Men's Society established in 1836 claimed 458 members by 1838.[34] In 1837, the Methodist abolitionist preacher Orange Scott spoke to a thousand at a crowded Methodist church, where a petition to Congress garnered over five hundred signatures.[35] Later that year, the Grimké sisters addressed fifteen hundred, a large percentage of them women.[36] "There is a very strong anti-slavery influence in this 'Manchester' of America," the *Liberator* commented.[37]

In rural Vermont, the Chittenden County Antislavery Society claimed in 1842 that abolitionism was "multiplying among our farmers and mechanics—the producers of [the] community." It was the Chittenden County society that called abolitionists "the bone and muscle of society." The productive classes therefore were "men who can sympathise with the toil-worn slave," they concluded, "men who feel that the product of their industry is suffering an intolerable depression in its competition with the produce of slave labor and by the irretrievable bankruptcy of the slave region."[38] Antislavery's valorization of productive labor made no clear distinction between wage earners and the members of other "professions," nor did it locate the enemies of free labor exclusively among slaveholders. In their clashes with opponents in the free states, abolitionists became powerful critics of growing class divisions that threatened their notions of republican equality.

Just before abolitionism appeared in the early 1830s, a workingmen's movement involving trade unions, independent workingmen's political parties, and newspapers had formed in the major Eastern cities. By the mid-1830s, this early alliance of working-class organizations had associated itself largely with the Jacksonian Democratic Party to press for hard money, antibanking measures, and other reforms. In Massachusetts, where a Workingmen's Party ran candidates for statewide office beginning in 1831, William Lloyd Garrison was unsympathetic. An editorial in the first issue of the *Liberator* entitled "Working Men" attacked efforts to inflame "our working classes against the more opulent," which he claimed were wrongly accused of being an oppressive, wealthy aristocracy. Since the reform of injustice had support among all classes, Garrison argued, it was "criminal, therefore, to exasperate our mechanics to deeds of violence, to array them under a party banner." Nor was it true that manual labor was held to be dishonorable, because, he argued, "in a government like ours," the industrious artisan "will always be held in better estimation than the wealthy idler."[39] In a republic where the people possessed power and hereditary distinctions counted for little, the *Liberator* insisted, the path to wealth was open to all. Inequality was inevitable, but not as a result of privilege or oppression. The wealthy were not the enemies, but the benefactors of the laboring classes. Their enterprise created jobs and reduced the cost of necessities.[40]

One of Garrison's readers quickly answered. Speaking in defense of the Workingmen's Party, the writer insisted on an affinity between the aims of abolitionism and those of the Workies. Garrison aimed to arouse Americans to the injustice of slavery, which deprived blacks of the fruits of their labor; the Workingmen's Party pursued the same objective on behalf of white labor. For blacks and whites, the causes of labor exploitation were the same: the assumption by a fortunate few from the beginnings of English settlement onward that they had the right to command labor from those they controlled, whether slaves, vassals, or operatives. To maintain that control, the exploited masses were kept in ignorance, and their ignorance and vice then became justifications for their subordination. As a consequence, the price of labor was set not by the value of labor's product, but by the raw power of those who commanded others to work. Just as abolitionists sought to persuade masters to liberate their slaves and compensate them fairly, so the Workingmen's Party appealed to the moral sense of the rich and powerful to pay the hard-working farmer and mechanic fairly and respect the nobility of their toil.[41]

Garrison was stung by the attack. He claimed sympathy for the Workingmen's Party, noting that he himself put in fourteen hours a day of arduous manual toil and that he never had defended perverted opulence. Still, he insisted, alluding to Edmund Burke, those who attempt to level never equalize because every society always had its upper class.

By the spring of 1832, Garrison's attitude toward the Workingmen's Party had changed radically. First, he welcomed the announcement by S. H. King that he was going to publish the *Workingman's Banner* in Boston to provide labor with a paper exclusively devoted to its rights and interests. "Employers need watching," he declared, because "in every branch of the mechanical business," there was "an exaction of labor altogether unequal to the reward, and a robbery of time from the laborers." God intended us to "invigorate and improve the human intellect." Ten hours was a reasonable day's work; any more was "oppression and robbery, unless the wages are commensurate."[42] Then, in the fall of 1832, Garrison praised the forthcoming New England Workingmen's Convention in Boston, which, he acknowledged, aimed to redress genuine grievances and promote mutual improvement.[43]

A month later, as Garrison traveled through a series of factory towns on his way to Providence, he became troubled by the universal "exorbitant exaction of labor and time" imposed on the operatives, the neglect of the education of the children employed, and the "unnecessary, severe regulations." Garrison again endorsed "the ten-hours-a day plan." Grinding "the face of the poor," he concluded, "injures the value of labor, begets resentment, produces tumults, and is hateful in the sight of God."[44]

For the rest of the decade, Garrison had little to say about the free labor question or about working-class movements, except to praise the workers in places like Lynn and Lowell who flocked to the abolitionist banners.[45] But other voices of abolition, especially Gerrit Smith, William

Jay, Charles Follen, William Goodell in the Utica *Friend of Man* and
James G. Birney and Gamaliel Bradford in the Cincinnati *Philanthropist*,
as well as Lucretia Mott and Angelina Grimké, expressed sympathy for
wage earners and appealed for their support.

When South Carolina governor George McDuffie set out in 1835
to defend slave labor by denigrating free labor, James G. Birney devoted
almost the entire first page of the first issue of the newly established
Philanthropist to McDuffie's message, and other abolitionist editors and
publicists quickly took notice. They recognized that McDuffie's explosive contention that slavery was appropriate for all poor men and
women, regardless of color, "bleached or not," gave abolitionists powerful new arguments for the conversion of the "laboring" classes.

The abolitionist Charles Follen, a German emigré devoted to the cause
of liberalism in his native land who had taught German language and
law at Harvard, penetratingly analyzed the threat slave labor posed to
free labor in the abolitionist movement's most intellectually substantial
periodical, the *Antislavery Quarterly* (1836–39). Slavery, he argued, was
not a local evil because its spirit and underlying assumptions infected the
entire society that tolerated it. A genuine republican regime rested on
moral principles rooted in the inalienable rights of man and in
Christianity's command that we "defend the innocent against violence
and contempt." Slavery justified theft, adultery, and murder if the victims were black, undermined the moral foundations of a Christian republic, and ultimately threatened people of all colors: "While citizens
can keep black slaves to serve them at the South, is it to be wondered at,
that they find white slaves to vindicate them [in] the North?"

Cruelty toward Native Americans and African Americans was the
most obvious example of the antirepublican tendencies of the United
States, Follen maintained. There were others: imprisonment of honest
debtors, the binding out of children as apprentices for longer terms than
allowed in many European countries, and the extension to women of
"fewer rights . . . than under civil law in Europe." The gulf between social classes also was growing. Class snobbery led parents to teach children to look down upon some citizens, equating them with poverty and
disgrace, and to prefer only members of their own rank. Schools further
encouraged "an artificial system of ambition and emulation . . . and an
arbitrary government." The result was an eager pursuit of wealth, not
so much for the comforts and luxuries it provided as to support a style
of life more elevated than others could sustain: "Our whole mode of life,
dress, dwelling, furniture, domestics, &, the society in which we move,

the party to which we belong, the church and the pew in which we worship, all must be conformed to that factitious standard of *respectability* by which the 'better sort of people' are distinguished from the vulgar."[46]

The growth and acceptance of class divisions in the North, Follen concluded, manifested the same antirepublican spirit expressed by color prejudice toward Native Americans and African Americans and opened the door to the Southern argument that free labor threatened social order. Slaves were property, and hence some men of property in the North felt it their duty to suppress a movement that threatened property anywhere. Follen closed with a warning of the dangers slavery posed to free labor: "Those who hold property in men, would persuade all those who hold property in things, that all attacks upon slavery are virtually assaults upon property; and that instead of trying to convert the slaves of the South to free laborers, the men of property should combine to convert all laborers into slaves."[47]

The common interests of all labor, free and slave, white and black, thus became an important theme in the antislavery appeal. Commenting on early efforts to recruit antislavery support in Lowell, Massachusetts, William Goodell urged manufacturing operatives to beware that "the aristocracy that grinds the colored man will soon break over the distinctions of color."[48] At the American Antislavery Society convention in 1836, Gerrit Smith warned that whites no longer should "flatter themselves" that color "will long continue to be the ground of enslavement." Southerners themselves, realizing the "absurdity" of that contention, now argue "for the enslavement of the laboring classes irrespective of color." Southerners urged "the aristocrats of the North to put the yoke of slavery on the necks of our farmers and mechanics," and Smith predicted that "those purse-proud and haughty amongst us who are displaying their pro-slavery spirit . . . would welcome the conversion of our independent Northern laborers into abject slaves." "It is the manifest doctrine of slavery," Smith concluded, "that labor becomes the slave only" and "closely connected with this, is the doctrine that the laborer is fit only to be a slave."[49] Abolitionism, therefore, was a movement in defense of "the life, liberty and happiness of all the lower orders of society in the land, especially at the North."[50] The mudsill theory, Rhode Island abolitionists pointed out, threatened the "day laborer on our wharves or on our farms," and they warned apocalyptically, "Shall our uneducated laboring people and operatives be shot down as dogs in the streets, for choosing and changing their places of employment and labor?"[51] From Connecticut, William Burleigh, an antislavery agent touring the state, reported that "the laboring classes, too, begin to feel that they have a mighty interest in this thing, inasmuch as slavery is bringing contempt upon honest labor, and burning *degradation* upon the brow of the laborers." "Connecticut," he predicted, "will be redeemed."[52]

For these reasons, the abolitionists argued, the laboring classes had a special stake in the defense of the civil liberties of antislavery men and women. The suppression of the abolitionists' rights to free speech, assembly, and petition threatened the liberties of all Americans. None had greater need to defend civil liberty than the working classes in a republic, since it provided them with an indispensable resource with which to combat the privileges of elites in the struggle for equal rights. "Let the poor man count as his enemy, and his worst enemy, every invader of the rights of free discussion," Gerrit Smith told the New York State Antislavery convention in 1835, because free speech and a free press "save him from being trampled upon in Republican America by the despotism of wealth and titles, as that despotism tramples upon him elsewhere, where he is not permitted to tell the story of his wrongs, and to resist oppression by that power, which even wealth and titles cannot withstand."[53]

In 1837, the *Philanthropist*, in noting the appearance of the *Boston Weekly Reformer*, a newspaper advocating the cause of the workingmen, insisted that although abolitionists gave top priority to the cause of the black slaves, who could not plead for themselves, they also sympathized with the cause of the white mechanics, operatives, and day laborers. "When the heavier oppressions of slavery are removed, they will be prepared to remove more effectively the lighter burdens that press on the free." For that reason, the *Philanthropist* concluded, Northern elites sought to repress the antislavery movement.[54]

Abolitionists went beyond these theoretical arguments in favor of the common bonds that united the cause of abolition and free labor by supporting wage earners in their struggles with employers. The New York State Antislavery Society in 1836 condemned the attempt to suppress strikes by prosecuting workers under conspiracy law, the first step in reducing free white labor to slave labor: "Already a northern judiciary stood ready . . . to visit with fines and imprisonment the *free laboring white citizens of New York,* who should have the audacity to fix the price of their own labor, while the aristocracy were combining under the sanctions and facilities of the law, to grind the faces of poor." William Jay came to the defense of the right of mechanics to strike, as well: "Journeymen mechanics, are indicted and punished for violations of law utterly insignificant in their character and tendency, compared with the outrages committed" by the mob organized by elites at Utica, yet a man "distinguished by his violence on that occasion" has been elected attorney general of New York, "in which capacity he will no doubt be ready to assist, when required, in prosecutions against Trade Unions."[55]

In July 1836, the *Philanthropist* analyzed critically Judge Edwards's decision in the conviction of twenty-one New York City journeymen tailors for attempting to raise wages. He held that trade unions that struck to impose terms and conditions of employment threatened not just the interests of masters and journeymen, but the rights of "the entire community and of every man who wants to live by the produce of his labor." If uncurbed, he argued, unions would allow small groups to advance their interests at the expense of the common good. The *Philanthropist* responded that if the judge had interpreted the law properly, the law should be repealed because it established a double standard. Master tailors were free to fix prices without penalty, but workers could not combine to fix wages. "This looks like anything but even handed justice" because "the law by which these journeymen tailors have been punished is one which violates the principles of justice." The application of conspiracy law to labor by "the aristocracy of New York" was "but the *initiation* of slavery," dictating "that those who are to receive wages, shall have nothing to do in fixing its amount." The *Philanthropist* concluded: "But let no class in the community be debarred of their just rights, merely that the convenience or interest of other classes may be advanced."[56]

Charles C. Burleigh, an abolitionist agent, speaking to an audience filled with mechanics and other wage earners, appealed to the self-interest of white laborers, whom slavery harmed more than any other class, save for the enslaved. Slavery reduced the markets for the products of Northern free labor and thereby lessened demand for free labor because slaves received no wages and masters maintained them at a low living standard. Once freed and paid wages, the blacks would increase demand for hats, shoes, and clothing and would insist on better quality than they received under slavery. Emancipation also would create a vast reading public, adding two and one-half million readers as literacy spread among bondsmen now kept in ignorance. Demands for books and other printed matter, he told them, would soar.

Southern white labor would also benefit from demand for improved housing and furnishings, which would provide employment for carpenters and other tradesmen. Many poor white men in the South now suffered from the exploitation of blacks and were as degraded as slaves, Burleigh argued, living on the margins, doing odd jobs, suffering from the tendency of land to concentrate in a few large estates and from a planter-dominated culture that made manual labor disgraceful. As a result, enterprising poor whites abandoned the region for the free states; emancipation would produce a new prosperity that would discourage emigration.

Slavery, Burleigh concluded, was the greatest enemy of equal rights because it spawned attitudes and values entirely at odds with an egalitarian democracy. Southerners who traveled in the North spread their contempt for manual toil along with their preference for aristocracy, their notions of the gentility of idleness, and their loathing of the poor. In the political arena, slavery's champions warned against allowing the propertyless to vote. These ideas had proved catching in the free states, as evidenced by the many who preferred to earn a living through fraud and extortion than through honest labor. "The contest is not between the slavery of white men and black men," Burleigh insisted, "but between liberty and slavery."[57]

The logic of the abolitionists' argument for equal rights led them to defend the rights of working women, as well as working men. Abolitionists supported the struggles of working women in New York City in December 1836. The *Philanthropist* endorsed "An Appeal to the People of New York in Behalf of the Oppressed Tailoresses and Seamstresses" published by the *Journal of Public Morals* and the *Advocate of Moral Reform,* organs of the antiprostitution movement. Scanty wages and grievous oppression by employers drove women to crime and to lives of ill repute. In New York City, an estimated ten thousand seamstresses depended on their needles. They could not strike because thousands stood ready to replace them. Some attempted to challenge the exclusive right of employers to set the price for labor. The *Advocate* agreed that allowing employers unilaterally to determine wages "goes directly to annihilate one of the fundamental principles of human rights, viz: the right that every man has to the products of his own labor." When employers fixed wages, they made workers vassals, forcing "woman, lovely woman" to labor fourteen to sixteen hours a day for a few shillings that were inadequate to support a family so that rich merchants and shopkeepers could live in luxury.[58]

Henry C. Wright, an abolitionist agent, attended the meeting of five thousand at the Broadway Tabernacle in New York City in support of the Society of Tailoresses and Seamstresses. The mayor and other speakers called for immediate action to relieve the suffering of the women by granting them just wages. Although the rhetoric reminded Wright of abolitionist protest against the exploitation of slaves, the speakers were hostile to claims by black labor for justice, whereas Wright, as an abolitionist, opposed slavery in all its forms, whether the victim was white or black, free or slave, male or female.[59] Far from being advocates of a single issue, by the 1830s abolitionists had articulated a comprehensive moral stand that demanded equal rights regardless of race, class, or gender.

Workers, Radical Jacksonians, and Abolitionism

The response of wage earners and their champions to abolitionism was as diverse as that of evangelical Protestants: a small number joined the movement, others sympathized and signed antislavery petitions that did not commit them to immediatism, but many more remained indifferent or hostile and bitterly prejudiced toward free African Americans. Most anomalous were the radical, egalitarian workingmen who flocked to the Jacksonian Party in coalition with slaveholders and planters who held them and all free labor in contempt.[1] A closer look at the responses to the journalistic champions of Northern workers in the 1830s reveals a complex relationship with the antislavery movement. Despite the alliance between many elements of Northern free labor and the Jacksonian Democrats, that relationship foreshadowed the desertion in the 1840s and 1850s of large fractions of native-born American farmers and workers from the Democratic party in favor of "free soil, free land, and free labor."[2]

In January 1837, the Methodist abolitionist minister Orange Scott reported a convergence of revivalism, abolitionism, and labor militancy. For the second time in the decade, in 1836, Lowell factory women struck, this time against efforts by employers to raise the fees in the boardinghouses. Having left independent farm families to enter the mills temporarily, having forged there a sense of sisterhood with other women, both in the workplace and in leisure time, having been steeped in the ideology of the American Revolution, which insisted that those born free

never should submit to "enslavement," the Lowell women displayed
a labor militancy that shocked the complacent paternalism of their
employers, who unilaterally altered the conditions of employment as
they thought the market and their interests required.[3] Though during
the strike "for their *just rights*" some women had left Lowell in order
to return home, Rev. Scott reported, others had returned, and the
Methodists had gained one hundred and fifty converts. One thousand
crowded into the Lowell Street Church on Watch Night, filling the
house entirely, to hear Scott plead "the cause of *human rights,* both as
it respects *Northern oppression* and *Southern slavery.*" Scott estimated
that more than seven-eighths of the church's eight hundred members,
men and women, were abolitionists.[4]

Elsewhere, abolitionists encountered among workers and their leaders unshakable indifference or violent hostility toward African
Americans, slave and free. In New York City, for example, trade union
leader Ely Moore, elected to Congress as a Jacksonian Democrat in the
1830s, loyally followed the party's anti-abolition line, as did other radical, "equal-rights" Jacksonians. Almost everywhere, skilled white
workers resisted the entry into the trades of skilled black workers. The
race riots that broke out periodically in the early nineteenth century in
cities with black populations illustrated the violent volatility of white
wage earners, whose own precarious hold on "respectability" fueled
racial violence to remind themselves and others, blacks and whites, that
the United States was a white man's *Herrenvolk* republic.[5] The abolitionist wage earners in Lowell and Lynn were hardly typical, though like
wage earners everywhere, their experiences in the marketplace shaped
their consciousnesses. Still, the ideas and experiences they brought to labor markets, the cultures of the workplaces and the communities in
which they settled, influenced their responses to the antislavery appeal.
The market revolution did not create a single, homogeneous "working
class," but rather many working classes, all composed of wage earners,
to be sure, but of wage earners with varied preindustrial backgrounds
and skill levels, confronting particular technologies and market conditions distinctive to their industries and occupations, undergoing also dif-
ferential geographic and occupational mobility experiences, and distinguished by regional, ethnic, religious, and community subcultures. For
these reasons, history can encompass the varieties of wage-earner responses to the market revolution only by acknowledging that some free
workers in the North preferred conformity instead of rebellion, conservatism instead of radicalism, faith in individual self-help instead of col-

lective action, and church membership instead of union membership. Many also resisted these polarities, employing instead pluralistic strategies for dealing with the problems that the market revolution posed.[6]

In New York City, home of the most important radical Jacksonian labor agitation in the country, workingmen with roots in the tradition of Thomas Paine exhibited natural sympathy for the antislavery cause, as did hundreds of mechanics who signed antislavery petitions circulated by abolitionists. As elite hostility to abolition hardened in the mid-1830s, working-class signers became proportionately more dominant.[7] Yet most workingmen willing to lend their names to the antislavery cause had more important matters on their mind, such as the relations between capital and labor and between government and the economy. That was also true of two of the most articulate and thoughtful advocates of "the producing classes," George Henry Evans and William Leggett. Both wrestled with the abolitionist challenge as they wrestled with the still greater challenge that the market revolution posed to their notions of social justice.

George Henry Evans was a leader of the short-lived New York City Workingmen's Party (1828–32) and editor of the *Workingman's Advocate*. By 1832, independent labor politics had collapsed, and Evans's paper focused on the struggles by radical workers for influence in the Democratic Party. Evans led the battle for hard money, favoring educational and land reform and a ban on banks and other corporate charters that gave state privileges to private interests. Evan's principal opponent was the New York County Democratic organization, Tammany Hall, since its professional party puppeteers fashioned and managed the rules of political engagement—such as the nomination process—to prevent popular control from the grass roots and to protect conservative business and banking interests. Evans and the radical workingmen also advocated strict separation of church and state, which was threatened, they believed, by evangelical forces such as the Sabbatarian movement that sought to use state power to promote Christian standards in public life. Since New York City's leading abolitionists, including the Tappan brothers, were active in a panoply of evangelical causes, among them the movement to close the post office on Sunday, Evans and other strict separationists had additional reasons to look on the antislavery movement, like other evangelically inspired movements, with suspicion.

Yet on a number of important issues, the interests of secularists like Evans and evangelicals like the Tappans converged. Thus, hundreds of skilled artisans signed Sabbatarian petitions in the hopes of establishing a national standard that limited the power of employers to force people to work seven days a week. In this case, evangelical businessmen such as the Tappans and working-class Sabbatarians agreed on the need to limit market freedom and business enterprise. Evans exhibited sympathy for a series of reform movements conventionally regarded as evangelical and middle class.

For example, he praised the manual labor movement in education, insisting only that the advantages should not be confined to the training of clergy.[8] Likewise, Evans endorsed Sylvester Graham's health-reform notions, defending him from the attacks of conservatives, who were offended by Graham's contentions that the frenzies of the marketplace contributed to the ruin of health.[9] Evans also endorsed the aims of the temperance movement, favoring teetotalism, though in a series of exchanges with William Goodell, editor of the *Genius of Temperance,* he attacked the effort to link temperance with piety.[10] Acknowledging that alcohol was a serious problem among workingmen, Evans argued for the deeper social causes: that people were more disposed to drink when unjustly deprived of the fruits of their labor or subject to oppressive and unequal laws.[11]

Evans was less sympathetic to the antiprostitution drive undertaken by the Magdalene Society, in which the Tappans and other Finneyites were active. Echoing the views of conservative critics anxious to preserve the double standard and keep the truth out of the public eye, Evans thought the antivice forces had exaggerated the extent of prostitution in New York City and had violated standards of decency, refinement, and patriarchy by frankly exposing the evils in direct appeals to women. Willing to concede good intentions to the Magdalene Society, Evans and other writers in the *Workingman's Advocate* nevertheless feared that this was one more "auxiliary to the one grand scheme of sectarian aggrandizement." Above all, he urged, those interested in rescuing women from degradation must rescue them from poverty, since low wages forced people to turn to vice for a living.[12]

Like many Northeastern evangelicals, Evans was sharply critical of Georgia's treatment of Native Americans: the friends of equal rights, he argued, must protect the Indians in possession of their lands. But Evans's sympathy did not extend to the white missionaries, whom he depicted as religious demagogues who ranted for political purposes to embarrass the Jackson administration.[13] When the Supreme Court ruled in favor of the Cherokee nation, Evans expected Georgia and President Jackson to obey the judges.[14] Nearly a decade later, Evans denounced the war against the

Seminoles in Florida and the continued despoliation of Native American lands, the result of national policy that promoted land speculation and concentration of ownership. By this time, Evans had made land reform— reserving free land on the public domain in limited amounts for actual settlers—the centerpiece of labor reform. Land reform that limited ownership to between 80 and 100 acres and prohibited speculation, he believed, would end the Indian wars and the white land grabs.[15]

Evans also expressed mild sympathy for the Antimasonic movement, since he believed Masonry was useless and he did not approve of secret societies in a republic. The Morgan case, which had exposed virtually all the elected officials in the state of New York as members of the secret order, proved that Masonry had led to abuses, but Evans insisted that the nation faced other, more important problems.[16]

Slavery, race, and abolition elicited only marginal comment by Evans and his contributors, but generally they expressed sympathy for abolitionism and racial equality, withering scorn for colonization, and hostility to attacks on the civil liberty of the antislavery movement. Evans praised Benjamin Lundy's *Genius of Universal Emancipation* and reprinted its prospectus.[17] On principle, all republicans and friends of equal rights, Evans editorialized, opposed forcible removal of free blacks and favored giving them educational opportunities such as envisioned by the proposed school at New Haven: "To send away forcibly the free blacks, or even the surplus of the slaves, would only perpetuate *slavery* in the United States, by rendering it easy for those who claim a property in human beings to maintain them as property." He had a practical argument, as well. The Southern economy depended on black labor; without it "there would be a lamentable deficiency of white male population."[18] Commenting on a meeting of the American Colonization Society in New York City in 1833, Evans scoffed at the delusory claims that colonization was a practical strategy for ridding the country of slavery by restoring blacks to their "*original* country." "Are not those born in this country, and would have never been out of it, *now* in their 'original country,' or have all our lexicographers given a lying definition of the term *original?*" However, Evans wryly approved of a colonization scheme for exporting American clergy to Africa, "but so far as it is considered a scheme of negro emancipation, we look upon it as a producing evil, by diverting the efforts of the benevolent for what is *practicable* in favor of emancipation."[19]

Among such practical efforts was the abolition of slavery in the District of Columbia. In October 1831, Evans endorsed the *Liberator*'s call for a new campaign to end slavery in the nation's capital, reprinting Garrison's editorial and petition. "All sects and parties should unite to accomplish the object," which would wipe out "one foul stain from our national escutcheon," he wrote.[20]

Evans's response to Nat Turner's rebellion was unusual for the sympathy and understanding with which he interpreted this bloody event. Deploring the violence, Evans reminded Americans that the rebels' objective was freedom and that they believed violence was their only hope of securing their birthright. Ignorance had deluded the Turnerites into thinking they could succeed, but it was the master class that kept them in such ignorance: Virginia law prohibited teaching slaves to read and write. The current generation of slaveholders, he argued, could not escape the guilt of violating the natural rights of mankind to "life, liberty, and the pursuit of happiness" by arguing that they had inherited an evil, because the slaveholders had expanded and protected that evil.[21]

Evans came under attack from the National Republican *New York Courier and Enquirer*, but he continued to defend abolitionists against charges that they had incited Nat Turner's rebellion. The antislavery movement, he insisted, did not exaggerate the sufferings of the slaves, nor did it spread hatred of whites among African Americans. Accepting the immediatist argument, Evans maintained that there was no reason why slavery could not be abolished in ten years, except for the unwillingness of slaveholders to renounce property in human beings and to suffer great losses in wealth. The notion that the Founding Fathers recognized the right to enslave human beings, he argued, was "monstrous," "too absurd for belief."[22]

Evans went further and defended the idea of racial equality. That naturally followed from his consistent belief in human equality: "In relation to the question of slavery our kindred are mankind—our color is the color of freemen," not the color of a particular race. Evans doubted the common contention that equality of the races would result in amalgamation, but said "if a mixture of the races *would* be the consequence of that equality which the immortal Jefferson declared to be the birthright of all mankind, we should still contend for equality."[23]

Twice the *Workingman's Advocate* reprinted a long attack entitled "Prejudice against Color" by "A Free Colored Floridian," who claimed to be a resident in one of the black settlements in Canada. He argued that prejudice can have no rational basis, that it is the result of ignorance, and that the fact it was much weaker in the other nations of the Americas proved it is not natural.[24]

Evans condemned the repression of white opposition to slavery in the South, just as he upheld the rights of Northern abolitionists to free speech.[25] He dismissed a wave of anti-abolitionist meetings in the Northern states in 1835 as the work of "a few sordid mercantile souls who feared that their business with the South would be injured in consequences of the proceedings of the Abolitionists."[26] And he condemned the anti-abolitionist riots in Utica and Boston while defending abolitionists against popular misrepresentation: "Their desire to *free* the slaves, so far as they can do so by the force of moral power, we believe to be a good and a just cause, and one that they have not attempted to advance by any but constitutional means."[27]

These examples of Evans's views on slavery, race, and abolition appeared scattered over several years, during which the *Workingman's Advocate* concentrated on the struggles of white labor for equal rights. For Evans, abolition was a just cause, but not the central cause. "I am as much an *abolitionist* as any man in the land," he wrote in 1841. "I think Slavery is a disgrace to the republic, black slavery as well as *white*." He would not "truckle to the southern slaveholders, by asserting *that the negro is not a man*." But Evans believed the cause of emancipation lay in the North: "If we would abolish southern slavery, let us set the slaveholders an example, by emancipating the white laborer, *by restoring his natural right to the soil*."[28]

While Evans championed the radical Jacksonian doctrine of equal rights as spokesman for organized wage earners, William Leggett, an editor of the *New York Evening Post,* the leading Jacksonian organ in New York during the Bank War, became one of the most powerful partisan journalistic voices of the urban, antimonopoly wing of the Democratic Party. His premature death in 1839 after a siege of bad health, bankruptcy, and persecution by his own party made him a martyr in the eyes of many Democrats. As a memorial, Theodore Sedgwick Jr. collected samples of his political writings from the *Post* and the *Plain Dealer,* which Leggett established after being forced out of the *Post* because of his defense of abolitionism.

"The foundation of his political system," Sedgwick explained, was "an intense love of freedom. . . . Liberty in faith—liberty in government—liberty in trade—liberty of action in every way." Convinced that government privilege was the source of inequality, Leggett opposed government-sanctioned banks, corporate charters, transport monopoly, tariffs—any departure from market freedom, including the post office monopoly. In New York, Leggett and the *Post* led the fight against conservative Democrats, Tammany, and the Albany Regency, all of whom resisted "equal rights." His powerful editorials, which ran for almost a decade, "constituted an education in political philosophy for New York Democrats" and made the *Post* for a time the leading organ of the Jackson administration in New York City.[29]

As a strongly partisan editor in the nation's metropolis, Leggett fervently advanced the electoral fortunes of Jackson, Van Buren, and the radical Democrats, and he shared at first the conventional misunderstanding and hostility of Democrats toward abolitionism. Though he was one of the earliest and most forceful voices demanding suppression of anti-abolition rioting in July 1834, he regarded immediatism and amalgamationism—which he linked together—as "preposterous and revolting alike to common sense and common decency." He also attacked abolitionists for "addressing their doctrines to the negroes themselves, whom they thus render discontented and wretched, but whose condition they cannot meliorate." By contrast, the American Colonization Society, he thought, pursued a rational, practical strategy. The abolitionists were "wholly wild and visionary," and their fanaticism had incited the mob.[30] Still, Leggett insisted that persecution was a violation of citizens' rights and was more likely to advance than to suppress abolitionist influence.[31]

As the presidential election of 1836 approached, the Whig opposition attempted to exploit antislavery agitation by sowing distrust in the South for Jackson's hand-picked successor, New York's Martin Van Buren. Abolitionist agitation, especially the petition campaign that led the House of Representatives to adopt the gag resolution in 1836, made slavery more salient politically and the South more insecure, especially now that a Northerner had replaced Old Hickory, a Tennessee planter and slaveholder, at the top of the Democratic ticket. Playing on Southern fears, insecurity, and guilt, the anti-Jackson forces raised doubts about the reliability of any Northern candidate for the presidency, an office that had been nearly dominated by slaveholders since the birth of the republic.

In 1835, the Southern states' rights faction, led by Governor George McDuffie, attacked Northern Democrats as supporters of the Garrisonians. Leggett answered that abolition found backing among "the aristocracy . . . of that party which has always been in favour of encroaching on the rights of the white laborers of this quarter." As in England, in the United States "the most violent opponents of the rights of the people" were the loudest champions of enslaved blacks, "as if they sought to quiet their consciences for oppressing one colour, by becoming the advocates of the freedom of the other."[32] Northern Democrats,

moreover, had interests in common with Southern planters, he said ap-
provingly, because freeing the slaves and admitting them to equal civil
and social rights, as abolitionists proposed, "would operate mainly to
the prejudice of the labouring classes among the democracy of the
north." The freedmen would migrate to the North in a search of equality, to which they never could aspire by remaining in the South, and
would compete for jobs with white labor, depressing wage levels to the
benefit of employers. For that reason, the white working classes in the
North had been faithful to the Democratic Party, a coalition devoted to
the protection of Southern slaveholders and Northern white labor. The
Whig campaign against Van Buren in the South, Leggett concluded,
aimed to divide and conquer the Democrats.[33]

This argument stands in conflict with Leggett's contention, from the
outbreak of the New York City anti-abolition riots, that leading Whig
newspapers such as the *Courier and Enquirer* and the *Journal of
Commerce,* far from supporting Garrisonianism, had encouraged riots
and the repression of abolitionist activities. This repression indeed had
intensified abolitionists' commitment and had won them new supporters, but it is clear that such was not their intent. Leggett's response to
McDuffie also conflicts with his views of New York City abolitionist
leaders such as the Tappans, because while most may have been Whigs,
most Whig "aristocrats" shunned abolition. Moreover, as Leggett became more familiar with the motivation of the city's abolitionist leaders
and read their literature carefully, he described them as "men of wealth,
education, respectability and intelligence, misguided on a single subject,
but actuated by a sincere desire to promote the welfare of their kind."[34]

By the winter of 1836, Leggett had undergone a transformation. In
the prospectus for the first issue of the *Political Plain Dealer,* he affirmed
his loyalty to the Democratic Party, but vowed never to place party above
principle. The cardinal principle of the party he defined as equal rights,
which he interpreted to include absolute freedom of discussion for abolitionists and the rejection of slavery as wicked.[35] Slavery was not a partisan issue, he insisted. Everywhere, citizens from both parties loathed
the peculiar institution, but particularly wherever "the moral leprosy of
slavery does not exist." Still, Democrats, he argued, had a greater affinity for abolition because slavery "is in more positive and utter violation
of the fundamental article of the creed of democracy, which acknowl-
edges the political equality, and unalienable right of freedom, of
all mankind."[36] Since anyone who condemned slavery and regarded
the poor, degraded blacks as fellow human beings was smeared as a

"fanatic," an "incendiary," and an "amalgamationist"—terms that Leggett once had thought appropriate—Leggett now proudly declared himself an abolitionist: "we therefore not merely admit that we are an abolitionist, but earnestly lay claim to that appellation."[37] As for the great body of abolitionists, Leggett now insisted that "there never was a band of men, engaged in any struggle for freedom, whose whole course and conduct evinced more unmixed purity of motive, and truer or loftier devotion to the great cause of human emancipation." Here were men and women "free from all taint of selfishness . . . personal ambition, and all sordid projects of ultimate gain."[38]

The sources of Leggett's shift are complex, but begin with his attack on Postmaster Amos Kendall's acquiescence in the suppression of mass mailings of abolitionist literature to the South in 1835. Once more, repression aroused Leggett as the champion of civil liberties. Finding no legal basis for Kendall's position or that of local postmasters, Leggett regarded the ban on antislavery publications as another, even more dangerous attempt to suppress free discussion. He warned Southerners, "we shall not permit our right to discuss the question of slavery, or any other question under heaven, to be denied."[39]

Kendall had acted with one eye on the 1836 presidential race: the suppression of the abolitionists' bold mass-mailing campaign directed at Southern whites was a test of whether slaveholders could rely on the Jackson–Van Buren administration to protect their vital interests. Leggett, however, found himself caught in a dilemma. "We cannot trample on the charter of our national freedom to assist the slaveholder in his warfare with fanaticism."[40]

By September 1835, Leggett had not shifted his view that it was unwise to agitate on the slavery question, yet he now expressed new sympathy for the antislavery movement: "We admire the heroism which cannot be driven from its ground by the manic and unsparing opposition which the abolitionists have encountered."[41] Government repression also unleashed his own hatred of slavery, which not only violated the rights of African Americans, but threatened the civil liberty of all Americans. No attempts to suppress antislavery sentiment, he vowed, would deter him from viewing slavery as "a curse, a monstrous and crying evil." Had Congress the power to abolish slavery, he would favor its "speedy and utter annihilation."[42]

Leggett had gone too far. The Democratic Party's semi-official organ, the *Washington Globe,* denounced him, and the New York County Democratic organization read him out of the party. The *Evening Post,* of which he was part owner with William Cullen Bryant, lost government patronage, which threatened the paper with bankruptcy and compelled Bryant to force Leggett out. In purging Leggett, the Democratic leadership hoped to shore up Van Buren in the South and beat back Whig charges that the Little Magician was soft on abolition. Earlier, New York's Democratic governor William L. Marcy had recommended legislation to criminalize abolitionist agitation in response to demands from the South that Leggett bitterly opposed.[43]

Leggett discovered that party loyalty required him to suppress his loathing of slavery and acquiesce in the suppression of freedom of speech, assembly, and the mails. He was proscribed, he explained, "for considering the poor negro a man and a brother" and for deploring slavery "on account of the prejudicial influence which slavery exercises on the morals of a people, for the manifold vice which it fosters, and for the paralyzing effects which it has on enterprise and industry in every walk of life."[44]

By the winter of 1837, Leggett had moved beyond antislavery to advocate racial equality. He supported the petition by New York blacks to the state legislature seeking equal voting rights. The constitutional reform of 1821 had imposed a property qualification on black voters at the same time that it removed one for white voters. Now blacks demanded parity. Leggett agreed: "May not the black man, who has only one hundred dollars, possess as much capacity, honesty, and love of country, as he who has twice or thrice that sum?"[45] Finally, Leggett attacked the argument that the greater longevity of enslaved over free blacks proved that Africans were better suited to slavery than to freedom. Leggett responded that cruel discrimination against free blacks denied them educational and occupational opportunities, so they could not demonstrate their potential to advance as a free people. Yet he remained optimistic: "The day will come when the claims of the American black race to all the privileges and immunities of equal political freedom will be fully acknowledged, and when the prejudices of society will give way before the steady influence of truth, enlightened reason, and comprehensive philanthropy."[46]

Toward the end of his life, Leggett wrote an editorial entitled "Jefferson's 'Fatal Legacy,'" inspired by the repudiation of human equality by the Charleston, South Carolina, *Southern Literary Journal* on the now familiar "mudsill" theory that the free laborers of the North occupied positions comparable to those of slaves in the South. In repudiating Jefferson's "fatal legacy"—"all men are created equal"—the defenders of slavery now made boldly clear the threat that the peculiar institution posed to free labor. "We must put down slavery," Leggett instructed his readers, "or it will put down us."

His own fate within the Democratic Party supported his warning. Leggett's acceptance of the abolitionist position was now complete. The battle for equal rights had originated in a crusade against the misuse of state power—such as the grant of bank charters to private interests—as the main engine of inequality in the era of the market revolution. At first, Leggett had ignored or tolerated slavery, but abolitionism, which he first thought "fanatical" and dangerous to the political fortunes of Jacksonian Democrats, became integral to his mature understanding of "Jefferson's 'Fatal Legacy'" and to the understanding of a growing fraction of the working classes, from leaders like George Henry Evans to shoemakers in Lynn and female factory workers in Lowell.[47]

PART 4

Women and Abolitionism

In July 1832, William Lloyd Garrison admitted that two errors had hindered the early progress of antislavery immediatism: men's depreciation of women's influence and women's depreciation of their own influence.[1] The "Ladies Department," an early feature of the *Liberator,* initially contended that women should not enter the public arena to expose slavery's brutal consequences for the domestic lives of white and black Americans because female opinion expressed within the home was sufficient to transform the views and behavior of men without trespassing on the norms of domesticity, separate male and female spheres, and female subordination.[2] Yet such a constricted notion of women's role in the struggle against slavery did not last long.

The male delegates who met to found the American Antislavery Society in December 1833 welcomed four female observers, including Lucretia Mott, a Philadelphia Quaker, who took the floor, hesitatingly at first, but with telling effect, to improve on the work of the men. The delegates in turn acknowledged the special contribution women brought to the struggle: God created woman "to point man away from sordid and selfish pursuits, to the high and holy object of doing good to his species." The delegates concluded: "Let the females of this nation organize themselves into Anti-Slavery Societies."[3]

Garrison had announced the formation of the first female antislavery society in Providence, Rhode Island, in July 1832, but in fact, not until 1835 did Providence women organize.[4] Garrison's own efforts to arouse them had proved abortive. In the winter of 1834, he pressed his future wife, Helen Benson, a daughter of the state's most prominent old anti-slavery family, to take the initiative in organizing women, though she knew only two families in the city with whom she could freely discuss the issue of slavery. In his efforts to arouse women's consciences, Garrison had blundered. "I am still under the ban of the ladies of Providence," he admitted to Helen, because he had violated the norms of polite society by speaking frankly about slavery's licentiousness. "Indeed, Miss Helen, I am grieved and surprised to learn the prevalence of this here refinement." It forced him to question whether "those females who are loudest in their denunciations of my unfortunate address, neither cherish nor evince any real sympathy for their poor enslaved sisters," victims of "those libidinous monsters" who robbed them "of that which is infinitely more precious than life."[5] Lydia Maria Child agreed. In tactfully introducing the subject of slavery and sexuality, she made it a matter of principle to violate the taboos against speaking the truth. "It is a matter of conscience not to be fastidious," she insisted.[6] Garrison's frustration did not last long. Some women soon overcame the constraints of "refinement" to rescue black women from "libidinous monsters," an especially compelling reason for white women to enlist in the cause.

For women, however, abolitionism bore special risks that differed from those faced by their male counterparts. Becoming an abolitionist was also unlike joining most of the other associations to which women flocked in the early nineteenth century. Bible, missionary, Sunday school, and temperance societies enjoyed popular respectability and the favor of elites, whereas membership in an antislavery society defied both popular and elite sentiment. And because immediatists also advocated racial equality and assisting free Northern blacks to uplift themselves, women defied nearly universal racial prejudice, as well.

In a much greater degree than men, women attracted to the antislavery movement had to possess independence, courage, and a willingness to defy convention and popular sentiment. Anti-abolitionists were quick to denounce female antislavery work as an unwomanly breach of the domestic sphere that plunged the fair sex into the forbidden political sphere. Nevertheless, a small fraction of American women took up the anti-slavery cross. A number of different reasons led them to do so. Most, however, had shared in the epochal transformation in female consciousness in the half-century after the American Revolution that led by midcentury to Seneca Falls and the formal opening of a long struggle for equality, including female suffrage. Thus, although they had much in common with male abolitionists in terms of social background, in important ways, for women, both the obstacles and the inducements to joining the abolitionist cause differed from those that brought men into the mass movement.

Anatomy of Female Abolitionism

If the experiences and influences that brought nineteenth-century male abolitionists into the fold are epitomized in the life of William Goodell, for female abolitionists the same might be said, despite their otherwise exceptional status, of the life experiences of Sarah and Angelina Grimké. In the 1830s, the abolitionist and protofeminist activities of these two Southern women, former slaveholders from Charleston, South Carolina, electrified the country. The protofeminism that emerged in their formative years led them to champion racial equality and the immediate abolition of slavery. Abolitionist experience in turn made that feminism manifest as a powerful movement in its own right, one that sometimes found itself criticized for pursuing its own agenda.

The early influences of home and hearth set them on the path of Christian moralism and republican virtue, just as they did most male abolitionists. And like them, the Grimké sisters and other female abolitionists struggled to find a morally legitimate and personally fulfilling career in what they had come to regard as a world corrupted by the decadence of commerce and luxury. But the female abolitionists also had to overcome the forces of the market revolution that defined women's roles in such a way as to deny them any career that would be equivalent to those open to men, despite their evident intellectual gifts and their desire to put them to good use.

Although some, like Lydia Maria Child, were able to confront head-on the obstacles they faced and overcome them, many, under the dual influence of the same moral convictions that eventually brought them to the forefront of the mass movement and the conventional moralizing of the limited "women's sphere," took a more indirect route to social reform. They began with a passion for self-education and self-fulfillment that frequently led to an emphasis on their own purification from the seductive attractions of the market revolution and the peculiar institution it sustained. Only by following this introspective inner path did they find the resources to begin to reform society. Beginning as ultraists of their own self-improvement and self-reform, they frequently saw the obstacles that they encountered as women in terms of personal trials, and it was by surviving these trials that they found their way to the national stage as abolitionists and as protofeminists.

Although this pattern appears in the experiences of many female abolitionists and reformers, it is present with particular clarity in the lives of the Grimké sisters. After a complex, tortuous pilgrimage that took them along this *via negativa,* Sarah and Angelina Grimké renounced slavery, moved to the North, and dramatically enlisted in the immediatist cause. Women ascending the platform and speaking for abolition were almost unheard of, but the Grimké sisters did so, lecturing first to women and then to mixed ("promiscuous") audiences. Between 1836 and 1838 they also published a series of powerful pamphlets addressed to Southern women, to Southern clergymen, to Northern women, and to free African Americans.[1]

In addressing Southern women, Angelina explained, "I will speak to them in such tones that they *must* hear me, and, through me, the voice of justice and humanity."[2] Copies of Angelina's appeal arrived in Charleston via the mails and were quickly burned, and she faced arrest if she returned home to what had become a closed society. The sisters' work, of necessity, therefore targeted Northern consciences. The Grimkés' lectures attracted thousands of men and women, some of whom converted to abolition, but they also aroused intense criticism from people who thought it improper for women to step so far beyond the domestic sphere and into the whirlwinds of politics. In defense of their participation in civic life on behalf of black people, Sarah Grimké wrote a searching, radical defense of female equality that foreshadowed the emergence of a feminist movement in the next decade.

They grew up in luxury, in an elite household served by numerous slaves, but the Grimké sisters differed markedly from most Southern women of their class.[3] That they chose to follow their own path owed much to the encouragement they received from their father and brother Thomas to develop their intellects and moral faculties. This had unintended consequences. They began to search for meaningful lives consistent with Christian duty, which led them to reject the model exemplified by their mother—the dutiful plantation mistress, manager of a household of numerous white children and black slaves, and faithful attender of the rituals of the Episcopal Church. Exhibiting early in life a dislike for the cruelties of slavery, the Grimkés embarked on a complicated search for an alternative life that led them to abandon the Episcopal and Presbyterian Churches for Quakerism, Charleston for Philadelphia, and domesticity for the public arena of abolitionist agitation. Sarah, much the senior to Angelina, initiated the process and provided a role model for her younger sister. Blessed with a superior intellect and driven by a thirst for knowledge, Sarah delighted her father with her intelligence and curiosity and received encouragement from her brilliant brother Thomas, who went off to Yale and came back something of an evangelical Yankee. There were limits, however, to male encouragement because Sarah's ambitions seemed to her father and brother doomed to be fruitless: when she begged to study Latin, she met opposition, though she persisted by studying in private.

Judge John Faucheraud Grimké, of Huguenot stock and prominent in Carolina's low-country elite, was a wealthy aristocrat who had occupied public office from the American Revolution, when he had served the patriot cause, until his death in 1819. He was something of a maverick, a man of independent thought and character. He opposed primogeniture, believed in serious education for women, rendered unpopular decisions that almost cost him his judgeship. Impressed by Sarah's love for learning and her private study of the law, the judge thought she would have made one of the best lawyers in the state were she a man. Her talent, ambition, and the encouragement she received from the men she most respected quickly came into conflict with the limited possibilities open to women for education and career.

The judge's piety and intellectual independence influenced his other children, too. Whereas many sons of elite Southern families attended college in the North without questioning the conservative religious and social beliefs they had brought to Harvard or Princeton, Thomas returned from Yale filled with enthusiasm for a career in the Presbyterian ministry and stirring with ideas for the improvement of society, which he developed in a series of publications on peace, education, and temperance reforms.

By contrast, Sarah's life seemed without purpose. Always conscious of her educational deficiencies, denied opportunities routinely available for affluent males such as her brothers, "her ambitions and independence were fired," paradoxically, by inequitable, artificial barriers that stunted human potential.[4] Later in life she recalled her thwarted ambitions: "With me learning was a passion," but convention had denied "her appropriate nutriment," crushing her aspirations.[5]

The judge departed from conventions of his class in many ways. He preferred to live economically and prudently, though he did not deny his wife and household the luxuries and affluent lifestyle that he could well afford and that members of his class expected. Whereas almost any kind of manual labor appeared degrading to slaveholders, Grimké taught Sarah the importance of being useful by showing her how to spin and weave "Negro cloth." She even went into the fields occasionally to pick cotton. Later, she speculated that "perhaps I am indebted partially to this for my life-long detestation of slavery, as it brought me in close contact with these unpaid toilers."[6] For Angelina too, performing manual labor, usually the work of slaves, symbolized her break with the system: "Today, for the first time I ironed my clothes, and felt as though it was an acceptable sacrifice" that prepared her for "removal to the North."[7]

Time pressed hard on Sarah as she matured into a young adult who would be expected to marry and become, like her mother, a plantation mistress. As a necessary step in entering the marriage mart, she was introduced to elite society, "into the circles of dissipation and folly," as she described them.[8] She never married, even after she freed herself from her family, her class, and slavery, a course shaped by a spiritual struggle tied to a desire to preserve her independence so she might find a worthy cause and career that would give meaning to her life.

When Angelina was born, Sarah insisted on becoming the child's virtual mother, usurping the role of her natural mother, with whom there were strained relations. Sarah was certain that the busy natural mother, overwhelmed with the management of household and slaves, was less fit to nurture the last of the Grimkés' fourteen children. The mother, Mary Grimké, managed an unhappy household in which sullen slaves repaid whippings and poor living conditions with grudging and poor service. This cycle of misery further strained the loyalty of Sarah and Angelina, who shuddered at the suffering endured by the victims of the cowhide. The whipping house (called "the Sugar House") in Charleston was centrally located, and for neighbors and passersby the screams and sobs of beaten slaves were as familiar as the sounds of the horses and wagons in the city's streets. Between Sarah and her mother there was no question where Angelina's sympathies lay: for decades, she referred to her older sister as "Mother."

Her adoption of this surrogate motherhood as a protest and a substitute career was just one sign of Sarah's troubled psyche. Her father and Thomas had encouraged her to develop a deep religious sensibility. She credited her brother for preventing her from succumbing to "this butterfly life" of her social set and for saving her from sinking along with other young women "in the stream of folly" and "the whirlpool of an unhallowed marriage," always at risk of betrayal by a slaveholding husband's irresistible sexual passions for dark women.[9]

Avoiding marriage and deeply troubled by slavery, Sarah embarked on a tortuous religious journey. She began to renounce the luxury and frivolity that were standard for members of her class; she abandoned Episcopalianism for Presbyterianism and threw herself into the new church's works of benevolence. Finally, she found temporary fulfillment by devoting herself exclusively to her dying father, whom she took to Philadelphia for medical treatment. There and in Long Branch, New Jersey, she nursed him lovingly until his death. She thus could repay him for having understood her independent nature. By caring for him all alone, far from the Grimké household, she found a new independence and self-sufficiency inspired by a "constant sacrifice of selfishness" that gave meaning to existence. "I regard this as the greatest blessing next to my conversion that I have ever received from God," she confessed.[10]

Philadelphia brought Sarah into touch with its large Quaker community. She found an affinity for the Quakers' modest dress, rejection of fashion, frivolity, and luxury, and for their devotion to self-denial and to works of benevolence. In Charleston, she had backslid after renouncing worldliness because the conventions of her class were so dominant and powerful. In Philadelphia, however, social pressure worked in favor of renunciation because the Quakers were numerous and associated mostly with their own kind. Her brother Thomas recognized that Quakerism had an appeal for his sister that his own Presbyterianism could not match: "Thee had better turn Quaker, Sally; thy long face would suit well their sober dress."[11]

Returning to Charleston only deepened her determination to make a radical break with her mother's world, which seemed unreformable. Becoming a Quaker and removing to Philadelphia to live in the household of Friends with whom she had struck up an acquaintance offered possibilities for a new life, since now she might aspire to become a

Quaker minister, the only Christian denomination that allowed talented women to preach. Later in life, Sarah showed remarkable understanding of her life's trajectory: "Oh had I received the education I desired, had I been bred to the profession of the law, I must have been a useful member of society," and "instead of myself and my property being taken care of, I might have been a protector of the helpless, a pleader for the poor and unfortunate."[12]

Sarah's departure left Angelina stranded, her "mother" now gone. But she left her with an example: she need not be trapped in Charleston or enter the world of the plantation mistress. In Philadelphia, Sarah hoped to put to good service her superior intellect, find an outlet for her "benevolent and unselfish disposition," and finally become "an active, useful member of society."[13] Philadelphia Quaker society proved frustratingly disappointing, however. Sarah's quest awaited her sister's arrival before both could find a way out of the maze.

Angelina, unlike her sister, had an exuberant, attractive, and self-confident personality and seemed more likely to fit into Charleston's elite society. Yet from an early age she revealed a compassionate sensibility for the suffering of slaves, together with an independent will difficult to thwart. She once fainted in school at the sight of a black boy crippled by whippings, and she remained sensitive to the victims of the lash, which seemed slavery's unavoidable, essential prop.[14] She came to share Sarah's loathing for the disorder and fear that permeated their mother's management of the household and its "servants."[15]

At the age of thirteen she demonstrated a fierce independence when she refused confirmation into the Episcopal Church, one of those rites of passage routinely expected of children in elite Charleston families. "I cannot promise what is here required," she insisted.[16] Not even the bishop could persuade her. She did not believe in the rites and doctrines of the church, and the cleric's reassurance that these were mere forms only made matters worse.[17] She later submitted to the family church, but not for long. Like Sarah, and under her sister's prodding, she underwent a religious crisis that culminated in conversion to Presbyterianism in 1826. Now she found what seemed like a genuine Christian community, not the ritualism and class snobbery of Episcopalianism. Now, too, she found support for her impulse to jettison the finery and luxury that marked her class and devote herself to the many works of benevolence her new denomination sponsored. Her conversion satisfied her spiritual needs as nothing had before: "Now I feel as if I could give up all for Christ, and that if I no longer live in conformity to the world, I can be saved."[18]

Believing that "Slavery is a system of abject selfishness," she searched her own heart. Angelina's guilt focused on her own character defects. "For a long time it seemed to me," she confessed, "I did everything from a hope of applause," a thoughtless child of privilege. And again she admitted, "My pride is my bane." Selfless sacrifice offered the only balm.[19]

Sarah returned temporarily from Philadelphia to Charleston in the hope of pushing her toward Quakerism. In January 1828, Angelina tore up her novels and renounced laces, veils, and other finery, which she gave Sarah for stuffing a cushion. "I do want, if I *am* a Christian, to look like one," she said.[20] Sarah's intellect and moral example proved powerful; Angelina abandoned the Presbyterians for the Quakers. The refusal to denounce slavery by the Presbyterian Rev. William McDowell, to whom she had been attracted, removed one of the obstacles to making that choice. "Every idol must be abolished in my heart," she declared.[21]

A summer in Philadelphia with Sarah that thrust her into Quaker society, with its moral seriousness, benevolence, and plain lifestyle, proved decisive. She returned home, but not for long. When a family "servant" was sold off, Angelina realized the household, and by implication the slave society as a whole, was unreformable from within. She had observed firsthand how selfishness, laziness, cruelty, and quarrelsomeness had deformed members of her own family.[22] With her mother's permission, she left Charleston, never to return.

As it had for Sarah, for Angelina Philadelphia became but a stage in a pilgrimage that had begun with an inchoate conviction that "there was work before me to which all other duties and trials were only preparation." She, too, hoped she might become a Quaker preacher, but the precise nature of the work beckoning she did not know. She was certain, however, that once found, it would "lead me and cause me to glorify my Master in a more honorable work than any in which I have been yet engaged."[23]

Hatred of slavery and the quest for fulfilling careers had driven the sisters to Philadelphia; hatred of slavery and thwarted ambition drove them away. The Grimké sisters painfully discovered that Quaker Philadelphia in the early 1830s was not the Promised Land. Sarah's hope of becoming a Quaker preacher succumbed to her lack of self-confidence and rhetorical gifts, as well as to crushing discouragement from Quaker elders. Angelina's attraction to Catharine Beecher's invitation to come to the Hartford Female Seminary for brief training in preparation for joining the teaching staff there ran into the obdurate opposition of Quaker authority to involvement with people and institutions outside

their community. Both sisters avoided marriage, though there was no
lack of Quaker suitors. Marriage would derail their search for independent lives, a search that still eluded them.

Removal to the North seemed to have changed nothing; it only dis-
tanced them from "the putrid carcass" of slavery. Though they had been
troubled by the peculiar institution from childhood, their disquiet and
guilt were diffuse because there seemed no way out of the system that
supported it. Both Thomas and Sarah Grimké sympathized with the
work of the American Colonization Society, though Thomas had no
illusions that colonization would solve the problem of slavery in the
United States. In Philadelphia, the sisters, under the influence of black
and white abolitionist objections to removal, abandoned any hope that
the American Colonization Society held the key.[24]

In particular, Sarah's friendship with Sarah Douglass and other
blacks clarified her thinking about colonization. It showed her the extent to which both slavery and its supposed remedy rested on assumptions of black inferiority. Like other white abolitionists, Angelina valued
black opinion: she consulted Sarah Forten for her views on Africa colonization, as well. Angelina subsequently taunted Catharine Beecher for
preferring colonization over immediatism, like her father, Lyman
Beecher. Instead of "protesting against that corrupt and unreasonable
prejudice, and living it down by a practical acknowledgment of their
right to *every* privilege, social, civil and religious which is enjoyed by
the white man," professed friends of the blacks like the Beechers and
other Northern colonizationists favored expulsion. "I have never yet
been able to learn how our hatred to our colored brother is to be
destroyed by driving him away from us."[25] In 1838, Angelina appealed
to black women for help in combating prejudice. Just as she and other
early abolitionists overcame bias by becoming acquainted with African
Americans and developing friendships with them, other white Americans
must undergo that same process of discovery. "It is only by associating
with you that we shall be able to overcome" racial prejudice, she wrote.[26]

In 1834, Angelina began reading the *Liberator*. In 1835, she attended
an abolitionist meeting to hear the charismatic British antislavery orator George Thompson. At last Angelina discovered what was in her view
a practical program and organization devoted to emancipation. The abolitionists' attack on racial prejudice and their devotion to the advancement of free blacks especially impressed her. She joined the Philadelphia
Female Antislavery Society, which is where she became friends with
Sarah Douglass. And she began to work on an appeal to Southern women

in the same conviction that other abolitionists initially shared, that appeals to reason and Christian faith could penetrate white consciousness in the slave states. Angelina should have been prepared for disillusionment by the response to her budding abolitionism among Quakers.[27]

Not only did most Quakers disapprove of joining a movement outside the sect, but abolitionist organizations employed inflammatory rhetoric and many thought they incited mob violence. Much safer and more appealing to the quietist, evasive sensibility of Quaker benevolence was the soothing anodyne of African colonization.[28] Even though there were many Quakers, especially Hicksites, who joined the abolitionist crusade, mainstream Quakers adamantly opposed racial mixing, relegating blacks to segregated pews in their meetinghouses. Quaker prejudice deeply disturbed Sarah and Angelina, and in defiance, they took seats on the benches reserved for African Americans. As it did with other abolitionists, male and female, the discovery of white prejudice among those oblivious to their own sinful bias played a role in the Grimké sisters' conversion.[29]

While Sarah timidly bowed before Quaker authority, Angelina rebelled against a new imprisonment and publicly endorsed abolitionism in an eloquent letter that Garrison published in the *Liberator*. When the Agency Committee of the American Antislavery Society in New York invited her to become an antislavery agent and join dozens of men training for the campaign to convert the North, Angelina agreed. Quaker efforts to dissuade her were of no avail. She had not escaped entrapment in Charleston to exchange it for entrapment in Philadelphia. At last she had found the cause, career, and religious crusade for which she had been searching. She dragged her older sister Sarah along, who was reluctant to leave even though she had not found the fulfillment she had hoped for in Quaker community.[30] "The door of usefulness among *others* seems to have been thrown open in a most unexpected and wonderful manner," Angelina explained as she embraced abolition. Looking back on a purposeless life that left her talents unused, she grasped at the new possibilities: "I sometimes feel frightened to think of how long I was standing idle in the market place."[31]

In New York City, the other agents accepted her as their equal. The master antislavery agent, Theodore Weld, her future husband, was preparing "The Seventy," the initial cadre of itinerant antislavery agents, for a nationwide campaign to spread the message. He brushed aside objections that it was risky to put a woman on the platform. Since neither sister had any experience as an agitator, Weld trained them in abolitionist doctrine and platform deportment. At first, the Grimkés spoke only to women in New York City parlors, but then they branched out to churches, the better to accommodate the crowds. Angelina proved a gifted platform speaker, and Sarah happily played second fiddle.

Angelina's reputation rapidly spread, and many calls came from towns in New York, New Jersey, and Massachusetts. The intense curiosity of men to hear a riveting female orator on the most contentious issue of the day soon forced acceptance of "promiscuous meetings," although abolitionists had not planned them. Mechanics and laborers walked great distances to hear her.

At first, Angelina found her abolitionist colleagues "as lovely as specimens of meekness and lowliness of the Great Master as I ever saw," but as she became immersed in the movement, the racial prejudice of white antislavery women in New York City disturbed her, and she took special care to stress the movement's commitment to racial equality, not just to immediate abolition. Angelina taught a black Sunday school class in New York City, and after appearing before a biracial audience in Poughkeepsie in response to an invitation from African Americans, Sarah swelled with pride: "I feel as if I had taken my stand by the side of the colored Americans, willing to share with them the odium of a darker skin." The sisters had a realistic understanding of why white Northerners so resisted abolitionist appeals. As Angelina wrote in her address to Southern women, "great numbers cannot bear the idea of equality" because once given opportunity, blacks "would become as intelligent, as moral, and as respectable and wealthy" as others. "Prejudice against color," she concluded, "is the most powerful enemy we have to fight with at the North."[32]

The logic of equal rights was irresistible, as some male abolitionists had found, and Angelina's concerns reached beyond the denial of equal rights to African Americans and women. The unjust conditions of the laboring classes also attracted her notice. "I believe it is our duty to visit the poor, white and colored . . . and to receive them at our houses," but not with paternalistic condescension, she said. "I think that the artificial distinctions of society, the separation between the higher and the lower orders, the aristocracy of wealth and education, are the very rock of pauperism," and just as the only way to eradicate racial prejudice was for whites and blacks to mix, the only way to eradicate class prejudice was "to associate with the poor" just "as our Redeemer did," and not "as our inferiors," but "as our equals."[33]

A lecture tour in Massachusetts proved triumphant. Angelina spoke
in dozens of towns to tens of thousands of men and women. Her appearance before a special meeting of a committee of the Massachusetts
legislature capped the campaign. "I think it was a spectacle of the greatest moral sublimity ever witnessed," Lydia Maria Child observed, not
just because of the eloquent, persuasive case made for immediate emancipation with telling effect on the solons, but because of the subtext, that
women were in the forefront of the struggle to extend human freedom.
It became difficult to escape the realization that women's unequal condition also deserved close scrutiny. Angelina put it best: "My idea is that
whatever is morally right for a man to do is morally right for a woman
to do. I recognize no rights but human rights. . . . For in Christ Jesus
there is neither male nor female." The day was past when a woman was
"a mere secondhand agent in the regeneration of a fallen world." Now
woman had become "the acknowledged equal and co-worker with man
in this glorious work." In the struggle against slavery and for personal
fulfillment, Sarah and Angelina Grimké had learned that "the rights of
the slave & women blend like the colors of the rainbow."[34]

The inward route to abolitionist social reform taken by the Grimkés
already had been followed by Elizabeth Chandler. "*She was the first
American female author that ever made this subject* [slavery] *the principal theme of active exertions,*" concluded Benjamin Lundy in his memoir of her, and "no one of her sex in America has hitherto contributed
as much to the enlightenment of the public mind." She was the daughter of Delaware Quaker parents, whom she lost in childhood. Lundy
speculated that being orphaned contributed to Chandler's "seriously reflective turn, which appears in her after-life as one of the most distin-
guishing traits in her character."[35] Raised by a pious, doting grandmother and by aunts, she attended a Friends school that, according to
Lundy, sought to resist the spread of consumerism and selfishness among
the pupils, which only reinforced Chandler's "seriously reflective" character by protecting her from "the giddy thoughtless votaries of fashion
and vitiating amusement in the gay metropolis of Philadelphia."[36]
Growing up almost entirely enclosed in Quaker subculture, Chandler
read widely and developed into a person who was "introspective and
sensitive beyond the normal, even for that age," someone "almost as a
matter of course . . . concerned with the injustices of the world."[37]

Chandler's exceptional intellectual and literary gifts became evident
early. Adults encouraged her to submit her writing for publication, which

she began to do at sixteen. Her pieces won reprinting in publications all over the United States and Europe. A poem on the slave trade brought her to Lundy's attention, and he invited her to write for the *Genius of Universal Emancipation*. Although she had thought little about slavery, what she learned in reading the newspaper soon changed her life.

Like most precocious and gifted writers, a love of reading helped prepare and inspire her own literary efforts. When later in life she came across the first book she had owned, she recalled that "I gave myself up resistingly to their fascination. It was like being ushered into the midst of a new creation—and I paused not to inquire whether it was one of imagination or reality. The recollection of what I had read, followed me to my pillow, and in my dreams."[38]

Chandler never married. She edited the women's department in Lundy's paper and wrote numerous antislavery poems and essays, which made her in the late 1820s and early 1830s the most powerful female antislavery voice in the United States. She joined the Philadelphia Female Antislavery Society, but then removed with relatives to the Michigan frontier, where she continued her antislavery work. In the forests, she found an "exquisite . . . *religious* stillness" that "must be felt in order to be understood." In the wilderness, she expressed an interest in writings of John Locke and Catharine Beecher, no doubt because they radically enlarged the possibilities for female development through education.[39] Reading them "would be like lifting the veil of another fresh and lovely world to gaze among the hidden feeling unveiled mysteries of the human mind," akin to being "endowed with a new intellect or gifted suddenly with another sense."[40] From the wilderness, Chandler remained in contact with her antislavery comrades in the East. In 1834, she died of fever, but not before encouraging her sisters in the Philadelphia Antislavery Society to persevere in the face of hostility. "I never expected to do 'great things' in this cause . . . yet I sometimes feel as if I had been a mere idle dreamer, as if I had wasted my time in nothingness—so disproportioned does the magnitude of the cause appear to all that I have done; so like a drop in the ocean are my puny efforts."[41]

The underlying forces that shaped her life were a deep piety, a belief in women's potential for education, and a desire to transcend the self by providing moral leadership that aroused others to follow. She published anonymously because she did not wish for public acclaim. She struggled against pride and selfishness and treasured humility and service for others, and though she admitted that admiration of her literary gifts gave her pleasure, she sought to curb ego satisfaction.[42] "I would wish myself *and all others,*" she confessed, "to reach the highest point of excellence that God has created human nature capable of attaining; and it is this which I feel myself fallen so far short of. Error and darkness wherever I discover them, whether in my own mind or those of others, are always painful to me."[43] Even when she wrote on purely literary subjects, Lundy remembered, she tried to "leave a moral impression on the mind of readers, favorable to the cause of humanity."[44]

Nothing so threatened "the cause of humanity" as much as human selfishness. Even patriotism—love of "country and friends because they are ours"—stood tainted by a narrowness of feeling, a form of "refined selfishness." Men and women were not put on earth to live solely for themselves, nor can they serve God as long as they are "regardless of the happiness of one human being." Though some calamities that mankind suffered were the result of God's punishment, she argued, slavery, the worst calamity, had "its origins wholly in the wickedness of man."[45]

It was a woman's office, in particular, Chandler believed, to be a powerful scourge of selfishness and its bitterest fruit, chattel slavery. "Woman was not formed to look upon scenes of suffering with a careless eye," she proclaimed: "it is alike her privilege and her duty to impart consolation to the sorrows of the afflicted."[46] Yet Chandler recognized that most women, Northern as well as Southern, remained indifferent to the suffering of those in bondage, even those of their own sex.[47] She hoped that female education would cultivate and strengthen women's potential for moral leadership "as the helpers, the companions of educated and independent men."[48] She remained convinced that when "selfishness irresistibly crept into man's heart," women could counter it with their selfless compassion, "herself forgotten, and her sex alone predominant."[49]

Yet formidable dangers threatened woman's fulfillment of her true nature. She could be easily swayed by a worldly desire "to win the transient admiration of the ball-room assembly" or to add "new admirers to her triumphant list of conquests."[50] Quoting the British abolitionist Hannah More, Chandler warned against taking as a role model "the fair, fluttering thing of fashion, the beautiful wonder and admiration of the hour." None stood in greater danger than Southern slaveholding women, especially the plantation mistresses "who have been accustomed from youth to the ready service of dependants," and consequently "rarely acquire habits of industry and extensive usefulness." Slavery not only made women lazy, but the profits from it encouraged extravagance, class snobbery, and competition in consumer display—a life of "selfish gratification." Nor were Northern women immune from slavery's baneful influence. As they met and mixed with slave-owning Southern women, they, too, became obsessed with "a fondness for showy ornament, and extravagance, almost to the exclusion of a desire for the better wealth of substantial acquirements and moral excellence."[51]

Chandler sought to arouse female conscience to active engagement and to deflect critics by arguing that slavery struck with brutal force against black women and families. To critics like Sarah Josepha Hale, Chandler argued that women were created as helpmeets to men in "every great work of philanthropy." By taking up the cause of emancipation, women did not seek to become "a race of politicians." To plead for the suffering "can never be unfeminine or unfitting the delicacy of woman!" She did not attack slavery for political reasons, she said, but because it violated "*humanity* and *morality* and *religion*."[52]

Yet Chandler also presented bolder arguments to justify female mobilization. Silence over slavery's sinfulness made women complicit and compromised their consciences. While females risked stepping beyond their sphere, "would it not be better that women should lose somewhat their dependent and retiring character, than they should become selfish and hard-hearted?"[53] Were white men to attempt to enslave white women, women would be justified in casting off the "softness and propriety of the female character" to resist tyranny. White women could not remain indifferent to the enslavement of black women because "their cause is our cause—they are one with us in sex and nature—a portion of ourselves." Since slaves could not protect themselves, that task fell to their white sisters.[54] Answering the argument that abolition work would lead women into the tawdry political sphere, Chandler replied that it was devotion to domestic rights that required women to struggle to extend the blessings of those rights to slaves: "We would have the name of *Woman,* a security for the *rights* of the sex. Those rights are withheld from the female slave; and as we value and would demand them for ourselves, must we not ask them for her?"[55]

Implicit in Chandler's defense of black women was a rejection of racial prejudice. Many, she acknowledged, believed slavery unjust, but thought African Americans were unfit for freedom. For Chandler, Negro intellect and character were at least an open question. "Let not his moral character be complained of, nor his intellectual powers be vilified, until the experiment of his instruction has been fairly tried," she argued. Admittedly, slaves were neither "wise or learned, nor possessed of high intellectual superiority," but whites who believed that blacks were inferior "by nature" were "adding sin to sin, by attempting to charge the effects of our own iniquity upon the hands of God!"[56]

Women had a special role to play as teachers and as mothers in rescuing blacks from darkness. Schools for blacks demanded women's labor. Rearing white children to be free of prevailing racial prejudice would enhance the possibilities of black success. Without ignoring the poverty and ignorance of free blacks, Chandler warned against insinuating "the idea into the mind of the child, that *all* are, and must ever remain" degraded. Some African Americans had risen to positions of respectability, overcoming handicaps; others remained behind, but white children must be taught to understand "that negroes have not risen to higher grade in society because their efforts to do so have been continually baffled and discountenanced, by the contempt and unrelenting prejudices of the whites."[57]

Chandler made her greatest contribution by turning her literary talents to the cause of racial equality and the abolition of slavery. But she understood the necessity of organization, believing that only through collective action could women rescue the republic from slavery by instilling in American men compassion for African Americans. That task, she believed, "should be the task of woman."[58]

While an exceptional number of immediatists were Friends, most Friends rejected abolition, some persecuting abolitionists in their ranks. In a letter to Lucretia Mott, Garrison ranked the Quakers among "the corrupt sects of the age." Although American Quakers had abandoned slavery among themselves in the last half of the eighteenth century, as the Grimkés discovered, most embraced neither racial equality nor immediate emancipation.[59]

Being raised a Quaker nevertheless played an important role in Lucretia Mott's development as one of the foremost female abolitionists in the country. Born on the island of Nantucket, Massachusetts, an old Quaker community, Mott early absorbed a keen sense of female strength from the example of her mother and the other women of the island. Because Quaker whaling men spent long periods at sea, wives managed businesses and households as "deputy husbands." Lucretia's mother made business trips to Boston to obtain stock for the family store.[60] Like other Quaker children, she worked closely as her mother's helper and was taught early to seek "the inward monitor," the inner light that brought one closer to God and His laws. At thirteen, her family sent her to Nine Partners, a Quaker boarding school for boys and girls in New

York State. There, women received demanding training.[61] Believing in
female education and recognizing his daughter's exceptional intelligence,
Lucretia's father, Thomas Coffin, permitted her to remain an extra year
in school. Recognizing her intellectual gifts, the school made her an as-
sistant teacher at fifteen and then advanced her to become a regular
teacher. Yet while female students paid the same tuition as males,
Lucretia received only half the pay of male teachers such as her
boyfriend, James Mott, whom she later married. The injustice rankled
as she experienced firsthand "the unequal condition of woman." Such
injustice made her resolve "to claim for myself all that an imperial
Creator had bestowed."[62]

James Mott and Lucretia Coffin married and settled in Philadelphia,
where James prospered in business, working for another and then for himself as a merchant. In 1818, at the age of twenty-five, Lucretia began her
career as a Quaker preacher. For the next several decades, she preached
to thousands of Quakers along the Eastern seaboard. Even though Quaker
women long had served as ministers and held separate meetings to carry
on the work of benevolence and consider questions of discipline, Quaker
men dominated governance, allowing women only an advisory role. When
the men's meeting in their church acted on questions of discipline without
consulting female opinion in 1820, James thought it "strange" and wrong,
a sign that the common opinions about women "prevalent with the 'people of the world'" had infiltrated Quaker precincts. Since Quakers professed to believe that males and females were one in God's eyes, how could
anyone doubt "that our labors would be superior if they involved both"?
Still, James remained hopeful that "as we become more enlightened and
civilized, this difference will be done away, and women will have an equal
voice in the administration of the discipline."

Whatever were the Quakers' failings in the treatment of women, they
remained light-years in advance of other denominations. Buoyed by her
belief in female possibilities and sustained by her understanding of the
Quaker faith, Lucretia Mott never faltered in her search for an autonomous life dedicated to social betterment.[63] "Women in particular,"
she lamented, "have pinned their faith to minister's sleeves. They dare
not rely on their own God-given powers of discernment." The "inner
light" had given her confidence in herself to preach the true gospel,
"resting on truth for authority, not on authority for truth," one of her
favorite apothegms, and one that struck a blow at patriarchy.[64]

In the formative years of her youth, before she joined the abolitionist
movement, Mott had developed a strong sense of self as a woman. She

was intellectually and morally engaged, organizing domestic life in ways that permitted her to travel and preach the gospel without neglecting responsibilities at home. In rejecting sexual stereotypes, Mott prepared herself to reject racial stereotypes.

Mott's protofeminism had roots in her discovery of her superior intellect and ability at Nine Partners, as well as in her egalitarian understanding of the Quaker way. Her egalitarianism extended beyond gender relations to broad issues of class relations. Its roots lay in lessons learned early in life, after the Coffin family moved from Nantucket to Boston. At first, Lucretia attended a Quaker school in Boston, as was common within this group, which kept together and disowned any who married outside the fold, a practice she came to oppose. Her parents, however, removed her to a public school so she could mix with children of all classes without distinction, thereby avoiding "a feeling of class pride, which they felt was sinful to cultivate in their children." Later in life, Mott expressed gratitude for her parents' decision "because it gave me a feeling of sympathy for the patient and struggling poor, which, but for experience, I might never have known."[65]

The unfolding of the market revolution in the early nineteenth century, especially the suffering caused by the crash in 1819, deeply troubled both James and Lucretia. As James prospered, he worried about succumbing to conspicuous consumption, which he observed spreading among other prospering Quakers. He received counsel from his grandfather in New York: "It is probably, in the present state of affairs in [Quaker] Society, as respects an unwarrantable, expensive manner of living, particularly as regards furniture, that the cross must be taken up by you" to "bear a noble testimony against the deviations from that moderation that characterized our early Friends, and which true humility still dictates."[66]

The panic of 1819 revealed how easily prosperity could turn to disaster. Lucretia and other Quaker women established the Fragment Society to aid the poor at a time of severe distress. And James worked in soup kitchens. He displayed ambivalence, if not profound doubts about the social costs of economic development. Observing that the depression had punctured real estate prices in Lancaster and Chester, he looked backward to an earlier, less volatile age: "Happy is the man who has a good farm clear of debt, and does not know how to write his name!" Such a person "knows little of the anxiety attendant upon mercantile life when perhaps the hard earnings of many anxious days and sleepless nights are swept away by failures and losses on almost every hand." James concluded: "I say let those who have been up in the country, stay there."[67]

The Motts' anxiety over the spread of worldliness and the departure from Quaker simplicity was a view widely shared by others and contributed to the split between the followers of Elias Hicks and orthodox Quakers. Hicks, a gifted Quaker preacher from New York, for some decades had preached against decline from the piety of the founding generation. He and his large following also resisted the orthodox desire to "Americanize" Quakerism, making it more like other Protestant denominations. The Motts regarded the trends that seemed to characterize what was becoming of orthodoxy—secularism, consumerism, and doctrinal innovation—as worldly corruptions of genuine Quakerism. In the struggle between the Hicksites and the orthodox, which culminated in a formal split in 1827, the Motts sided with the Hicksites. They found themselves increasingly alienated from the decline of personal piety and the spread of consumer display and ritualism among the more affluent. Though they lived in the metropolis until the 1850s, they sided with the country Quakers, farmers and small-scale mechanics and shopkeepers, among whom the Hicksites were strongest. The strength of the orthodox, by contrast, lay especially with the urban Quaker bourgeoisie.[68]

In siding with the Hicksites, the Motts were seeking to reconcile their faith with the moral challenges of the market revolution. Slavery posed one of the strongest challenges. Neither had given much thought to slavery until the 1820s, though Lucretia remembered her schoolbook accounts of the suffering caused by the slave trade and the heroism of Quaker opposition. However much they may have deplored slavery, that did not stop James from entering the domestic commission trade, in which he handled the sale of cotton. Elias Hicks had been preaching for years that Quakers must avoid any complicity with slavery, and he set an example by refusing to purchase cotton goods or sugar produced by slave labor.[69]

The Hicksite schism had a profound impact on Lucretia Mott and her husband. In the course of the struggle she "was obliged to judge even of herself what was right, and to abide by that decision at whatever sacrifice." The result was that "her whole spiritual vision widened, and she beheld directly before her extended fields of labor wherein honest workers were sorely needed." Where she previously had viewed slavery primarily as an issue of Quaker piety, she now came to see it as a national problem. This was in keeping with the Motts' rejection of Quaker sectarianism, which they thought inhibited a person's ability to do good in the world. Doing good became their litmus test of true piety. They now felt irresistible pressure to set an example. They renounced the consumption of the products of slave labor, and James switched his commission business from cotton to woolens.

While remaining faithful to Quakerism, as they understood it, the Motts grew increasingly antidoctrinal and ecumenical, increasingly willing to work with others outside the Quaker fold. Lucretia joined the Philadelphia Female Antislavery Society, and though its members were mostly Friends, the Society was nonsectarian and operated without the patronage of any church or elite organization. Organization was a bracing learning experience. "I had no idea of the meaning of preambles, and resolutions, and voting. Women had never been in any assemblies of the kind," Lucretia remembered. "I had attended only one convention—a convention of colored people—before that."[70] At Quaker business meetings, voting and parliamentary procedure were unknown.

For the next two decades, Lucretia Mott became one of the abolitionist movement's most important leaders. She did not stop preaching abolitionism as a Quaker itinerant, but now she acted on a much larger stage. She worked together with whites from all denominations who shared her principles and with African-American men and women, with whom she socialized in her home. Her advocacy of antisectarianism and antidoctrinalism while still holding to her Quaker principles touched a deep chord among many evangelicals who gravitated to the antislavery struggle. J. Miller McKim, a young Presbyterian minister sent as a delegate by an entirely black antislavery society in Carlisle, Pennsylvania, to attend the founding of the American Antislavery Society, encountered Lucretia Mott and explained her effect on him: "I never before heard a woman speak at a public meeting," McKim recalled. "She said but a few words, but these were spoken so modestly, in such sweet tones and yet withal so decisively, that no one could fail to be pleased." Mott's presence seemed wrapped in an aura of piety: "The evidence of the Divine presence and the Divine approval was palpable."[71]

McKim was deeply immersed in the theological debate then raging between Liberals such as the Unitarians and evangelical defenders of Christian orthodoxy in his own denomination. Mott, who long had rejected the concept of human depravity, advised him to read the Bible for himself and not be swayed by sectarian argument.[72] Garrison, she later recalled, was "never attached to any sect."[73] The notion that sectarian doctrine and theology were at the center of Christian belief tended "to lower the estimate of practical righteousness, and rational Christian duties." She pointed to McKim as a stunning example of one who, as he

abandoned the "bigoted sectarianism and gloomy superstition" of
Presbyterianism, came to exhibit "all that is truly 'pious' and valuable."
As for McKim, he looked back on the collapse of the Second Great
Awakening in the early 1830s as the beginning of an era of a social
Christianity, "when the feelings of the sincere and enlightened . . . began
to take a new turn." People previously had dwelled on the state of their
own souls, their desire for salvation. Now, "their attention was called
away from themselves to the condition of others." Some, even if only a
minority, had progressed far enough in Christian faith to understand
now "that cardinal injunction: 'Let no man seek his own, but every one
his neighbor's weal.'" For McKim, as for Mott, the struggle against slavery now became the test.[75]

Reviewing Lucretia Mott's career in 1858, the republic's leading female editor, Sarah Josepha Hale of *Godey's Ladies Book,* acknowledged
Mott's gifts as a preacher, but cautioned that "her sermons *sound* better
than they read, because her persuasive manner prevents the listener from
noticing the fallacies of her reason, so easily detected in her printed productions."[76] Garrison had another view of Mott: "She dwelt with emphasis and power upon the wide difference which exists between a cer-
emonial religion and practical godliness."[77]

A similar religious trajectory, though not from Quakerism, but from
orthodox Congregationalism, appears in the evolution toward abolition
of Lydia Maria Child, the country's foremost female author in the 1820s
and 1830s. Child produced a stream of short stories and novels, the first
children's magazine, the *Juvenile Miscellany,* advice books such as the
Frugal Housewife (1829) and *The Mothers' Book* (1831), and a two-
volume history of women (1835). By the end of her career, over forty
volumes had poured from her pen. None caused such an explosion as
An Appeal in Favor of that Class of Americans Called Africans (1833),
the most powerfully written, comprehensive extended argument for immediatism and racial equality produced by the antislavery movement.
Among those it influenced were Rev. William Ellery Channing,
Unitarianism's leading light, the antislavery senator Charles Sumner, the
editor and critic Thomas Wentworth Higginson, Wendell Phillips, and
countless others.

Child realized that the *Appeal* faced tough going in persuading a skeptical public that preferred evasion and that was steeped in ignorance and
prejudice toward African Americans. She worked three years to gather
data, reading widely in the Boston Athenaeum, the city's leading library,
carefully and soberly putting the argument together. In the preface, she

exhorted readers inclined to avoid the subject "not to throw down this volume as soon as you have glanced at the title." She pleaded with them to read it, "if your prejudices will allow, for the very truth's sake" or if not, only to find new reasons "to sneer at the vulgarity of the cause." Finally, she appealed to people's "sheer curiosity to see what a woman (who had much better attend to her household concerns) will say upon such a subject."[78] For her trouble, Child paid a steep price in public displeasure orchestrated by her Boston elite boosters. Sales of the *Juvenile Miscellany* collapsed as parents sought to protect their children from a disseminator of subversive doctrine. Sales of the advice manuals plummeted, and now Child faced life among the marginal folk devoted to abolition. Former Boston boosters even banned her from the Boston Athenaeum.[79]

William Lloyd Garrison and her husband, David Lee Child, a newspaper editor Garrison earlier had converted, were the immediate sources of Child's conversion in 1830. She was a likely prospect, however, because formative experiences before 1830 made her susceptible to the antislavery appeal. Protofeminism, exceptional intellectual and literary gifts, which pushed her toward a career and an independent life, a restless search for religious truth, and a critical view of commercial values combined in Child, as they did in others, to open her mind to radical notions on race and slavery.

From an early age, Child demonstrated a love of reading, which her brother, Convers, encouraged. He recognized that his sister possessed a powerful intellect, perhaps more powerful than his own. By ten, she knew much of Shakespeare and Milton and revealed "intellectual boldness and self-assurance."[80] But whereas her brother was sent to Harvard, and previously to an academy to prepare him, her own formal education was limited, although her father judged it sufficient. Convers Francis was a prosperous Medford, Massachusetts, baker with little sympathy for "reading women" and none for his daughter's intellectual ambitions. By contrast, Medford's Rev. David Osgood taught his three children, among them two girls, Hebrew, Greek, and Latin, and encouraged vigorous intellectual exchange within the family. Lucy Osgood, Child's friend, provided a role model of women's intellectual potential. It became clear to Child that only her sex, not her ability, denied her the benefits her brother received. Such injustice "sowed the seeds of a feminist consciousness," as it did in other women of her generation.[81]

However unsympathetic her father was to Lydia's protofeminist aspirations, he harbored a rough-hewn egalitarianism. He was proud of his service in the American Revolution, and of not looking down on the less fortunate members of society, white or black. Lydia recalled that her father treated Col. Middleton, a black veteran of the American Revolution who lived nearby, "with uniform kindness."

Exiled by her father to the Maine frontier to live with a married sister, she nevertheless had access to books and continued her self-education. At nineteen, she moved to Gardner, Maine, to teach school and live on her own: "All I expect is, that, if I am industrious and prudent I shall be *independent.*"[82] In 1821, she returned to Massachusetts to live with her brother, now a Unitarian minister in Watertown. His recognition of her literary gifts encouraged her to write. "I consider such intellectual culture as I have mainly attributed to your influence," she told him.[83] As with the other female abolitionists, for Child male respect for female talent facilitated the search for autonomy. None proved more important or more frustrating than David Lee Child, whom she married in 1828. David Lee Child was a farmer's son who had attended Harvard and who had become a lawyer and editor of the *Massachusetts Journal,* a National Republican weekly that vigorously supported the administration of John Quincy Adams. His respect for her talents and acceptance of her career as a writer softened the loss of independence that marriage brought. Her earning capacity rescued her feckless husband from repeated failures as a breadwinner and gave her an autonomy that allowed them to live apart when their careers diverged or when remaining together became too much to bear for this issueless couple.[84]

In 1824 Child published at her own expense *Hobomok,* a novel that challenged patriarchy and racial prejudice, two causes that prefigured the ideals that shaped the rest of her life. The title page boldly asserted that *Hobomok* was written "By an American," and the narrative voice was male.[85] Even as she felt it necessary to disguise her sex, Child's protofeminism buttressed her self-confidence. She believed that she possessed an uncommon voice that deserved a hearing. "I know not how it is," she explained, "but my natural temperament is such that when I wished to do any thing I seem to have an instinctive faith that I can do it."[86]

At the same time that Child's protofeminism pushed her toward a career as a writer, she searched for religious beliefs that would provide a moral compass. She rejected the Calvinism of the family's Congregationalist faith, unable to swallow the doctrine of original sin. Her brother's Unitarianism, however, was too rational and cold to satisfy her sense of the mystical. She found a spiritual home in Swedenborgianism, with its pantheistic tendency to see the Divine in all things. Swedenborg's "doctrine of Correspondences seemed a golden key to unlock the message gate between material and spiritual world," she recalled. "I then *experienced religion; and for a long time lived in a mansion of glories.*"[87] She joined Boston's New Jerusalem Church, but abandoned it later when she discovered that these Swedenborgians had no affinity for brotherhood with African Americans. Still, Swedenborgianism's optimistic view of the world bolstered her belief in gender and racial equality. Eventually, Child gravitated toward an ecumenical conception of religion that stressed the centrality of ethical obligation as the authentic expression of spirituality. She sought to downplay denominational sectarianism, a difficult position to take in a highly sectarian age. These views found their most extended statement in *The Progress of Religious Ideas* (1855).

In the antislavery movement she found a true church, where sect and doctrine did not matter, only a willingness to take risks in the struggle for justice. As with so many antislavery people, the gospel became a social gospel. In her farewell in the last issue of the *Juvenile Miscellany,* she reminded the children that "all true excellence and happiness consists in living for others, not for yourselves."[88] These views meshed with her egalitarian predilections. Child cast a critical eye on the growing inequality and class pretensions associated with the market revolution and the power of elites. At first, she basked in the attention paid to her by men like George Ticknor, one of Boston's toniest cultural leaders. So impressed was fashionable Boston society with her talent that she gained invitations to some of their homes. She expressed astonishment that she had acquired "terms of intimacy—nay that I even regard with contempt some of these great people, who used to frighten me at a distance." There also were practical reasons for her delight in being lionized by "the rich and fashionable people." She expected to remain single owing to lack of beauty or fortune and therefore would have to support herself. Elite sponsorship was immensely valuable. "I am an American enough to prefer money to fame," she confessed.[89]

Elite sponsorship, however, was a foundation built on sand. She was the daughter of a self-consciously proud artisan family, and her parents taught her not to look down on the disadvantaged and always to remember those in need. She would remain an outsider in fashionable circles. When in 1824 Lydia met David Lee Child, he expressed a gloomy view of the prospects of the republic at their first meeting. He "spoke of the tendency to decline which marks all institutions, particularly republican," especially given the power of "the tremendous *squirearchy* of

America."[90] The attempt to repress free expression by means of the anti-abolition riots of the 1830s revealed its brutally antidemocratic agenda.

The conventional explanation of those riots was that they were the fault of the working classes and evidence of the excesses of democracy. Lydia Maria instructed her brother Convers, who held this view, that the real cause was "the lack of republicanism" among elites. The aristocratic principle, "unable to act openly, disguises itself, and sends its poison from under a mask." The riots aimed to prevent free discussion of abolitionism among the farmers and mechanics because "the majority of their voices would be on the right side if the question were fairly brought before them." Behind the mobs stood "manufacturers who supply the South, merchants who trade with the South, politicians who trade with the South, ministers settled at the South, and editors patronized by the South." The root of the evil traced back to the beginning of the republic, when "the principle of despotism was admitted in the very formation of our government, to sanction which our consciences have been continually silenced and sealed." There would be no mobs, Child insisted, "if people called respectable did not give them their sanction."[91] When the Massachusetts legislature, by one vote, granted use of its hall for an antislavery meeting in 1837, Child reaffirmed her opinion about the class character of the opposition: the city members, especially those from Boston, stood opposed, but "the country members" had saved the day. "God bless the yeomanry," she exclaimed.[92]

Even before the anti-abolition riots sharpened Child's sense of class, she revealed an acute awareness of the corrupting influence that the process of modern class formation had on republicanism in the era of the market revolution. In 1826, she published her second novel, *The Rebels, or Boston Before the Revolution,* a work that intertwined an overly complicated tale of romance and betrayal with a celebration of Boston's Whig patriots and with dark depictions of the Tory enemies of freedom and of republican values.[93] A Tory British army officer, nephew of the Tory lieutenant governor Thomas Hutchinson, and his outspokenly misogynist sidekick, the Tory Rev. Byles, throws over the beautiful daughter of a patriot preacher for another woman in the Hutchinson circle who has suddenly inherited wealth. In the end, Tory avarice is exposed and defeated, and the Whig lovers are rewarded by marriage. The same avarice that led the British to tax the Americans without their consent drives Tory men to betray women.[94] Child's protofeminism also surfaces as patriot women rebut Tory denigration of their sex and demonstrate their devotion to liberty.[95] The rich heiress who barely escaped a loveless marriage to an aristocratic fortune seeker wrings out the final lesson: "Wealth, with all its imposing pageantry, and rank with its embroidered baldrick and blazing star, had been idols before which her imagination had bowed with scarcely inferior homage." Recognizing "their utter insufficiency to satisfy the soul in its hour of trial . . . she now began to estimate men and things according to their real value,— to appreciate qualities according to their usefulness, not according to their lustre."[96]

Though *The Rebels* is set fifty years in the past, the celebration of republican virtue in its formative period held special salience for those sensing the decay of republicanism as commercial values threatened the purity of both civic and personal relations, not just for Lydia Maria Child, but for other female converts to abolitionism. Lydia Child's two widely read advice books helped spread her critical view of consumer display, of competition in the service of class snobbery, and of selfish values in conflict with Christian republicanism.

The Frugal Housewife (1829) neither celebrated nor disparaged women's work in the home. Nor was it directed, like its British predecessors, at the comfortable middle and upper classes. Rather, Child aimed to assist the less affluent, who relied on their own labor, not that of servants, in managing their households by stretching limited funds. She offered practical advice about repairing old clothing, removing stains, preventing food spoilage, and, most of all, gave recipes for inexpensive meals that contrasted with earlier books whose recipes only the better off could afford. The book proved immensely popular with a public that valued domestic management without pretension, but it displeased Sarah Josepha Hale, who objected to Child's preoccupation with saving money and minimizing household expenses, vulgar attitudes that she believed her own upper-middle and upper-class readers should disdain. Hale seemed oblivious to the very different audience at which Child aimed.[97]

Child dedicated *The Mother's Book* (1831) "To American Mothers, on which intelligence and discretion the safety and prosperity of our Republic so much depends."[98] Again addressing an audience among the less affluent, Child offered a system for raising children appropriate to a democratic republic. She began with the Lockean assumption that God created all children as vessels "empty and pure—ready to receive, and always receiving."[99] The best way to curb evil or "bad passions" in youngsters was for parents to curb them in themselves. The best way to stimulate a child's intellectual development was to encourage it by satisfying curiosity. She rebutted the common view that everyday responsibilities left little time for women or their daughters to develop their intellects, arguing that fashionable women devoted more time to their dress than "reading women" to their books. Parents should encourage children to love books, but not foolish, escapist novels.[100]

Child denied that women must suffer from weak physical constitutions if they engaged in appropriate exercise and manual labor, which she respected at a time when disdain was a characteristic attitude of upwardly mobile middle-class people, who thought freedom from physical toil was evidence of their social ascent. And she deplored other characteristics of the emerging modern middle class. Training children to value clothing and domestic display was unrepublican, as was a patronizing disrespect of others. Genuine politeness was natural and extended to all strata. Parents who encouraged snobbish disdain for servants forgot that in a republic, those who "are servants now may be mistresses next year; and those who *keep* domestics may *be* domestics hereafter." In the United States, "half our people are in a totally different situation from what might have been expected in their childhood."[101]

Throughout the advice books, Child argued for the preservation of republican values that had fallen under attack. "Do not suffer your mind to brood over the external distinctions of society," she argued. "One should measure peoples' worth by their characters." "If the inordinate love of wealth and parade be not checked among us," she warned, "it will be the ruin of our country, as it has been the ruin of thousands of individuals."[102] She deplored the pride and insolence of the affluent and the jealousy and envy of the poor.[103] And she argued for the importance of personal independence: it was better for young women to work than to live off the largess of others; it was likewise preferable for women to remain single than to enter unhappy marriages.[104]

As early as 1829, recognizing Child as a powerful social critic, Garrison anointed her as "the first Woman in the Republic." He praised her efforts to "reform the manners of the age" and to restore "the simplicity of the good old days of our fathers."[105] No reform so distinguished Child's pre-abolitionist career as her opposition to racial prejudice. In short stories, a novel, and a book-length historical argument that humanized Native Americans, she justified their resistance to European invasion and offered an alternative to dispossessing and murdering Indians—their peaceful assimilation into white culture through a blending of the races by miscegenation.

Hobomok, her first novel, took aim at patriarchy and racial prejudice. In Puritan Massachusetts in the early days of white colonization, the heroine, Mary Conant, is prevented by a bigoted Puritan father from marrying an Anglican priest. Forced to leave the colony, the lover is thought to have been lost at sea in a shipwreck. The heartbroken daughter punishes her father by running away to live with Hobomok, a Native American who long had admired her. Learning in turn to admire Hobomok for his kindness, strength, and beauty, Mary goes native and gives birth to a son, whom she raises in Hobomok's teepee, aided by his devoted mother. All is serene until Hobomok learns that Mary's first love has returned, now welcomed by her repentant father, whose suffering because of his cruel patriarchalism and Calvinist bigotry have finally enlightened him. The noble savage then makes the great sacrifice. He returns Mary and his son to white "civilization" and disappears forever into the wilderness. Mary and her former lover are united, the son goes to Harvard, and all live happily ever after.

A contemporary critic regarded the interracial relationship as distasteful, but praised *Hobomok* for its attempt to fashion a story out of American materials. Other contemporaries of Child also had made Native Americans central characters in their novels, but with very different perspectives: James Kirke Paulding celebrated the disappearance of Native Americans as clearing the land for the advance of "civilization"; James Fenimore Cooper regarded the decline of the natives as tragic but unavoidable.[106] Child, however, was truly visionary, modern critics have pointed out: "If we are to understand *Hobomok* and her alternative visions of race and gender relations . . . we must take as our starting point the defiance of patriarchy which governs its fictional strategies."[107] Mary's defiance echoed Child's defiance of her father's view of what was proper for women. Child's rejection of gender stereotypes made her open-minded about racial stereotypes and led her to reject the idea of the inherent inferiority of women and people of color.

Five years later, Child further developed her radical, revisionist views of Native Americans in a book-length dialogue between a mother and her two daughters, *The First Settlers of New England, or Conquest of the Pequods, Narragansets and Pokanokets* (1829), by "A Lady of Massachusetts."[108] Based on an original, critical reading of seventeenth-century Puritan historical sources, Child, speaking as Mother, argued that avaricious "Invaders" rewarded friendly, cooperative, and courteous Native Americans with cruel warfare in order to dispossess and destroy them. Every act of warfare or retaliation by natives was triggered by the Invaders' aggression and crimes. The daughters listen in shocked horror as Mother explains how the monstrous doctrines of Calvinism made such brutality possible. The Native Americans could not count on the compassionate intercession of Puritan women because Calvinism deformed their minds and hearts, too, not allowing expression of women's benevolent nature.[109]

Child, via Mother, then sets forth an alternative that was more relevant in the 1820s in the face of the contemporary betrayal and dispossession of the Cherokees. The New England natives in the seventeenth century had remained conciliatory, Child argued. The Europeans would have been better off "by intermixing with the natives" and assimilating them to the Invaders' superior culture. Had that occurred, Child concluded, "we should have gained more than would have been lost" because "the primitive simplicity, hospitality, and generosity of the Indians would gradually have improved and softened the stern and morose feelings" of the Calvinists. Racial mixture thus would purge whites of a religion-borne viciousness, allowing ascendancy of "the pure religion of Jesus."[110]

When daughter Caroline questions the practicality of racial intermixture because of white aversion to dark skins and belief in black inferiority, Mother, anticipating the historical arguments in the *Appeal*, insists that civilization had its roots among dark-skinned peoples in Asia and Egypt, from whom the Europeans learned. Yet whatever history taught, Child reminded her readers, Christians were obliged to honor the will of God, "who had made of one blood all the nations of men, that they may dwell together."[111]

Child's book may never have reached the public, for no reviews appeared in the press. Child may have suppressed the book to protect her career and her livelihood. Her radical views put her at odds with powerful forces, not just advocates of Indian removal, but their Northern evangelical foes, heirs of the Puritans, who she cried out came into court with bloody hands. *The First Settlers of New England* remains a remarkable register of Child's bold analysis of racial injustice and its cure, racial intermixture, prefiguring an assault on prejudice against African Americans in the coming years.[112]

One fact emerges from this survey of the routes that the most prominent early female abolitionists took in their journeys toward the cause. Generalizations are as difficult to make as they are about the ways in which male abolitionists came to advocate the immediate end of slavery. Like their male counterparts, female abolitionists were a heterogeneous lot. Clearly, however, also like their male counterparts, many were disturbed by what they took to be the morally defined social, political, and economic consequences of the market revolution. But because of the circumscribed place that women occupied in antebellum America, the terms in which they experienced such concerns were different, and the ways in which they found ways to attempt to do something about them were different as well. Whether they came to their public roles via an inward turn toward self-cultivation and self-purification, like the Grimkés and Elizabeth Chandler, or stepped boldly forth on the public stage like Lydia Maria Child, or took some route that veered between these private and public spheres, each had to contend with a form of discrimination that their male counterparts, however supportive they were, did not. And from the experience of contending with that discrimination, like many of their male counterparts, they tended to find their way to an overarching vision of American society, a vision premised on equal rights for all, regardless of class, color, and gender.

Roots of Female Abolitionism

From a handful of early female converts to immediatism, the numbers of women forming women's antislavery societies swelled. Black women in Salem led the way in 1833, soon joined by their white sisters. By 1838, abolitionists claimed over one hundred and ten female societies, 8 percent of the total, with over sixty-four hundred members. In Britain, there were at least seventy-three women's societies formed between 1825 and 1833, when the movement achieved emancipation in the West Indies.[1] In Ohio and perhaps elsewhere, there were some mixed societies before the antislavery movement split on the role of women. Massachusetts alone accounted for 38 percent and New York for 27 percent of the female societies, whereas Vermont boasted only one. These variations suggest that some local political cultures were more encouraging of female efforts than others. Sarah and Angelina Grimké moved from New York City to Massachusetts, where they expected a more favorable reception when they ascended the antislavery platform in 1836 and 1837, for example. In the Bay State, support by women for abolitionism was notable in industrial communities such as Lowell and Lynn and among women who belonged to conservative Calvinist churches such as the Hopkinsian congregations in the southeastern part of the state, whose ministers and male leaders were especially attracted to the immediatist cause.[2]

The reasons why women joined the antislavery movement are complex. Like their male counterparts and like the early female abolitionist leaders, rank-and-file women formed a heterogeneous group. Female

TABLE 5   FEMALE ABOLITIONISM

Number of Female Antislavery Societies

	1832	1833	1834	1835	1836
Maine	0	0	1	0	0
New Hampshire	0	0	2	2	2
Vermont	0	0	0	0	0
Massachusetts	0	3	3	7	9
Rhode Island	0	0	1	0	1
Connecticut	0	0	1	0	1
New York	0	2	1	8	0
Pennsylvania	0	1	0	0	2
Ohio	0	0	0	6	1
Total	0	6	9	23	16

	1837	1838	Undated[a]	Total	Members, 1838
Maine	2	0	0	3	140
New Hampshire	4	0	0	10	895
Vermont	1	0	2	3	—
Massachusetts	13	4	9	48	2418
Rhode Island	1	0	1	4	260
Connecticut	1	0	3	6	133
New York	7	0	1	19	1711
Pennsylvania	0	0	0	3	152
Ohio	1	2	6	16	671
Total	30	6	22	112	6380

[a]Female societies without founding dates.

SOURCE: *Fifth Annual Report of the Executive Committee of the American Anti-Slavery Society* . . . (New York, 1838), 129–52. Because membership data were not reported for many female antislavery societies, the figure in the table substantially underreports actual membership.

abolitionists included the evangelical and the nonevangelical, Hicksite Quakers much more than orthodox Quakers, leisured as well as working women, and both married and single women. Many of the social influences that we have seen operating on female abolitionist and protofeminist leaders like the Grimké sisters, Elizabeth Chandler, Lucretia Mott, and Lydia Maria Child also affected many other women who became abolitionists. But those influences, in turn, were part of larger social and historical developments that affected the status of women in antebellum America.

The seeds of the transformation in women's understanding of their role in a supposedly egalitarian society were sown in the latter half of the eighteenth century, when environmental explanations of human differences gained wider acceptance. The Lockean notion that each person enters the world with a clean mental slate to be filled up by experience unsettled notions of inequalities based on class, race, and gender.[3] But Enlightenment environmentalist assumptions only slowly became part of public discourse and even more slowly altered social relations, facing as they did formidable resistance from those who benefited from tradition.

In the United States, the American Revolution stimulated new ideas about women's role in the public sphere. Women provided support for the resistance movement before 1776, especially in the consumer boycotts, and after fighting began, they contributed to the war effort as "deputy husbands." But the Revolution's greatest effect on the status of women was the result of the emergence of a cult of republican motherhood as the foundation for a republican form of government. The cult of republican motherhood charged women with rearing children prepared to assume the responsibilities of republican citizenship. It was a vague, amorphous concept without clear functional consequences. It did not challenge the conventional view that women were only half citizens, not entitled to vote and not expected to hold opinions on public issues, let alone to voice them in the public arena. Still, notions of republican motherhood gave some women a glimpse of an alternative, enlarged conception of their role in society.[4]

Even more important were the long-term economic, demographic, and cultural changes that generated a series of conflicting new conceptions of womanhood. "I regret the trifling narrow, contracted Education of the female of my own country," lamented Abigail Adams. "You need not be told how much female Education is neglected, nor how fashionable it has been to ridicule Female learning."[5] A minister's daughter with access to her father's library, Abigail Adams educated herself, encouraged further by a husband who relished a "reading woman" with whom he could engage in intellectual exchange. Her well-stocked mind helped her to form opinions on a broad array of subjects, from politics to religion, and to engage as an intellectual equal with some of the best-educated men of her generation. She was, however, exceptional.[6]

For the next generation of women, coming of age in the half-century after the birth of the republic, there were new opportunities. A communications revolution gave all Americans, but especially more women than ever before, the chance to cultivate their minds. An expansion in the quantity and accessibility of print literature, newspapers, periodicals, and books and the spread of "social libraries" in hundreds of towns in the Northeast helped make "reading women" more common, although the phrase remained a term of derision for many. As women discovered the power of their intellects, they no longer would accept conventional views of the female mind as weak, its cultivation a threat to fragile female bodies and psyches.[7]

The "democratization of the written word" that made reading an important part of everyday life also produced a genre of the novel that challenged sexual stereotyping and empowered "individual readers in ways innately inimical to social authority," Cathy N. Davidson has argued.[8] These novels "tended to proclaim a socially egalitarian message" and "spoke for . . . orphans, beggar girls, factory girls . . . and . . . repeatedly advocated the general need for 'female education.'"[9]

As we already have seen, in becoming "reading women," some discovered that they possessed intellects superior to those of many men. And as we also have seen, such discoveries inevitably affected everyday interpersonal relations. Some women were readier to express strongly held opinions on various subjects, including religion, politics, and public affairs. It was the beginning of a quest for autonomy. Women searched for lives, careers, and marriages different from those customarily led by the wives of peasants, farmers, artisans, and petty shopkeepers. The subversive effects of this literary genre gave women a new sense of choice. By "reading about a female character's good or bad decisions in sexual and marital matters, the American woman could vicariously enact her own courtship and marriage fantasies."[10]

Improvements in female educational opportunity, first at the basic level and then by the establishment of academies (secondary schools for more advanced instruction) intensified the transformation in women's consciousnesses. Now, women were thrown together with other young women, and collectively their experience reinforced confidence in their ability, intellect, and possibilities. The hundreds of academies founded in the decades following the American Revolution were diverse: some were finishing schools whose only end was to improve marital prospects, but others, including those founded by Emma Willard, Catharine Beecher, Zilpha Grant, and Mary Lyon, took seriously the religious, moral, and intellectual development of women. Rev. Joseph Emerson insisted that female education be rigorous, much like men's, that women study science and mathematics, not just literature. Catharine Beecher had visions that women first would transform themselves and then transform society, not realizing the radical directions some women might take, such as abolitionism and feminism, much to her later horror.[11]

The impact on some women was transformative: "After Emily Howland's parents brought her home from school in Philadelphia she struggled for years to recapture the self-esteem, the sense of potential, and the independence that she had experienced at school." Howland, like Mary Grew, who attended Beecher's school, eventually found worthy work in a commitment to antislavery and to the improvement of free African Americans, a result not intended by the early champions of female education.[12]

Woman's nature and woman's destiny no longer were settled questions, but had become highly contentious matters. Urbanization, industrialization, and the processes that were forming a middle class further meant that farming no longer set the parameters of female aspiration, even though a majority of females remained in agriculture. The growth of manufactures created jobs for women that allowed them to leave home, even if only temporarily, and to earn cash wages. The strikes by women against the textile manufacturing companies in Lowell, the organization by Lynn female shoemakers of a union to agitate for better pay, and more generally, the decision to leave or enter labor markets, gave women a place among the emerging wage-earning classes. Even women who remained on farms carved out domains, such as dairying, that made their labor more notable in a market economy.[13]

Like farming, marriage no longer exclusively shaped women's lives. While women expected to marry, and most did, remaining single slowly emerged as an attractive and fruitful alternative for a small, but growing minority because it allowed for the autonomous development of the self while still serving God, family, and community. Spinsterhood or delayed marriage, once confined to a few, now became more common and more accepted by society. Indeed, it could be hard to avoid in a region such as the Northeast, where land shortages pushed many men west, leaving surpluses of marriageable females. At the same time, women were becoming able to support themselves, as factory operatives or as school teachers, for example. Single women thus "struggled to free themselves from the constraints of domesticity—or more accurately, to define themselves and their calling in opposition to the domestic—so that they might explore the realms of imagination, spirituality, or human experience."[14]

In the realm of spirituality, women long had found a special role as exemplars of piety and purity. Continuing a long-term trend, women outnumbered men among church members in evangelical denominations that required a conversion experience. This involved abject submission before God, a sensibility at odds with male experience in the nineteenth-century marketplace, where assertiveness and the will to power paid off with survival and success. The feminization of religion gained greater saliency as the market revolution sharpened notions of sexual difference. But as pious women discovered, the routine celebration of domesticity as a bastion of purity immune from the temptations, worldliness, and corruptions of the marketplace did not immunize families from the evils lurking beyond, and popular social movements such as temperance became increasingly militant as women struggled to control recalcitrant male behavior that violated Christian precepts. Although males dominated the governance of churches and most reform societies, the feminization of piety challenged one of the chief claims of patriarchy—to reserve moral leadership for men.[15]

The Finneyite revival, in particular, eroded patriarchy and emboldened women to sponsor evangelism in their communities, pray in mixed meetings, and develop the antinomian and perfectionist strains in Finney's preaching. As a result, "women were freed within the church and encouraged to fill larger roles in society by the revivalist impulse," joining temperance, moral reform, antislavery, feminist, and other movements. As one explained: "I was under bondage to authority, dogmas and conservative ideas until I married into a family of strong anti-slavery convictions, who had the courage to stand for these convictions." Like others swept up by the great revival, her "family seceded from the old Presbyterian church of the town, because we could no longer sit conscientiously under a preacher, or in a fellowship, where the golden rule of Christianity was not recognized as applicable to all men, whatever the color of their skin."[16]

In the face of transforming experiences such as these, defenders of patriarchy sought to persuade Americans that women's nature and social role remained fixed. The cult of "true womanhood" posited woman's mental inferiority, physical frailty, and her duty to remain outside the marketplace and public arenas. This conception of women, however, now faced challenges at every point. Many women and some men concluded that women's intelligence deserved cultivation, and that women are often more gifted than men. Nor are women inherently physically frail, as hard-working women on farms and in factories demonstrated. Even privileged women, women of leisure aided by servants, could strengthen their bodies through exercise. Work, whether paid or not, as in charitable or benevolent activities, was as important in the fulfillment of female lives as it was in men's. In fact, for many women, employment had become a necessity when their male breadwinners had failed in the dynamic and volatile marketplace. Such dissent added up to a rival notion of "real womanhood."[17]

The nature of womanhood thus was an issue in contention. Even conservative women who formally subscribed to the notions of female subordination and "true womanhood" could not consistently maintain their
position. Sarah Josepha Hale condemned female antislavery agitation
because it brought women into the political arena, yet she herself advocated African colonization at a time when it was an important political
issue between Jacksonian Democrats and Clay's National Republicans.
Moreover, in 1827 she wrote a novel, *Northwood*, that attacked evangelical Yankee antislavery sentiment, yet finally achieved sectional rec-
onciliation between "good" Northerners and "good" Southerners
through the invention of labor-saving machinery, which replaced slave
labor and allowed repatriation of the surplus African American population to its ancestral home. Hale's book was reissued in the 1850s as an
antidote to *Uncle Tom's Cabin*.[18]

Likewise, Catharine Beecher, a pioneer in educating women to become
the nation's school teachers, could not resist the impulse to carve for women
a larger sphere than the domestic. At the Hartford Female Seminary that
she directed in the 1820s, she operated almost as a lay preacher, encouraging born-again teachers and pupils to press the cause of conversion
among students by humanizing God, downplaying theology, and advocating belief in freedom of the will. Swept away by the excitement of witnessing the moral and intellectual development of her pupils, Beecher led the
students to circulate petitions protesting the removal of the Cherokees from
Georgia, an issue that came to a head in the election of 1828: "The girls
come and tell us such marvelous stories about a circular for the Cherokees
around in Hartford" and "public meetings and petitions are getting up in
New York and other places." Beecher herself never embraced immediatism;
in 1837, she wrote a pamphlet attacking the Grimké sisters for mounting
the antislavery platform. They violated the norms of the separate spheres,
and by demanding access to the church, undermined male clerical authority, she argued. Though no activity by abolitionist women was perhaps
more noteworthy than their circulation of antislavery petitions to Congress
and the state legislatures, Beecher saw no conflict between her hostility to
female antislavery agitation and her own earlier circulation of petitions on
behalf of Native Americans. The real difference was that one cause boasted
considerable elite support among leading ministers and politicians, whereas
immediatism was beyond the pale of respectability. Still, Catharine
Beecher's devotion to female intellect, education, and teaching as a woman's
profession had unforeseen consequences that she could not fully anticipate,
let alone control. By "training women for useful lives, in an experimental

educational setting, she prepared them neither for entrance into a male sphere nor for confinement to a traditional women's sphere."

Many causes competed for the commitment of awakening women, but two in particular, abolitionism and the movement against prostitution known as "moral reform," ran afoul of respectable opinion and encountered intense opposition. Between moral reform and immediatism there were close affinities. When the moral reformers faced intense attacks, abolitionists were among the few to rush to their defense. Moral reform had begun under male auspices, led in New York by Arthur Tappan and his friends, but they could not surmount either the lack of resources or the opposition. Eventually, women assumed control and rebuilt the moral reform movement, defying elites and men of all classes, ignoring clerical hostility, and establishing their own organization, raising funds, publishing an immensely successful newspaper, and recruiting thousands of women into societies throughout the North. By 1840, the New York Moral Reform Society claimed five hundred and fifty-five local organizations.[19]

The initial work began with efforts by the Tappan group and the Presbyterian minister Rev. John McDowall. Frustrated by the expense and the difficulty of reforming women taken from the streets, the early reformers regrouped. Aided by women, McDowall persisted by raising funds and issuing publications that exposed the magnitude of vice. Increasingly, McDowall focused on the customers: without the patronage of "respectable" men from all social classes, there would be only limited demand for commercial sex. Widespread prostitution had become the dirty little secret that good manners required good citizens to ignore, just as they ignored the cruelty and immorality of slavery.

Tappan and McDowall had broken the silence, and as a result incurred widespread community censure. McDowall's detailed revelations of prostitution, including the theaters where customers were recruited and the houses of assignation where they were entertained, led to charges that he was violating standards of public decency and catering to prurient interests. Especially irking was his exposé of the "respectable" customers. When Presbyterians in New York City brought suit against McDowall on the grounds that he improperly diverted funds for publication purposes, outraged women charged that male religious leaders, lay and clerical, were attempting to cover up the double standard and suppress both the truth and the movement dedicated to it. McDowall's death shortly after his conviction made him a martyr in the view of abolitionists, another victim of "gentlemen of property and standing."

Such repression galvanized women: only they could press the cause of moral reform. "This work must be begun with the ladies. They are the injured and they must rise and assert their rights." Licentiousness was "a regular crusade against our sex," protected by the powerful in church and state. Since men suffered no loss of respectability by corrupting women, fairness required that the harlots be welcome in respectable parlors and drawing rooms. "All we ask is equal privileges where there is equal guilt." Moral reformers thus framed their argument slyly in the rhetoric of "equal rights."[20]

Moral reform taught women that women's poverty, low wages, and consumerist desire for finery and other luxuries made them vulnerable to sexual exploitation. The efforts to repress reform revealed the extent to which men would go to perpetuate the enslavement of white women. In addition, the fight against prostitution taught women to "identify with females entirely different from themselves," with "*all women* as the victims of society's oppression."[21] Finally, in the struggles against vice, according to the *Advocate of Moral Reform,* the movement's leading publication, women had learned "to feel that they have a personal responsibility in *all* that concerns the . . . *good* of society."[22]

Moral reform attracted many more women as members of organized societies than did abolition, but there were striking common experiences both faced: opposition in the churches; opposition from those who argued that activist women violated their proper sphere; the thankless work of challenging a code of silence that sought to shield conscience from sin; repression, including the efforts by the United States Post Office to curtail access to the mails; and the mobilization of petition campaigns that recruited thousands of women in favor of legislation such as antiseduction laws to advance the cause.[23]

There also was an overlap of membership and leadership. In 1834, the American Seventh Commandment Society unsuccessfully sought the services as general agent of Theodore Weld, then heavily committed to the antislavery cause at Lane.[24] In Boston, the abolitionist Free Church, formed by Christians alienated from evangelical churches hostile to their cause, was also a hotbed of moral reform.[25] In New York, the Tappan circle took the initiative in launching the movement, and later, prominent male abolitionists such as Beriah Green and William Goodell were leaders of the American Seventh Commandment Society. The New York Female Moral Reform Society became an affiliate of the national organization and purchased the *Female Advocate,* the antivice paper edited by William Goodell. The women who ran the new paper, the *Advocate of*

Moral Reform, made clear that they would be as relentless in exposing the sins of vice as abolitionists were in exposing the sins of slavery, and equally defiant of public hostility: "For there is nothing covered that shall not be revealed; neither hid that shall not be made known."[26] No abolitionist pressed the linkages between antivice and antislavery more cogently than William Goodell. One could measure the moral character of any society, Goodell argued, by the treatment of its women. Christianity had been the first movement in history to rescue and elevate women from degradation and servility, but what was the position of women in the United States today? Were they "the menial slave" or "the rational companions of man?" Goodell asked, "the object, *not* of his brutal sensuality, but of his tender and sacred affection, not the idol of his vanity, but the sharer of his joys, and soothers of his sorrows—*not* the corrupter, but the purifier of his morals." As the world progressed, women progressed in dignity and influence, and no beneficial reforms were possible without the influence of women: "It is *among* the imperfections of the present state of society, that woman is not expected, nay, scarcely *permitted* to exert that *proportion* of moral influence on society to which she is entitled, for which the Creator designed her." Goodell therefore warned against the unthinking, habitual denigration of women by males: "Every biting sarcasm, every silly jest, every contemptuous sneer, every invidious innuendo . . . that ever *was* or ever shall be uttered" against women illustrated "that the lower the tone of public morals, the greater the dread of female elevation, female improvement, and *female influence.*"[27]

Goodell linked the growth of prostitution to the corruption corroding the society emerging from the market revolution. Among the affluent, idleness led to love of luxury, indolence, and "epicurean indulgence," which in turn produced vice and crime. The example of the wealthy and fashionable men corrupted others, including women. Good character no longer was the basis of respectability, which was why a man could indulge his erotic appetite with no loss of standing, any more than he would suffer for shady business practices in the marketplace.[28]

In January 1834, William Goodell informed moral reformers of the discontinuance of the *Female Advocate* and his assumption of the editorship of the *Emancipator,* the weekly organ of the American Antislavery Society. He urged women to write to him at his new post because the cause of black women was the cause of white women. "Few topics connected with the welfare of the sex can assume a higher importance than the emancipation of the suffering slave" because "a nation that degrades and brutalizes more than a million females, on no stronger provocation than is offered by the hue of their complexion, can hardly be expected . . . to be very solicitous to assign the female sex in general the elevated stand the God of nature designs them to occupy." The "deep and foul licentiousness which invades the purity of the domestic circle, pollutes the atmosphere of our splendid cities, and infects the whole land with the leprosy of Sodom, can never be removed while two millions of our population are virtually denied the purity of the family state."[29]

Like other women, the minority who became moral reformers or abolitionists experienced many if not all the transformative experiences that altered conceptions of womanhood and gender relations. Abolitionist women were set apart by the intensity with which they experienced the conflict between old and new notions of womanhood and the conclusions they drew. For deeply religious women, racial equality and abolitionism became the ultimate test of Christian conversion, the hardest and most demanding, especially as the intensity of revivalism waned after 1831 and most clerical authority stood steadfastly hostile. For women especially gifted with intellectual and leadership skills, developing and devoting their talents to remedy the most intractable social problem in the republic was a formidable challenge, but one that filled their lives with an sense of unrivaled purpose. Abolitionist women did not reject domesticity, but sought to redefine it. Domestic duty could not be confined to one's home, nor did meeting its obligations free one from meeting obligations as citizens of a Christian republic.[30] Fallen or impoverished white women, poor and uneducated free black women, enslaved black women, their children and families broken apart and sold as commodities, beckoned to all who venerated the holy sanctity of the home, where God's families dwelled, submissive to His law.

For the four spinster Weston sisters of Weymouth, Massachusetts, stalwarts for decades in the Boston-area abolitionist movement, their "shared lives provided a firm foundation upon which to build prominent vocations in the antislavery campaign."[31] Another spinster, Sarah Pugh, declared that antislavery work was the "blessing of my life," providing fulfillment along with other, more mundane responsibilities such as taking care of her parents.[32] The thousands of immediatist women, married or single, participating in antislavery work forged ties of sisterhood made particularly intense by the intense hostility, even violence, that they faced. In the process of taking up the anti-slavery cross, women challenged hierarchies of gender and race that made them threats to conservative notions of social order.

Female Abolitionist Activism

"The destiny of American slaves is in the hands of the American woman, and complete emancipation can never take place without her coopera- tion," Garrison confided in March 1833, before much female support had materialized.[1] Securing women's cooperation, however, faced for- midable obstacles. "Some do not dare to do anything for fear that they may get rid of their 'sphere,'" reported Abby Kelley.[2]

Opposition to female abolitionism was fierce. In Boston in 1835 and in Philadelphia in 1838, women faced mobs. T. R. Sullivan, a Massachusetts Unitarian clergyman, in a broad attack on popular agi- tation in general and on antislavery associations in particular, denounced "measures adopted to inflame the passions of the multitude, including the women and children, the boarding-school misses and factory girls." Attending a meeting in a factory town, Sullivan had heard an abolition- ist preacher arouse an audience, mostly of women, with provocative at- tacks on the South for permitting slaveholders "to break the conjugal tie and separate family relations at will." Sullivan believed women to be es- pecially susceptible to antislavery agitators, who elicited tears with sto- ries of cruelty and blushes with tales of sexual exploitation. The intru- sion of women into the political arena imperiled sober, rational discourse, Sullivan added, because men were too inclined to yield influence, thereby forfeiting "true mental independence." In her proper domestic sphere, woman "is as lovely as the evening star," but "when woman leaves her place" and "mingles with men in the struggles of ambition and power," the consequences are as dangerous as "the disastrous shock of comets."[3] The *Boston Centennial and Gazette* agreed: female abolitionists were a "parcel of silly women" acting as "petticoat politicians."[4]

Congressman Henry Wise of Virginia, provoked by antislavery petitions signed by thousands of women, also spoke for many in both sections: "Woman in the parlor, woman in her proper sphere, is the ornament and comfort of man; but out of the parlor—out of her sphere—" she becomes "a devil incarnate." He compared an abolitionist woman to "a fiend riding on the blast of strife and ruin, hissing rage and rapine, and rape and murder," who threatened "our lives and property and matrons and maidens of the South." Slavery was "a delicate political question," Wise insisted, and only those "who have some common sense as well as experience as statesmen, and who are honest patriots" should express an opinion.[5]

Abolitionists assured women that activism was both appropriate and their duty. They were certain to exert a wholesome influence on their brothers, fathers, and husbands "at the fireside" as well as on those "in the halls of legislation."[6] "We need *your* aid—your sanction—your interests and prayers—your wakeful concerns—your heart-beating sympathies—the encouragement of your unwavering faith" in the struggle "in behalf of perishing humanity," Ohio male abolitionists proclaimed.[7]

The abolitionists' argument for female activism knit together a fresh interpretation of the ideology of female domesticity and separate spheres with a conception of women's nature that rebutted conservative opinion by turning conventional assumptions about women upside down. In time, Sarah Grimké and others broke free from the constraints of familiar gender assumptions to lay the foundations of female abolitionism on the bedrock of human equality. Few, if any, foresaw where the abolitionists' argument about the role of women and the work of the pioneer female abolitionists would lead.

None denied that God had endowed women with a special measure of piety and benevolence, the abolitionists insisted. The advent of Christianity restored "woman to that moral and intellectual standing for which she was originally designed, when God pronounced her a help *meet* for man."[8] In the nineteenth century, the feminization of evangelical churches in which women constituted the great majority of born-again Christians underlined their peculiar moral and spiritual nature, as did their fund-raising for foreign and domestic missionaries, their Sunday school teaching, their pleas for the Native Americans, and countless other efforts of female religious benevolence. Few objected to these activities outside the home, abolitionists pointed out. Only a hypocritical, irrational double standard declared female benevolence on behalf of the slave off limits.[9] Silencing woman turns her into "a mere thing; an instrument to prepare the grain for the foul grinders of men to pulverize." A defiant female abolitionist refused to be "bound to conciliate the affections of any man" who crushed her moral impulses.[10] From this perspective, becoming an abolitionist was only fulfilling the nature of "true womanhood." "I have no hope of converting Catharine Beecher [to abolitionism]," explained Angelina Grimké, "because she does not have the heart of a woman."[11] Nor did Beecher ever become a born-again Christian.

By nature and religious obligation, women were especially sensitive to cruelty and injustice, according to abolitionist argument, and never more so than when the victims were families—mothers, husbands, and children. Slavery posed a dark threat to the sanctity and purity of home and family. Its sins against the family were its greatest sins. It broke up families, separating children from their parents and fathers from their wives, sons, and daughters. Even when families remained intact, slavery undermined a father's authority in the household. "Those who sell mothers separately from their children" claimed "a legal right to human flesh," like Shylock, "and they too cut it nearest to the *heart*," asserted Lydia Maria Child.[12] What was equally sinful, slavery led to the sexual exploitation of black women and the betrayal of white wives, also victims of the unlimited authority slavery gave white men.

Abolitionist propaganda focused keenly on the sins of slavery against the black family. It enabled women to fulfill what was supposed to be their natural, moral impulse to labor on behalf of the most needful, to defend domesticity and the family, and to rescue their Southern white sisters from betrayal and dishonor. George Bourne dedicated abolitionism's definitive exposé of slavery's effect on the family to "those sisters of philanthropy" working to liberate "the twelve hundred thousand Women, who are now chained in the American House of Bondage." In one hundred and twenty-seven pages, Bourne exposed a chamber of horrors, the most "melancholy facts in the annals of human depravity." False notions of delicacy and decorum long had shielded from exposure slavery's "social degeneracy," an "everflowing fountain of all uncleanness," Bourne wrote. The slave states were a vast brothel in which "multiform incest, polygamy, adultery and other uncleanness are constantly perpetrated." In the face of such horrors, the Lynn female abolitionists asked:

"When women's heart is bleeding,
Shall woman's heart be hushed?"[13]

Opponents of female abolitionism failed to understand that "the *primary duties and responsibilities of woman*" unavoidably brought her into the public arena and into one of "the great moral movements of the day." Slavery was not just a political issue, it was also a moral and religious issue, and as such lay well within the sphere of female benevolence. "The chief end of woman" no less than of man is to "glorify God," which compels her to become "active in furthering every moral enterprise." To restrict women to the home "is to sacrifice the *rational* to the *animal* part of woman" and to deny her the possibilities to fulfill "the *peculiar happiness* of intelligent beings." Woman was not meant to be a mere drudge, or "a *painted puppet or a gilded butterfly*," or "a mere *subservient* to the *purposes and pleasures* of man, or . . . the *passive recipient* of the *pleasures* of man." God intended "that woman should exert an immense control," which explains her "constitutional susceptibilities" for compassion and benevolence. In short, God made woman "the guardian angel of the world's hopes."[14]

Appeals to history buttressed the case for female activism. The examples of female leaders such as Miriam, Esther, and others in the Old Testament and of the women who attended Christ on the cross in the New Testament, as well as the heroism of women in ancient Greece and Rome, illustrated women's public activism in the distant past. More recently, patriotic women active in the American Revolution furnished further examples, boycotting British goods, substituting household manufactures, and running businesses, farms, and households while husbands and sons were away. As descendants of the Revolution's Daughters of Liberty, "the mothers and daughters of the land" had a duty to preserve "the heritage of freedom which our fathers purchased with their blood and which we had hoped to transmit unimpaired to our posterity." A woman had converted William Wilberforce to lead the antislavery forces in Britain, abolitionists argued. Another Englishwoman had discovered the principle of immediatism, and abolitionists claimed that Garrison's mother, living alone in Baltimore and grateful for care by a loving black nurse who attended her at the end of her life, had set in motion her son's conversion to racial equality and immediatism.[15] More recently, abolitionists pointed out, the mobilization of thousands of British women behind immediatism, converting men from gradualism, raising substantial sums of money, and gathering hundreds of thousands of signatures on petitions to Parliament, culminating in West

Indies emancipation in 1833, offered American women an example worthy of emulation.[16]

Abolitionists insisted that American women simply had no moral choice but to enlist in the antislavery crusade. As New York abolitionists argued, "the females of our country are especially responsible for the prevalence and continuance of the cord of caste, which is fearfully withering and destructive in its bearing on our colored brethren."[17] In the North, women's indifference, apathy, and silence gave legitimacy to the peculiar institution; in the South, white women acquired leisure and luxury from the labor of slaves, much to the ruin of their character. When plantation mistresses traveled in the free states, they spread their manners there, which Northern women imitated with "a fondness for show, ornament and extravagance, almost to the exclusion of a desire for the better wealth of substantial acquirements and moral excellence," an attitude that "invades all classes of society."[18] Abolitionists thus could blame slavery for the spread of consumerist display in the free states and link the opposition of one to the opposition of the other.

North and South, women had "joined themselves with the oppressors and it is by their supineness" that slavery had endured, the abolitionists argued. Slavery ministered "to their pride, to supply their luxuries, to provide for their comforts," and thus deeply engulfed them in the guilt of oppression.[19] There was surely something wrong with the education and rearing of women "when they prefer assembling themselves together for the gratification of display and vanity, or the uneasy excitements of fashion and gaiety, rather than for the noble purpose of alleviating the condition of helpless wretchedness."[20]

Still, many Northern women hesitated to violate the code that expected women to be meek, genteel, and deferential if they wished to be regarded as "ladies." Even a female abolitionist such as Julia Tappan, daughter of Lewis Tappan, felt torn: "On the one hand, we are in danger of servile submission to the opinion of the other sex, and on the other hand, in perhaps equal danger of losing that modesty and instinctive delicacy of feeling that our Creator has given us as a safeguard, to protect us from danger, to which on account of our weakness we are continually exposed."[21]

Because they were endowed with special sympathies for suffering, free women could not escape either their duty or their guilt, abolitionists argued, and must defend those enslaved women who could not defend themselves.[22] "We felt that we could no longer enjoy our comfortable homes, or rest in peace upon our pillows," claimed abolitionist women in Fall River, Massachusetts, "while we neglected our whole duty toward these sufferers." They could not forget that God had commanded that "inasmuch as ye have done it not unto one of the least of these, my brethren, ye have done it not to me."[23]

The argument for female abolitionism gave a radical twist to the ideology of separate spheres. Women are different from men, abolitionists insisted, because they are God's moral and spiritual elite, less scarred by ambition, selfishness, and political partisanship and more governed by disinterested benevolence. Their special role as exemplars of piety, compassion, and benevolence inevitably enlarged their sphere and sometimes required that they enter the public arena to protect other women, the family, and the home from lust and avarice. It was an error to assume that women could not combine "a meek and quiet spirit" with "an upright and enlightened intellect," a gentle heart that remained "open to the claims of humanity." Far from subverting women's separate sphere, women who took up the cause of abolition demonstrated female devotion to the home, argued Catharine Sullivan, vice president of the Boston Female Antislavery Society: "The more closely our hearts cling to our altars and our homes, the more fervent are our aspirations that every inhabitant of our land may be protected in his fireside enjoyments by just and equal laws."[24]

Like their male counterparts, only a small minority of American women accepted the argument for female abolitionism or sought its rewards. In Boston and Philadelphia, there were important contingents of black women, but the New York society discouraged them from joining the antislavery movement. The class status of abolitionists also varied considerably. In the greater Rochester area, the movement attracted both farm women from the surrounding small towns and the wives and daughters of city merchants and master mechanics. The New York society drew heavily on the wives of prosperous merchants and others aspiring to the middle class; the Boston society attracted a few elite women and many more middle-class and working women. Some forty-five worked for a living, as did the factory operatives in Lowell and Amesbury and the shoebinders in Lynn. Among factory operatives there was a cadre of strong, independent, undeferential women who valued wage labor for the independence it gave them and who were not afraid to strike or resist employers if they thought their treatment unfair.[25]

In Amesbury, Massachusetts, the Grimkés debated a man who argued that the slaves were better off than free Northern labor. A woman who had worked in the local mills for eleven years stood up to defend free labor from "base slander." Proudly, she proclaimed, "I speak as a free woman and not a slave; possessing the rights of a free-born citizen to think, to act, to speak for myself, my country and my God." And she never cringed "to obtain a day's labor." She called no man master and no one had the right to command her labor.[26]

Abolitionist women tended to come from the younger age groups. The average age of the Boston society was thirty-two, relatively high compared with Lynn and the Kent County, Rhode Island, society, where over 50 percent were under thirty and the Dover, New Hampshire, society, where over 40 percent were under thirty at the time of the group's founding. Younger women were more likely to have absorbed the transformations in female consciousness caused by social change, such as the advent of employment in mills and cities and the greater acceptability of delaying marriage or remaining single.[27]

Because the marital status of female society members or convention delegates is usually not given in the sources, precise information is not available, but fragmentary evidence suggests that single women were especially prominent, to some extent a result of the youthfulness of the group. In ten societies that reported the marital status of officers, single women constituted nearly 40 percent.[28] A majority of the officers of the Boston society were single,[29] while 55 percent of the membership of the Philadelphia society were not married in 1838.[30]

Women tended to join abolitionist societies together, as members of a group that shared similar affinities and provided support for an unpopular decision. The family was one of the most important sources of group support. In Lynn, certain family surnames stand out in the membership rolls, such as the ten Breed women, the twelve Newhalls, and the eight Buffums, families that also stood prominently in the male ranks. In all, eight surnames account for 27 percent of the entire Lynn female membership; in the Kent County society, thirteen family surnames that appear four times or more constituted 25 percent of the membership. Typically, men formed societies first and women followed. Only four of the nation's one hundred and twelve female societies by 1838 had preceded the male society in the same community. Nor was it very common for female societies to form in communities without male societies (16 percent of all societies). One wonders if the women in these communities acted in opposition to male opinion. Membership in the male societies tended to exceed that of the female societies. In only nineteen towns where there were male and female societies in 1838 was membership larger in the female than in the male society.[31]

Religion was the most important demographic variable in determin-
ing the sorts of women who became abolitionists, but here again, there
was a good deal of heterogeneity. Hicksite Quakers like Lucretia Mott
were numerous in the founding of the Philadelphia society and among
farm folk outside Rochester, though some Hicksites, like the orthodox
Quakers, were hostile. In Rochester, proper Baptists and Presbyterians
influenced by the Finneyite revival were prominent, as were the Finneyite
women in New York City. Antinomian Quakers stood out in Lynn,
together with Methodists; Baptists were prominent in Providence.
Congregationalists (56 percent) and Baptists (20 percent) were the most
numerous group in the Boston society, though there were also some
Liberals from the Unitarian camp. Nearly one-fifth of the Weymouth society belonged to the Congregationalist Union Church of Weymouth and
Braintree. But the denominations were deeply divided over abolitionism.

More important than denominational affiliation was the attitude
of the local minister. In Providence, the Baptist minister of the Pine
Street Church, Rev. John Blair, gave strong encouragement to men and
women to enlist in the cause, as did Rev. Jonas Perkins, licensed by the
Hopkinsian-Emmonsite Mendon Association to preach in Weymouth-
Braintree. In Rhode Island, Rev. Henry Tatem, one of the few abolitionist
clergy to sign the 1834 Phelps appeal, opened the Tatem meetinghouse
to the Kent County antislavery women. Often the leading officers of the
female societies were the wives of ministers and deacons, suggesting that
fractions of a church took the lead, with the minister's encouragement,
to form a society.[32]

A closer look at the Kent County Female Antislavery Society in
Rhode Island sheds further light. Founded in 1835, the society attracted
two hundred and fifty women inhabiting six towns, five in Kent and
one in Providence County, just across the county line. It was one of five
female societies in Rhode Island in 1838. In all, the five societies accounted for one-third of the total reported abolitionist membership.
When male abolitionists formed the Rhode Island Antislavery Society in
1836, the Kent women elected seven men as their delegates, but the
state society did not include any women among the eight hundred and
fifty who signed the call to hold a founding convention. The sexes still
remained apart.

For thirty-eight months, beginning in August 1835, the Kent County
women met on an average of once a month, rotating meetings among
schools and churches in the six villages, though the Phoenix and
Coventry village centers hosted more than half the meetings. Meetings

offered members a liberating experience in self-expression and self-government. At each of the first thirteen meetings, one member read the society's constitution, even when there were no new members to subscribe. Each reading reaffirmed the women's founding faith: "We believe that all men are created equal. . . . We believe that slavery . . . violates these sacred rights." The ritualistic reading of the constitution probably reflected the novelty of female participation in civic culture. For these Americans, reaffirming the words of the Declaration of Independence month after month must have been a bracing experience.

In March 1838, the society changed its name from the "Ladies" to the "Female" Antislavery Society. The members gave no explanation, but a rising tide of feminist consciousness and conservative reaction offers clues. The Grimkés had stormed the platforms, exhausting the patience and tolerance of many conservative Congregationalists, Baptists, and others who sought to stem the assault on patriarchy. "Female," a generic term for all kinds of women, was more inclusive than "ladies," a term laden with age and class connotations. From a conservative perspective, real "ladies" did not become abolitionists, intrude into the political sphere by circulating petitions to legislative bodies, speak in public, or participate in "promiscuous" meetings with men. The Kent society, however, was sympathetic to the feminist abolitionism of Maria Weston Chapman, Angelina Grimké, and Elizabeth M. Chandler, reading aloud their addresses at meetings. It also heard addresses that had been delivered to other female societies in Muskegon, Michigan, and Putnam, Ohio, and speeches by two of their own members. In October 1837, the society condemned the *Clerical Appeal* of the Massachusetts Congregationalist clergy, which sought to crush the movement begun by the Grimkés by closing the churches to female speakers and by reminding women of their subordinate sphere. The substitution of "females" for "ladies" may have been a protest against that narrow, conservative understanding of women's roles in judging who were "ladies."

Tracing the Kent women to the United States Census of 1850 has produced information for only twenty-six of the two hundred and fifty members, hardly a reliable sample. Most were under forty in 1835, with the largest group in their twenties. Judging their social status by the households to which they belonged in 1850—the real wealth and occupations of fathers and husbands—most came from humble circumstances. Four were related to farmers, eleven to manual workers, and only three possessed real estate, all in modest amounts. Such fragmentary data may be unreliable, however.

More suggestive are religious and kinship networks. Clusters of surnames suggest that membership spread along familial networks, as we have seen. Nine Sisson women and seven Cranstons joined six Gardiners, Greenes, and Anthonys. Together with other surname clusters of four or more, they accounted for just over one-third of all Kent female abolitionists. Though many related men and women joined their respective societies, there were no male counterparts in seven of the nineteen female surname clusters, hinting at independent female decision-making.

Church membership was another source of clustering. In Phoenix village in Warwick, the society usually met at the Tatem meetinghouse. Eight of the church's ten incorporators in 1833 signed the call for founding the state society, including Cyrus Babcock, chosen by the Kent women to represent them at the founding. Elder Henry Tatem was an iconoclastic preacher, one of three in Rhode Island who signed the Amos Phelps appeal in 1834. He was an independent, tied to no denomination, an outspoken Antimason, and an ally of a fellow abolitionist and Antimason, Rev. Ray Potter of Pawtucket. The Bethel Six-Principle Baptist Church, a branch of the large Maple Root Baptist Church in Coventry, contributed at least six men and nine women to the local antislavery societies. In addition, Regular Baptist preachers in Warwick and Coventry were abolitionists, and some of their female members may have joined the society, as did Quaker women such as Susan Sisson, one of the nine Sisson women who joined.

What united women as diverse as those in Kent, Weymouth, Dover, and Lynn, women who came from mainline and fringe, from nonevangelical denominations as well as evangelical (although the evangelicals were by far the more numerous), was a nonsectarian piety at odds with the worldliness they found in the great body of Christians. Like the male abolitionists, the female abolitionists defined themselves in opposition to those whose lives and behavior stood in sharp conflict with applied or social Christianity. The active pursuit of the clear dictates of Scripture and conscience, not ritual or theology, abolitionists believed, was the true measure of a person's commitment to gospel teaching.

Once female antislavery societies had been formed, the work awaiting them usually exceeded their resources. Dues alone (Lynn charged eight cents per month) could not fund the many activities these societies undertook: hiring agents to proselytize other women, bringing speakers to town, subscribing to abolitionist newspapers, purchasing propaganda for an antislavery library, and assisting in the work of educating African Americans. To increase their funds, societies voted for voluntary sub-

scriptions for designated purposes, and women knit and sewed to produce items for annual fairs, such as those in Boston and Philadelphia,
which raised substantial sums that helped to support the state society.

At first, meetings of the Dover women's society were infrequent and
attendance sparse. When the members turned themselves into a sewing
circle, however, they had an energizing activity with specific goals, such
as making clothing for poor African Americans attending Oneida
Institute. The social spirit of this aspect of antislavery society activity is
suggested by the decision of Dover to admit men as honorary members of
the "Sewing Circle." In 1844, Weymouth voted to unite with the "Sewing
Corall." The Weymouth society, after dispatching its business, devoted
the rest of the afternoon to making handicrafts for the Christmas Fair in
Boston. That fair became a big moneymaker, thanks to the enterprise of
Maria Weston Chapman, the strikingly handsome and forceful wife of a
rich Boston merchant. She was familiar with the latest fashions and able
to obtain unusual items from European suppliers before Bostonians could
purchase them from retailers. When the Boston society split and the less
affluent and sophisticated Congregationalist women tried their hand at a
fair, they could not match the success of Weston's Garrisonian faction, led
by Chapman. Many who came to Chapman's fairs had no sympathy for
abolitionism, but wished to enjoy the beautiful decorations and purchase
the unusual Christmas presents, which were available nowhere else.
Chapman's mastery and exploitation of consumerist display stood in
sharp conflict with the attacks by Garrison, Goodell, and other abolitionist leaders, especially the clergy, on fashion, frivolity, and consumerist
excess, though the prophets of asceticism welcomed the funds.

Women also solicited contributions from sympathizers in their communities and in their churches. The Weymouth society, driven by ambitious activities, doubled its dues, assessed members who did not con-
tribute items to the antislavery fair, and appointed a seven-person
committee to go after delinquents.

The Kent women met an average of nine to ten times a year between
1835 and 1838, in contrast to the Dover society, which met an average
of five to six times a year between 1834 and 1846, and in contrast to
Weymouth, which met an average of three to four times a year between
1835 and 1846. The first ten meetings of the Lynn society in 1837
attracted an average of twenty-one members, only a small fraction of the
total. There are no attendance data for the other three societies.

The women's societies held meetings in churches, vestries, schools,
and homes. The frequent use of residences suggests low turnouts.

Inviting outside speakers sparked interest, but they were sometimes difficult to obtain, and meetings substituted reading antislavery pamphlets aloud. In the larger cities, abolitionist women patronized "free produce" stores that offered alternatives to slave-grown cotton and sugar, but the substitutes usually were of inferior quality, and abolitionists disagreed over the value or practicality of boycotting the fruits of slave labor. Between 1816 and 1862, fifty-three free produce stores catered to people of conscience, especially among the Quakers.[33] For those who lived in small towns or in the country, free produce was simply not available. The free produce movement built on female abolitionists' roles as homemakers and shoppers.

Societies typically subscribed to antislavery publications. Weymouth regularly appointed distributors to circulate the *Liberator,* the *Herald of Freedom,* and the *Antislavery Standard* in their neighborhoods to promote maximum access. Meetings usually opened with prayer and Bible reading, and the Weymouth women closed theirs with songs such as Garrison's "I Am an Abolitionist."

Among all the activities engaged in by female abolitionists, none required more energy and commitment or elicited more criticism than the circulation of antislavery petitions. From the beginning, the abolitionist movement had encouraged petitions to Congress, but not until the mid-1830s did petitioning become a mass movement. The growth of abolitionist organization and membership made that possible, while incendiary issues such as Texas annexation and the admission of new slave states opened new battlegrounds. The abolition of slavery in the District of Columbia gave Northerners a constitutional and practical means of containing slavery's expansion, which became more salient as Southern resistance to moral suasion became impenetrable. The recruitment of women into societies also gave the movement a valuable new resource for gathering signatures, since many women, especially single women, had more time than men to canvass systematically. Abolitionist newspapers printed samples of petitions to Congress and the state legislatures on various subjects and gave directions for their distribution and return.[34] In 1837, Ohio abolitionists, who had sent thirty thousand signatures the previous year, vowed to gather ten times that number. They vowed that there was "not a spot in the state, where a human being dwells, that should not be traversed in search of signers."[35]

Female antislavery societies took petitioning work seriously and appointed committees with responsibility to cover each section of the town or county. The results were spectacular. Hundreds of thousands of

Americans signed petitions, most of them not abolitionists. Women accounted for about 70 percent of the signers in the latter half of the 1830s, according to some analysts, but they accounted for 59 percent of the signers of the 1837 petitions for abolishing slavery in the District of Columbia.[36]

The gag resolution first adopted in 1835 by the House of Representatives to prevent debate on antislavery petitions stimulated renewed activity and helped to trigger the calling of the first national women's antislavery convention in 1837 to encourage the continued mobilization of societies for gathering signatures on fresh petitions. The data in table 6 suggest that female societies were largely responsible for the majority of female signatures. Vermont, which had few female societies, produced few female signers; Massachusetts, which had many female societies, produced over twenty thousand female signers, more than double the number of male signers. The absence of any male signers from Rhode Island in the face of over thirty-two hundred female signers suggests that the women, unlike the men, conducted the campaign and sought support only among females.

TABLE 6   SIGNERS BY GENDER,
1837 PETITION TO ABOLISH SLAVERY
IN THE DISTRICT OF COLUMBIA

	Towns/ Counties	Males	Towns/ Counties	Females	Females %Total
Maine	6	472	4	1340	74
New Hampshire	19	1806	37	3510	66
Vermont	21	4143	12	1945	32
Massachusetts	60	9157	108	21214	70
Rhode Island	—	0	—	3253	100
Connecticut	13	1456	3	173	11
New York	67	10227	29	6805	40
New Jersey	3	855	0	0	0
Pennsylvania	21	3863	6	4966	56
Ohio	42	10780	16	19786	64
Michigan	2	782	0	0	0
Indiana	4	199	1	78	28
Illinois	1	121	0	0	0
Tennessee	—	107	—	108	50
Total	259	43968	176	3178	59

SOURCE: *Emancipator,* 20 April 1837. The geographic units from which data were reported are not comparable because in New England the reports are from towns and cities, whereas in Ohio and New York, for example, the reports come from cities, towns, and counties. Omitted are reports from a small number of "male and female" categories not broken down by gender.

Female canvassers who traveled from door to door seeking signers had reason to hope for positive responses, since they presented themselves as engaged in religious and benevolent work, not as political activists. Petitions were addressed to "fathers and rulers," professing outward deference to male authority while implicitly asserting citizenship rights for females. Citizens who might not respond to a male canvasser were more likely at least to listen to a female. Canvassers did not ask citizens to endorse abolitionism outright, but presented petitions that had much broader popular appeal, such as the abolition of slavery in the nation's capital or opposition to the annexation of Texas. Often they engaged in discussions to persuade people to sign, which meant that canvassers had to be prepared with data and arguments to make a strong case. In Fall River, Massachusetts, canvassers collected six hundred and thirty signatures, from both men and women, and left copies of antislavery publications at every house.

Whether people signed or not, canvassing was a way to bring the slavery question to the doorstep of that great mass that preferred to evade the issue. As Abby Kelley put it, "many who would not otherwise think at all about it [slavery] are induced to give it a little place in their minds, and some are brought to embrace Abolition principles."[37] Canvassing, however, was not without its risks, according to Maria Weston Chapman: "Young women, whose labors depended on public opinion, laid the claims of the enslaved to freedom before those whose simple word might grant or deny their own means of subsistence."[38]

Canvassers encountered predictable resistance. Elderly men reminded them that they were transgressing their appropriate sphere. A young woman accused them of advocating amalgamation. Another wanted nothing to do with any paper of any kind, while her husband shouted from an easy chair in the parlor that "they were opposed to ladies doing delicate business." Still another, who had signed the previous year, now refused because it was degrading and not ladylike. Men sometimes spoke for the women in the household, not allowing them to decide for themselves. A "Mrs. X" knew and cared nothing about slavery, never wanted to, and thought that slavery never harmed her.[39] Acknowledging that circulating petitions was "weary work," the Third Antislavery Convention of American Women (1839) urged persistence in spite of "how painful it is to endure the scornful gaze, or rude repulses of strangers."[40]

In Congress, Southern hostility to female petitioning was fierce. Virginia's John Tyler warned that "woman is to be made the instrument of destroying our political paradise. . . . She is to be converted into a fiend."[41] "On what other occasion, on what other great question, have females thought it their imperious duty to step forth as the asserters and champions of the great right of petition?" asked an enraged congressman from Virginia in 1837.[42]

The *New York Sunday Morning News* denounced Northern female petitioners for making war against the women of the South and denounced New England men for hiding behind the petticoats of women, who on their own would not participate in such disgraceful, abominable activity. Abolitionist women were, in fact, more dangerous than men, the newspaper claimed. They were slaves to fanatic ministers and religious leaders, yet as females they aroused less suspicion and hostility, and consequently "the excitement may be spread with as little opposition as possible."[43]

Abolitionists, abetted by Congressman John Quincy Adams, defended the right of women to petition. New York City women, denying that they were stepping beyond their sphere, said they never would petition on political and economic issues, but only on religious and benevolent grounds. Slavery disrupted the family, "the primeval institution," and exposed the nation to God's judgment.[44] Pointing to the immense petition campaign by women in Great Britain, abolitionists argued that even monarchical governments welcomed female petitions. America was a republic with white male suffrage, but women had no electoral voice. All that was left was the petition. "The right of petition is the only political right women have," they pointed out. An abolitionist woman renounced "glittering baubles" in order to claim "her high prerogatives as a moral, intellectual, an accountable being," argued Angelina Grimké.[45]

Ohio's female abolitionists issued a stirring defense of the right to petition against slavery in the District of Columbia in an address to the women of the state. Those who would deny their right to petition in defense of black women "subject to the most cruel and humiliating bondage" would narrow the sphere of female action and return to the Dark Ages. God held women no less accountable than men for the sins of slavery. "We should be less than women, if the nameless wrongs of which the slaves, of our sex, are made defenseless victims" did not elicit our protests, they declared. By petitioning, women "shall at least clear our skirts of the blood of souls." Moreover, women, who acted "untrammeled by party politics, unbiased by the love of gain," countervailed men's selfishness and opened "afresh the fountains of human sympathy and lofty patriotism."[46]

Against these defenses of female activism, conservative opinion stood obdurate. Despite her support of the petition campaign against the removal of the Cherokees a decade earlier, Catharine Beecher now instructed women that they could join abolitionist societies or sign antislavery petitions only at risk of violating the woman's sphere and sacrificing their Christian natures. The petitions from females only would "exasperate" those who deemed them "obtrusive, indecorous, and unwise" and would thereby increase the evil of slavery. Signing a petition was just "the opening wedge" to involve women in "every political measure." Beecher was certain that the right to petition Congress "IN ALL CASES" fell "entirely without the sphere of female duty," because men alone were "the proper persons to make appeals to the ruler whom they appoint."[47]

Thousands of women ignored such warnings. They became active in abolitionist societies, and tens of thousands signed the petitions female activists circulated to advance the struggle for emancipation. That struggle faced its toughest test as Americans wrestled with the future of those African Americans already freed, living mostly in the North and battling prejudice there. In that struggle, abolitionist women pledged to "continue to act in accordance with our profession that the moral and intellectual character of persons, and not their complexion, should mark the sphere in which they are to move." Such a pledge required increased "efforts to improve the condition of our free colored population, by giving them mechanical, literary, and religious instruction, and assisting to establish them in trades, and such other employments as are now denied them on account of color." As with slavery in the South, so with racial bias in the North did women possess the power "to roll back this tide of cruel prejudice."[48]

PART 5

Of One Blood

A black preacher from New York City rose at the 1837 annual meeting of the New York State Antislavery Society to sound the alarm against white abolitionist neglect of the struggle for racial equality for free blacks. Recounting the key role African Americans had played in converting Garrison, Tappan, Jocelyn, and others from colonization to immediatism, Rev. Theodore S. Wright reminded the convention that combating racial prejudice and elevating free blacks to civic equality—affirming the possibility of an egalitarian, biracial republic—once had seemed a moral and logical imperative if immediatism was to replace colonization. Colonization now stood discredited, while abolitionism attracted tens of thousands of members into hundreds of societies scattered across the free states.

That influx, Wright warned, was precisely the danger: many among the mass now flooding the movement did not share the founders' commitment to racial equality. Wright sketched the discrimination free blacks in the North faced in virtually every facet of life, from childhood to death. Three years ago, he said, to be an abolitionist was to oppose racial prejudice. Too often it now meant only hostility to slavery and an enthusiasm for free speech, the right of petition, and keeping Texas out of the Union. It was easy to hate slavery, but hard to treat black people as equals. That was why the constitutions of many recent antislavery societies, unlike earlier ones, failed to make the advancement of racial equality a central aim of the organization. Wright, therefore, proposed interrogating each new member to ascertain "whether he looks upon man as man, all of one blood and one family" and teaching recruits that "the giant sin of prejudice" was "at once the parent and offspring of slavery." Unless prejudice was destroyed, slavery never could be abolished. If the North treated free blacks as pariahs, the slave states would be confirmed in holding their blacks in chains.

Then Wright softened his criticism. The abolitionist movement, he acknowledged, was "the first institution which has combined its energies for the overthrow of this heaven-daring, this soul-crushing prejudice." Still, he could not forget that even the most pious, such as the Quakers, the first to take up the cross of emancipation, discriminated against free African Americans. Immediate abolition was not enough, Wright insisted: "Let every man take his stand, burn out this prejudice, live it down, talk it down, everywhere consider the colored man as a man, in the church, the stage, the steamboat, the public house, in all places and the death blow to slavery will be struck."[1]

White abolitionists in the movement's first decade wrestled with racial prejudice as no earlier generation had and as few subsequent generations of Americans would. They faced formidable odds, however, and achieved only limited success. But they began the complicated, tortuous process of building a society committed to racial justice in an age when people seriously questioned the humanity of colored people, when intensifying racial conflict periodically unleashed white mobs against free blacks in the Northern cities, and when pervasive discrimination in schools, churches, housing, theaters, museums, and public transportation debased colored people, no matter how respectable. The intensification of racial conflict was to a considerable degree a response to the advances made by African Americans in the North, which inspired rising expectations among blacks and rising anxieties among whites. It was also a response to the unprecedented challenges white abolitionists launched against white supremacist ideas, behavior, customs, and laws.

The American Peculiarity

American abolitionists and perceptive European travelers in the United States agreed that racial prejudice was more intense and pervasive in the United States than anywhere else in the world. "Travellers have told us that in England (and so throughout Europe)," Garrison reported in 1834, "the malignant prejudices which reign in this country against persons of colored or black complexion, do not exist; or, if cherished at all, they are scarcely perceptible and practically inert." Judging people not by their "worth and claims" as "human beings," but by the "tinge of their skin," Garrison insisted, was "the American peculiarity." At the 1821 New York State Constitutional Convention, which eliminated the property qualification for whites while disenfranchising all but propertied blacks, Chancellor James Kent, in opposition, noted that "the distinction of color is unknown in Europe."[1] Simeon Jocelyn echoed Garrison and Kent: "the prejudice peculiar to our country . . . subjects our colored citizens to degrading distinction."[2]

The English traveler Edward Abdy agreed: the American people were equal to other nations in their love of justice, religion, and kindness, yet they condemned one-fifth of their people to contempt and debasement only because of their skin color, "to the shame of human nature." Though the United States was the world's leading egalitarian republic, "the history of no age and no country exhibits more preposterous contradictions to the spirit of the times, the advancement of intelligence, and the spread of Christianity." In Britain, Abdy claimed, "a sable complexion is a passport, almost everywhere, to kindness and liberality," whereas in the United States, treating blacks decently or breaching "the inexorable *tabu*" of "despotic custom" threatened whites with "losing caste."[3]

Combating prejudice in such a country was all the more difficult because few would admit to it. That made it more insidious, Abdy pointed out, because people "do not perhaps even suspect its existence in their own minds."[4] The prejudiced did not regard their views of blacks as prejudice, but as a rational, unavoidable inference from firsthand observations, backed by the teachings of Scripture and history. And though this view of Africans conflicted with the Christian doctrine that God had created a single human race "of one blood" and was contradicted by the scientific argument that dark skins are not linked to character or intelligence, universalistic views never dominated public opinion. In time, popular, informal, pervasive, unthinking prejudice drew fresh support from scriptural interpretation. After 1840, the emergence of an American school of "scientific" racism rejected the environmentalist presuppositions of Enlightenment natural science, which had confirmed Enlightenment belief that all races are human and all men created equal. Racial prejudice, however, depended on no argument from Scripture or science, because it flowed from "the secret feeling of the heart, which blinds the mind, and blunts the moral perception."[5] Historians err in inferring that before 1830, because few challenged the views of high culture—the Enlightenment and Christian doctrines that people of all colors belong to a common species of equal capacity—public opinion accepted that doctrine. The public and private treatment of blacks reveals attitudes about color that belie the universalism of high culture. Even such a striking devotee of Enlightenment beliefs and the ethics of Christianity as Thomas Jefferson questioned racial equality because it conflicted with observation, interest, prejudice, and conscience.

Because there were no serious challenges to slavery in the South or to racial prejudice against free blacks in the North before 1830, the question of racial equality lacked the salience it acquired after abolitionism's assault. An abolitionist leader combating prejudice in his own ranks recognized that "the single object of all our meetings and societies" was "to impress upon the community this one principle, that *the colored man is a* MAN." One of the most ubiquitous abolitionist slogans, engraved on disks and in print, affirmatively asserted, "Am I not a Man & Brother?" Yet, privately, if not publicly, large numbers questioned the claim of blacks as members of humanity and believed their views "natural." For some whites, blacks were not just mentally and morally inferior, but aesthetically loathsome, more akin to monkeys, baboons, or orangutans than to human beings, which explained white tolerance for the debasing treatment of free and enslaved African Americans in both the North and the South.[6]

"A Nigger is a Nigger, and will be a Nigger, do what you will for him." This was the common view, reported Arnold Buffum from his earliest forays as an antislavery itinerant.[7] Anecdotes captured the extent to which whites went to dissociate themselves from blacks. An African American bought a pew in a Randolph, Massachusetts, church only to find it locked on Sunday. Next time the seats had been removed, and subsequently the floor torn up. The pewholder gave up. Similar incidents elsewhere confined blacks to obscure corners or galleries, unseen.[8] A black youth risked his life to save two white boys from drowning, but none of the whites standing around went to the aid of the black child when he went under. For months afterward, none of the relatives consoled or thanked the grieving mother.[9] A cultured, well-dressed New York City African American, Thomas van Rensselaer, took his family in a carriage to the New York Zoological Institute, but their skin color barred entry. Any black servant attending whites or a white gambler or prostitute could enter, but independent blacks, Henry C. Wright, exploded, were treated like dogs.[10] In Worcester, Massachusetts, passengers on a stage coach objected to admission of a genteel, well-dressed African-American woman. "I don't like the perfume," one complained. In another community, blacks were not allowed to take water from the communal well, yet some whites still insisted "that there is no prejudice existing against the colored man."[11] Abolitionists denounced racial prejudice as "absurd," "pitiful," "silly," unmanly, cruel, and sinful, but more than indignation, their epithets suggest frustration in combating a widespread popular belief that was so deep-seated it even infected their own ranks.

In the early 1830s, at the moment that immediatism was emerging, three Europeans visited the United States to examine the young republic's prison system. Each found the system of race relations an even more compelling subject, one deserving description and explanation for a European public mystified by the racial obsessions of the world's leading republican country. It was difficult for Europeans to comprehend "the insurmountable gap" between whites and blacks in the United States, Alexis de Tocqueville observed. He ominously concluded in *Democracy in America* that "the most formidable evil threatening the future of the United States is the presence of blacks on their soil." Even if Americans found a way to end slavery (and de Tocqueville regarded

African colonization as a mirage), prejudice would remain to fuel racial war: "You may make the Negro free, but you cannot prevent him from facing the European as a stranger." Slavery irremediably had debased its victims, and consequently "this stranger brought by slavery into our midst, is hardly recognized as sharing the common features of humanity." To Americans, "his face appears hideous, his intelligence limited, his tastes low." He seemed like "some being intermediate between beast and man." Echoing Jefferson, de Tocqueville predicted, "I do not think that the white and black races will ever be brought anywhere to live on a footing of equality." Only if African Americans changed radically, adopting the culture and mores of the dominant race, might they persuade whites to abandon prejudice, but prejudice itself made such a transformation impossible.[12]

De Tocqueville's traveling companion, Gustave de Beaumont, reached equally gloomy conclusions. In a novel that he claimed to be true to life, Beaumont explored the irrationality and tragic consequences of color prejudice. The first theatrical event he attended in the United States astonished him and persuaded him not to duplicate his friend's study of American institutions, but to focus on its racial mores. In the theater, whites occupied the first balcony, mulattoes the second, and blacks the third. As an American explained, "the dignity of white blood demanded these classifications." Among the mulattoes he observed a beautiful woman who was virtually white, but stamped as of mixed blood. Among the whites, Beaumont noticed a dark-skinned woman, regarded as "white" by local tradition, owing to her Spanish origins. This color code illustrated Beaumont's central theme: color prejudice persisted after slavery's demise because bondage permanently degraded those with the merest tincture of African blood, even those whiter than many whites.

In Beaumont's novel, *Marie, or Slavery in the United States* (1835, in France), Ludovic, a French liberal disillusioned by the triumph of reaction in his homeland, takes refuge in America, a "society which is new yet civilized" and of "virgin nature."[13] He visits a friend in Baltimore and falls in love with his beautiful daughter, Marie, an exemplar of goodness, piety, and benevolence who works in the city's almshouse, where "she knows the secret of healing the wounds of the spirit" and where "her name is blessed" (43). Only Marie is able to subdue a mad African American inmate. "Never, since I had been in America," Ludovic asserts, "had I seen a white person take pity on a Negro." Whites regarded black people as "not worthy of commiserations, deserving nothing but contempt" (46).

Marie's father, Daniel Nelson, son of a Boston trader, refuses to sanction their union because Marie has mixed blood, and color prejudice is certain to doom a mixed marriage. The Nelson family had fled from New Orleans, where Marie and her brother George had passed as "pure" white until Marie refused to become the mistress of a wealthy Spaniard, Don Fernando d'Almanza, who made public her mixed ancestry. Though Marie is dazzling white in appearance, she thus becomes a black person, and Nelson loses his friends, his credit, his social position, and his wife, who dies (54–55). The inflexibility of racial prejudice, Nelson explains, is essential "to the very dignity of the American people." Confronted with two different races, Negroes and Indians, Americans have mixed with neither and kept the blood pure. "To prevent all contact with these races they must stigmatise them in public opinion," and "the stigma remains even after color disappeared" (63). Marie, too, pleads with Ludovic to desist, but he refuses to bow to American prejudice.

Nelson challenges Ludovic to travel through the country for six months to observe racial mores, especially the treatment of free blacks, and if he still wishes to marry Marie, the father will give his consent (68). In New York City, Ludovic finds that free blacks suffer disgrace "perhaps worse than slavery." There, "all people of color [are] branded by public contempt, overwhelmed with abuse, more degraded by shame than by misery" (70). Everywhere in the free states, Ludovic finds, a black is free in name only. In reality, "he has no place in human society" (72). George Nelson, Marie's mulatto brother, joins Ludovic in New York, and they go to the theater, where the relentless persecutor, Fernando d'Almanza, exposes George, warning that there is a mulatto sitting among the white patrons (87–88). Returning to Baltimore, George and his father attempt to vote, and again d'Almanza exposes the mulatto, whose single ballot had determined the election (108).

Having learned firsthand the depths of white prejudice, Ludovic still persists, and Marie's father relents. The marriage arouses the mob, which takes it as an insult against "the dignity of whites" (124). The rioters level black homes and churches while the couple flees. Together with Marie's father, they take refuge in the Michigan wilderness, where "we may behold man in his primitive dignity" (213). There, Marie sinks toward death. In an apocalyptic ending, George goes south to join an uprising of slaves and Indians that proves abortive. He kills d'Almanza, but loses his own life. After witnessing this succession of melodramatic events, Ludovic concludes that his chief error "was my belief that man is greater than he is" (184).

240 Of One Blood

In crafting a story of racial tragedy, Beaumont exposed the irrationality of color prejudice. The content of Marie's character counts for nothing. Only her "color" matters, though none would have suspected she was anything but "white" were it not for a crazed, relentless persecutor bent on sexual plunder. In the United States, Beaumont showed, there was no escape from racial prejudice.

The English traveler Edward Abdy arrived in the United States in 1833 and wrote a three-volume travel memoir that reported in great detail the consequences of white prejudice toward free blacks. From city directories and asylums to potters fields and churches, in employment and on stage coaches, African Americans were set apart. Whites heaped such insult on these unoffending "creatures . . . as would not be credited in England or in any part of Europe," Abdy reported. A young driver on a carriage headed for Albany told Abdy that while the Irish laborers were "an ugly set of people . . . there are no people I hate so much as the *niggers*—I always drive over 'em, when they get in my way." When Abdy protested that they were the same as other human beings, the driver responded: "So they are, to be sure:—I don't know why I hate em:—but I do hate em." Abdy repeatedly was astonished by the inability of whites to understand or acknowledge that characteristics they saw as inherent and attributed to the color of African Americans were largely the result of formidable barriers that undermined black self-esteem and blocked black self-improvement. There were hardly any black mechanics in Boston or other cities because white mechanics would not allow them to learn the trade and would not work side by side with blacks who had acquired skills. Discrimination, not laziness and shiftlessness, kept blacks mired in the poorest-paying occupations or without work. American racial prejudice, Abdy concluded, was "a psychological anomaly that I could not comprehend." The white American's mind, he judged, had been so degraded by racial prejudice that "he can never be respected for moral excellence."[14]

Americans were as "clear-headed and acute as other people" on all "common subjects," but when it came to the subject of race, even the "the best educated man amongst them will utter more nonsense among them in a given time than the most unlettered clown in the three kingdoms."[15] Abdy's prime example was Rev. William Ellery Channing, the nation's leading Unitarian minister, pastor of a Boston church that attracted members from among the metropolis's business and professional elites. Channing was widely admired as a saintly and powerful preacher, the foremost exponent of rational Christianity in the United States, and the man who was rescuing the country from the "brutal superstition" and irrationality of Calvinism.[16] Channing kept aloof from the controversy swirling around abolitionism in the early 1830s, recognizing that race and slavery were contentious and divisive issues capable of breaking up united churches. Channing also knew that abolition was not an issue the "gentlemen of property and standing" in his own congregation wanted him to press. Still, his personal opposition to slavery as a violation of Christian teaching strained his silence, and finally, in 1835, as antislavery sentiment and organization mounted and mobs threatened free speech and public order, Channing realized that to remain silent risked his claims to moral leadership. He spoke out in an eloquent pamphlet that denounced slavery and virtually endorsed immediatism, but Channing kept his distance from the organized antislavery movement. Among his objections were that it accepted black members and fought for racial equality. When Abdy met Channing, the Englishman probably was unaware of the minister's ambivalent position and expected to find the Unitarian eminence sympathetic to his own views. The confrontation that ensued is a high point in Abdy's journal.

Abdy began by inquiring of Channing his view of such common customs as the refusal by whites to eat at the same table with blacks. Channing defended the practice, arguing that it was no different from masters remaining apart from servants, or feudal lords from serfs. Abdy protested that Channing missed the point: discrimination fell on all blacks, no matter how educated, refined, and accomplished. Moreover, not even the serf was a victim of contempt and insult wherever he went.[17] Channing replied that there were other prejudices that deserved redress besides color prejudice and wished that abolitionists devoted more attention to the condition of the white poor (3:219).

While disavowing color prejudice, Channing revealed little sympathy for free African Americans. All the black people he had observed "were men of indifferent character." He thought them remarkable for want of sympathy with each other's misfortunes. According to the evidence of a correspondent in Philadelphia, "the generality of those of African descent in that city, were degraded to the lowest state" (3:219). Abdy insisted that one man's observation was hardly a reliable basis for generalization. His own observations of African Americans contradicted Channing's Philadelphia authority. On the defensive, Channing resorted to the classic defense of prejudice, personal example ("some of my best friends are . . . ") as evidenced by his intervention with a stage driver who refused to take a black passenger. He declared himself willing to eat with blacks, although his own black and white servants ate apart. Abdy recalled that after Channing read Lydia Maria Child's *Appeal in Favor of that Class of Americans Called Africans,* Channing told Child that he agreed with her about slavery, but not about racial equality. It would lead to racial mixture, a result he abhorred just as much as his rival, Boston's leading evangelical preacher, Lyman Beecher: "Would you have us sully the pure blood we have received from our English ancestors, by such alliances as a closer intimacy with the other race would produce?" Beecher asked, expressing a common point of view (3:221).

Channing affirmed Christian orthodoxy: "We undoubtedly feel our-selves to be all of one race; and this is well: we trace ourselves up to one pair, and feel the same blood flowing in our veins" (3:221 n). Yet at the same time he believed that phrenology had proved that blacks have smaller brains and more limited intellects than whites. Abdy reminded him that the issue was color, not brain size, pointing out that "no one's reception in general society depended on the quantity or the quality of his brain" (3:222).

Channing then shifted ground, admitting that color prejudice was widespread, but insisting that only the uneducated harbored it. Abdy was too polite to contradict, but cited instead the color bias one found in sermons, speeches, and literary productions in the United States, hardly the work of the uneducated (3:222). The lofty *North American Review,* the country's leading arbiter of high culture, insisted that cli-mate is destiny: isothermal lines, it declared, determine skin color, and skin color determines human potential.[18] Abdy acknowledged that prej-udice was common among the lower classes, but he insisted that it "was encouraged by the similar prejudice of the wealthy" (3:231). Finally, Channing blamed color prejudice on slavery, which debased Africans and caused prejudice against them. Abdy would not relent: Native Americans, rarely enslaved, he argued, still suffered from the color prej-udice that dogged African Americans. Prejudice was wrong, the clergy-man acknowledged, but only time and self-improvement by blacks could reduce it. But prejudice, Abdy countered, stood in the way of education and good jobs, matters about which Channing professed ignorance.

Further discussion was fruitless. Abdy concluded that "Channing as-sumed that the blacks were inferior," always referring to them "as ser-vants whose proper place was in the kitchen." If prejudice was irreme-diable, as many contended, it was because "truth and reason have no influence on the rational mind," not even on that of the illustrious Channing, who twisted and turned every which way to justify racial bias

(3:231). Abdy concluded that Channing's attempts to blame the victim and "to find in the extent and intensity of a prejudice a reason for its continuance" were the most striking and discouraging outcomes of the interview (3:233).

Realizing that he had strained Channing's patience, which he detected from the minister's cold and reserved manner, Abdy apologized for his combativeness and withdrew. Abdy's friends, who read this account in manuscript, advised against publishing it because it might hurt the abolitionist cause by annoying Channing's many friends and admirers, especially Unitarians. Abdy decided otherwise. He believed Channing was representative. Abdy doubted that a single distinguished American man of letters "was willing to sacrifice the paltry ambition of the hour to principle" or was able to "rise above the infected atmosphere around him" (3:237–38).

In seeking to explain "the American peculiarity," these visiting analysts of American racial prejudice identified characteristics distinctive to American society. The absence of racial slavery in Europe went far to explain why Europeans did not associate blacks to the same degree with the debasements of bondage, especially after they became free. Because those Europeans who held slaves were colonizers in the New World, few Old World Europeans shared the burden of guilt that in the United States afflicted some conscientious Christian slaveholders and Northerners bent on preserving sectional peace. In addition, the small numbers of blacks in Europe meant there was no competition for jobs and made tolerance and acceptance unthreatening to white dominance. The African Americans who were lionized in Britain were often formally educated or self-educated and gifted members of their race, belying racial stereotypes.

De Tocqueville, Beaumont, and Abdy saw American racial prejudice as a cultural norm that transcended class differences. De Tocqueville generalized and made no distinctions among social strata in his analysis. Beaumont noted that while workingmen formed the destructive mob in Baltimore, they were encouraged by the middle and upper classes. Abdy was the most keenly aware of the variety of views on race among different classes and was careful to report exceptions to the widespread prejudice among elements of the working and middle classes.

Abdy had visited Rev. Peter Williams, a black Episcopal minister in New York City, who reported that prejudice was less prevalent in rural districts than in cities "and stronger among the wealthy than the less fortunate portion of the society." Abdy agreed from his own observations and added that prejudice was "more bitter in women than in men—in the clergy than in the laity—in the North than in the South." Abdy also reported less bias among farmers, who not only were more ready to employ blacks, perhaps because of labor shortages, but also more apt to eat at the same table with them. And he found some laboring men in rural areas surprisingly in favor of racial equality and opposed to ill treatment of free blacks. Abdy speculated that when it came to racial prejudice, the humble tillers of the soil and rural workmen possessed "more real dignity of character than the purse-proud merchant, or the flippant shopboy from whom the small vulgar borrow opinions and habits." The Irish were everywhere the most prejudiced. Everywhere, amid competition for scarce jobs, a belief that blacks drove down wages and supplied scabs to break strikes gave white workers grievances against freedmen. Commenting acerbically on the cross-class character of racial prejudice, Abdy concluded: "I may just observe that the same people cannot well be burthen to the rich by their idleness, and nuisance to the poor by their industry." [19]

One clue for understanding "the American peculiarity" was the peculiarity of American social structures. Some observers like Abdy and de Tocqueville noted that racial prejudice appeared more intense in the North than in the South. In the South, slavery delineated clear racial lines. The Southern social order was more aristocratic, less republican, and less egalitarian (despite Southern claims to the contrary). [20] In the North, the market revolution had inspired a more pervasive and intensive material drive for fortune, which brought not just increased social mobility, but an increased uncertainty of status. Movement up beckoned to almost everyone, but movement down also threatened everyone. Under such conditions, ordinary human vanity and pride took vicious forms: an anxious white majority could erect a safety net through racial prejudice below which no white ever could fall. The social system, otherwise fluid, drew a caste line for blacks, no matter how prosperous, educated, or morally upright.

Abdy noted how sensitive Americans were about social status. This was because class distinctions were less clear. Thus, sensitivity to fashion in dress was greater in the United States among all classes than in Europe. Fashion could mask or bolster one's precarious social status. That also explained why, much to the annoyance of puritanical abolitionists, blacks took such pride in clothing, inspiring brutal caricatures depicting apelike creatures decked out in tuxedos and other fancy finery. The joke was that clothes never could help them. And it explained, too, why Americans had such an aversion to work as servants. For an anxious white population always concerned about social standing, imposing caste on blacks seemingly uplifted whites, as if the humiliation of one race testified to the perfections of the other.[21]

In such a social setting, fear of amalgamation, of racial intermixture, was the preferred allegation against abolitionists for whipping up riots. Southerners took racial mixing in their stride. In New Orleans, handsome mixed-blood women were the open paramours of men who came to the Crescent City to seek their fortunes. For Northerners, amalgamation was another matter. As Beaumont's tale suggests, interracial mixture could produce white "blacks" who threatened a caste system based on skin color alone. Marie might apply her benevolent compassion to the inmates of a white-run asylum; George might attend the theater in the white balcony. But passing as Marie and George did make them vulnerable to perpetual persecution. And although breaches in the color line might be not be permissible, they were hard and sometimes impossible to detect, leaving an edge of uncertainty about who was white or black.

Beaumont regarded Americans as among the world's great hypocrites. Here was a nation obsessed as no other with human liberty, resting its very foundations on it, while it enslaved millions of its people. Americans condemned distinctions based on birth, but made whiteness the sign of nobility. Here, too, was a nation obsessed as no other with the accumulation of money, since nothing else could provide a badge of superiority.[22] They are "a race of businessmen who consider themselves honest because what they do is legal," Beaumont observed, "but their integrity is trickery countenanced by law, usurpation without violence," and "their weapons are guile, fraud, and bad faith, with which they enrich themselves." Even worse, however, was "their hypocrisy even in their good deeds!" The Northern states offered "independence to a whole unhappy race; and on those negroes whom they free they inflict . . . a persecution more cruel than slavery!"[23]

De Tocqueville observed the enormous satisfaction that white Americans took from being citizens of the land of "democratic liberty." Yet there was a considerable gap between the promise of equality of opportunity and the results of competition in the marketplace. Racial superiority was a great consolation prize that American democracy guaranteed to all its white citizens. In that enormous pride of nation and race, there could be no equal place for those who might detract from it, reminders of "the American peculiarity."[24]

Of One Blood

The white abolitionist commitment to racial equality flowed from the rejection of colonization and from the effect of black opinion and example on the consciousnesses of the immediatist pioneers, as we have seen. Colonizationists assumed that color prejudice was irremediable and that emancipation would flood the country with an immense outcast population whom whites would never accept as fellow citizens. "Perhaps nothing shows more clearly the leprous deadly effects of slavery," observed an abolitionist, "than the common remark, 'I am opposed to slavery but what will you do with them?'"[1]

As we also have seen, immediatists assumed that "this deadly negro hatred" was vulnerable to religious and secular argument and to the example of improvement among free blacks.[2] As serious Christians, they grounded their belief in human equality in faith. Scripture taught that God had created the nations of one blood, that He was no respecter of persons, and that He required Christians to do unto others as they would have others do unto them. As serious republicans, abolitionists also took the promise of equality in the Declaration of Independence as another absolute command. These beliefs and obligations, they believed, formed the foundation of a distinctive American national identity. And since most Americans professed to be Christians and republicans, abolitionists insisted that they could be persuaded to abandon racial prejudice.

Yet disdain for black people persisted on aesthetic, intellectual, and moral grounds, whatever their legal status, free or slave. As one African

American leader explained: "The truth is, that the real ground of prejudice is not the *color of skin*, but the *condition*. We have so long associated *color* with *condition, that we have forgotten the fact, and have charged the offence to the wrong account*."[3] Abolitionists understood that the condition of free blacks in the Northern states gave empirical support to racial prejudice. Few whites there acknowledged that their own behavior toward the emancipated was largely responsible for the lowly state of black people. Treated like pariahs in the churches, denied access to jobs as skilled labor, kept out of schools or segregated in all-black schools, barred from voting in some states, and treated with contempt in almost every facet of everyday life, African Americans seemed fated to remain at the bottom of the social order. Relentlessly grinding down free blacks, whites nonetheless held them to exemplary standards of behavior, oblivious to how prejudice contributed to the lowly condition of those they scorned.[4]

From this gloomy picture, white and black abolitionists plucked hope. By improving their condition, they believed, the free blacks of the North could contradict the assumptions upon which prejudice rested. That would not be easy. It would require an abandonment of prejudice among a vanguard of whites. And it would require heroic efforts by African Americans, aided by white abolitionists, to better their character and condition despite white prejudice. It would require white abolitionists and free blacks to show the prejudiced by concrete acts that all were in fact "of one blood."

There were grounds for optimism. Blacks already had made remarkable progress since the end of slavery in the North, building their own churches, cultural and benevolent institutions, and producing a small cadre of property-owning and literate leaders. Most whites professed ignorance of that progress, but the abolitionist movement would seek to replace ignorance with knowledge. By the 1830s, blacks were more eager than ever to speed the tempo of racial progress, and now as never before there were growing numbers of whites ready to aid them.

The Antislavery Women's Convention in 1837 put the case clearly: "The abandonment of prejudice is required of us as a proof of our sincerity and consistency. How can we ask our Southern brethren to make sacrifices if we are not even willing to enter inconvenience? First cast the beam from thine own eye, then will thou see clearly to cast it from his eye." And the appeal concluded with these lines from Philadelphia black abolitionist Sarah Forten:

"We are thy sisters. God has truly said
That of one blood the nation he has maid."[5]

By working together with free blacks, abolitionists not only conquered their own prejudices, as we have seen, but began to reintroduce
black Americans to white Americans. Just as they had been converted to
the antislavery cause by their encounters with free African Americans,
they believed that other white Americans would have their prejudices
shattered by the example of interracial cooperation on a larger scale.
Reporting from an extended tour of upstate New York, William Goodell
identified the dimensions of the task: "O how little are these despised
people known by the population with which they are surrounded! How
little have we known them ourselves, in the past! How imperfectly are
they still known and appreciated even by abolitionists themselves."
   In the logic of the antislavery cause, with its progression from colonization to emancipation, from gradualism to immediatism, from prejudice to respect, there thus was one more step: from segregation to an
integrated society. Goodell put in perspective the pioneering nature of
interracial collaboration in the 1830s, especially when one considers the
extent to which the races remain distant and apart in everyday life and
interpersonal relations a century and a half after he lamented "how little have we known them."[6]
   Integration had to begin first among abolitionists, white and black.
When the Massachusetts General Colored Association joined the New
England Antislavery Society, it was a first step toward creation of a biracial, integrated movement.[7] From time to time blacks presided at meetings of antislavery organizations, and thirteen served as officers of the
American Antislavery Society in the 1830s, not an impressive number,
but a beginning. The older antislavery societies had not admitted blacks.
There were only a small number of black antislavery societies affiliated
with the American Antislavery Society, six by 1838, either because blacks
joined integrated societies, thought it too dangerous to join such societies at all, or preferred to invest their energies in the various self-improvement enterprises that proliferated in the 1830s.[8]
   Oberlin and Oneida led the way, opening their doors to blacks seeking advanced training and to a new level of biracial interaction. "It is important to make the two races feel kindness and respect for each other,"
explained Rev. Theodore Wright, referring to Oneida's racial integration,
"even if but few do, so it will have an effect on others. Get two men to

love each other, though of two nations, and it will make them love the whole class."⁹ "This prejudice was never reasoned up and will never be reasoned down," Wendell Phillips said. "It must be lived down."¹⁰

There was no substitute for interracial relations in overcoming racial prejudice. This was recorded in a small way in the *Emancipator* in an account of a visit by a white woman abolitionist and her biased great aunt to Miss Paul's School for blacks in Boston, run by the black school-teacher Susan Paul, daughter of Rev. Nathaniel Paul. Fifty pupils were present, mostly seven to eight years old, all well dressed and cheerful. Miss Paul boasted that there were as many good heads among her class as among comparable numbers of whites, and she had that on the authority of the great European phrenologist Dr. Spurzheim, who, after examining the children, declared: "These little tawny children of humanity with their mild sparkling eyes, their broad open foreheads, and their quiet, orderly deportment and behavior are even now before me. Such discipline, such undeviating obedience and docility, I have never witnessed in a white school." But the real proof lay in performance. The children promptly answered questions in their various lessons; whites hardly could do better. And when they sang sweetly, the visitor and her great aunt were deeply moved, exulting at the victory, even if only temporarily, "over aunt's prejudices." In the afternoon, the pair visited an African-American church, where "the sight was truly gratifying." She rejoiced to be an "abolitionist, for it has given me an opportunity to see a portion of the human family to which I have too long been a stranger." For the first time in her life, she found herself in a black congregation, where she observed "that distinction which mind, cultivated mind, always gives, whether to white or black." And when the Methodist minister, Rev. Snowden, preached powerfully, she wished she could convey his earnestness and fervor, for "your heart would be touched."¹¹

In 1835 the schoolteacher in this interracial encounter, Susan Paul, authored *The Memoir of James Jackson, The Attentive and Obedient Scholar, Who died in Boston, Oct 31, 1833, aged Six years and Eleven Months* (Boston, 1835). Paul aimed to bring the interracial experience enjoyed by her visitors to a larger white audience and to provide an example of black potential to white and black readers alike. Why a child who lived less than seven years deserved a memoir became evident at the outset. Written in a simple, didactic style easily comprehended by children, the memoir aimed to use the life of Master Jackson to convince Americans "that the moral and intellectual powers of colored children

are inferior to the power of others, only as their advantages are inferior."
Paul hoped that "this little book [will] do something towards breaking
down that unholy prejudice which exists against color."[12] The target
audience was not just children, but adults, since in both cases, whites
were more inclined to suspend their prejudice against black children,
given common views of the innocence and goodness of children and the
winsomeness of youth.

James Jackson was a model of Christian piety, industry, obedience, a
figure not unlike Little Eva in Harriet Beecher Stowe's epic nearly twenty
years later, a being filled with Christian love who was too good to live
long in a world of Christian sinners. "In this life," Paul explained to
African-American readers, "you shall see your children growing up to
be respected in society, and in the world to come, they shall be acknowledged by our Lord as heirs to life eternal" (viii). The most remarkable quality in James was the development before the age of three
of a moral and religious sense that led him to ask questions about Heaven
and goodness that astonished people. He always obeyed his mother,
"tried to *do* as well as he knew how," and never was happier "than when
he made *others* happy" (12). He was also mentally precocious, desiring
to become literate at an early age so he could read the Bible (25). From
the time he learned to talk, he started to pray. He entered school before
he was four and learned more in one year than other children learned in
three. Other children loved him and gave him gifts, which he always
shared. "This was benevolence," Paul exulted (30). He preached to the
children and led them in prayer. Despite his gifts and accomplishments,
James never became proud and helped the slower children to learn how
to read and spell (58–59). On the Sabbath he refrained from work as
much as possible, living by the verse

> I must not work,
> I must not play,
> Upon God's holy Sabbath day. (64)

In October 1833, he became ill and died a Christian death, singing
hymns, longing for God, and forgetting his physical suffering. Paul ap-
pended to her heroic story a black mother's answer to a child's query,
why do "people slight me so?":

> Tis this my child; your Maker gave
> To you a darker skin;
> And people seem to think that such

Can have no mind within.
Am I to blame? It cannot be:
What God has done is right;
And he must be displeased with those
Who little black boys slight. (87)

Such appeals to original goodness were part of a strategy of combating prejudice. Susan Paul's focus on children was not unique. "It is in
our childhood that this prejudice is imbibed, of which we are so tenacious in after-life," observed an abolitionist.[13] As a result, "we grow up
to manhood with a feeling of hatred and scorn burning in our bosoms
against the negro." White children were especially vulnerable to viewing blacks either positively or negatively, since none was born with prejudice and all were entirely dependent on upbringing.[14] Prejudiced mothers transmitted fear and loathing of African Americans when they treated
or regarded them as outcasts, attitudes that children readily absorbed.
White parents used black folk as bogeymen to frighten their children if
they misbehaved. "See nigger's thick lips—see the flat nose—nigger eye
shine—that slick looking nigger . . . are sounds emanating from little
urchins of Christian villagers, which continually infect the feelings of
colored travellers," reported the black preacher Hosea Easton.[15]
    In order to help prevent children from being infected with the preju-
dice of their elders, the American Antislavery Society appointed Henry
C. Wright as a traveling agent to organize youth. By 1838, the American
Antislavery Society claimed thirty-three juvenile societies in twenty-eight
cities and towns, nineteen of which had female societies, suggesting that
antislavery women played an important role in their formation.[16]
Abolitionists pointed out that mothers had a vital role to play in this
process as well, and that they could do so without stepping beyond the
most conventional notions of women's proper sphere. Mothers could
crush such prejudice in the bud by teaching children that blacks are children of God, their skin color no reason to treat them any differently
than whites.
    White abolitionists also paid a great deal of attention to black edu-
cation, helping blacks to found or improve schools by providing funds
and teachers. Traveling antislavery agents visited black schools, praised
children, and uplifted the hearts of parents and youth. These biracial
relations affirmed the importance of working hard to improve the
condition of blacks, and they made a dent in breaching the isolation of
black communities. Now, for the first time, the races came together on
more than a token basis. Now, for the first time, there was a nationwide

movement that cared for the welfare of America's lowliest citizens. Abolitionists believed that few who observed the performance of African American children could remain prejudiced. Enter these schools and you "will see as much evidence of sprightliness, mental activity, and intelligence, as in any other schools," one abolitionist wrote.[17] And none were more open to conversion than white children. In September 1836, the children of Miss Paul's school received greetings from the Union Evangelical Sunday School in Amesbury and Salisbury: "Wicked men tell us that black children have no souls. But we know that you have souls—and we are glad to hear that your souls are growing and filling up with wisdom and goodness under the instruction of a kind teacher." The white children sent three dollars, the candy money they received from their parents every Fourth of July: "We do this to show our respect for you and your teacher, and the interest we feel in your welfare. We hope that you will grow up to be very wise and good people, and so put to shame those wicked men who say that colored people have no souls."

The black students thanked their benefactors for the money and the confidence placed in them: "We know of some little children who do not love us because we are colored; but we pity them and pray for them." The letter was "the first one we ever received," they said, and the money went "for children in school who were most destitute." They invited the Amesbury and Salisbury students to visit them, "for we love you very much, although we never saw you," and they promised to sing songs about the enslaved, about Sunday school, and about the evils of intemperance.[18]

Exhibiting black talent before white audiences could have a telling effect. In July 1835, Garrison brought four young men ranging in age from sixteen to twenty-one from Boston to Plymouth, New Hampshire. They impressed whites with the simplicity and power of their oratory, besting earlier itinerant temperance speakers. The young men also attended a white church, where "the pew doors of our yeomanry, too respectable to be sneered down by all the dandyism and pomposity of the land, were opened to them, and they enjoyed the pleasure of associating with their brethren and countrymen and fellow sinners, on a proper and Christian footing." Here was an example of "Abolition in the *concrete*," Garrison wrote. Opposition to prejudice was the real test and required a willingness by whites to "walk the streets in friendly association with this object of public aversion and contempt—to ride in the chaise with him—to sit in the pew with him in the house of God—at your own table, in your social circle in the exercise towards him of the rites of hospitality."

Garrison reported success. The black youth "afforded us ample opportunity to disperse much, if not all of our remaining pro-slavery prejudices, and that inhuman, unchristian uneasiness, which we are wont to feel at the free presence of our colored brethren."[19]

Nowhere did white abolitionists work as hard on behalf of black education than in Ohio, a state that had attempted to drive out its free people of color in 1829 and that taxed them, but barred them from public schools. In 1835 and again in 1837, the Ohio Antislavery Society made social surveys of the state's black population in order to gauge its numbers, conditions, and resources. The 1835 survey counted seventy-five hundred, one-third in Cincinnati, a majority having been born in slavery, with many purchasing their freedom and that of their loved ones. As was the case everywhere, the Ohio abolitionists found "among this people, a latent intellect, not a whit behind that of white citizens."[20]

Since so many lived in Cincinnati, educational work centered there. Lane students concluded their great debate by devoting themselves to Sunday and grammar schools for blacks. As children and adults crowded the first school, abolitionists established three more to accommodate demand. The teachers found their work gratifying, as students, old and young, acquired the ability to read and write, some with startling rapidity. A nine-year veteran teacher in the city's public schools testified "that the colored people are not only equal to white people in natural capacity to be taught, but that they exceed them—they do not receive instruction, they seize it as a person who had been long famishing for food, seizes the smallest crumb."[21] Only a few seemed slow. The proof was in samples of students' compositions. One twelve-year-old wrote: "Dear School-master, I now inform you in these few lines, that what we are studying for is to try to get the yoke of slavery broke and the chain parted asunder. . . . O that God would change the hearts of our fellow men." And a sixteen-year-old pointed to the Britons, Saxons, and Germans who once "had no learning and had not a knowledge of letters. But now look, some of them are our first men." King Alfred "at one time did not know his a,b,c, but before his death he commanded armies and nations." Blacks must take heart: "He was never discouraged but always looked forward and studied harder. I think if the colored people study like King Alfred, they will soon do away with the evil of slavery."[22]

In countless ways and places, blacks and whites mixed together repeatedly, and not just in schools. In Utica, a biracial group celebrated the Fourth of July with a procession, music, church services, and then dinner in a display that aimed "to beat down the prejudice which has long existed in regard to the moral elevation of the colored people" by proving that "there is a dignity in the character of the colored population."[23] In New York City and elsewhere, integrated Phoenix Societies, organized and mainly run by blacks, encouraged the formation of new free black societies devoted to uplift. Here, free blacks could hear a white minister recall the glory of Africa when barbarian, uncivilized people inhabited much of Europe and the Greeks and Romans sent their sons to Africa for education.[24] In 1834, the American Antislavery Society praised the anniversary meeting of the New York City Phoenix Society: "the audience was composed of the most opposite complexions" and "the speakers were about equally divided." This model meeting operated "on many minds like an admission to the general assembly of the universe," teaching whites to abandon "any conscious superiority on the ground of color, or any lingering doubts as to the native ability of the colored race."[25] In 1836, Rhode Island's white abolitionists invited blacks to sit together with them at the annual meeting of the state antislavery society.[26]

Churches offered another important platform for integrating the races. Driven by humiliating treatment in the white churches, blacks formed their own, either within existing white denominations or by creating new black denominations. More important was the founding of "free churches." In free churches, attenders or members did not have to purchase or rent pews. Instead, worshippers were expected to donate funds according to their means. Some also repudiated common practices of racial segregation in seating. The Boston Free Church announced: "We believe the day has fully come when the most unchristian and wicked prejudice which refuses to receive men of different complexions to equal privileges in the house of God, ought to be laid aside fore ever."[27] Free churches tended to be most popular among "Presbygationalists," heirs of the missionary efforts following the Presbyterian-Congregationalist Plan of Union, especially under Finneyite influence. New York City had several, but racial integration remained a very contentious issue among Presbyterians there.[28] Abolitionist efforts to integrate Christian worship hardly made a dent, especially since African Americans were developing their own distinctive worship styles and preachers, which they preferred. But they added one more arena, along with schools and Phoenix Societies, in which the two races could come together.

Modern readers should not dismiss these efforts as flawed by tokenism or white paternalism. For both races, the social and cultural gulf was immense. One gains a more realistic appreciation of these pioneering bira-

cial encounters when one considers how much the races today remain
strangers in everyday life, in interpersonal relations. To gauge the reaction of blacks to these new relations with whites, one has to remember
how isolated African Americans were from the dominant race, except as
menial employees. That is why the creation of the schools by white abolitionists in Cincinnati and elsewhere had such a dramatic effect.[29]

At first, blacks were suspicious of these white do-gooders. By living
in black homes, taking meals together, and worshipping together in black
churches, the white teachers from Lane quickly made clear that they were
different from most white folks. Female abolitionists in Ohio intending
to work for the betterment of local blacks received warnings that white
prejudice toward blacks had fostered black prejudice toward whites.
That required whites to be patient in seeking black confidence. Working
with blacks briefly on a token basis never would pass muster. Only long-
term commitments by whites could be productive.[30]

Such commitments, once made, such confidence, once gained, paid
off. Soon blacks responded in kind. A pious mother in Cincinnati "was
delirious with joy for more than a week, at the bright prospect for her
children." She revealed that "many times I have lain awake all night,
and prayed for just such things, but when they came, I couldn't stand
it." A black woman recently arrived from Virginia was equally astonished: "If we should go back and tell . . . how we have the white people
to teach us, and how they treat us like brothers,—they couldn't believe
us. . . . It is just like changing out of one world into another." When
one of the "most strong minded . . . colored men" returned to the city
to witness a lecture hall crowded by his race, he was dumbfounded: "I
was in a perfect maze, to see a man get up, and speak to a colored congregation on such subjects,—to hear such sentiments from white men,—
to have them talk in such a way to *us*,—was too much for me believe. I
thought I was dreaming." For whites, too, these were transforming experiences: "The gratitude which at time flows out from their *full*, warm
hearts, is rich in blessing, and lightens all our labors."[31] One Lane
worker in Cincinnati's black schools wrote happily that "this is the best
place I have ever lived in."[32]

Antislavery agent Henry C. Wright recalled lecturing on a steamboat
from New York to Providence, Rhode Island, on behalf of racial equality. While seven or eight black waiters stood by, a white Southerner seized
a black passenger, pushed him forward, and demanded to know if Wright
regarded him as a brother and would walk, eat, and sleep with him.
Wright stood by his views, only to be cursed as an amalgamationist. The

contrast with the reaction of blacks was telling. Wright declared that "the looks given me by the colored men I never can forget. It amply made up for the scowling contempt of the insolent white. The colored man's heart is a deep fountain of gratitude."[33]

As whites visited and mingled with them, blacks "became guarded and circumspect in all their demeanor" and "as they become intelligent, they lose their relish for gaudy tinsel and display." They become "convinced that character is based on mental and moral worth." Yet there was much pain in the process. After living with blacks for a year "on terms of perfect friendship and equality," whites reported that blacks displayed "an increased sense of moral and intellectual distance" as they now for the first time fully appreciated how much hard work lay ahead. "I feel as though I did not know anything, and never had done anything," one black man sadly confessed. Responses to prejudice varied as blacks gained a new sense of self-worth. A majority felt "pained and depressed" by white prejudice, but others tried to ignore it or looked down upon it "with utter contempt."[34] Most important, the new opportunities for biracial communication and cooperation enhanced black self-esteem, which strengthened the will and incentives for self-improvement. "The sympathy which has been exhibited towards the free people of color, for the last few years," explained abolitionists, "has led them to feel a greater respect for themselves, and has excited them to great exertions to elevate their condition."[35] Sarah Forten testified that she was "wholly indebted to the Abolition cause for arousing me from apathy and indifference, shedding light into a mind which has been too long wrapt in selfish darkness."[36]

The deepest harm slavery and prejudice inflicted on African Americans was to brainwash them and rob them of confidence in themselves. "Many among us have tacitly consented to admit that we were an inferior race," acknowledged an African-American delegate to the American Antislavery Society convention in 1837. In the process of recovering a sense of self-worth, the respect of some white people was indispensable.[37] Summing up the progress of his race, Rev. Theodore Wright insisted in 1837 that "considering the proscription we labor under, would it be a wonder if we are all a debased set of wretches, involved in the greatest vice and misery that can be expressed? We ought to be better than we are—that is clear. But would it be a wonder if we were a thousand times worse?"[38]

Two years after the first encouraging reports from Cincinnati came troubling accounts of difficulty. The novelty of amiable relations between the races eventually wore off and no longer dazzled the eyes of the blacks as at first. "To break up old habits and form new ones . . . to root out growing jealousy and cold-hearted neglect, and to cherish brotherly love, kindness, meekness, benevolence and humility" proved difficult. When black people "supposed their *friends* were about to take them in their arms, and *carry* them up the hill of elevation, their united voice was '*we will go*'; but when they understood that they must *climb* the ascent," some faltered, "loving their sins too well to be elevated." To be sure, slavery and Northern prejudice were the ultimate sources of their failings, but that did not make any easier overcoming the harmful attitudes and behavior oppression had generated.[39] As much as students, young and adult, hungered for knowledge, when work beckoned as steamers pulled up to the piers at the riverside, they took off from school, to the teachers' frustration. One Cincinnati teacher, even during the first heady months of instructing blacks, sensed trouble ahead. "I fear sometimes that our hopes are too sanguine, for observation teaches us the colored people are not good to keep promises."[40]

Abolitionists seriously underestimated the difficulties of helping the grossly disadvantaged and of converting the prejudiced, including those in their own ranks. As the movement rapidly expanded, many who joined proved far more committed to ending slavery than to racial equality. Abolitionists had to argue continually that one was not possible without the other. And the gulf between the races did not suddenly vanish. Phoebe Matthew welcomed the departure of some of her colleagues in the Cincinnati schools because "they do wish us to stoop so often to prejudice, to shake hands and say how do you do to it. And they feel so bad if per chance we lay our hands on a curly head, or kiss a colored face." It embarrassed Matthew "to be in society of the colored people with such lingering bias" among the other whites present.[41] In 1836, Lewis Tappan reported to Weld differences even within the Executive Committee of the American Antislavery Society, which refused to invite black leaders to speak at the forthcoming meetings of the society. Some may have been afraid of offending new converts to the cause, others of arousing more intense opposition from outside the movement, especially from mobs fearful of amalgamation. Even Tappan himself came under attack from fellow abolitionists as an amalgamationist for his personal relations with African Americans.[42] Sarah Forten, a member of the Philadelphia Female Antislavery Society, reported that even professed friends of African Americans found it difficult to rid themselves of prejudice.[43] "It will be a long time, we fear," wrote one immediatist, "before even abolitionists themselves will entirely get rid of the remaining prejudices which make us almost start with admiration, when we read an able production of a *colored man!*"⁴⁴ The editor of the *Emancipationist* reported that white delegates to antislavery conventions were astonished at black delegates who made impressive speeches, rudely staring at them as if they suddenly had dropped from the moon. Such talents long had existed, but prejudiced whites had failed to recognize their worth. The rise of the antislavery movement had encouraged manly independence and self-possession among blacks, but it took time for reality to penetrate biased consciousnesses: "The blessing of God on the labors of the Anti-Slavery Society, has now broken the charm of caste, and we find those whom we disliked once 'men and our brothers,'" observed one editor.⁴⁵ But Rev. Samuel Ringgold Ward, writing in 1840, attacked abolitionists "who have yet to learn what it is to crucify prejudice against color within their own bosom. Too many best love the colored at a distance." Such friends, remarked Ward, sustained proslavery parties and laws that "disfranchise us." In social life, when with other white persons, "they find it difficult to see a colored man, though they have spectacles on their noses," and in churches, they go along with "negro-pewism" and allowing sextons "*to seat them near the door.*"⁴⁶

Outside their ranks, abolitionists had almost no success persuading master mechanics to train blacks and give them jobs in the skilled trades. Even a sympathetic master mechanic could not ignore the refusal of whites to work with black mechanics. Most white churches did not welcome black worshippers. In 1838, Pennsylvania took away the right of blacks to vote, and the campaign to restore it in New York in the later 1830s was just the beginning of a long, frustrating struggle. Most advanced schools—academies and colleges—remained for whites only, while public education for blacks either was not available or the schools were scandalously poor. In the 1830s, the gospel of self-help yielded meager rewards and tangible penalties. Nothing so inflamed the big-city mobs as the efforts by blacks to raise themselves and claim their rightful place in "respectable society."

Yet the resort to force by the mobs was also a sign of weakness. In the long run, violence could not entirely obscure improvements in the conditions of blacks or prevent the emergence of talented, impressive representatives of the race. The first statewide referendum in New York to give propertyless blacks the right to vote in 1846 lost, but found wide support in upstate New York, in communities where abolitionism and the Liberty Party were relatively strong. This suggests the substantial inroads against prejudice that had been made among a sizable minority.[47]

Though the antislavery press and lecturers endlessly trumpeted the advances of African Americans, their voices had to compete with thousands of newspapers, magazines, ministers, and politicians who sang another song. Abolitionists had enormous faith in the example of African American schools to overcome prejudice, but there were severe barriers to spreading such experience beyond antislavery ranks.[48] For two decades, the American Colonization Society and its influential supporters relentlessly had affirmed that blacks never could improve in the United States and required expatriation. Abolitionists credited the ACS with steeping the country in prejudice. William Goodell remembered that a black had attended school with him in Connecticut a generation earlier. Now, thanks to the work of the colonizationists, that experience was less common. In 1837, Henry Clay reasserted the colonizationist doctrine on racial difference in order to refurbish his campaign for the presidency.[49] The black-faced minstrel show, which became increasingly popular by the 1840s, was potent entertainment that refuted abolitionist claims of the real progress made by African Americans. From the age of the minstrel show to the reign of *Amos and Andy* in the twentieth century, purveyors of racist humor made comedy out of malapropisms and mispronunciations of black English that assured whites of the blacks' ignorance and fecklessness, while depictions of efforts by blacks to imitate whites depicted blacks futilely pressing the limits of their color-bound inferiority.[50]

By 1840—only ten years after it became committed to racial equality—the abolition movement could claim much progress, yet the record of its achievement was mixed. Tens of thousands within the movement had embraced the principle that God had created mankind "of one blood" and had worked, often heroically, to advance that principle. Outside the movement, their example inspired numerous fellow travelers. Blacks received an electric shock from white efforts at integration, especially by white schoolteachers in black schools. These efforts breached the isolation of a pariah people, raised their self-esteem, encouraged the formation of reform societies that fought gambling and licentiousness, and advanced the educational and cultural level of African Americans.

The truly perplexing problem, however, was white inconsistency. As long as white people practiced racial prejudice in all its cruel, debilitating forms, they made it extraordinarily difficult, except for an especially talented or lucky few, to climb the mobility ladder that beckoned whites.

Whites still attributed black poverty, crime, and lack of cultivation to the inherent inferiority of colored people, and they did so without any real willingness to put that theory to the test. And although few blacks questioned the ideology of uplift through education and moral reform, Peter Paul Simons criticized these as false remedies because they made blacks subservient and passive in the face of continuing white prejudice. Whatever their schooling, he pointed out, most blacks still could obtain only mean employment.[51]

In spite of limited gains, white abolitionists took pride in their work. "As we have claimed more for the colored man than any class of abolitionists have in our country heretofore, we have created a deference to colored persons which never existed before," the pioneers Simeon Jocelyn and Beriah Green announced to a convention of the faithful.[52] Black leaders agreed. The abolitionists were not just against slavery. They actively worked to make freedom and equality a reality.[53]

Notes

PREFACE

1. Quoted by William G. McLoughlin in Gilbert H. Barnes, *The Antislavery Impulse, 1830–1844* (1993; reprint, New York, 1965), xxiii.
2. The recent extended debate over abolitionism, humanitarianism, and the rise of capitalism in the *American Historical Review* illustrates the disagreements. See Thomas L. Haskell, "Capitalism and the Origins of the Humanitarian Sensibility: Part I," *American Historical Review* 90 (April 1985): 339–61; Part 2, ibid., (June 1985): 457–566; Thomas L. Haskell, "Convention and Hegemonic Interest in the Debate over Antislavery: A Reply to Davis and Ashworth," ibid., 92 (October 1987): 829-78; David Brion Davis, "Reflections on Abolitionism and Ideological Hegemony," ibid.; and John Ashworth, "The Relationship between Capitalism and Humanitarianism," ibid., 797-828.
3. *The Letters of Theodore Dwight Weld, Angelina Grimke Weld, and Sarah Grimke, 1822–1844*, 2 vols., ed. Gilbert H. Barnes and Dwight L. Dumond (1934; reprint, Gloucester, Mass. 1965).
4. Edward Magdol's *The Antislavery Rank and File: A Social Profile of the Abolitionists' Constituency* (New York, 1986) studied mainly signers of abolitionist petitions who were mostly not members of abolitionist societies and many, if not most, were not strictly speaking abolitionists.

PART 1

1. William C. Nell, *The Colored Patriots of the American Revolution* (1855; reprint, New York, 1968), 350–51; Garrison to Ebeneezer Dole, 14 July 1830, *The Letters of William Lloyd Garrison*, ed. Walter M. Merrill, 6 vols. (Cambridge, Mass., 1971–81), 1: 106; David E. Swift, *Black Prophets of Justice: Activist Clergy before the Civil War* (Baton Rouge, La., 1989), 93.

2. "An Address Delivered to the Colonization Society of Kentucky," in *African Repository,* March 1830, 12. See also William Jay, *Miscellaneous Writings on Slavery* (Boston, 1853), 372 and 372 n.

3. Philip J. Staudenraus, *The African Colonization Movement, 1816–65* (New York, 1961); Early Lee Fox, *The American Colonization Society, 1817–1840,* Johns Hopkins University Studies in Historical and Political Science, series 37, no. 3 (Baltimore, 1919).

CHAPTER 1

1. Winthrop D. Jordan, *White over Black: Attitudes towards the Negro, 1550–1812* (New York, 1977); Arthur Zilvermsmit, *The First Emancipation: The Abolition of Slavery in the North* (Chicago, 1967).

2. Gary Nash, *Forging Freedom: The Formation of the Philadelphia Black Community, 1720–1840* (Cambridge, Mass., 1988); Shane White, *Somewhat More Independent: The End of Slavery in New York, 1770–1810* (Athens, Ga., 1991).

3. Gaillard Hunt, "William Thornton and Negro Colonization," *Proceedings of the American Antiquarian Society* 40 (April 1920): 41; John Daniels, *In Freedom's Birthplace: A Study of the Boston Negroes* (Boston, 1914), 24–29.

4. Leonard P. Curry, *The Free Black in Urban America, 1800–1850* (Chicago, 1981), 103–5.

5. Ira Berlin, *Slaves without Masters: The Free Negro in the Antebellum South* (New York, 1974), 15 ff., 79 ff.

6. This is based on the *Minutes of the Proceedings of a Convention of Delegates from the Abolition Societies... Assembled at Philadelphia....* (Philadelphia, 1794–1803). *Minutes of the Proceedings of the Seventh Convention of Delegates from the Abolition Societies...* 1801 (1801), 37; *Minutes of the Proceedings of the First Convention of Delegates from the Abolition Societies...* 1794 (1794), 14–15. See Sylvia R. Frey, *Water from the Rock: Black Resistance in a Revolutionary Age* (Princeton, 1991); and Mechal Sobel, *The World They Made Together: Black and White Values in Eighteenth-Century Virginia* (Princeton, 1988).

7. Leon Litwack, *North of Slavery: The Negro in the Free States, 1790–1860* (Chicago, 1961), 187–213; Gary Nash, *Forging Freedom: The Philadelphia Black Community, 1720–1840* (Cambridge, Mass., 1988), 66 ff. For Quakers, see ibid., 28–29, 180; Carol V. R. George, *Segregated Sabbaths: Richard Allen and the Emergence of Independent Black Churches, 1760–1840* (New York, 1973).

8. Curry, *The Free Black in Urban America,* 15–36, 147–73; Nash, *Forging Freedom.* For education, see ibid., 22–23, 31, 36, 202–20, 262–71, and for economic conditions, see 72–78, 144–46, 148–59, 161–63, 214 ff., 246 ff.; James O. and Lois E. Horton, *Black Bostonians* (New York, 1979), 39 ff. Litwack, *North of Freedom,* 113–86.

9. Litwack, *North of Slavery,* 64–112; James Truslow Adams, "Disenfranchisement of Negroes in New England," *American Historical Review* 30 (1924–25): 543–47.

10. George S. Brookes, *Friend Anthony Benezet* (Philadelphia, 1937), 45–46, 49–52.

11. Jordan, *White over Black,* 276, 283, 298–99, 550; Stanley K. Schultz, "The Making of a Reformer: The Reverend Samuel Hopkins as an Eighteenth-Century Abolitionist," *Proceedings of the American Philosophical Society* 115 (October 1971): 350–65; David S. Lovejoy, "Samuel Hopkins: Religion, Slavery, and the Revolution," *New England Quarterly* 40 (June 1967): 227–43.

12. See Jordan, *White over Black,* 286–87, 305–6, 416–17, 423–24, 448–49, 517–22, for Rush, and 442–44, 460, 486–88, 513–16, 516–17, 532–33. Samuel Stanhope Smith, *An Essay on the Causes of the Variety of Complexion and Figure in the Human Species,* ed. Winthrop D. Jordan (Cambridge, Mass., 1965); Henry Gregoire, *An Enquiry Concerning the Intellectual and Moral Faculties of Negroes,* trans. D. B. Warden (1810; reprint, College Park, Md., 1967); John C. Greene, "The American Debate on the Negro's Place in Nature, 1780–1815," *Journal of the History of Ideas* 15 (June 1954): 384–96.

13. Jordan, *White over Black,* 431–32, 434–40, 453–60, 477–81; Louis Ruchames, ed., *Racial Thought in America* (Amherst, Mass., 1969), 162–69, 256–57.

14. Berlin, *Slaves without Masters,* 51.

15. White, *Somewhat More Independent,* 24 ff., 147–49, 152–56. For the Baltimore cartmen's battle, see the *Genius of Universal Emancipation,* 12 January and 10 May 1828.

16. Nash, *Forging Freedom,* 172–211, esp. 177, 275–77; Paul A. Gilje, *The Road to Mobocracy: Popular Disorder in New York City, 1763–1834* (Chapel Hill, 1987), 143–70; Robert J. Cottrol, *The Afro-Yankees: Providence's Free Black Community in the Antebellum Era* (Westport, Conn., 1982), 53–57; Emma Jones Lapsansky, "'Since They Got Those Separate Churches': Afro-Americans and Racism in Jacksonian Philadelphia," *American Quarterly* 32 (spring 1980): 54–78; Carl E. Prince, "The Great 'Riot Year': Jacksonian Democracy and Patterns of Violence in 1834," *Journal of the Early Republic* 5 (spring 1985): 1–19.

CHAPTER 2

1. Gaillard Hunt, "William Thornton and Negro Colonization," *American Antiquarian Society,* new series, 30 (April 1920): 32–61, esp. 51; Drew McCoy, *The Last of the Fathers: James Madison and the Republican Legacy* (Chapel Hill, 1989), 44–45, 308–10, 317–22, 221–26, 230–33, 265–66, 277–81, 282–86, 296–99, 301–3, 306–8, 363–65.

2. John Chester Miller, *The Wolf by the Ears: Thomas Jefferson and Slavery* (New York, 1977); Donald Robinson, *Slavery and the Structure of American Politics, 1765–1820* (New York, 1971); Drew McCoy, "James Madison and Visions of American Nationality in the Confederation Period: A Regional Perspective," in *Beyond Confederation: Origins of the Constitution and American National Identity,* ed. Richard Beeman, Stephen Botein, and Edward C. Carter II (Chapel Hill, 1987), 226–60.

3. For the fugitive slave problem in Pennsylvania, see Lydia Maria Child, *Isaac T. Hopper: A True Life* (Boston, 1853). For John Adams, see John R. Howe Jr., *The Changing Political Thought of John Adams* (Princeton, 1966), 223.

4. McCoy, "James Madison and Visions of American Nationality in the Confederation Period."

5. Glover Moore, *The Missouri Controversy, 1819–1821* (Lexington, Ky., 1966); Charles Sellers, *The Market Revolution* (New York, 1991), 103–36.

6. Early Lee Fox, *The American Colonization Society, 1817–1840,* Johns Hopkins University Studies in Historical and Political Science, series 36, no. 3 (Baltimore, 1919); Philip J. Staudenraus, *The African Colonization Movement, 1816–65* (New York, 1961); Douglas R. Egerton, *Charles Fenton Mercer and the Trial of National Conservatism* (Oxford, Miss., 1989); Douglas R. Egerton, "'Its Origin Is Not a Little Curious': A New Look at the American Colonization Society," *Journal of the Early Republic* 5 (fall 1985): 463–80; Lawrence J. Friedman, "Purifying the White Man's Country: The American Colonization Society Reconsidered, 1816–40," *Societas* 6 (winter 1976): 1–24; David M. Streifford, "The American Colonization Society: An Application of Republican Ideology to Early Antebellum Reform," *Journal of Southern History* 45 (May 1979): 201–20; Charles I. Foster, "The Colonization of Free Negroes in Liberia, 1816–1835," *Journal of Negro History* 38 (January 1953): 41–66. George M. Frederickson, *The Black Image in the White Mind: The Debate on Afro-American Character and Destiny, 1817–1914* (New York, 1971). Sylvia R. Frey, *Water from the Rock: Black Resistance in a Revolutionary Age* (Princeton, 1991). Mechal Sobel, *The World They Made Together: Black and White Values in Eighteenth-Century Virginia* (Princeton, 1988).

7. Michael Tadman, *Speculators and Slaves: Masters, Traders, and Slaves in the Old South* (Madison, Wisc., 1989).

8. Daniel Walker Howe, *The Political Culture of the American Whigs* (Chicago, 1979), 133–37; Thomas Brown, *Politics and Statesmanship: Essays on the American Whig Party* (New York, 1985), 138–40.

9. Staudenraus, *The African Colonization Movement, 1816–65* (New York, 1961), 69–81; Early Lee Fox, *The American Colonization Society, 1817–1840,* Johns Hopkins University Studies in Historical and Political Science, series 37, no. 3 (Baltimore, 1919), 75 ff.

10. Douglas R. Egerton, *Charles Fenton Mercer and the Trial of National Conservatism* (Oxford, Miss., 1989), 161–73; see Egerton, "'Its Origin Is Not a Little Curious': A New Look at the American Colonization Society," *Journal of the Early Republic* 5 (fall 1985): 463–80, for the relationship between Mercer and Finley and their respective claims to being the father of the ACS.

11. Staudenraus, *The African Colonization Movement,* 94–116. Fox, *The American Colonization Society,* 77 ff., 82 ff.

12. Fox, *The American Colonization Society,* 9 ff.

13. William Lloyd Garrison, *Thoughts on African Colonization . . .* (Boston, 1832), part 2, 48. For Garrison, see the preface, 1; for Birney, see *Letter on Colonization* (New York, 1834), 20.

14. This and the following discussion are based on the *African Repository,* the quarterly publication of the American Colonization Society.

15. *The Sixteenth Annual Report of the American Society for Colonizing the Free People of Colour of the United States* (Washington, 1833), vii–viii.

16. The author noted the source of these quotes as *"African Repository,* annual reports" without further elaboration—Eds.

17. *African Colonization: Proceedings of the Formation of the New-york State Colonization Society . . .* (Albany, 1829), 8–9.

18. Frederickson, *The Black Image in the White Mind,* 15 ff.

19. *Memoirs of John Quincy Adams,* 12 vols. (Philadelphia, 1874–77), 4:292–95, 4:353–56, 4:475–76, 5:10–12; William Jerry MacLean, "Othello Scorned: The Racial Thought of John Quincy Adams," *Journal of the Early Republic* 4 (summer 1984): 143–60.

20. Staudenraus, *The African Colonization Movement,* 169–87; Fox, *The American Colonization Society,* 85 ff.

21. *Memoirs of John Quincy Adams,* 8:309.

CHAPTER 3

1. Jeremiah Gloucester, *An Oration Delivered on Jan. 1, 1823 in Bethel Church on the Abolition of the Slave Trade* (Philadelphia, 1823), 16.

2. Leonard P. Curry, *The Free Black in Urban America, 1800–1850* (Chicago, 1981), 200 ff.; Gary Nash, *Forging Freedom: The Formation of the Philadelphia Black Community, 1720–1840* (Cambridge, Mass., 1988), 148–53.

3. *Genius of Universal Emancipation,* October 1821; February 1822; September 1823; October 1823; March, October, November, and December 1824; January, February, March, May, and 10 December 1825; 21 January, 4 March, and 2 December 1826; 24 March, 12 June, 4, 14, and 21 July, and Dececember 1827; 14 June 1828; and January 1832. For Texas, see addenda to vol. 12, August 1832, June 1833, and November 1835.

4. Sheldon H. Harris, *Paul Cuffe, Black America and the African Return* (New York, 1972), 41–51, 64–66, 69–71, 191–93, 198–204, 221–23; *Resolution and Remonstrance of the People of Colour against Colonization on the Coast of Africa, 1818* (Philadelphia, 1818); Peter Williams, *A Discourse Delivered on the Death of Capt. Paul Cuffe before the New York African Institution . . . Oct 21, 1817* (New York, 1817), in Black Abolitionist Papers, ed. C. Peter Ripley (Sanford, N.C.: Microfilming Corporation of America, 1981), microfilm, reel 16. On Russwurm, see the New York *Freedom's Journal,* 14 February, 7 and 14 March 1829 and the New York *Rights of All,* 29 March 1829. Leroy Graham, *Baltimore, The Nineteenth Century Black Capital* (Lanham, Md., 1982), 70, 77–78.

5. A memorial of free blacks who met on 7 December 1826 at Bethel Church, Baltimore, endorsed African colonization. *Genius of Universal Emancipation,* 16 December 1826. For the allegation on C. C. Harper, see Graham, *Baltimore, The Nineteenth Century Black Capital,* 100–101. Subsequently, Lundy, insisting that his paper was open to all points of view, refuted a challenge that alleged a procolonization piece claimed to have been

written by a black was in fact written by a white, but this may have been a different piece than the one Watkins rebutted. See *Genius of Universal Emancipation,* 7 December 1828 and an earlier rebuttal of colonization by "A Coloured Baltimorean" in *Freedom's Journal,* 6 July 1827.

6. David E. Swift, *Black Prophets of Justice: Activist Clergy before the Civil War* (Baton Rouge, 1989), 27.

7. *Freedom's Journal,* 16 March 1827.

8. The following paragraphs are based on *Freedom's Journal.*

9. *Freedom's Journal,* 23 March 1827.

10. Ibid., 2 November 1827.

11. Ibid., 24 August; 7, 28 September; 5 October; 2 November 1828.

12. James O. and Lois E. Horton, *Black Bostonians* (New York, 1979), 57. For Cornish, see Swift, *Black Prophets of Justice,* 44. For criticism of the Adams administration's support of colonization, see *Freedom's Journal,* 22 January 1828.

13. Swift, *Black Prophets of Justice,* 39–40; American Colonization Society, *Fourteenth Annual Report,* xiii; *Freedom's Journal,* 21 September 1827.

14. Charles H. Wesley, "The Negroes of New York in the Emancipation Movement," *Journal of Negro History,* vol. 24 (January 1939): 81.

15. *Freedom's Journal,* 14 April 1828.

16. *Freedom's Journal,* 19 December 1828.

17. Walker, *Appeal,* in Herbert Aptheker, ed., *"One Continual Cry," David Walker's Appeal to the Colored Citizens of the World* (1829–30; reprint, New York, 1965), 74.

18. Ibid., 89.

19. Ibid., 109 ff.

20. Ibid., 80.

21. Ibid., 121; Wendell Phillips Garrison and Francis Jackson Garrison, *William Lloyd Garrison: The Story of His Life Told by His Children,* 4 vols. (Boston and New York, 1885 and 1889).

22. Aptheker, ed., *"One Continual Cry,"* 45–53.

23. *African Repository,* March 1830, 29; *Genius of Universal Emancipation,* 26 February and 5 March 1830.

24. Aptheker, ed., *"One Continual Cry,"* 38–44.

25. Ibid., 3–4.

26. Garrison et al., *Life,* 1:161 n.

27. *Minutes and Proceedings of the First Annual Convention of the People of Colour* (Philadelphia, 1831), title page, in Howard H. Bell, ed., *Minutes of the Proceedings of the National Negro Conventions, 1830–1864* (New York, 1969).

28. Ibid., 1831: 5.

29. Ibid., 1831: 5; 1832: 8, 15–20; 1833: 23.

30. Ibid., 1831: 13.

31. Ibid., 1832: see 23 for Jocelyn, 24 for Tappan.

32. *College for Colored Youth. An Account of the New-Haven City Meeting and Resolutions . . .* (New York, 1831), 2.

33. Bell, ed., *Minutes,* 1831: 14.

34. Ibid., 1832: 9, 12.
35. Ibid., 1834: 21.
36. Ibid., 1834: 29.

CHAPTER 4

1. *Colored American,* 13 May 1837.
2. William Lloyd Garrison, *Address at Park Street Church, Boston July 4, 1829,* Old South Leaflet, no. 180 (n.p., n.d.). This is an extended excerpt that also appears in Wendell Phillips Garrison and Francis Jackson Garrison, *William Lloyd Garrison: The Story of His Life Told by His Children,* 4 vols. (Boston and New York, 1885 and 1889), 1:124–37. The full text appears in the *National Philanthropist,* 22 and 29 July 1829, but I have not succeeded in getting copies. For accounts, see Archibald Grimké, *William Lloyd Garrison* (New York, 1891), 65 ff.; John L. Thomas, *The Liberator* (Boston, 1963); R. Jackson Wilson, *Figures in Speech* (New York, 1989).
3. Garrison et al., *Life,* 1:122.
4. Ibid., 1:81, 1:84, 1:114, 1:122; Thomas, *The Liberator,* 57, 62, 69, 71.
5. Lundy published from time to time wide-ranging, penetrating analyses of the long-range development of American politics in which Southern slaveholders maintained dominance over the nation. See, for example, *Genius of Universal Emancipation,* November 1823; March 1824; 8 January, 4 July, 15 and 29 September, 20 October, and 29 December 1827; 9 February and 24 May 1828. For Garrison's postelection views, see 4 December 1829, and for Garrison's reassessment of Clay, see 12 and 19 February and 5 March 1830.
6. Garrison, *Address at Park Street Church,* 2–3
7. Ibid., 5.
8. Ibid., 5.
9. Ibid., 7.
10. Ibid., 8–9.
11. Ibid., 5.
12. Ibid., 6.
13. *Genius of Universal Emancipation,* 2 September 1829. Leroy Graham, *Baltimore, The Nineteenth Century Black Capital* (Lanham, Md., 1982), 93 ff. For "A Colored Baltimorean," see *Genius of Universal Emancipation,* 27 November and 18 December 1830 and 7 February 1828.
14. *Genius of Universal Emancipation,* 2 September 1829.
15. Ibid., 30 October 1829.
16. Ibid., 8 January 1829.
17. Ibid., 4 December 1829. For Clay, see 12 and 19 February and 5 March 1830. There were few who had regarded Clay more highly than Garrison did, he confessed in reviewing Clay's important Address to the Kentucky Colonization Society in December 1829. Clay, he thought, had more political honesty and patriotism than any man since George Washington. One could never forget his efforts to outlaw slavery at the outset of Kentucky's statehood. Even now, Garrison did not repudiate Clay for his shortcomings. No reasonable

person could expect Clay to denounce slavery, as might a nonslaveholder, a Northerner, or a man of smaller ambitions. Yet Garrison no longer could permit Clay's racial prejudice to go unchallenged: his insistence on the physical and mental superiority of whites over Native Americans was simply unphilosophical and absurd, pandering to the same contempt that undergirded Jacksonian policy on their removal. The same bias applied to blacks, Garrison complained. In one respect, Clay was the same as other slaveholders: prejudice warped his mind, however much he discoursed eloquently on the evils of the system. As soon as one presses the slaveholder, Clay included, Garrison declared, he tells you how ignorant and helpless the slaves are, how freedom would be a disaster, and how all the blame for slavery rests with the British, who imposed it on innocent colonists. Clay boasted of the ban on the foreign slave trade in 1808 as evidence of American philanthropy, but he was silent on the domestic slave trade, which vastly overmatched the criminality of the foreign importations. Surely, Clay knew that Maryland and Virginia raised slaves like swine or cattle to be driven in chains hundreds of miles and suffer cruel treatment on plantations in the Deep South, Garrison added. Ibid., 12 February 1830.

Clay claimed that slavery was ultimately doomed because free labor was more efficient than slave labor, but since he could not contemplate emancipation without removal, slavery was destined to be eternal, since African colonization, Garrison concluded, was impractical. Yet even in March 1830, Garrison did not entirely break with colonization, but urged that it not be overrated or allowed to spread delusions.

18. Oliver Johnson, *William Lloyd Garrison and His Times* (Boston, 1880), 41.

19. Lewis Tappan, *The Life of Arthur Tappan* (New York, 1879), 135–47.

CHAPTER 5

1. Garrison to Simeon S. Jocelyn, 30 May 1831, *The Letters of William Lloyd Garrison*, 6 vols., ed. Walter M. Merrill (Cambridge, Mass., 1971–81), 1:119.

2. For Taylor's theology and his circle, see Sidney E. Mead, *Nathaniel William Taylor, 1786–1858* (Hamden, Conn., 1967), and the pages of the *Christian Spectator* published in New Haven, edited by Rev. Leonard Bacon.

3. Theodore D. Bacon, *Leonard Bacon: A Statesman in the Church* (New Haven, 1931), 31 ff., 55 ff., 62 ff., 100–143, 179–241; Leonard W. Bacon, *Anti-Slavery before Garrison* (New Haven, 1903); Leonard Bacon, *A Plea for Africa* (New Haven, 1825); *Slavery Discussed in Occasional Essays, from 1833 to 1846* (New York, 1846); "Northern Colonizationist and Free Blacks: Leonard Bacon as a Test Case," unpublished paper.

4. *Freedom's Journal*, 20 April 1927.

5. David E. Swift, *Black Prophets of Justice: Activist Clergy before the Civil War* (Baton Rouge, 1989), 57.

6. *College for Colored Youth: An Account of the New-Haven City Meetings and Resolutions . . .* (New York, 1831).

7. Ibid., 5.

8. Ibid., 4–5.
9. Ibid., 5.
10. Ibid., 10.
11. Ibid., 11.
12. Ibid., 11–12.
13. Robert A. Warner, *New Haven Negroes: A Social History* (New Haven, 1940), 65.
14. *African Repository,* August 1832.
15. *College for Colored Youth,* 12–13.
16. Ibid., 5.
17. Ibid., 18–19.
18. Ibid., 20.
19. Ibid., 21.
20. Ibid., 17–18.
21. Samuel J. May, *Letters to Andrew T. Judson, Esq., and Others in Canterbury, Remonstrating with Them on Their Unjust and Unjustifiable Procedure Relative to Miss Crandall and Her School for Colored Females* (Brooklyn, Conn., 1833).
22. Philip S. Foner and Josephine F. Pacheco, *Three Who Dared* (Westport, Conn., 1984), 9.
23. Ibid., 14.
24. Ibid., 16, 20.
25. Ibid., 38.
26. Ibid., 38–39.

CHAPTER 6

1. Oliver Johnson, *William Lloyd Garrison and His Life* (Boston, 1880), 133.
2. William Lloyd Garrison, *An Address Delivered before the Free People of Color, Philadelphia, New York, and other Cities, during the Month of June, 1831,* 2d ed. (Boston, 1831), 3–4, 12–13. And see Elizur Wright Jr., *The Sin of Slavery, and Its Remedy, Containing Some Reflections on the Moral Influence of African Colonization* (New York, 1833): "In view of this subject [African colonization] I must be permitted solemnly to say, that I do confess my own guilt, in the cold and cruel prejudice with which I have suffered myself, in time past, to advocate the unchristian principles, and the mischievous plans, of the American Colonization Society" (23).
3. Garrison, *Address Delivered before the Free People of Color,* 17–18.
4. Ibid., 18.
5. Garrison, *Thoughts on African Colonization,* part 2, 14.
6. John Jay Chapman, *William Lloyd Garrison* (New York, 1913), 65.
7. Garrison, *Thoughts on African Colonization,* 5.
8. Ibid., 151 ff.
9. Johnson, *William Lloyd Garrison,* 118.
10. Lydia Maria Child, *An Appeal in Favor of That Class of Americans Called Africans* (New York, 1836), 138.

11. Child, *Appeal,* 134; Charles Olcott, *Two Lectures on the Subject of Slavery and Abolition* (Masillon, Ohio, 1837), 52–53.

12. Garrison, *Thoughts on African Colonization,* 12–13.

13. Wright, *The Sin of Slavery,* 26.

14. Garrison, *Thoughts on African Colonization,* 120, 144.

15. American Anti-Slavery Society, *Prejudice against Color* (New York, n.d.), 7.

16. *African Repository,* March 1825, 7; January 1827, 331. For an example of an abolitionist citing the colonizationist historical argument, see Samuel J. May, *Letters to Andrew T. Judson, Esq., and Others in Canterbury, Remonstrating with Them on Their Unjust and Unjustifiable Procedure Relative to Miss Crandall and Her School for Colored Females* (Brooklyn, Conn., 1833), 21–22.

17. American Antislavery Society, *Prejudice against Color,* 19.

18. Child, *Appeal,* 176.

19. Ibid., 169.

20. Ibid., 162.

21. Ibid., 169.

22. Ibid., 171.

23. Ibid., 208.

24. William Jay, "On the Condition of the Free People of Color in the United States," *Miscellaneous Writings on Slavery* (Boston, 1853), 373.

25. Child, *Appeal,* 208.

26. Garrison, *Thoughts,* part 1, 131.

27. Child, *Appeal,* 215.

28. Ibid., 133.

29. Olcott, *Two Lectures on the Subject of Slavery,* 156.

30. Garrison, *Thoughts,* part 1, 146.

31. May, *Letters to Andrew T. Judson,* 9, 13.

32. Garrison, *Thoughts,* part 2, 17.

33. Ibid., part 2, 28. For the decisive impact the discovery of black opinion had, see the repudiation of colonization by Dr. S. H. Cox, *African Repository,* vol. 10 (June 1834).

34. Wright, *The Sin of Slavery,* 34.

35. Johnson, *William Lloyd Garrison,* 37, 94–95.

36. American Colonization Society, *Fifteenth Annual Report,* 1832, xxi.

37. *Christian Spectator* 14 (June 1832): 318, 320, 323, 324.

38. Ibid., 334. G. B. Stebbins, *Facts and Opinions Touching the Real Origin, Character, and Influence of the American Colonization Society . . .* (Boston, 1853; reprint, New York, 1969), 61.

39. Garrison, *Address Delivered before the Free People of Color,* 6–8.

40. Wright, *The Sin of Slavery,* 28.

PART 2

1. *The American Anti-Slavery Almanac for 1837* (Boston, n.d.), 7.

CHAPTER 7

1. Garrison to William Goodell, 26 February 1836, *The Letters of William Lloyd Garrison*, 6 vols., ed. Walter M. Merrill (Cambridge, Mass., 1971–81), 1:22, 1:44.

2. Quoted in M. Leon Perkal, "William Goodell: A Life of Reform" (Ph.D. diss., City University of New York, 1972), 12.

3. *Investigator and General Intelligencer*, 8 November 1827. In January of 1829 this paper combined with another to form the *National Philanthropist and Investigator*. Hereafter citations referring to *Investigator* will designate the former for the period before January of 1829 and the latter for later dates.

4. William Goodell, *Slavery and Anti-Slavery: A History of the Great Struggle in Both Hemispheres* (1852; reprint, New York, 1970), 389.

5. Ibid., 389–90.

6. *Investigator*, 16 January 1829, reprints the original prospectus; the editorial on parties is in 9 April 1829.

7. Ibid., 19 June 1828.

8. Ibid., 8 November 1827; 17 April 1828.

9. Ibid., 17 April 1828; 9 April 1828.

10. Ibid., 15 and 22 November 1827.

11. Ibid., 4 December 1828. For antibanking, see 12 March, 21 May, 11 June, and 1 July 1829, and the "Mr. Buy Cheap" editorial, 3 February 1830.

12. Ibid., 11 November 1829.

13. Ibid., 25 November 1829, and see a reprinted piece, "Village Aristocracy," from 17 June 1829.

14. Ibid., 8 and 15 November 1827.

15. Ibid., 20 November 1828. See also ibid., 9 April 1829; 16 January 1829, "Letter from a Laboring Mechanic in One of Our Country Villages"; 9 April 1829, "Hard Times" (see this issue also for more on consumerism); 31 March 1830, "The Dancing School"; 28 April 1830, "Recipe for Making a Dandyette"; 16 December 1829, editorial on "Gentlemen."

16. Ibid., 4 and 11 June 1829.

17. Ibid., 8 July 1830. This appeared in an editorial on slavery in Washington, D.C.

18. Ibid., 23 January and 26 March 1829.

19. Ibid., 28 May 1829.

20. Ibid., 4 April 1828; 5 February 1829; 5 March 1829; 2 December 1829. For worker support, see John B. Jentz, "Artisans, Evangelicals, and the City: A Social History of Abolition and Labor Reform in Jacksonian New York" (Ph.D. diss., City University of New York, 1977). For worker opposition, see the *Working Man's Advocate* and Sean Wilentz, *Chants Democratic: New York City and the Rise of the American Working Class, 1788–1850* (New York, 1984). For workers and religion, see Teresa Anne Murphy, "Labor, Religion, and Moral Reform in Fall River, Massachusetts, 1800–1845" (Ph.D. diss., Yale University, 1982).

21. *Investigator*, 30 June 1830.

22. Ibid., 3 November 1830, quoted in Perkal, "William Goodell," 51; 12 June 1830, from the *Mechanics from Essex Gazette;* see 16 June 1830 for a report from the *Philadelphia Mechanics Free Press.*

23. *Investigator,* 29 November 1827, 3 February 1830, 28 May 1830.

24. Ibid., 28 April 1830 and 5 May 1830, "To Mothers."

25. Ibid., 21 May 1829, 3 February 1830.

26. Ibid., 5 February 1829.

27. Ibid., 13 and 27 November 1828.

28. Ibid., 24 June 1829.

29. Ibid., 1 July 1829.

30. Ibid., 15 July 1829.

31. Ibid., 12 August 1829.

32. Perkal, "William Goodell," 28.

33. Ibid., 77.

34. Ibid., 78.

35. Goodell, *Slavery and Anti-Slavery,* 142 n. See 139–40, 347–49, for the ACS and prejudice.

36. Ibid., 473.

37. William Goodell, *The Democracy of Christianity,* 2 vols. (New York, 1849–52), 1:244. Subsequent page references will appear in the text.

38. See also Paul Goodman, "The Emergence of Homestead Exemption in the United States: Accomodation and Resistance to the Market Revolution, 1840–1880," *Journal of American History* 80 (September 1993): 470–98.

39. George Fitzhugh used Goodell's criticisms of Northern society for proslavery purposes in *Cannibals All! or, Slaves without Masters* (Richmond, 1857).

40. Goodell, *Slavery and Anti-Slavery,* 474.

CHAPTER 8

1. Elizur Wright to Amos Phelps, 16 July 1835, Elizur Wright Papers, Library of Congress.

2. Quoted in Philip G. Wright and Elizabeth Q. Wright, *Elizur Wright: The Father of Life Insurance* (Chicago, 1937), 17. For biographical material, see also Lawrence B. Goodheart, *Abolitionist, Actuary, Atheist: Elizur Wright and the Reform Impulse* (Kent, Ohio, 1990).

3. Elizur Wright to Susan Wright, 26 February 1829, Elizur Wright Papers, Library of Congress.

4. Elizur Wright, *Lecture on Tobacco* (New York, 1833), 12.

5. Quoted in Wright and Wright, *Elizur Wright,* 61.

6. Quoted in Goodheart, *Abolitionist, Actuary, Atheist,* 80.

7. Elizur Wright to William Lloyd Garrison, 6 November 1837, Elizur Wright Papers, Library of Congress.

8. For an extended discussion of the links between abolitionism and the manual labor movement, see Paul Goodman, "The Manual Labor Movement and the Origins of Abolitionism," *Journal of the Early Republic* 13 (fall 1993): 355–88.

9. Beriah Green, *Sermons and Other Discourses* (New York, 1850), 50. For biographical material, see Milton C. Sernett, *Abolition's Axe: Beriah Green, Oneida Institute, and the Black Freedom Struggle* (Syracuse, 1986).

10. For biographical material, see William Birney, *James G. Birney and His Times* (New York, 1890), and Betty Fladeland, *James Gillespie Birney: Slaveholder to Abolitionist* (Ithaca, N.Y.,1955).

11. James G. Birney, *Letter on Colonization* (New York, 1834), 6–7.

12. Quoted in Robert A. Trendel Jr., *William Jay: Churchman, Public Servant, and Reformer* (New York, 1982), 25, 31. For biographical material, see also Bayard Tuckerman, *William Jay, and the Constitutional Movement for the Abolition of Slavery* (New York, 1893).

13. Quoted in Trendel, *William Jay,* 47.

14. Ibid., 140.

15. Tuckerman, *William Jay,* 43–80.

16. Ibid., 99.

17. For biographical material, see Hugh Davis, *Joshua Leavitt, Evangelical Abolitionist* (Baton Rouge, 1990).

18. For biographical material, see Edward H. Madden and James E. Hamilton, *Freedom and Grace: The Life of Asa Mahan* (Metuchen, N.J., 1982).

19. Samuel Joseph May, *Memoir of Samuel Joseph May* (Boston, 1876), 3. For biographical material, see Daniel Yacovone, *Samuel Joseph May and the Dilemmas of the Liberal Persuasion, 1797–1871* (Philadelphia, 1991).

20. May, *Memoir,* 93.

21. Ibid., 126.

22. Ibid., 136–37.

23. Samuel Joseph May, *Some Recollections of Our Antislavery Conflict* (Boston, 1869), 12.

24. Ibid., 19.

25. Yacovone, *Samuel Joseph May,* 38.

26. Ibid., 55.

27. May, *Some Recollections,* 28–29.

28. Bertram Wyatt-Brown, *Lewis Tappan and the Evangelical War against Slavery* (New York, 1971), 17.

29. Wyatt-Brown, *Lewis Tappan,* 102. For biographical material on Arthur Tappan, see Lewis Tappan, *The Life of Arthur Tappan* (New York, 1870).

30. Diary of Lewis Tappan, 2 November 1822, Lewis Tappan Papers, Oberlin College Library.

31. Lewis Tappan, *Arthur Tappan,* 337.

32. Ibid., 145–46.

33. Gerrit Smith was another example of a moralizing capitalist. His inherited wealth left him uneasy all his life. He asked his wife to pray for him to overcome his selfishness. At twenty-five he thought he wanted to become a minister. Then he found the antidote to his uneasiness in benevolence. Smith was active in the Sabbatarian movement, joined the American Colonization Society in 1827, and started a manual labor school for blacks in Peterboro, New York, in 1834, which Beriah Green wanted integrated. Temperance was his first enthusiasm. Smith concluded that the ACS had no interest in free blacks and left it in 1835.

For biographical material, see Ralph V. Harlow, *Gerrit Smith, Philanthropist and Reformer* (New York, 1939).

34. Ibid., 25.

35. Ibid., 31.

36. Ibid., 145.

37. Quoted in James B. Stewart, *Wendell Philllips, Liberty's Hero* (Baton Rouge, 1986), 145.

38. Ibid., 57.

39. Ibid., 66.

40. Ibid., 68.

41. Quoted in Robert Vincent Sparks, "Abolitionist Silver Slippers: A Biography of Edmund Quincy" (Ph.D. diss., Boston University, 1978), 14, 18.

42. Ibid., 49.

43. Ibid., 49.

44. Ibid., 51, 52.

45. Ibid., 99.

46. Ibid., 200.

47. Theodore Dwight Weld, *First Annual Report of the Society for Promoting Manual Labor in Literary Institutions . . . January 28, 1831* (New York, 1833), 74 nn. 59 and 60. Also 66–67, 87–88, 94, 96, 115–16 n. For Weld's own appearance, see Robert Abzug, *Passionate Liberator: Theodore Dwight Weld and the Dilemma of Reform* (New York, 1980), 3–4; Benjamin P. Thomas, *Theodore Weld, Crusader for Freedom* (New Brunswick, N.J., 1950), 8–9. On the topic of masculinity, see Joseph Kett, *Rites of Passage: Adolescence in America* (New York, 1987); David G. Pugh, *Sons of Liberty: The Masculine Mind in the Nineteenth Century* (Westport, Conn., 1983); Paul Goodman, *Towards a Christian Republic: Antimasonry and the Great Transition in New England, 1826–1836* (New York, 1988), 50–53, 87 ff.; David Leverenz, *Manhood and the American Renaissance* (Ithaca, N.Y., 1989); Mary Ann Clawson, *Constructing Brotherhood: Class, Gender, and Fraternalism* (Princeton, 1989); Mark C. Carnes, *Secret Ritual and Manhood in Victorian America* (New Haven, 1989). Jonathan A. Glickstein, in *Concepts of Free Labor in Antebellum America* (New Haven, 1991), also found concerns with effeminacy in the disdain for manual labor. See 41, 493 n. 41.

48. Weld, *Report,* 66–67, 87–88, 94. For the importance of consumerist display to the new middle class, see Karen Halttunen, *Confidence Men and Painted Women* (New Haven, 1984).

49. Lawrence T. Lesick, *The Lane Rebels: Evangelicalism and Antislavery in America* (Metuchen, N.J., 1980), 168; Abzug, *Passionate Liberator,* chapters 1–4.

50. See Donald M. Scott, *From Office to Profession: The New England Ministry, 1750–1850* (Philadelphia, 1978). For artisanal manhood, see David Leverenz, *Manhood and the American Renaissance* (Ithaca, N.Y., 1989), 3, 72–85.

51. Leverenz, *Manhood and the American Renaissance,* 3 ff., 47.

52. Ann Douglas, *The Feminization of American Culture* (New York, 1977); Richard D. Shiels, "The Feminization of American Congregationalism,

1730–1835," *American Quarterly* 33 (spring 1981): 46–62; Mary P. Ryan, *Cradle of the Middle Class: The Family in Oneida County, New York, 1790–1865* (Cambridge and New York, 1981); Goodman, *Towards a Christian Republic,* 69.

53. Mary P. Ryan, *Women in Public* (Baltimore, 1990).

54. Anthony J. Barker, *Captain Charles Stuart, Anglo-American Abolitionist* (Baton Rouge, La., 1986), 65 ff.; Charles Stuart to Weld, 26 March 1831 and June 1831, *The Letters of Theodore D. Weld, Angelina Grimké Weld and Sarah Grimké,* 2 vols., ed. Gilbert H. Barnes and Dwight L. Dumond (1934; reprint, Gloucester, Mass., 1965), 1:42–44, 1:48–49; Philip G. Wright and Elizabeth Q. Wright, *Elizur Wright: The Father of Life Insurance* (Chicago, 1932), 61 ff.; Sernett, *Abolition's Axe,* 25; Frederick C. Waite, *Western Reserve University: The Hudson Era* (Cleveland, 1943), 96 ff.

CHAPTER 9

1. *Second Annual Report of the Board of Managers of the New England Anti-Slavery Society* (Boston, 1834), 7.

2. *Liberator,* 21 September and 5 October 1833.

3. Elizur Wright Jr., *The Sin of Slavery and Its Remedy, Containing Some Reflections on the Moral Influence of African Colonization* (New York, 1833), 5.

4. Herman R. Muelder, *Fighters for Freedom* (New York, 1959), 54.

5. John R. McKivigan, *The War against Proslavery Religion* (Ithaca, N.Y., 1984), 203–20.

6. *Liberator,* 14 December 1833.

7. John Greenleaf Whittier, *Justice and Expediency: Slavery Considered with a View to Its Rightful and Effectual Remedy, Abolition* (Haverhill, 1833), 1.

8. Amos Phelps, *Lectures on Slavery, and Its Remedy* (Boston, 1834), xi.

9. Ibid., v–ix.

10. Ibid., 13–17.

11. See Amos Phelps Papers, Boston Public Library.

12. *Liberator,* 26 July 1834.

13. Phelps, *Lectures,* vi.

14. Ibid., 284.

15. Ibid., 88.

16. Ibid., 237, 238.

17. Ibid., 155. See also David Brion Davis, "The Emergence of Immediatism in British and American Thought," *Mississippi Valley Historical Review* 49 (September 1962): 209–30.

18. Beriah Green, *Antislavery Quarterly* 1 (October 1835): 53.

19. See Phelps, *Lectures,* 18–20, and the antislavery press, especially the *Emancipator.* Robert S. Fletcher, *A History of Oberlin* (1943; reprint, New York, 1971), 297; *Friend of Man,* 1 December 1836.

20. Paul Goodman, *Towards a Christian Republic: Antimasonry and the Great Transformation in New England, 1826–1836* (New York, 1988), 234.

21. Ibid., chapter 4.

22. Phelps, *Lectures,* 181.

23. Ibid., 186. See also George B. Cheever, "The Principle of Expediency," *Liberator,* 23 August 1833; David T. Kimball Jr., "Apology for Anti-Slavery," Andover Theological Seminary, 22 August 1833 (n.p., n.d.); and for an abolitionist account of an attack on ultraism, see *Friend of Man,* 15 September 1836, and another defense of "modern radicalism," 13 October 1836.

24. *Philanthropist,* 30 December 1836.

25. *Philanthropist,* 22 July 1836.

26. Beriah Green, *Antislavery Quarterly* 1 (October 1835): 57, 61; also ibid. (January 1836): 158–62, 170–71.

27. *Philanthropist,* 1 January 1836.

28. Asa Rand, *The New Divinity Tried, Being an Examination of a Sermon Delivered by C. G. Finney on Making a New Heart* (Boston, 1832), 11, 17.

29. David Oliphant, *What a Minister Must Do to Remain Pure* (Beverly, Mass., 1817), 121.

30. David Oliphant, *The Happy Nation* (Beverly, Mass., 1825), 16.

31. David Oliphant, *Why Sinners Cannot Come to Christ* (Beverly, Mass., 1831), 15.

32. Charles J. Warren, *Memorial for Posterity* (Boston, 1831), 24.

33. David T. Kimball, *Sermon on the Utility of a Permanent Ministry* (Ipswich, Mass., 1839), 4–6, 11–13.

34. David T. Kimball, *The Pastor's Jubilee* (Ipswich, Mass., 1857), 28, 44.

35. *Emancipator,* 19 May 1835.

36. *Friend of Man,* 13 October 1836.

37. *New England Telegraph and Eclectic Review* 1 (1835–36): 11. For an attack on Beecherism, see 373.

38. Ibid., 112.

39. Ibid., 213–14, 450.

40. Garrison to Helen E. Garrison, 10 May 1836, *The Letters of William Lloyd Garrison,* 6 vols., ed. Walter M. Merrill (Cambridge, Mass., 1971–81), 2:94.

41. Thomas Williams, *A Sermon on the Conclusion of the Second Century, from the Settlement of the State of Rhode Island and Providence Plantations* (Providence, 1837), 19.

42. Ibid., 20, 21.

43. Thomas Williams, *A Discourse on the Ordination of Reverend Emerson Paine* (Middleborough, Mass., 1816), 9.

44. Williams, *Second Century,* 28.

45. *Emancipator,* 16 September 1834.

46. Williams, *Second Century,* 28.

47. Ibid., 17, 18.

48. Thomas Williams, *A Discourse for the Month of April, A.D. 1816* (Providence, R.I., 1816), 17.

49. Williams, *Ordination,* 20; Thomas Williams, *The Mercy of God: A Centurial Sermon on the Revival of Religion A.D. 1740* (Hartford, Conn., 1840), 18.

50. Thomas Williams, *A Discourse on the Ordinances of Divine Appointment* (Providence, R.I., 1855), 24.

51. George Hathaway, *A Sermon Preached at the Funeral of Reverend Josiah Peet* (Portland, Maine, 1852), 15.

52. Joseph C. Lovejoy, *The Alliance of Jehoshaphat and Ahab* (Boston, 1844), 2, 3.

53. Swan C. Pomroy, *Arguments in Favor of Missions* (Portland, Maine, 1833), 8.

54. Ibid., 12.

55. Ibid., 16.

56. *Congregational Quarterly* 9 (October 1867): 313–28.

57. David Thurston, *A Sermon Delivered in Saco, June 26, 1816, before the Maine Missionary Society* (Hallowell, Maine, 1816), 5, 6.

58. Ibid., 18.

59. David Thurston, *A Sermon Preached at the Ordination of Rev. David Smith* (Hallowell, Maine, 1811), 12.

60. David Thurston, *A Discourse Preached in Winthrop, April 3, 1823 at the Annual Fast, in Maine* (Hallowell, Maine, 1823), 12, 20.

61. David Thurston, *A Sermon Preached at the Ordination of the Rev. David Starret* (Hallowell, Maine, 1821), 14; David Thurston, *A Discourse Preached in Winthrop, April 12, 1821, at the Annual Fast in Maine* (Hallowell, Maine, 1821); David Thurston, *Causes of an Unsuccessful Ministry* (Hallowell, Maine, 1819).

62. Thurston, *The Annual Fast* (1823), 6, 7.

63. David Thurston, *A Sermon Delivered at the Third Annual Meeting of the American Missionary Association* (New York, 1849), 7, 9.

CHAPTER 10

1. *Friend of Man,* 5 April 1837.

2. *Second Annual Report of the American Anti-Slavery Society* (New York, 1835), 62.

3. Theodore Dwight Weld to Birney, 28 May 1834, in *The Letters of James Gillespie Birney, 1831–1857,* ed. Dwight L. Dumond (New York, 1938), 113.

4. *Proceedings of the First Annual Meeting of the New York State Anti-Slavery Society* (Utica, 1836), 44.

5. *Emancipator,* 25 March 1834, and Augustus Wattles letter to the *Emancipator* on 22 April 1834.

6. *Second Annual Report of the Board of Managers of the New England Anti-Slavery Society* (Boston, 1834), 27.

7. Garrison to the *Liberator,* 7 September 1832, *The Letters of William Lloyd Garrison,* 6 vols., ed. Walter M. Merrill (Cambridge, Mass., 1971–1981), 1:163.

8. Garrison to the *Liberator,* 2 October 1832, *Letters,* 1:187.

9. Ibid., 22, 151 ff.

10. *Emancipator,* 8 June 1833.

11. Ibid., 4 March 1834.

12. Garrison to Henry E. Benson, 29 August 1831, ibid., 1:128, and William Lloyd Garrison, *Thoughts on African Colonization* (Boston, 1832).

13. Garrison to Henry S. Benson, 30 July 1831, *Letters,* 1:124.

14. Ibid.

15. Garrison to Henry E. Benson, 31 May 1832, ibid., 1:151.

16. *Liberator,* 1 and 8 September 1832.

17. Ibid., 7 and 12 July 1832.

18. Ibid., 8 September 1832.

19. Garrison to Henry E. Benson, 21 July 1832, *Letters,* 1:159.

20. *Liberator,* 17 November 1832.

21. *The Report and Proceedings of the First Annual Meeting of the Providence Anti-Slavery Society* (Providence, 1833), 5–10.

22. There were earlier abortive efforts from the *Liberator* and Garrison. The figure of 101 members comes from the *Third Annual Report of the American Anti-Slavery Society* (New York, 1836), 93.

23. John L. Myers, "Antislavery Agencies in Rhode Island, 1832–1835," *Rhode Island History* 29 (summer and fall 1970): 82–93, and John L. Myers, "Antislavery Agents in Rhode Island, 1835–1837," ibid. (winter 1971): 21–31.

24. *Proceedings of the Rhode Island Anti-Slavery Convention* (Providence, 1836), 76, 86.

25. See table 3.

26. Weld to Elizur Wright Jr., 2 March 1835, in *The Letters of Theodore Dwight Weld, Angelina Grimké Weld and Sarah Grimké, 1822–1844,* ed. Gilbert H. Barnes and Dwight L. Dumond (1934; reprint, Gloucester, Mass., 1965), 206.

27. Samuel Galloway to Weld, 9 August 1835, in ibid., 228.

28. Weld to Lewis Tappan, 5 April 1836, in ibid., 288.

29. *Emancipator,* 28 July 1836.

PART 3

1. *Proceedings of the Rhode Island Anti-Slavery Convention* (Providence, 1836), 15, 34; John B. Jentz, "The Antislavery Constituency in Jacksonian New York City," *Civil War History* 27 (June 1981), 121.

2. *Proceedings of the First Annual Meeting of the New York State Anti-Slavery Society* (New York, 1834), 54–55; *Liberator,* 25 July 1835; *Friend of Man,* 18 August 1836.

3. *Friend of Man,* 6 October 1836.

CHAPTER 11

1. *Proceedings of the Rhode Island Anti-Slavery Convention* (Providence, 1836), 33–35. See *Friend of Man,* 6 October 1836, for a detailed analysis of the social composition of the Cincinnati mobs that exonerates most German, Irish, and working-class people, and see *Anti-Slavery Record* 2 (July 1836): 3–4, on antislavery mobs.

2. *Sixth Annual Report of the Board of Managers of the Massachussets Anti-Slavery Society* (Boston, 1838), xiv; "The Commercial Aristocracy of the North," *Liberator,* 11 October 1834.

3. *Friend of Man,* 18 August 1836.

4. *Fourth Annual Report of the American Anti-Slavery Society* (New York, 1837), 60.

5. Quoted from the labor reform newspaper *Daily Reformer,* "By a Democrat," in *Liberator,* 14 November 1835; *Fourth Annual Report of the American Anti-Slavery Society,* 60.

6. *Emancipator,* 21 July 1836; *Proceedings of the Rhode Island Anti-Slavery Society,* 30–32, 33, 36; *Liberator,* 7 November 1835.

7. *Proceedings of the Rhode Island Anti-Slavery Convention,* 31; *Fifth Annual Report of the Board of Managers of the Massachussets Anti-Slavery Society* (Boston, 1837), xix; *Liberator,* 1 September 1832.

8. *Fourth Annual Report of the Board of Managers of the Massachussetts Anti-Slavery Society* (Boston, 1836), 63; *Philanthropist,* 17 February 1835.

9. Charles Stuart to Birney, 30 September 1836, in *The Letters of James Gillespie Birney, 1831–1857,* ed. Dwight L. Dumond (New York, 1938), 362–63.

10. Birney to Ezekial Webb, Thomas Chandler, and Darius C. Jackson, 6 October 1836, in ibid., 363–64.

11. Ralph R. Gurley to Birney, 21 August 1833, in ibid., 84; Jentz, "The Antislavery Constituency in Jacksonian New York City," 117.

12. *Proceedings of the Rhode Island Anti-Slavery Convention,* 7.

13. *Liberator,* 21 June 1834. On dispensing with titles at a Pennsylvania antislavery meeting, see *Philanthropist,* 24 February 1837.

14. *Philanthropist,* 29 May 1838.

15. *Liberator,* 12 October 1838. See also 21 September 1838, which quotes Thomas Jefferson saying that the work of emancipation is for the young.

16. See table 3.

17. See table 3.

18. See table 4.

19. *Lynn Mirror,* 19 March 1831; *Lynn Record,* 11 July 1832.

20. All but one member of the Antimasonic ticket in Lynn were members of the abolitionist society in 1834; see Paul Goodman, *Towards a Christian Republic: Antimasonry and the Great Transition in New England, 1826–1836* (New York, 1988), 181–88.

21. Lynn Anti-Slavery Society Records, Lynn Historical Society; *Liberator,* 7 January 1832.

22. Marie-Pierre Brasseur, "Chaos or Community: Abolitionism in Lynn, Massachussets, 1832–1839," Seminar Paper, University of California, Davis, 1982, 9.

23. *Philanthropist,* 18 November 1836.

24. *Lynn Record,* 11 January 1837.

25. Lynn Anti-Slavery Society Minutes, 4–21 June 1838. Not paginated.

26. Based on ibid.

27. Ibid., 4 December 1839.

280 Notes to Pages 151–156

28. *Liberator,* 2 April 1831.

29. *Friend of Man,* 29 March 1837. See Eric Hobsbawm, *Workers: Worlds of Labor* (New York, 1984), on the radicalism of shoemakers. He attributes this in part to the work process, which enabled one to read while the others labored, and which thus stimulated discussion and political thought.

30. Alan Dawley, *Class and Community: The Industrial Revolution in Lynn* (Cambridge, Mass., 1976), 56–57.

31. See table 3.

32. Amos Phelps, *Lectures on Slavery, and Its Remedy* (Boston, 1834), viii.

33. *Liberator,* 19 September 1833; *Emancipator,* 23 January 1834.

34. *Liberator,* 11 January 1835. See the annual reports of the American Anti-Slavery Society for the years 1836–38.

35. *Liberator,* 4 February 1837.

36. *Emancipator,* 10 August 1837.

37. *Liberator,* 4 February 1837.

38. Chittenden County Anti-Slavery Society Records, Vermont Historical Society.

39. *Liberator,* 1 January 1831. See also a reprint from the Unitarian *Christian Examiner* arguing against class conflict, *Liberator,* 22 January 1831, and praise for the Harvard commencement orator who attacked "the wild spirit of jacobinism" that aroused the working classes, *Liberator,* 3 September 1831.

40. Ibid., 29 January 1831.

41. Ibid.

42. Ibid., 5 February 1831.

43. Ibid., 1 September 1832.

44. Ibid., 13 October 1832.

45. See ibid., 20 December 1834, which commended a letter from Philadelphia to Northern laboring men attacking the use of slave labor in cotton manufacturing in Virginia. Also see ibid., 14 November 1835, which reprinted an editorial from the Boston labor newspaper the *Daily Reformer* attacking the rich for organizing the anti-abolition mob in Boston, and an editorial in ibid., 30 July 1836, that defended the workingmen's movement against Lyman Beecher's attack on them as "agrarians" and "infidels."

46. *Philanthropist,* 1 January 1836, and also 17 March 1837. See an earlier argument in favor of disenfranchising white labor in the Virginia Constitutional Convention, *Emancipator,* 23 September 1834.

47. *Antislavery Quarterly* 2 (October 1836): 61–73. The quotes are from 65, 66, 67, 69, and 72. See also the attack on New York City Whig merchants for their attempt to forge an alliance with planter elites to defeat Van Buren's bank policy, *Philanthropist,* 2 June 1837. See also Beriah Green's attack on clerical apologies for slavery as rooted in "factitious distinctions" based on wealth and status-seeking consumption styles that led "some bloated creatures" to look down on those whose skin was "darkened by the sun, or pinched by poverty." *Antislavery Quarterly* 1 (October 1835): 34–67; the quote is at 56–57. "Address by A. A. Guthrie," *Philanthropist,* 21 October 1836: "Pride, selfishness, and love of gain, have been nourishing a pro-slavery spirit at the north. . . . The constant

intercourse between the north and the south has not only made slavery familiar but has rendered *labor* disreputable."

48. *Emancipator,* 28 January 1834.

49. *Third Annual Report of the American Anti-Slavery Society* (New York, 1836), 17–18; "An Address before the Union Evangelical Antislavery Society of New York City," *New York Evangelist,* 4 January 1840; editorial on Lyman Beecher, *Liberator,* 30 July 1836. The Otsego County Antislavery Society in New York echoed Gerrit Smith's warning: "That as the south have founded the defense of slaveholding,—not on the color of the slave principally, but on his *asserted inability* to take care of himself; and the superior happiness of his present condition over that of a state of freedom . . . therefore the extension of this principle will involve the whole lower and laboring class in our land in a state of bondage to the rich."

50. *Emancipator,* 25 August 1836.

51. *Proceedings of the Rhode Island Anti-Slavery Convention,* 40, but see also 23, 25, 37, 39, 57.

52. *Emancipator,* 6 April 1837. See also the powerful appeal to farmers and mechanics in the *Friend of Man,* "The Hope of the Slave," 5 April 1837, which argued that the spirit of Mammon of which slavery was only a particular expression threatened free labor, that workers were coming to understand that slavery was not just "a domestic institution of the South, and they have nothing to do with it" and therefore "the Hope of the slave is in the free laboring population in the North."

53. *Proceedings of the First Annual Meeting of the New York State Anti-Slavery Society* (Utica, 1836), 20, reprinted in *Herald of Freedom* (Concord, N.H.), 14 November 1836.

54. Reprinted in the *Liberator,* "Working Men," 4 February 1837.

55. *Proceedings of the First Annual Meeting of the New York State Anti-Slavery Society,* 55–56.

56. *Philanthropist,* 1 and 22 July 1836. See also Christopher Tomlins, *Law, Labor, and Ideology in the Early American Republic* (New York, 1993).

57. *Philanthropist,* 2 June 1837.

58. *Friend of Man,* 1 and 22 December 1836.

59. Paul Goodman, "The Emergence of Homestead Exemption in the United States: Accomodation and Resistance to the Market Revolution, 1840–1880," *Journal of American History* 80 (September 1993): 470–98; Eric Foner, *Free Soil, Free Labor, Free Men: The Ideology of the Republican Party before the Civil War* (New York, 1970); William Gienapp, *The Origins of the Republican Party, 1852–1856* (New York, 1987).

CHAPTER 12

1. *Emancipator,* 2 February 1837.

2. *Philanthropist,* 18 December 1838.

3. Thomas Dublin, *Women at Work: The Transformation of Work and Community in Lowell, Massachussets, 1826–1860* (New York, 1979), 86–107.

4. *Zion's Herald,* 18 January 1837.

5. David Roediger, *The Wages of Whiteness: Race and the Making of the American Working Class* (New York, 1991); Alexander Saxton, *The Rise and Fall of the White Republic: Class Politics and Mass Culture in Nineteenth-Century America* (New York, 1990); Bruce Laurie, *Artisans into Workers: Labor in Nineteeth-Century America* (New York, 1989); Eric Foner, *Tom Paine and Revolutionary America* (New York, 1976); Sean Wilentz, *Chants Democratic: New York City and the Rise of the American Working Class, 1788–1850* (New York, 1984), 333, 264.

6. Alan Dawley and Paul Faler, "Working Class Culture and Politics in the Industrial Revolution: Sources of Loyalism and Rebellion," *Journal of Social History* 9 (June 1976): 466–80.

7. Wilentz, *Chants Democratic,* 161, 186, 263–64, 263; John B. Jentz, "Artisans, Evangelicals, and the City: A Social History of Abolition and Labor Reform in Jacksonian New York" (Ph.D. diss., City University of New York, 1977).

8. *Working Man's Advocate,* 11 January 1831; 18 June 1831; 20 April 1833.

9. Ibid., 2 July 1831.

10. See ibid., 2 July 1831, for health reform; for temperance, see 6, 13, and 20 August 1831.

11. Ibid., 9 June 1832.

12. Ibid., 23 June, 27 August, and 24 September 1831.

13. Ibid., 17 September 1831.

14. Ibid., 10 March 1832.

15. *The Radical, in Continuation of the Working Man's Advocate,* November 1841, 169.

16. *Working Man's Advocate,* 11 June 1831.

17. Ibid., 22 December 1832.

18. Ibid., 3 December 1831; 15 October 1831. See 28 January 1832, which argued that allowing the slave states to force free blacks to move to the North would help perpetuate slavery.

19. Ibid., 15 October 1831; 22 June 1833.

20. Ibid., 1 October 1831.

21. Ibid., 24 September 1831.

22. Ibid., 15 October 1831.

23. Ibid.

24. Ibid., 1 October 1831; 1 October 1832. The *Working Man's Advocate* also publicized the Convention of Free Persons of Color to meet in Philadelphia, reporting that the delegates were opposed to colonization, 27 April 1833.

25. Ibid., 17 December 1831; 15 October 1831.

26. Ibid., 19 September 1835.

27. Ibid., 31 October 1835; 21 November 1835.

28. *The Radical,* March 1841. See Roediger, *Wages of Whiteness,* 65–92.

29. Theodore Sedgwick Jr., in *A Collection of the Political Writings of William Leggett,* 2 vols., ed. Theodore Sedgwick Jr. (New York, 1840), 1:vi, xii; Arthur M. Schlesinger Jr., *The Age of Jackson* (Boston, 1945), 186, 189–91,

259–60, 265; Edward Pessen, *Jacksonian America: Society, Personality, and Politics* (Homewood, Ill., 1969), 295–96.
    30. William Leggett,*Writings,* 1:28–33, 38–39. See also 35–36.
    31. Ibid., 1:398.
    32. Ibid., 1:207.
    33. Ibid., 1:204–9.
    34. Ibid., 2:10, and also see his earlier criticism of the press, ibid., 1:28–29.
    35. *Political Plain Dealer,* 3 December 1836.
    36. Ibid., 24 December 1836.
    37. Ibid., 14 January 1837. See Leggett to James G. Birney, 22 November 1838, in *Writings,* 1:477–78, affirming his abolitionism and giving Birney permission to reprint his antislavery writings.
    38. *Political Plain Dealer,* 14 January 1837.
    39. Leggett, *Writings,* 2:25, and see 2:14, 17–18.
    40. Ibid., 2:34, 39–47.
    41. Ibid., 2:53–55.
    42. Ibid., 2:55, and also 2:60, 2:67.
    43. Ibid., 2:71–75, 77–79, and Sedgwick's account, ibid., 1:xiv–xv. Schlesinger, *Age of Jackson,* 190–91.
    44. Leggett, *Writings,* 2:77–78.
    45. *Political Plain Dealer,* 11 February 1837.
    46. Ibid., 4 March 1837.
    47. Ibid., 3 June 1837.

PART 4

    1. *Liberator,* 14 July 1832.
    2. Ibid., 5 May 1832.
    3. Ibid., 28 December 1833.
    4. Ibid., 14 July 1832.
    5. Garrison to Helen E. Benson, 18 February 1834, *The Letters of William Lloyd Garrison,* 6 vols., ed. Walter M. Merrill (Cambridge, Mass., 1971–81), 1:284, and see also Garrison to Helen E. Benson, 18 January 1834, 1:280.
    6. Jean Fagan Yellin and John C. Van Horne, eds., *The Abolitionist Sisterhood: Women's Political Culture in Antebellum America* (Ithaca, N.Y., 1994), 8.

CHAPTER 13

    1. For a convenient collection of the Grimkés' writings, see Larry Ceplair, ed., *The Public Years of Sarah and Angelina Grimké: Selected Writings, 1835–1836* (New York, 1989).
    2. Catherine H. Birney, *The Grimké Sisters: Sarah and Angelina Grimké, the First American Women Advocates of Abolition and Woman's Rights* (Boston, 1885; reprint, Westport, Conn., 1969), 138.
    3. Gerda Lerner, *The Grimké Sisters from South Carolina: Pioneers for Woman's Rights and Abolition* (New York, 1967); Birney, *The Grimké Sisters;*

Katherine Du Pre Lumpkin, *The Emancipation of Angelina Grimké* (Chapel Hill, 1974). For Southern white women's support of slavery, see Jean Friedman, *The Enclosed Garden: Women and Community in the Evangelical South, 1830–1900* (Chapel Hill, 1985), and Elizabeth Fox-Genovese, *Within the Plantation Household: Black and White Women of the Old South* (Chapel Hill, 1988).

4. Birney, *The Grimké Sisters*, 17, 7–13; Lerner, *The Grimké Sisters*, 16, 18, 21, 27–29.

5. Lerner, *Grimké Sisters*, 29.

6. Ibid., 9.

7. Ibid., 78.

8. Ibid., 18.

9. Ibid., 19.

10. Lerner, *The Grimké Sisters*, 45.

11. Birney, *The Grimké Sisters*, 30.

12. Ibid., 38.

13. Ibid., 27.

14. Lumpkin, *Emancipation*, 4.

15. Ibid., 13–15.

16. Birney, *The Grimké Sisters*, 40.

17. Lumpkin, *Emancipation*, 14; Birney, *The Grimké Sisters*, 42–43.

18. Ibid., 43, 49; Lerner, *The Grimké Sisters*, 69.

19. Lumpkin, *Emancipation*, 81, 89, 82.

20. Birney, *The Grimké Sisters*, 53.

21. Lumpkin, *Emancipation*, 36, and see 31–36.

22. Ibid., 42–46.

23. Birney, *The Grimké Sisters*, 55–56.

24. Ibid., 144, 122.

25. Gerda Lerner, "The Grimké Sisters and the Struggle against Race Prejudice," *Journal of Negro History* 46 (October 1963): 280–81, 283.

26. Ibid., 286.

27. Birney, *The Grimké Sisters*, 123–30.

28. Ibid., 105–9.

29. Lerner, *The Grimké Sisters*, 132–33, 160.

30. Lerner, *The Grimké Sisters*, 109–10, 118–19, 132–33; Lumpkin, *Emancipation*, 77–91.

31. Gilbert H. Barnes, *The Antislavery Impulse: 1830–1844* (1933; reprint, New York, 1964), 154.

32. Lumpkin, *Emancipation*, 97, also 99–105; Birney, *The Grimké Sisters*, 170–71; Ceplair, ed., *Selected Writings*, 69, 71–73.

33. Lumpkin, *Emancipation*, 168.

34. Ibid., 120; Birney, *The Grimké Sisters*, 175–78.

35. Benjamin Lundy, *Memoir*, in Elizabeth Margaret Chandler, *The Poetical Works of Elizabeth Margaret Chandler, with a Memoir of her Life and Character by Benjamin Lundy. Essays, Philanthropic and Moral* (Philadelphia, 1836), 1–2.

36. Ibid., 9.

37. Merton L. Dillon, "Elizabeth Chandler and the Spread of Antislavery Sentiment to Michigan," *Michigan History* 39(December 1955): 484.

38. Chandler, *Works*, 66.

39. Dillon, "Elizabeth Chandler," 484–85.

40. Lundy, *Memoir*, 36.

41. Ibid., 39.

42. Ibid., 11. On anonymity and humility, see 16.

43. Ibid., 37.

44. Ibid., 25.

45. Chandler, *Works*, 66–68.

46. Ibid., 34.

47. Ibid., 13, 39.

48. Ibid., 9.

49. Ibid., 51.

50. Ibid., 64.

51. Ibid., 116.

52. Lundy, *Memoir*, 18, 21, 22.

53. Ibid., 23.

54. Ibid.

55. Ibid., 24.

56. Chandler, *Works*, 52, 60.

57. Ibid., 82.

58. Ibid., 69.

59. Anna Hallowell, *James and Lucretia Mott: Life and Letters* (Boston, 1884), 145, 201–15.

60. Ibid., 19–27; Lloyd C. M. Hare, *The Greatest American Woman: Lucretia Mott* (New York, 1937), 24, 33; Otelia Cromwell, *Lucretia Mott* (Cambridge, Mass., 1958), 5–6, 125.

61. Hare, *Greatest American*, 35.

62. Hallowell, *James and Lucretia Mott*, 35–47.

63. Ibid., 65. For her age, see 74.

64. Hare, *Greatest American*, 61, 48. She also read Mary Wollstonecraft and kept *A Vindication of the Rights of Woman* on display on a table for forty years. Cromwell, *Lucretia Mott*, 27.

65. Ibid., 35.

66. Hallowell, *James and Lucretia Mott*, 57, 65–66.

67. Ibid., 68, 71; Hare, *Greatest American*, 67.

68. Hallowell, *James and Lucretia Mott*, 65, 76, 79–80, 82, 100–103; Robert W. Doherty, *The Hicksite Separation: A Sociological Analysis of Religious Schism in Early Nineteenth-Century America* (New Brunswick, N.J., 1967); Hare, *Greatest American*, 70–75.

69. Ibid., 77–80.

70. Cromwell, *Lucretia Mott*, 122, 108–9.

71. Hallowell, *James and Lucretia Mott*, 114.

72. Ibid., 117.

73. Ibid., 224.

74. Ibid., 120.

75. Ibid., 114, 122; Cromwell, *Lucretia Mott*, 39–43, 109–11. Garrison credited Mott with helping him to overcome attachment to theological dogma. See

Blanche Hersh, *The Slavery of Sex: Female Abolitionists in America* (Urbana, Ill., 1978), 12.

76. Hare, *Greatest American*, 98.

77. Cromwell, *Lucretia Mott*, 41.

78. Lydia Maria Child, *An Appeal in Favor of That Class of Americans Called Africans* (New York, 1836), iii.

79. Editors' introduction to *Lydia Maria Child: Selected Letters, 1817–1880*, ed. Milton Meltzer and Patricia G. Holland (Amherst, Mass., 1982), 25, 28–29.

80. Carolyn Karcher, *The First Woman in the Republic: A Cultural Biography of Lydia Maria Child* (Durham, N.C., 1994), 2.

81. Deborah P. Clifford, *Crusader for Freedom: A Life of Lydia Maria Child* (Boston, 1992), 6–12. Child did attend an academy for one year, but it did not offer a rigorous curriculum. Karcher, *First Woman*, 3–4; William C. Nell, *The Colored Patriots of the American Revolution* (Boston, 1855; reprint, New York, 1968), 25.

82. Karcher, *First Woman*, 13; Clifford, *Crusader*, 21–30.

83. Karcher, *First Woman*, 36.

84. Ibid., 80–150; Clifford, *Crusader*, 61–85.

85. It was common for women to publish anonymously.

86. Clifford, *Crusader*, 49.

87. Ibid., 37–38; Helene G. Baer, *The Heart Is Like Heaven: The Life of Lydia Maria Child* (Philadelphia, 1964), 38.

88. Ibid., 68.

89. Child to Mary Preston, 6 January 1827, *Letters*, 8.

90. Child diary entry, 3 May 1825, ibid., 6.

91. Child to Convers Francis, 19 December 1835 and 25 September 1835, ibid., 39–42.

92. Child to Lydia B. Child, 27 January 1837, ibid., 61–62.

93. Karcher, *First Woman*, 41–53.

94. For the theme of avarice in Lydia Maria Child, *The Rebels, or Boston before the Revolution* (Boston, 1825), see 43, 46–47, 84, 101, 185, 229, 242, 279.

95. Ibid., 94, 151, 175, 208.

96. Ibid., 300.

97. Karcher, *First Woman*, 133–34.

98. Lydia Maria Child, *The Mother's Book* (1831; reprint, New York, 1972), 141–48.

99. Ibid., 9.

100. Ibid., 17–18, 86.

101. Ibid., 117, 141.

102. Ibid., 127.

103. Ibid., 129.

104. Ibid., 136, 166.

105. Karcher, *First Woman*, 173.

106. Carolyn Karcher, ed., *Hobomok and Other Writings on Indians* (New Brunswick, N.J., 1986), xvii.

107. Ibid., xx. Karcher's intoduction is a penetrating analysis.

108. Karcher, *First Woman*, 90–99, suggests that marrying David Lee Child helped to politicize Lydia Maria. The Indian question had fresh saliency because of its important role in the struggle between President Adams and his challenger, Andrew Jackson, who was leading the forces in the South and Southwest pressing for final removal of the so-called five civilized tribes from the Southeast, where they blocked the expansion of the Cotton Kingdom.

109. Lydia Maria Child, *The First Settlers of New England, or Conquest of the Pequods, Narragansets and Pokanokets* (Boston, 1829), 36, 109–19. For a fascinating discussion of women, see 241, where Child adheres to an environmentalist explanation of women's moral superiority: "I would not, however, have it imagined that I suppose women to possess superior talents for governing, but think it unquestionably arises from their being early taught to exercise and cherish the gentle virtues of kindness, forbearance, and desire to please."

110. Ibid., 65.

111. Ibid., 66–70.

112. Karcher, *First Woman*, 94.

CHAPTER 14

1. Clare Midgely, *Women against Slavery: The British Campaigns, 1780–1870* (London, 1992), 44.

2. See table 5.

3. Jay Fliegelman, *Prodigals and Pilgrims: The American Revolution against Patriarchal Authority, 1750–1800* (New York, 1982); Gordon Wood, *The Radicalism of the American Revolution* (New York, 1992).

4. Linda Kerber, *Women of the Republic: Intellect and Ideology in Revolutionary America* (Chapel Hill, 1980); Mary Beth Norton, *Liberty's Daughters: The Revolutionary Experience of American Women, 1750–1800* (Boston, 1980).

5. Keith E. Melder, *Beginnings of Sisterhood: The American Woman's Rights Movement, 1800–1850* (New York, 1977), 14.

6. See Lester Capon, ed., *The Adams-Jefferson Letters: The Complete Correspondence between Thomas Jefferson and Abigail and John Adams* (Williamsburg, Va., 1959); Edith Gelles, *Portia: The World of Abigail Adams* (Bloomington, 1992).

7. For a satirical treatment of apprehensions of female advanced literacy, see William Wirt, *The Old Bachelor* (1814), described in Paul Goodman, *Towards a Christian Republic: Antimasonry and the Great Transition in New England, 1826–1836* (New York, 1988), 96.

8. Cathy N. Davidson, *The Revolution and the Word: The Rise of the Novel in America* (New York, 1986), 44, and more generally, see the first sections of the book. William Gilmore, *Reading Becomes a Necessity of Life: Material and Cultural Life in Rural New England, 1760–1830* (Knoxville, 1988); Lee Virginia Chambers-Schiller, *Liberty, a Better Husband? Single Women in America: The Generations of 1780–1840* (New Haven, 1984), 124.

9. Davidson, *Revolution and the Word*, 73.

10. Ibid., 123.

11. Ira V. Brown, *Mary Grew, Abolitionist and Feminist, 1813–96* (Selingsgrove, Pa., 1991), 13.

12. Chambers-Schiller, *Liberty, a Better Husband?* 93.

13. Joan Jensen, *Loosening the Bonds: Mid-Atlantic Farm Women, 1750–1850* (New Haven, 1986); Thomas Dublin, *Transforming Women's Work: New England Lives in the Industrial Revolution* (Ithaca, N.Y., 1994); Mary Blewett, *Men, Women, and Work: Class, Gender, and Protest in the New England Shoe Industry, 1780–1910* (Urbana, Ill., 1988).

14. Chambers-Schiller, *Liberty, a Better Husband?* 105.

15. Ann Douglas, *The Feminization of American Culture* (New York, 1977); Goodman, *Towards a Christian Republic,* chapter 5.

16. Nancy A. Hardesty, *Your Daughters Shall Prophesy: Revivalism and Feminism in the Age of Finney* (Brooklyn, 1991), 47–48, 49–78, 79–93, 113–29.

17. For the classic argument for the "cult of true womanhood," see Nancy Cott, *The Bonds of Womanhood: "Woman's Sphere" in New England, 1780–1835* (New Haven, 1977). For a critique that posits a competing conception of "real womanhood," see Frances B. Cogan, *All-American Girl: The Ideal of Real Womanhood in Mid-Nineteenth-Century America* (Athens, Ga., 1989). Many specialized studies and biographies provide empirical support for Cogan's claim that the cult of domesticity faced challenge. Though she focuses on the period from 1840 to 1900, had she researched in the earlier period, she would have found additional support for the idea of "real womanhood."

18. *Ladies Magazine and Literary Gazette* 2 (December 1829): 515–17; Goodman, *Towards a Christian Republic,* 99–101.

19. See Barbara Berg, *The Remembered Gate: Origins of American Feminism* (New York, 1978), 145–213, for the New York data. For moral reformers in Boston, see Barbara M. Hobson, *Uneasy Virtue: The Politics of Prostitution and the American Reform Tradition* (New York, 1987).

20. Berg, *The Remembered Gate,* 152–75.

21. Ibid., 175; for the work of the female moral reform movement, see 177–222; Hardesty, *Your Daughters Shall Prophesy,* 123–27.

22. Berg, *The Remembered Gate,* 194.

23. For the postal problems of the moral reformers, see ibid., 185; for the petition campaigns for antiseduction legislation, see ibid., 211.

24. William Brown and D. Fanshaw to Weld, 17 March 1834, in *The Letters of Theodore Dwight Weld, Angelina Grimké Weld and Sarah Grimké, 1822–1844,* 2 vols., ed. Gilbert H. Barnes and Dwight L. Dumond (1934; reprint, Gloucester, Mass., 1965), 1:130.

25. Hobson, *Uneasy Virtue,* 55.

26. *Friend of Man,* 23 June, 15 and 22 September, 1 December 1836, and 31 May 1837. William Goodell gave extensive and friendly coverage to the moral reformers in the *Genius of Temperance* in New York and later as editor of the *Emancipator* between 1834 and 1836. See also the *Liberator,* 30 July 1831, 17 August 1833, 5 April 1834, and 17 September 1836. Bertha-Monica Stearns,

"Reform Periodicals and Female Reformers, 1830–1860," *American Historical Review* 37 (July 1932): 681–84.

27. *Emancipator,* 8 June 1833, from an address to a Pennsylvania temperance society previously reprinted in the *Female Advocate,* a New York City moral reform journal that Goodell edited. In September 1833, a column devoted to moral reform appeared in the *Emancipator.* In 1833, Goodell was president of the city's moral reform society. *Emancipator,* 13 July 1833; Stearns, "Reform Periodicals and Female Reformers," 678–99.

28. *Emancipator,* 28 September 1833.

29. Ibid., 14 January 1834. For other examples of support for moral reform, see 7 September 1833 and 9 December 1834. Debra Gold Hansen, "Blue Stockings and Blue Noses: Gender, Class, and Conflict in the Boston Female Anti-Slavery Society, 1833–1840" (Ph.D. diss., University of California, Irvine, 1988), 121.

30. Many of the leading abolitionists were excellent housekeepers and devoted child rearers, among them Lucretia Mott and, in their later careers, Lydia Maria Child and Abby Kelley. Blanche Hersh, *The Slavery of Sex: Female Abolitionists in America* (Urbana, Ill., 1978).

31. Chambers-Schiller, *Liberty, a Better Husband?* 133–38.

32. Ibid., 159.

CHAPTER 15

1. Garrison to Harriott Plummer, 4 March 1833, *The Letters of William Lloyd Garrison,* 6 vols., ed. Walter M. Merrill (Cambridge, Mass., 1971–1981), 1:208.

2. Dorothy Sterling, *Ahead of Her Time: Abby Kelley and the Politics of Anti-Slavery* (New York, 1991), 88.

3. T. R. Sullivan, *Letters against the Immediate Abolition of Slavery* (Boston, 1835), 7–9, 18–19.

4. Debra Gold Hansen, "Blue Stockings and Blue Noses: Gender, Class and Conflict in the Boston Female Anti-Slavery Society, 1833–1840" (Ph.D. diss., University of California, Irvine, 1988), 24.

5. *Antislavery Record* 2 (1836): 21. For John Tyler, see Jean Fagan Yellin, *Women and Sisters: The Antislavery Feminists in American Culture* (New Haven, 1989), 3.

6. John Greenleaf Whittier, *Justice and Expediency: Slavery Considered with a View to Its Rightful and Effectual Remedy, Abolition* (Haverhill, Mass., 1833), 20.

7. *Report of the First Anniversary of the Ohio Anti-Slavery Society* (Cincinnati, 1836), 26.

8. *Philanthropist,* 18 March 1836.

9. *Genius of Universal Emancipation,* June 1831; *Report . . . of the Ohio Anti-Slavery Society,* 29.

10. *Liberator,* 19 December 1835.

11. Yellin, *Women and Sisters,* 40.

290   Notes to Pages 219–223

12. Quoted in George Bourne, *Slavery Illustrated in Its Effects upon Woman and Domestic Society* (Boston, 1837), 1.

13. Ibid. Quotes are from dedicatory page and 12, 13, 22, 23, 27; *Philanthropist*, 24 June 1836, 14 April 1838; *Genius*, April 1832; *Report . . . of the Ohio Anti-Slavery Society*, 30–37; Yellin, *Women and Sisters*, 4–5; Ronald G. Walters, *The Antislavery Appeal: American Abolitionism after 1830* (Baltimore, 1976); Records of the Lynn Female Antislavery Society, Lynn Historical Society.

14. *Report . . . of the Ohio Anti-Slavery Society*, "Address to the Ladies of Ohio," 26–28; "Address to the Females of the State of Ohio by Female Antislavery Society for Muskingum C.," *Philanthropist*, 24 June 1836; *Genius*, December 1832.

15. *Genius*, March 1832.

16. *Philanthropist*, 24 June 1836; 14 November 1837; 10 April 1838; *Genius*, May and June 1831.

17. *Proceedings of the First Annual Meeting of the New York State Anti-Slavery Society* (Utica, 1836), 10.

18. *Genius*, July 1831.

19. Ibid., June 1831. Garrison reprinted a flattering portrait of the typical plantation mistress by a Northern female traveler that Sarah J. Hale had printed in *Ladies Magazine* in order to attack it. *Liberator*, 6 August 1836.

20. Amy Swerdlow, "Abolition's Conservative Sisters," in *The Abolitionist Sisterhood: Women's Political Culture in Antebellum America*, ed. Jean Fagan Yellin and John C. Van Horne (Ithaca, N.Y., 1994), 42.

21. *Genius*, February 1831.

22. *Philanthropist*, 24 June 1836; 14 August 1838.

23. *Friend of Man*, 6 October 1836.

24. Hansen, "Blue Stockings and Blue Noses," 25.

25. Efforts were made to trace to demographic sources the members of five large antislavery societies, those in Lynn and Weymouth, Massachusetts, Kent County, Rhode Island, and Dover and Concord, New Hampshire. Those efforts proved frustrating, yielding only fragmentary data. Towns with city directories, like Lynn, did not include most women. The census of 1850 did include most women, but few female abolitionists could be found because of name changes following marriage and because of residency changes, which were very common, given geographic mobility patterns and the difference of ten to fifteen years between the dates of the membership lists, mostly from between 1835 and 1840, and the census of 1850. For a demographic analysis of female abolitionist leaders, see Blanche Hersh, *Slavery of Sex: Feminist Abolitionists in America* (Urbana, Ill., 1978), 121–47.

26. *Liberator*, 18 August 1837. See Edward Magdol, *The Antislavery Rank and File: A Social Profile of the Abolitionists' Constituency* (New York, 1986), 72. Magdol reports that skilled women in the mills were more likely to sign antislavery petitions because they were at once more independent and more socialized, both into the female wage-earning world and into the politics of the boarding houses and labor conflict.

27. The foregoing and following demographic and other data come from the manuscript records of four female abolitionist societies with membership lists that have been traced to the United States Census of 1850 and church records. These are: Records of the Ladies Anti-Slavery Society of Dover, New Hampshire, in the New Hampshire Historical Society; Records of the Kent County Female Antislavery Society, in the Rhode Island Historical Society; Records of the Female Antislavery Society of Lynn, in the Lynn Historical Society; and Records of the Weymouth and Braintree Ladies Antislavery Society, in the Massachusetts Historical Society.

28. From reports in the *Liberator*.

29. Hansen, "Blue Stockings and Blue Noses," 109.

30. Jean Solderland, "The Philadelphia Female Anti-Slavery Society," in Yellin and Van Horne, eds. *The Abolitionist Sisterhood*, 74.

31. *Fifth Annual Report of the Executive Committee of the American Anti-Slavery Society* (New York, 1838), 129–51.

32. Based on the officers listed in the *Liberator* and in female antislavery society manuscripts. Child to Charlotte Phelps, 2 January 1834, *Lydia Maria Child: Selected Letters, 1817–1880*, ed. Milton Meltzer and Patricia G. Holland (Amherst, Mass., 1982), 28.

33. Margaret Bacon, "By Moral Force Alone: The Antislavery Women and Nonresistance," in Yellin and Van Horne, eds., *The Abolitionist Sisterhood*, 277; *Genius*, May and August 1831.

34. *Philanthropist*, 7 July 1837; *Emancipator*, 21 July 1836.

35. *Philanthropist*, 30 June 1837.

36. See table 6. Lori Ginzberg, *Women and the Work of Benevolence* (New Haven, 1990), 83, and see 71–90 for a broader treatment of women and politics.

37. Sterling, *Ahead of Her Time: Abby Kelley*, 35.

38. Maria Weston Chapman, *Right and Wrong in Massachusetts* (Boston, 1839; reprint, New York, 1969), 13.

39. *Liberator*, 4 August 1837.

40. Judith Wellman, "Women and Radical Reform in Antebellum Upstate New York: A Profile of Grassroots Female Abolitionists," in *Clio was a Woman: Studies in the History of American Women*, ed. Mabel E. Deutrich and Virginia C. Purdy (Washington, D.C., 1980), 117.

41. Yellin, *Women and Sisters*, 3.

42. Wellman, "Women and Radical Reform," 124.

43. *Philanthropist*, 10 February 1837.

44. *Emancipator*, 17 February 1835.

45. *Genius*, January 1833; Yellin, *Women and Sisters*, 36.

46. *Emancipator*, 21 July 1836.

47. Catharine E. Beecher, *An Essay on Slavery and Abolition with Reference to the Duty of American Females* (Philadelphia, 1837), 103–5.

48. "An Appeal to American Women, on Prejudice against Color," in *Proceedings of the Third Anti-Slavery Convention of American Women* (Philadelphia, 1838), 7–8, 21–24; *Report . . . of the Ohio Anti-Slavery Society*, 38–40.

PART 5

1. *Emancipator,* 12 and 26 October 1837. See Gerrit Smith, in ibid., 3 February 1835, and for another black minister, see Rev. Hosea Easton's plaintive voice, sounding much like Wright's, in the *Fifth Annual Report of the Board of Managers of the Massachusetts Anti-Slavery Society* (Boston, 1837), xxxix.

CHAPTER 16

1. *Second Annual Report of the New England Anti-Slavery Society* (Boston, 1834), 33; *Friend of Man,* 29 March 1837; Garrison to Gerrit Smith, 7 March 1835, *The Letters of William Lloyd Garrison,* 6 vols., ed. Walter M. Merrill (Cambridge, Mass., 1971–81), 1:460; Kent is quoted in Edward Abdy, *Journal of a Residence and Tour in the United States of North America from April, 1833 to October, 1834,* 3 vols. (1835; reprint, New York, 1969), 1:epigraph on title page.

2. *Third Annual Report of the American Anti-Slavery Society* (New York, 1836), 29. For the Tappans, see *Emancipator,* 29 June 1833.

3. Abdy, *Journal,* 1:45, 1:55. See Gustave de Beaumont, *Marie, or Slavery in the United States* (1835; reprint, Stanford, Calif., 1958), where a Frenchman in America says, "In Europe we do not have this prejudice. . . . All humanity is equal" (59).

4. Harvey Newcomb, *The "Negro Pew": Being an Inquiry Concerning the Propriety of Distinctions in the House of God, on Account of Color* (Boston, 1837), 8–9; Abdy, *Journal,* 1:123. For the claim by the anti-abolitionist *New Hampshire Observer,* a Congregationalist weekly, that blacks were not victims of prejudice, see the *Herald of Freedom,* 22 August 1835, and for the contention of the Boston Unitarian *Christian Examiner* that there were no castes in the United States, see Abdy, *Journal,* 1:144 n, and also Abdy's contention that many of the prejudiced were "quite unconscious of their injustice and absurdity" (1:123).

5. Newcomb, *The "Negro Pew,"* 9.

6. For the comparison of blacks to animals, see William Yates, *Rights of Colored Men to Suffrage, Citizenship and Trial by Jury* (Philadelphia, 1838), 32; *Fourth Annual Report of the Board of Managers of the Massachusetts Anti-Slavery Society* (Boston, 1836), 50; *Third Annual Report of the American Anti-Slavery Society* (New York, 1836), the statement of Swan Pomroy, 9. For blacks compared to frogs, see the *Emancipator,* 28 July 1836.

7. *Liberator,* 8 September 1832.

8. Abdy, *Journal,* 1:131.

9. Ibid., 2:48.

10. *Emancipator,* 9 March 1837; *Friend of Man,* 29 March 1837.

11. *Emancipator,* 8 June 1837; *Friend of Man,* 29 May 1837. Gerrit Smith's speech is in the *Fifth Annual Report of the Executive Committee of the American Anti-Slavery Society* (New York, 1838), 330–36.

12. Alexis de Tocqueville, *Democracy in America,* ed. J. P. Mayer and Max Lerner (New York, 1966), 342, 340, 341, 360, 342, 342 n. 32.

13. Beaumont, *Marie,* 30. Subsequent page references will appear in the text.

14. Abdy, *Journal,* 1:122, 1:251, 1:361, 1:374.

15. Ibid, 1:363.

16. Quoted in ibid., 3:235. For Unitarians and slavery, see Daniel Walker Howe, *The Unitarian Conscience: Harvard Moral Philosophy, 1805–1861* (Cambridge, Mass., 1970).

17. Abdy, *Journal,* 3:218, 3:219. Subsequent page references will appear in the text.

18. *North American Review* 12 (April 1821).

19. Abdy, *Journal,* 1:47, 1:196, 1:218, 1:159, 1:117, 3:246, 3:331. See 3:317–35 for a Philadelphia riot with details of involvement by white groups, including landlords who encouraged the riot because they wished to get rid of black tenants who paid lower rents than the more "respectable" people the landlords wished to bring in.

20. Edward Abdy, *American Whites and Blacks* (London, 1842), 37.

21. Abdy, *Journal,* 1:50; Abdy, *American Whites and Blacks,* 43. For racist Negro caricatures, see Gary Nash, *Forging Freedom: The Formation of Philadelphia's Black Community, 1720–1840* (Cambridge, Mass., 1988). See Beaumont, *Marie,* 99–101 for a comparison of European and American social structures.

22. Beaumont, *Marie,* 30–36, but especially 36.

23. Ibid., 120–21.

24. Tocqueville, *Democracy in America,* 357. For an excellent anthology of key writings on slavery and race, with shrewd editorial introductions, see Donald L. Noel, *The Origins of American Slavery and Racism* (Columbus, Ohio, 1972).

CHAPTER 17

1. *Philanthropist,* 3 March 1837.

2. Ibid.

3. C. Peter Ripley, ed., *The Black Abolitionist Papers,* 5 vols. (Chapel Hill, 1985–92), 4:227; *Friend of Man,* 26 January 1837; *Philanthropist,* 8 May 1838. For an argument that slavery, not color, caused prejudice, since it did not abate in freedom, see Rev. Hosea Easton, *A Treatise on the Intellectual Character and Civil and Political Condition of the Colored People of the United States and the Prejudice Exercised towards Them* (Boston, 1837), 47.

4. *New York Evangelist,* 9 November 1833. For an appeal to white mechanics to relent in prejudice, see *Antislavery Record,* December 1837; *New Hampshire Herald,* 7 March 1835.

5. William C. Nell, *The Colored Patriots of the American Revolution* (1855; reprint, New York, 1968), 350–51.

6. *Emancipator,* 10 February 1835.

7. Nell, *Colored Patriots,* 346.

8. The count of black antislavery societies comes from the *Fifth Annual Report of the Executive Committee of the American Anti-Slavery Society* (New York, 1838), 129–52.

9. Nell, *Colored Patriots,* 352.

10. Ibid., 7–8.

11. *Emancipator,* 2 July 1836.

12. Susan Paul, *The Memoir of James Jackson, the Attentive and Obedient Scholar, Who Died in Boston, October 31, 1833, Aged Six Years and Eleven Months* (Boston, 1835), vi. Subsequent page references will appear in the text.

13. *New Hampshire Observer,* 7 March 1835.

14. David Lee Child, "The Despotism of Freedom," in *Abolitionist's Library, No. 1* (Boston, 1833), 11; Harvey Newcomb, *The "Negro Pew": Being an Account of the Propriety of Distinctions in the House of God, on Account of Color* (Boston, 1837), 63.

15. Easton, *A Treatise,* 41.

16. The statistical evidence is from the *Fifth Annual Report . . . of the American Anti-Slavery Society* (1838), 129–52. Lewis Perry, *Childhood, Marriage, and Reform: Henry Clarke Wright, 1797–1870* (Chicago, 1980). For an appeal for juvenile support, see the *First Annual Report of the New York State Anti-Slavery Society* (Utica, 1835), 17.

17. Newcomb, *The "Negro Pew,"* 30.

18. *Emancipator,* 15 September 1836.

19. *Herald of Freedom,* 25 July 1835.

20. "Report of the Condition of the People of Color in the State of Ohio," in the *Proceedings of the Ohio Anti-Slavery Convention, Held at Putnam on the 22d, 23d, and 24th of April, 1835* (n.p., n.d.), 1–2; *Report of the Second Anniversary of the Ohio State Anti-Slavery Society* (Cincinnati, 1837), 58–62.

21. "Report of the Condition of the People of Color in the State of Ohio," 4 n.

22. Ibid., 5.

23. *Emancipator,* 12 August 1833.

24. Ibid., 15 April 1834.

25. *First Annual Report of the American Anti-Slavery Society* (New York, 1834), 46.

26. *Emancipator,* 16 November 1837.

27. *Emancipator,* 9 November 1837. For the opening of the Free Church of Schenectady, see ibid., 28 December 1837.

28. See Keith J. Hardman, *Charles Grandison Finney, 1792–1875: Revivalist and Reformer* (Syracuse, 1987), and Bertram Wyatt-Brown, *Lewis Tappan and the Evangelical War against Slavery* (Cleveland, 1969).

29. "Report of the Condition of the People of Color in the State of Ohio," 8.

30. *Philanthropist,* 20 January 1837.

31. "Report of the Condition of the People of Color in the State of Ohio," 7.

32. William T. Allan to Theodore Weld, 15 December 1834, in *The Letters of Theodore Dwight Weld, Angelina Grimké Weld and Sarah Grimké, 1822–1844,* 2 vols., ed. Gilbert H. Barnes and Dwight L. Dumond (1934; reprint; Gloucester, Mass., 1965), 1:182.

33. *Emancipator,* 13 April 1837.

34. "Report of the Condition of the People of Color in the State of Ohio," 11.

35. *Second Annual Report of the Board of Managers of the New England Anti-Slavery Society* (Boston, 1834), 17.

36. Ripley, ed., *Black Abolitionist Papers,* 4:221.

37. *Fourth Annual Report of the American Anti-Slavery Society* (New York, 1837), 13; Nell, *Colored Patriots,* 345–48; Evan Lewis, *Address to the Colored People of Philadelphia* (Philadelphia, 1833), 12–17.

38. *Fourth Annual Report of the American Anti-Slavery Society* (1837), 15.

39. *Report of the Second Anniversary of the Ohio State Anti-Slavery Society* (1837), 57–58; Nell, *Colored Patriots,* 345, 248.

40. Emeline Bishop to Weld, March 1835, in *The Weld-Grimké Letters,* 1:214.

41. Phoebe Matthew to Weld, March 1835, in ibid., 1:217.

42. Tappan to Weld, 15 March 1836, in ibid., 1:277.

43. Sarah Forten to Angelina Grimké, 15 April 1837, in ibid., 1:380.

44. *Friend of Man,* 6 October, 1836.

45. *Emancipator,* 31 August 1837.

46. Ripley, ed., *Black Abolitionist Papers,* 4:340–41.

47. Phyllis F. Field, *The Politics of Race in New York: The Struggle for Black Suffrage in the Civil War Era* (Ithaca, N.Y., 1982).

48. *Friend of Man,* 1 February 1837; Lewis, *Address to Colored People,* 12.

49. *Philanthropist,* 3 April 1837.

50. Robert Toll, *Blacking Up: The Minstrel Show in Nineteenth-Century America* (New York, 1974); Alexander Saxton, *The Rise and Fall of the White Republic: Class, Politics, and Mass Culture in Nineteenth-Century America* (New York, 1990); David Roediger, *The Wages of Whiteness: Race and the Making of the American Working Class* (New York, 1991). The last two authors argue for the working-class character of the minstrel show by assuming it, not proving it. The nature of the class character of such entertainment is unclear from the data in Toll and questionable from the pervasiveness of color prejudice among all classes. Moreover, one wonders how these authors distinguish among upper-class, middle-class, lower middle-class, and wage-earning social strata.

51. Ripley, ed., *Black Abolitionist Papers,* 4:287–93.

52. *Emancipator,* 10 November 1836.

53. *Emancipator,* 15 December 1836. For Robert Purvis's thanks to abolitionists, see the *First Annual Report of the American Anti-Slavery Society,* 15.

Index

Abdy, Edward, 235, 240–43
Abolitionists: agency system and, 104, 133; aristocrats vs., 139–60; Democrats and, 168; growth in numbers of, 35, 248; female, 97, 159, 173–232; integration and, 35, 248; limits of, 5; racial equality and, 62, 246, 255; recruitment by, 143; religious commitment and, 67; social characteristics of, 138, 145–48; workers and, 153–54, 161–72. *See also specific leaders, organizations*
ACS. *See* American Colonization Society
Adams, Abigail, 208
Adams, John, 13, 143
Adams, John Quincy: on colonization, 17, 22; defeat in 1828 election, 37–38; defends women's right to petition, 231; support of, 85, 198; views on slavery, 21–22.
Adams, Samuel, 6
Address Delivered before the Free People of Color (Garrison), 54
Advocate of Moral Reform, 159, 214
African Americans: ACS and, 23–35, 48; colonization and, 2, 11–35, 47, 54, 57, 67, 233, 246; community development and, 28; education and, 83, 99, 117, 227, 248, 253; Garrison and, 51, 54, 61–62; immediatism and, 10, 27, 48, 233; manual labor and, 50–51, 63, 99, 102, 143, 156; racial equality and, 23–35, 62, 246, 255; racial prejudice and, 49–50, 60, 155, 233–34; self-

improvement campaigns, 26, 32–34, 46–47, 55, 63; suffrage and, 7. *See also specific leaders, organizations*
African Improvement Society, 46
African Repository, 17
African Temperance Society, 42
Agents, 104, 133
Allan, William, 101
Allen, Richard, 30, 32
Amalgamation, vs. integration, 126; opposition to, 137, 230, 245, 257. *See also* Integration
American Antislavery Almanac, 65
American Antislavery Society: agency system, 133–34; Child publication of/by, 57; Christians and, 105; Garrison and, 82–83; Goodell and, 215; May and, 93; Mott and, 195; Phoenix Society and, 254; prejudice and, 256–57; Thurston and, 119; Weld and, 99, 105; Williams and, 117; Wright and, 82, 251
American Colonization Society (ACS): Adams and, 21; African Americans and, 23–35, 48; aristocrats and, 61; Bacon and, 46; Birney and, 85; Evans and, 165; formation of, 12, 16–17; Garrison and, 33–34, 55–57; Goodell and, 77; immediatism and, 10, 34; Liberia and, 16; May and, 90; most important function of, 18; prejudice and, 10, 126, 259; Russwurm and, 46; southerners and, 14
American Revolution, 5, 208

297

Compositor: BookMasters, Inc.
Text: Sabon
Display: Sabon
Printer and Binder: Haddon Craftsmen